The Art of Building

FRONTISPIECE
Tram depot for the
Amsterdam Omnibus
Company, Amsterdam
(by Adolf L. van
Gendt, 1893), with
stables for eighty-one
horses and living
quarters for the
foreman. The art of
building is a
sophisticated game
with complex
semantics, even in a
relatively simple
building such as this,
which incorporates
the design skills of
the architect and the
operating efficiency of
his practice, the skills
of the building
workers and the
intentions of the
client, as well as
public taste, the
expression of
local pride, a
representation of the
social order, and
references to 'higher'
values such as
nationhood,
made visible by
interpretations of
Dutch Renaissance
architecture. Photo:
Jacob Olie, 1893.

Auke van der Woud

The Art of Building

From Classicism to Modernity:
The Dutch Architectural Debate
1840–1900

ASHGATE

The publisher gratefully acknowledges the support of The Netherlands Organisation for Scientific Research (NWO), The Hague and the Prins Bernhard Cultuurfonds, Amsterdam.

Published by
Ashgate Publishing Limited
Gower House
Croft Road
Aldershot
Hants GU11 3HR
England

Ashgate Publishing Company
131 Main Street
Burlington VT 05401–5600 USA

Ashgate website: http://www.ashgate.com

British Library Cataloguing in Publication Data

Woud, Auke van der.
   The Art of Building: From Classicism to Modernity:
   The Dutch Architectural Debate 1840–1900.
   (Reinterpreting Classicism series)
   1. Architecture, Modern—19th century—Netherlands.
   2. Architecture, Modern—19th century. 3. Architecture—
   Philosophy—History—19th century. 4. Classicism in
   architecture—Netherlands.
   I. Title.
   720.9'492'09034

Library of Congress Cataloging-in-Publication Data

Woud, Auke van der.
   [First English-language edition (revised) of *Waarheid en karakter.
   Het debat over de bouwkunst 1840–1900*, Rotterdam, 1997]
   The art of building: from classicism to modernity: the Dutch
   architectural debate 1840–1900/Auke van der Woud [translated
   from the Dutch].
      p. cm. (Reinterpreting Classicism)
   Includes bibliographical references and index.
   ISBN 0–7546–0254–0
   1. Architecture—Netherlands—19th century. I. Title. II. Series.
NA1147.W613   2001
720'.9492'09034—dc21   2001022526

ISBN 0 7546 0254 0

This book is printed on acid free paper
Typeset in Ehrhardt by Bournemouth Colour Press, Parkstone
and printed in Great Britain by Biddles Ltd, Guildford.

Contents

Acknowledgements

When I was invited to join the staff of the Architectural History Group at the Vrije Universiteit, Amsterdam, in 1990 Dr Erik de Jong and his students had created an intellectual atmosphere where the study of nineteenth-century Dutch architecture could thrive and flourish. Without the context of this group this book could not have been written. My main debt of gratitude is to its members, including the growing number of PhD students and post-doctoral members. Our many meetings and discussions are the common substratum in which our ideas and books grow; this book being a specimen. I owe a special thanks to Hetty Berens for permitting me to use important information on Willem Nicolaas Rose that enabled me to see his very special position in Dutch architectural history. My book rests upon a mass of material collected mainly from the Dutch architectural journals of the nineteenth century. I am greatly indebted to Imke van Hellemondt for assisting me with her excellent research.

This book was first published in Dutch in 1997. For their strong support of the idea of preparing an English edition I thank Professor Ed Taverne, Rijksuniversiteit of Groningen, and Professor Luc Verpoest, Catholic University of Leuven. For their generous and decisive subsidies I sincerely thank The Netherlands Organisation for Scientific Research, The Hague, and the Prins Bernhard Cultuurfonds, Amsterdam. I am grateful to Yvette Blankvoort and Bard Janssen, who translated my original text, which is full of ideas and concepts that belonged to an earlier intellectual and aesthetical world. Such ideas are not easily explained to the average present-day Dutch reader. However, to translate them into contemporary English quite often seemed almost impossible. I am very grateful to Sue Phillpott, who with a marvellous understanding and an astonishing intuition copy-edited the translation, elegantly building the linguistic and mental bridge connecting times past with times present, and English minds with continental ones. In the preparation of the illustrations I owe a debt to Sophie Ploeg, who suggested fascinating material to me.

At Ashgate, I thank Pamela Edwardes and Caroline Cornish for their support, precision and great care, and Alan Bartram for the design. But above all I wish to express my gratitude to Dr Caroline van Eck, Ashgate's Series Editor and a colleague at the Vrije Universiteit for many years. I thank her for her valuable editoral work, and, perhaps more important, for so many inspiring and clarifying discussions on architectural theory, for sharing with me her ideas and her vast knowledge of the problem of 'style' in architecture – the essential theme of this book.

The Art of Building: From Classicism to Modernity:
The Dutch Architectural Debate 1840–1900
is published in the series
Reinterpreting Classicism: Culture, Reaction and Appropriation
Edited by Caroline van Eck, Vrije Universiteit, Amsterdam

IN THE SAME SERIES

Producing the Past
Aspects of Antiquarian Culture and Practice 1700–1850
Edited by Martin Myrone and Lucy Peltz
Preface by Stephen Bann

Sir John Soane and the Country Estate
Ptolemy Dean

Building on Ruins
The Rediscovery of Rome and English Architecture
Frank Salmon

Allan Ramsay and the Search for Horace's Villa
Edited by Bernard D. Frischer and Iain Gordon Brown

The Built Surface, Volume 1
Architecture and the Visual Arts
from Antiquity to the Enlightenment
Edited by Christy Anderson

Introduction

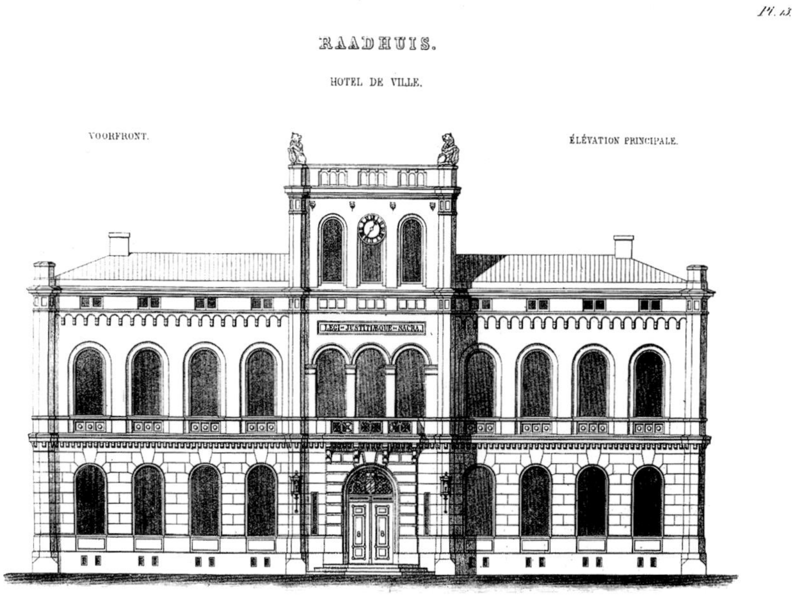

Building is a practice: the art of building is the subject of theory. For a long time the fundamental characteristics of European architecture had been provided by the tradition of classicism, focusing upon the five classical orders and their derivations. The eighteenth century felt the need to reinvestigate the fundamentals; to define them, by means of philosophical reasoning, as they 'really were'. In their quest for the essentials of the art of building, the architects of the nineteenth century found that philosophical reasoning was insufficient, and turned their attention to the empirical, comparative study of historic buildings. In handbooks of architectural history the conspicuous absorption of their results into nineteenth-century architecture is usually referred to as historicism; a term suggesting that history was the architect's predominant concern. In following this art-historical convention, we fail fully to take account of the fact that the problems for which architects were seeking solutions did not, in fact, belong to the past, but to their own age and to the future. The architecture of the past was, for them, not primarily a respected silent witness of a bygone era. Far more importantly, it was a representation of beauty – sometimes an unusual, strange beauty, sometimes an ideal beauty. The architecture of the past, it was generally thought, would provide study material for inquiries into the aesthetic 'laws' that, objective and universal like the laws of nature, would give the nineteenth century a splendid contemporary architecture. This last consideration had more implications than we tend to realize today. Of all the arts, the art of building was the most public, and it was its pre-eminent task – and that of the architect – to edify society by means of its beauty. Architectural theory, showing the way to realize this lofty purpose, was therefore of the utmost importance.

This book takes the importance of architectural theory as its starting point. From this viewpoint, it is not buildings and architectural design that are its subject matter, but ideas, theories, ideals, opinions, debates – precisely because ideas precede the material form. However, general cultural or political concepts do not result directly in specific architectural designs. There has to be an intermediate conceptual stage that in the following chapters I call the

'concept of form', a concept that relates cultural and political values to specific characteristics of architectural design. Classicism, for example, is such a concept of form, as are the neo-Gothic and the neo-Renaissance, and eclecticism. But the art-historical tradition of referring to these as 'styles' has not been adhered to in this book, because to use this term would be confusing in a book about debates on architectural theory. For about a hundred years 'style' did have a very wide cultural meaning, until in the late nineteenth century this was reduced by art critics to a set of common formal elements. Another reason for introducing the term 'concept of form' is to break with our habit of associating style with visual characteristics only. This has more than a theoretical significance. If one concentrates exclusively on the visual form of classicism, eclecticism or neo-Gothic architecture and on the debates on these subjects, one sees only differences and contrasts (the 'battle of the styles'). But focusing on the cultural content of these concepts of form reveals connections between them, and sometimes even unity. Many ideas

Fig.1
A competition design for a small village town hall by Abraham Nicolaas Godefroy (1849). Godefroy's maxim was: 'The highest to which we can aspire is for our buildings to clearly convey their function to any intelligent human being.' The adjudicators praised the design for its 'character', which expressed seriousness, dignity and strength.

which were traditionally associated with classicism lived on when classicism itself no longer played a role of any importance as a design concept; and they lived on in its arch-rival, neo-Gothic architecture, in much of the neo-Renaissance (1860–1900), and even in the radical innovatory movement of the 1890s that wanted to free itself from architectural history in order to make a fresh start. All these, to differing degrees, were concerned with one cultural ideal: architecture with objective, universal aesthetic principles, nationally understood and supported – what was called *style*. It was this same ideal that in 1917 induced Theo van Doesburg, Piet Mondrian and J. J. P. Oud to found the Dutch art group known as De Stijl.

The outsider here was eclecticism, which considered the quest for a uniform style irrelevant. It is not improbable that the reason why art historians have shown so little interest in eclecticism is precisely because of this indifference to the notion of style, and it may well be, too, that this is why they have often marginalized the subject when writing about the nineteenth century. In this book eclecticism occupies a more important position, because it sought the future of architecture not so much in aesthetic 'laws' but in the specific requirements of contemporary society. It not only accepted the cultural multiformity of the nineteenth century, but emphasized it and made it more explicit by means of its multiform view of concepts of form. Thus it laid the foundation for twentieth-century architecture, which would display far more individualism and multiformity as well as very much less interest in history.

Indeed, by the end of the nineteenth century eclecticism was the only concept whose principles were still robustly in evidence and which enjoyed the wide support of the architectural community – and its clients. Only a few architects, who through their wealthy clients were protected against the economics of the building market, continued to maintain that the aesthetic rules of the past applied to the future, and would result in one national style. By then, the majority of architects knew better. The architectural practice of the rapidly changing nineteenth century had long since ceased to conform with aesthetic rules as expounded in books on the subject, or with aesthetic principles from the past. Also, it was evident that the quest for a generally accepted style representing the unity of the entire nation had turned out to be illusory. Back in 1840, multiformity, individualism and subjective and emotional aesthetic judgements were still very rare, the collective ideal of unity suppressing such personal forms of expression. By 1900, however, they had become ubiquitous characteristics of both social and architectural reality. Architectural theory, considered the common objective

guide for architectural design for more than half a century, had become obsolete. Architecture was still thriving, but architectural design was no longer determined by words, but more than ever by images. Images became responsible for explaining and justifying design – a tautology that was to be even more forcibly felt with the breakthrough brought about by photography after 1900.

The ideas behind this book make it necessary to devote much attention to the activities of Hendrik Petrus Berlage (1856–1934) and his presumed spiritual father, 'the Dutch Viollet-le-Duc', Pierre J. H. Cuypers (1827–1921). This is not only because they generated many controversies in their time and were vociferous in these controversies, but also because for many decades there has been a consensus in Dutch historiography that regards them as the father and grandfather of modern Dutch architecture. It is my contention that this consensus should be reconsidered. And the strongest arguments against it are the ideas of Cuypers and Berlage themselves, as well as the context in which these two reputations were formulated, defended and contested around 1895. Cuypers' reputation was at that time the product of twenty-five years of continuous propaganda; Berlage was a man who lived in the past as far as his ideals on architecture and 'style' were concerned, and an opportunist who impressed his audience with his references to a variety of philosophers and his many – if somewhat stray – statements on modernity.*

This book considers the idea that the development of such an extensive phenomenon as architecture, with all its social ramifications, cannot be attributed to the achievements of just one or two individuals. On the contrary, it sees the activities of individual architects as not so much the cause but the expression of movements that have continuously changed the face of architecture; movements inspired by collective ideas and ideals concerning artistic representation, popular taste and fashion, the dynamics of building technology, the availability of building materials, new functional requirements and the demands of economic expansion. In fact, the situation is even more complex. It is not just a question of architects expressing those movements: there is also an essential interaction – individual architects can also *change* fashion, building technology and representational conventions, and in so doing have an effect on the building market.

---

* The Dutch edition of this book elaborates on some points more than seemed desirable for the English edition. This applies especially to the critical assessment of the way in which Cuypers' and Berlage's reputations were constructed around 1900.

What applies in this context to the relation between the individual and the architectural scene as a whole applies just as much to the relation between the national and the international. Gothic architecture was an international cultural concept that manifested itself in buildings that, in their visual characteristics, usually referred to both the international and the regional context. This also applied to nineteenth-century architecture. Dutch architects, while part of an international community, related to a 'national' public taste, a national building technology and building market, and national political and religious ideas. In a sense this was also true of London, Berlin, Paris and Vienna, and to some extent of Chicago and New York. Dutch architects read the same journals as their foreign colleagues: the writings of Karl Bötticher, Gottfried Semper, Viollet-le-Duc and Ruskin, and the illustrations of the buildings of Henry Hobson Richardson and the many reports of the miraculous American efficiency, made concrete certain ideas that were generally felt – consciously or unconsciously – in the Netherlands as elsewhere. The enthusiasm with which these ideas were received testifies to this.

At the same time it cannot be denied that there was an incongruity in Dutch nineteenth-century architecture as compared with foreign architecture. Architects frequently complained of the unflamboyant Dutch national character that, uninterested in monumental art, failed to provide them with the means that enabled their colleagues in the major foreign cities to apply their art in a more opulent way. The conventional theological explanation of the typical Dutch soberness is inadequate here: was it really the result of the long-established popularity of Calvinism in the Netherlands, or did Calvinism become so popular there in the sixteenth century precisely because it provided the right spiritual dimension to this national character?

The idea of beauty has a strange tradition in the Netherlands. For centuries urban design was a form of hydro-engineering, in which constructing a house could easily be compared to building a ship. A silent majority of the Dutch architects of the nineteenth century followed in this tradition: for them, visual beauty was not the result of philosophy and aesthetics, but of the visible success of technical intelligence and creativity. Beauty stood not so much for the representation of a splendid abstract ideal, but for the expression of superior functionality in a purely practical sense. The grand nineteenth-century themes discussed in this book, although earnestly considered and debated in the Netherlands, were perhaps at a fundamental level somewhat un-Dutch. They originated not from a set of traditional, pragmatic ideas, but from another architectural culture, an idealist, intellectual tradition.

It may be that Dutch architecture was only able to make its appearance on the international stage when, shortly after 1900, it discovered how to link these two traditions. The result was there to be seen not only in the well-known contributions to the Modern Movement of such architects as J. J. P. Oud, Johannes Duiker, Willem van Tijen, W. M. Dudok and Mart Stam, but also in the rapid growth and influence of the Dutch architecture profession, especially in the field of social housing and urban and regional planning, which immediately attracted international interest. Two traditions – ambiguous results. Even today, a hundred years later, the Netherlands is a country where the leading architects fulfil a prominent cultural function, yet refuse to consider themselves artists or to discuss architectural beauty; while on the other hand, without irony or cultural pretension, locks, bridges, quays, viaducts and pedestrian subways are referred to as *kunstwerken* (works of art). With the exception of the nineteenth-century interlude that is one of the subjects of this book, Dutch architecture is not a matter of theory; it is the art of building – a matter of practice.

Preamble

Around 1900 a fundamental change took place in collective ideas about architecture, a change apparent among other things in the common parlance. The term 'art of building' was now old-fashioned, evoking nineteenth-century artistic ideals and systems in which most architects were no longer interested. 'Architecture' became the neutral, more or less technical, designation. The cause of this change must not be sought merely in the rejection of ornament, the search for a pure simplicity, or any of the other 'modern' external characteristics of architectural design. Design concepts result from ideas, and so it is those changing ideas that we should examine.

The first question to ask is how in the collective architectural mind the essence of architecture was perceived. Nineteenth-century science demonstrated that each area of empirical reality had rational and therefore knowable fundamentals which, once they had all been mapped, would reveal a system. This happened in the field of biology, economics and sociology, of health and disease, in industrial processes and technology. Was there any reason why architecture should be an exception to this universal logic? Certainly, architects recognized that like painting and sculpture it was an art, but, unlike painting and sculpture, it was also a science. To look for the fundamentals of architecture in its history was therefore as sensible, it seemed, as geologists studying the history of the earth in order to understand the geological processes of the present. And as with geologists, the historical interest of the leading architects was a means, not an aim in itself; it was, for them, the only way to discover the laws of architecture. The essential characteristic of these architects, great theorists such as Gottfried Semper and Eugène Viollet-le-Duc, was that, just like geologists in *their* field, they were searching for the solution of the problem of contemporary architecture *within architecture itself*.

Towards 1900 many architects became aware that this solution could not, in fact, be found in the past. Architecture could only become contemporary if it searched for the laws, the conditions for its existence, *outside* itself. It is from that moment that architects ceased to feel the need to study the history of architecture. Rather, they now saw themselves as detached from it. It is to eclecticism that this fundamental change in the collective thinking, this radical orientation away from the internal and towards the external relations of architecture, can be attributed.

Perhaps the metamorphosis of the art of building into architecture can be highlighted in another way. To a large extent architecture withdrew from the cultural reference system in which it had remained in the nineteenth century to make a place for itself in the technical frame of reference of the twentieth. Whereas the old system was a cultural ideal fostered by an elite, a system of values and standards that owed its authority to a respectable tradition, the new system was a source of boundless technical potential, an ideal of progress that was to be professed so universally in the twentieth century that we called it mass culture; a culture of progress, directed not by history but by expectations for the future.

Part 1

The Enlightenment Inheritance:
Character, Truth and Style

I

Europe and the Netherlands: The Years before 1840

The common European view of the art of building held in the eighteenth and most of the nineteenth century was that architectural design could not be seen as an isolated phenomenon. Design as an aim in itself was meaningless and was therefore not accepted as art. Design always referred to a specific content – was, rather, an expression of the content. Design was the means through which the content, the 'ideal', materialized. According to this view, a successful design of the idea would result in beauty.

In order to understand why and how design in architecture changed, we must look for changes concerning the 'idea' of architecture, and changes concerning the question of what is to be considered a successful design. According to long-standing tradition, beauty was art's highest ideal; it deeply moved the observer and made him or her yearn for the loftiest human ideals. Art's exalted social position resulted from this: through its beauty it uplifted society. In the eighteenth and nineteenth centuries this view of architecture was hardly disputed. The debate focused not on the function of beauty, but on how beauty could be created – which rules to follow, which mistakes to avoid – and on the experience of beauty. The proliferation of architectural theories in the nineteenth century reflected the diminishing consensus on the characteristics of beauty.

Classicism required the rules of beauty to have a high degree of *objectivity*. The increasing focus on the role of the observer, which in the eighteenth century became the driving force behind the process of individualism and greater multiformity and which would terminate classicism's supremacy, can already be discerned in the architectural theory of Claude Perrault (1613–88). In his *Ordonnance des cinq espèces de colonnes selon la méthode des anciens* (Regulation of the Five Kinds of Columns after the Method of the Ancients, 1683) he proposed that the fixity and absoluteness of the rules of beauty derived from systems of proportion were not self-evident. He made a distinction between on the one hand 'positive', more or less objective, beauty, based on demonstrable characteristics of a building itself, and on the other hand 'arbitrary' beauty, based on the associations and habits of the observer or on the authority of the client or architect. Rules of beauty based on proportions were not

'positive', according to Perrault, but 'arbitrary', because there was no consensus on what was an ideal proportion. The perception of beautiful proportions in architecture is fundamentally different from that in music. Whereas in music even the slightest deviation from the proper relationship between tones sounds incontrovertibly out of tune, deviations in architecture are often not even noticed, and so do not detract from the experience of beauty.[1] Perrault was by no means an insignificant architect, and neither was he an anti-classicist. He published a learned and famous translation of the Roman architect Vitruvius' *De Architectura*, and built a new colonnade on the east side of the Louvre, commissioned by Louis XIV. His *Ordonnance* demonstrates an odd characteristic that Vitruvianism continued to display until the early nineteenth century – namely, the ability to maintain its monopoly by incorporating all criticism and contrasts.

Perrault distinguished between beauty that is the result of rules similar to the laws of nature, and beauty based on convention. This dichotomy became more prominent in the course of the eighteenth century. The *genre pittoresque* in French painting and the picturesque in English landscape gardens offered the opportunity to explore – so different from classicist, 'regulated' art – the new beauty of the apparently unregulated, the coincidental, the 'natural' and the 'naive'. This fundamental renewal in the view of art coincided with a similarly fundamental reconception of nature, which found expression in a variety of ways. The authority of nature was now pitted against the authority of Vitruvianism, resulting in new views on the rationality, functionality and aesthetics of a building in general and on structure and ornamentation in particular.

The new study of nature also implied the study of the nature of man himself. It was in philosophy, the discipline that played a primary role in the study of the as yet little understood human condition, that the study of aesthetics, concentrating on the definition, creation and experience of beauty, originated. Francis Hutcheson (1694–1746), for example, studied what it is that determines beauty. His answer was that beauty comprised the primary properties of objects that can activate a feeling in relation to these objects in the observer's psyche (*An Inquiry concerning Beauty, Order, Harmony, and Design*, 1725). This subjective (that is, belonging to the subject) faculty of cognition, *taste*, is the capacity to discern *unity in diversity*.

The relationship between the observer's soul, or psyche, and beauty as a characteristic of an observed object was defined in a pioneering way by Edmund Burke (1729–97) in his *Philosophical Enquiry into the Origin of our Ideas of the Sublime and the Beautiful* (1757), 'a diligent examination of our passions in our own breasts'. Burke was interested not only in the passions generated by delicate, classical beauty captured in rules ('the beautiful'), but also in experiencing beauty together with the 'terror' that accompanies it, resulting from something breathtakingly spectacular, something that is beyond comprehension and that can only be defined as 'the sublime'.

Burke broadened the range of objects and experiences that can be referred to in terms of beauty. And he transferred the inquiry into the object of beauty to the psychological mechanisms and laws on which the experience of the beautiful and the sublime is based. The development of architectural theory in France, on the other hand, remained dedicated to the classical tradition by incorporating in it the subjective, the 'natural', and thereby using it to modernize classicism. The subjective feelings of the observer were classified into a number of precisely described, and therefore more or less objective, feelings. These feelings in turn were categorized in precisely argued concepts, such as the 'elegant' (the 'graceful'), the 'sombre', the 'dignified', the 'strict' and the 'sublime'.

This theory of aesthetics, that was in principle a codification of perceptions, centred on the concept of *character*. A work of art, a building, has character, if it expresses its function and status through its form, ornamentation and location (which can be, for example, 'sombre', 'graceful', 'dignified' or 'sublime'). The architect and theorist Germain Boffrand (1667–1754) was the first to systematically describe *caractère* in his *Livre d'architecture* (1745).[2] The theorist Nicolas le Camus de Mézières (1721–c.1793) in his *Génie de l'architecture; ou L'analogie de cet art avec nos sensations* (The Genius of Architecture; or, The Analogy of that Art with Our Sensations, 1780) summarized thus the generally held view: 'Fixed and invariable rules govern the formation of taste and the process by which we manipulate, in a manner both distinct and sublime, the mechanism that gratifies the senses and conveys into the soul that delicious emotion that ravishes and charms us.'[3] In 1788 the theorist Antoine-Chrysostome Quatremère de Quincy (1755–1849) discussed the concept of character in great depth in his contribution to Charles-

Joseph Panckoucke's *Encyclopédie Méthodique* (1788–1825). His central idea was that in architecture the concept of 'character' has three meanings. A building has 'a specific character' (*un caractère*) when the observer discerns a certain degree of originality, an out-of-the-ordinary exterior form. It has 'character' (*caractère*) when it has characteristics that strike the observer, especially through grandeur or through the audacity or solidity of anything approaching magnificence or strength. A building has its 'its own character' (*son caractère*) if its exterior, visible characteristics proclaim its purpose.[4] This classification had a relevance more theoretical than practical – in practice the three definitions are interwoven. Seen from the perspective of the theoretical developments that were to follow in the nineteenth century, the last definition is the important one: character is the expression of 'the purpose' (the *destination*, the *pourquoi il est fait*), of what nowadays we would call 'the function' of the building.

Perrault's *Ordonnance* demonstrated that 'character aesthetics' was based on the Vitruvian tradition. Vitruvius taught that *venustas*, or beauty, consisted of six elements that were divided into three categories: *ordinatio*, *eurythmia* and *symmetria*, referring mainly to a building's proportions; *dispositio*, the constituent part of the design; and *decor* and *distributio*, which described the proper form of a building in relation to its function. The theory of character developed from the three latter elements in particular.

Apart from the theory of asthetics that put the sensory experiences and feelings of the observer first, there was another that saw architectural beauty basically as an intrinsic characteristic of the object itself, a characteristic that existed in essence independently of personal, subjective perception. This view was in line with the tradition of the aesthetics of proportion that Perrault had questioned, but which had been strongly defended by Perrault's learned and eminent opponent, the mathematician and architect François Blondel (1617–87), in his *Cours d'architecture* (1675–83). This theory focusing on the supra-individual, objective system was expounded in 1753 in the treatise by the French abbot Marc-Antoine Laugier (1713–69) entitled *Essai sur l'Architecture*. This influential treatise also aimed to reform classicism and adapt it to the demands of the new era. Like so many other innovators, Laugier reverted to the original 'pure' basic principles of classicism, principles which, with the advent of the decorative late baroque, had disappeared from sight. '[I]t is to be hoped that some great architect will undertake to save the art of building from eccentric opinions by disclosing its fixed and unchangeable laws,' he stated, concluding that 'absolute beauty [*beautés essentielles*] is inherent in the art of building independent of mental habit and human prejudice'.[5]

The work by the Parisian architect Jean-Nicholas-Louis Durand (1760–1834 see pp. 19, 22), the *Précis des leçons données à l'École Polytechnique* (first edition 1802–5), fits into this tradition. It reduced architecture to a simple modular design system, based on a quadrantal floor plan and round-arched openings (windows, doors, arcades) in the elevations. Ornamentation played only a minor role. Durand's method was in his time a radical modernization and rationalization – perhaps we could even say a democratization of the Vitruvian tradition. In a sense, architecture became civil engineering, less a question of erudition and culture and more a question of simple common sense and technique.

Conscious anti-classicism came into being two decades later, in Germany. Formulated by the architect Heinrich Hübsch (1795–1863) in his treatise *In welchem Style sollen wir bauen?* (In What Style Should We Build?, 1828), it met with wide approval. He concluded that imitating ancient Greek architecture was preposterous for climatic and technical reasons, and from an art-historical point of view quite outmoded – after all, classical antiquity did not constitute an ideal for modern drama, poetry or any of the other arts. Hübsch argued that a building should be designed according to objective basic principles and solid data: the function, and the mode and materials of construction to be employed. What remained was 'free art'. A theory intended to point the way for this free art should consist not of a collection of philosophical concepts, but of a system of concepts originating from architecture itself: a *style*, in other words. Hübsch understood 'style' to mean the general form that is developed in a special way by the artist and that is based on the 'national aspect' (for example, a Greek, Egyptian or Moorish style), the climate, building technique and function.[6]

Hübsch was not the first to expound this definition of the concept of style, and he used the definition of 'character' in the way that it had been established in late-eighteenth-century France. The architect Jacques-François Blondel (1705–74) further refined the concept of *caractère* as a continuation of the ideas of Boffrand, in 1771 linking it to the concept of *style*. 'Style', he said, was the highest guiding principle that determined the form of a building, character was one of the components of that principle, and the various styles originated from the various types of character. These types of character could be determined by the characteristics of peoples – for this reason Egyptian architecture, for example, differed from Greek architecture, and Roman from Gothic.[7] For the headword 'character' in the *Encyclopédie Méthodique* (published in 1788) Quatremère de Quincy wrote: 'As for the immediate influence of physical or natural causes on the character of the various architectural outputs of various peoples, nobody will deny that there is a close interrelationship between on the one hand the way of life, the climate and the materials available, and on the other hand the characteristic architectural forms.'[8]

Shortly afterwards Quatremère de Quincy also made the connection between character and style. The entry 'style' in the *Encyclopédie*, probably written in about 1790 but not published until 1825 on account of the prevailing social turmoil, contains two definitions. The first refers only to literature. Then:

According to the second view, *style* is defined in a much more general sense, as that typical and characteristic form that through very general causes is attributed to products of the mind, in accordance with the differences in climate, customs, acts of governments, and political or moral attitudes. In this latter sense *style* becomes synonymous with *character*, i.e. with a special way of doing things and with the specific appearance peculiar to each work, each creator, each genre, each school [of thought], each country, each century, et cetera.[9]

This definition used by Quatremère de Quincy and Hübsch – that style expresses the character of a people, the climate and the geographical and geological circumstances, which are expressed in the building materials – may go back as far as the famous archaeologist Johann Joachim Winckelmann (1717–68), who in the first chapter of his *Geschichte der Kunst des Altertums* (History of the Art of Antiquity, 1764) attributed the diversity of art in the world to the differences in climate and geography, and the customs and traditions of peoples.[10] As with Quatremère de Quincy's definition of character, the definition of style as postulated by him and by Hübsch remained in use throughout the nineteenth century.

However, Hübsch added an important new dimension, which the confirmed classicist Quatremère de Quincy did not. In the course of a study tour of many years' duration through southern Europe, Hübsch learned that during the period after the fall of the Roman Empire there had been two styles, the round-arch style (*Rundbogenstil*) and the pointed-arch style (*Spitzbogenstil*). The round-arch style, a characteristic of Byzantine, Lombard and Roman buildings, was then displaced by the pointed-arch style of the Middle Ages. To Hübsch, the construction and the decorative simplicity, the functionality and 'truth' of the round-arch style, seemed eminently suitable for further development in his own era. After the major revolutions and wars that took place around 1800, Europe was experiencing a period of recovery and reconstruction. And since this change occurred slowly and in conditions of great austerity, and demanded a simple, functional architecture, the pointed-arch style, which was far from simple, he considered less suitable.

Hübsch's plea was for a combination of rational and pragmatic arguments and Romantic ideas, and it introduced a quest for a national - that is to say, German - and contemporary style stemming from a shared past. Hübsch regarded the Romanesque Maria Laach Abbey at Koblenz as the best study model for his time. But whereas Durand in France upheld the Vitruvian tradition with his own round-arch style, Hübsch loosened the tie with Vitruvianism. The typically Vitruvian aspect of Durand lay in the fact that he saw style as an intrinsic characteristic of architecture; the anti-Vitruvian aspect of Hübsch was that style was for him a contingent characteristic, one that could vary in accordance with the determining historical and geographical circumstances.[11]

Hübsch also introduced a new aesthetic concept which he proclaimed to be one of the principal laws of the art of building: *truth*. Truth implied, for example, that construction and decoration were not to contradict each other: 'Because the first principle in art must be truth, we must not overlay bare yet functional walls with feigned constructions.' Walls had to be made rich and beautiful through the careful treatment of materials and by ensuring that exterior, functional, structural features were linked to the construction of the interior.[12] It would seem plausible that Hübsch based this rule on the essence of neoclassicist aesthetics, the standard of beauty derived from Greek temples, as expressed by, among others, the archaeologist Aloys Hirt (1759–1837) in 1809. Hirt argued that 'Architectural beauty cannot be created at the expense of the construction, or at the expense of a functional layout and interior. The nature of beauty must arise from the construction and from a functional arrangement, and must be based on these.'[13]

Truth was to remain a fundamental principle in the architectural theories of the nineteenth and twentieth centuries. For Hübsch it also dominated the relationship between the main form (based on objective basic principles and functional requirements) and the so-called 'free art' that supplemented it – a dichotomy already encountered in Laugier's references to the primary, load-bearing structure and the secondary 'additions'. Later, Karl Bötticher (1806–99), professor at the Bauakademie in Berlin since

1844, reformulated in his book on Greek architecture *Die Tektonik der Hellenen* (1844–52) the principal dichotomy that Hübsch had formulated as *Kernform* ('core-form') and *Kunstform* ('art-form'), the first being the invisible structural and functional essence of the building and the second the explicit artistic expression.[14]

Truth and character, then, were two members of the same family: the Vitruvian *decor*, the rule which, if a building was capable of expressing its function and its social status, led to beauty. In the concept of character, *decor* was represented by the subjective (but codified) perception of beauty. And we could say that, in the concept of truth, *decor* was to a greater degree objectified. While character presupposed a necessary relationship between the building and the observer, truth was an expression of characteristics within the object itself. Character related to the senses and feelings, truth was more closely associated with reason. An overemphasis on character opened the door to brilliant design, but also to superficiality, as the history of the nineteenth century would prove. An overemphasis on truth, on the other hand, was the characteristic of those who believed in a supra-personal, metaphysical truth and considered architecture to be instrumental in representing this higher truth.

These essentially eighteenth-century notions evolved outside of the Netherlands. However, from quite early on various prominent Dutch scholars and men of letters, including Frans Hemsterhuis (1721–90), Hiëronymus van Alphen (1746–1803), Bernard Nieuhoff (1747–1831) and Rhijnvis Feith (1753–1824), and architects such as Jacob Otten Husly (1735–95) and Abraham van der Hart (1747–1820), were acquainted with the latest theoretical concepts of art: these included the picturesque and the sublime, the aesthetics of character, and notions of national style and of the 'simple' style that Winckelmann had demonstrated so felicitously in Greek art. The Dutch architect Pieter de Swart (1709–73), much sought after in the highest circles, had studied at Jacques-François Blondel's École des Arts. Indeed, around 1800 in the Netherlands the theory of character was not unfamiliar, and certainly not in the dramatic arts where the rhetorical tradition and the doctrine concerning the appropriate use of style were still flourishing. The new concepts were also being expressed, albeit on a small scale, in architectural design – in the layout of gardens as well as in the construction of buildings.[15] Thus the state of affairs at the start of the nineteenth century was that Dutch theorists and architects were acquainted with the disintegration of Vitruvianism, which, though, had never become as

monolithic a doctrine in the Seven Provinces as it had in France. And they were also familiar with the new ideas. But the reality was that the Netherlands was being presented with solutions to problems that hardly existed. Because building activity, in particular regarding buildings in which there was scope for architectural expression, had come to a virtual standstill in the decades around 1800, a period of fifty or sixty years, the very small Dutch community of architects was more or less dormant.

The Batavian Revolution and the foundation of the Batavian Republic (1795) brought the old confederated Republic of the Seven Provinces to an end. It was the start of a new united state. The Revolution was inspired by the French Revolution of 1789, and the French actively supported the Batavian Republic and exploited the new situation for the benefit of their foreign policy against England. In 1806, Napoleon Bonaparte was responsible for turning the Batavian Republic into a seemingly independent monarchy headed by his brother Louis as its

king. In 1810 the monarchy was annexed by France, after which it became an integral part of the French Empire until 1813.

In the 1840s, the French art of building still set the tone in the Netherlands for the small number of monumental commissions that were awarded, thus continuing a long-standing tradition. In the eighteenth century, the main Dutch architects and their clients had abandoned the tradition of seventeenth-century Dutch classicism and turned to late French classicism. At the end of the eighteenth century the 'Louis XVI' fashion was replaced by the first examples of neoclassicism, while at the same time prominent architects rediscovered the architectural qualities of seventeenth-century Dutch classicism. The inevitable outcome was that new hybrids were created from these two prevailing design concepts and the new trends that supplanted 'Louis XVI' architecture were not just a new fashion. They entailed an essentially different view of architecture, corresponding with the French theories in which decorative abundance was suppressed in favour of

tectonic, structural characteristics that had more to do with notions of supporting, enfolding and covering.

In 1810 the ties with the French art of building had been strengthened when King Louis Bonaparte enabled several talented young Dutch architects to study in Paris on a grant. After the Empire had fallen in 1813 and the Kingdom of the United Netherlands had been founded, headed by the first Dutch king, Willem I, those same young architects became men of standing. Some became court or municipal architects (Bartholomeus Willem Hendrik Ziesenis, Jan de Greef, Tilleman François Suys, Charles Vander Straeten), while others became town architects (Abraham van der Hart in Amsterdam, Zeger Reijers in The Hague) or teachers at art academies, as did De Greef and Suys. The works of such architects reflected the whole panorama of late eighteenth-century Parisian architecture: the heavy sculptural treatment of Jacques-Germain Soufflot, the elegant empire style of Charles Percier and Pierre-François-Léonard Fontaine, the somewhat mannerist wilfulness of Claude-Nicholas Ledoux, the

Fig.5–6
Abraham van der
Hart's entry for a
French competition to
design a monument in
honour of Napoleon
(1814) at the Mont
Cenis, the place where
the road from Paris to
Turin passes the
French Alps. View of
the main façade
(below left) and side
wall, cross-section
and floor plan. The
design exemplifies the
theory of *architecture
parlante* –
'architecture with a
narrative exterior' –
a language then
understood
throughout Europe.
The building evokes
an impressive, noble
simplicity and a
representation of the
sublime, by virtue of
the almost terrifying
dimensions of its
pyramid (100 X 100
X 100 metres) with a
Gothic interior.

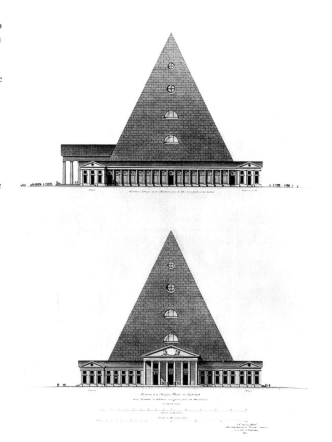

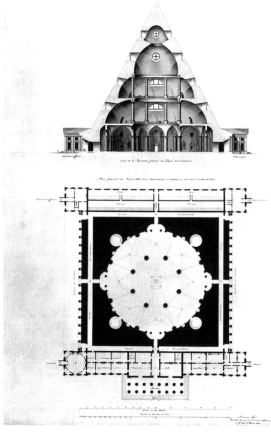

literary evocations of Étienne-Louis Boullée or the simplicity of Durand. Jan David Zocher the younger (1791–1870), who had also been sent to Paris by King Louis, started a flourishing private practice, and became famous for his designs of country houses and parks. Together with a few other colleagues, the Dutch architects made up a select but very small group. As for monumental architecture, hardly any commissions were forthcoming in the decades following 1813. Architecture in the eighteenth century had been patronized by the court of the Stadholder, or governor, in The Hague and by the Amsterdam aristocracy, but at the start of the nineteenth century, in face of the protracted economic depression, these two groups exercised more restraint. Neither did King Willem take on the role of client. Thus architecture lacked incentives at this time, due on the one hand to the lack of challenging commissions and, on the other, to the fact that intellectual interchange on the subject was still minimal.

The main links between the French concepts of the art

of building and Dutch practice were the French books on architecture such as the ten-volume *Recueil élémentaire d'architecture* [Elementary Architecture], *contenant des distributions de bâtimens bourgeois* by Jean-François de Neufforge (1757–80), the *Cours d'architecture ou traité de la décoration, distribution et construction des bâtimens* by Jacques-François Blondel (1771–7, six volumes of text, three of illustrations), mentioned earlier, and Durand's works. Occasionally Dutch works were published which, without any significant annotation, incorporated examples of modern French architecture, such as Johannes van Straaten's (1781–1858) *Illustrations of Ancient and Modern Structures, Borrowed from Greek, Roman and Eastern Temples, Palaces, Theatres, Baths and Other Extant Buildings or Parts Thereof, including Ruins* (1828–32).[16]

The same intellectual reticence applied in the Netherlands to aesthetics. In 1830, Friedrich Bouterwek's *Principles of the Theory of Aesthetics* was published, translated from the German. According to the editor's foreword, it was with some hesitation that the work was being published at all, despite the

Fig.7
Residential buildings at the Van Asch van Wyckskade, Utrecht (1833–9), by Jan David Zocher. These houses are part of a much larger project of Zocher's that was not built – a new district in Utrecht for the working class (1829–30), a modular, geometrical design recalling Durand's influential *Précis* (Summary of Lectures on Architecture).

fact that the only Dutch work available on the subject of aesthetics dated to as far back as 1802 – *Euryalus on Aesthetics* by J. F. van Beeck Calkoen. Bouterwek (1768–1866), a professor at Göttingen University, was not one of the leading philosophers of his time. Rather, he reworked the prevailing philosophical views into educational material. Only because Dutch books on the subject of aesthetics were extremely rare is it significant to mention his *Principles*, in particular with regard to his definition of aesthetics, which he called a *science*, a system of knowledge that allowed insight into man and the world around him; beauty, despite its metaphysical essence, was according to Bouterwek a rational, even a systematic, phenomenon. The issue that the main theories on architecture would now start to focus on was this: how could the architect *idealize* the physical reality of a building (materials, construction, function), transform the materials into an idea, and thus create a work of art? What tools were available to him? We shall discover that these questions were invariably associated with the categories of truth and character.

At the beginning of the nineteenth century, apart from the select group of architects whose canon was French architecture, there was a much larger number who were less talented, had fewer artistic ambitions and poorer social standing. They were the craftsmen, master carpenters or master bricklayers who acted as contractors, and they were often also involved in designing. These designer-craftsmen were no new phenomenon: they were merely carrying on a centuries-old Dutch tradition which would continue throughout the century. Apart from the odd town architect, they would not refer to themselves as master builders, let alone architects. There was, though, a category of designers who were not architects in the usual sense but who did establish a new profession; these were mainly officials who had a civil engineering background and who were employed by what could be described as the Ministry of Public Works.[17] They were involved mainly in the construction of public buildings, either as designers or as assessors of the building plans of others.

This heterogeneous group of craftsmen and officials

Fig.8
Dordrecht Town
Hall: George Nicolaas
Itz's design for the
reconstruction of the
medieval façade 'in
accordance with
ancient Greek taste'
(executed 1835–41).
As Dordrecht town
architect, during
1832–65 Itz also built
there the corn
exchange, the
weighhouse, the
orphanage, the post
office, the lunatic
asylum, schools, a
number of churches
and many new iron
bridges.

OPPOSITE
Fig.9
The promotion of
culture and religion:
classicism with
pointed arches, the
public expression of
the function of the
building. The
Evangelical Lutheran
Church, Amersfoort,
in the province of
Gelderland, by
B. Ruitenberg (1837).

with a technical background was responsible for most of the more important, representational buildings. And together they created an architectural picture that was just as heterogeneous, composed as it was of classical elements integrated into otherwise sober brick buildings. As far as churches were concerned, these classical elements would often be combined with Gothic details: Gothic windows, decorative vaults or stucco moulding.

The works of these lower-ranking designers did not suggest any underlying architectural theory – rather the opposite. Neither does it lead one to suspect that any notable buildings, Dutch or foreign, served as sources of inspiration. This does not mean, however, that these designers did not have distinct views on aesthetics or on architecture. In fact, the archives of the Ministry of Public Works reveal a profound interest in structural strength and functionalism, in addition to simplicity, which was a pivotal requirement. To regard this insistence on simplicity – on *firmitas* and *utilitas* – as a question of cost control would do little justice to the matter, although economy is usually the only motive that is referred to in the archives. It is, however, the case that simplicity as a consequence of the stringencies imposed by an economically difficult period played a major role not only in the minds of the Dutch Ministry of Public Works officials, but also in the opinion of Durand and Hübsch. Simplicity in architecture was the spirit of the age, and economic depression did not stop at the Dutch border.

It may very well be that the Public Works officials and the master craftsmen with their haphazard handling of columns, frontons, Gothic arches, cornice fronts and mouldings were continuing a tradition of long standing. In any event, until 1760 or 1765, strict application of the rules of the five classical orders – the Doric, Ionic, Corinthian, Tuscan and the Composite – had been uncommon in the Netherlands. The growing influence of neoclassicism had changed this only slightly – that is to say, change was noticeably only amongst the small group of architects who favoured theoretical reflection and were interested in foreign architecture. But the plea for rules in architecture, as well as for a more accurate interpretation of and adherence to those rules, was also directed towards less scholarly practitioners, as set out in *The Vignola of Craftsmen, or a Simple Way to Draw the Five Orders* (1825) by the builder-architect Johannes van Straaten, already mentioned. The book was a translation of the French architect and engineer Charles Normand's *Le Vignole des ouvriers* (1821); reprinted in 1835 and then in 1851, it was a traditional continuation of Vitruvianism in architectural education. The title refers to the *Rules of the Five Architectural Orders* by Jacopo Barozzi (known as 'Vignola'),

published in 1562, with many editions up to the nineteenth century. Van Straaten's *Vignola* contained some neoclassicist insights, but did not provide the necessary practical tools for designing. *Theoretical and Practical Building* (1827–34) by the engineer Willem Christiaan Brade (1791–1858) made references to Durand, but here, too, classical tradition was still adhered to. Until the 1850s, the Dutch classicist translation of the sixteenth-century Italian architect Vincenzo Scamozzi by Symen Bosboom, dating from c.1760 and republished in 1821 and 1854, was still being used for instructional purposes.

An outline of Dutch architecture in the first thirty years of the nineteenth century cannot end without a mention of the notion already current in the period, and which would remain widely accepted until quite late in the twentieth century – namely, that these first three decades were a period of decline. It would require a whole other study to reconstruct exactly what this 'decline' implied, but there was no shortage of suggestions as to the causes. In 1843, for example, a clergyman proposed, amongst other things, that the decline was due to the fact that for so many years the Netherlands had been a republic and that the prevalent

have been conducive to growth or advances in architecture. It was not until after 1840 that political, cultural and economic changes began to be witnessed, along with a new élan. 'Decline' would soon become a thing of the past.

Notes

1.　For this text from Perrault: Caroline van Eck 1994, 84–9.
2.　For the the theoretical development of the concept in France, see W. Szambien 1987, ch. 9. For the reception of *caractère* in eighteenth-century Germany: U. Schütte 1981, 30–4, and *Untersuchungen* 1788 (1986). Following Szambien the theory of character is usually associated with the studies of physiognomy by the Swiss writer and theologian Johann Kaspar Lavater (1741–1801). For the relationship between the theory of character and the philosophical tradition of rhetoric would appear to be more fundamental: Caroline van Eck 1994, 57–62; Caroline van Eck 1995.
3.　Nicolas le Camus de Mézières 1992, 74.
4.　Antoine-Chrysostome Quatremère de Quincy 1788–1825, Part V, vol. 1, 490. For the rhetorical background: Caroline van Eck 1995, 98–101.
5.　Marc-Antoine Laugier 1977, 2–3.
6.　Heinrich Hübsch 1992, 66–8.
7.　Jacques-François Blondel 1771–7, I, 373.
8.　Antoine-Chrysostome Quatremère de Quincy 1788–1825, Part V, vol. 1, 492.
9.　Antoine-Chrysostome Quatremère de Quincy 1788–1825, Part V, vol. 3, 411.
10.　Johann Joachim Winckelmann 1994, ch. 1, 'Von dem Ursprunge der Kunst und der Ursachen ihrer Verschiedenheit unter den Völkern', in particular 35ff.
11.　For the distinction between style as an intrinsic and style as a contingent characteristic: Caroline van Eck 1995.
12.　Heinrich Hübsch 1992, 96–7.
13.　Aloys Hirt 1809, 13, quoted by Georg Germann 1972, 37: 'Das architektonische Schöne kann weder auf Unkosten der Konstruktion, noch zum Nachteil einer zweckmäßigen Anlage und Einrichtung stattfinden; vielmehr muß das Wesen des Schönen aus der Konstruktion und einer zweckmäßigen Anordnung hervorgehen und gleichsam darauf ruhen.'
14.　Karl G. W. Bötticher 1874, 2nd edn, 20, 24–5, 34, 36; Caroline van Eck 1994, 164–7.
15.　Erik de Jong 1989a and 1989b; Paul Knolle 1989; Erik de Jong 1992; C. A. van Swigchem 1965; Freek H. Schmidt 1999. (The catalogue of Dutch publications on art theory by J. de Man et al. (ed.) 1993 is incomplete as far as architecture is concerned.)
16.　A list of French and other foreign books used in the Netherlands: C. A. van Swigchem 1965, esp. appendixes 1 and 3.
17.　For both groups: Coert P. Krabbe 1998, chs 1–3, *passim*.
18.　A. A. Stuart 1843, 8–11.

religion was Protestantism. Since neither of these factors had been conducive to any form of splendour, so the argument went, they were unable to stimulate any artistic sense. Other causes he suggested were the lack of beautiful natural building stone; the Dutch climate, which created a tradition of solidity rather than opulence; the poor training opportunities for craftsmen; and the sloppiness, idleness and addiction to alcohol of the typical Dutch workman, which resulted in workmen from abroad rather than the local workmen being employed on the more important Amsterdam buildings.[18] Such were the views of a contemporary, the author of a book entitled *The Advancement of the Art of Building in relation to the Moral Education of Builders*.

Today we would perhaps draw different inferences. Could the general decline be attributed to the low level of building activity and to the constant call for economies, as a direct result of the long economic depression? Certainly, the climate for investment until 1840 was unfavourable. Furthermore, from 1830 to 1839 the northern Netherlands kept the army mobilized against the southern provinces which, in 1830, had declared their independence under the name of Belgium – another circumstance that could not

2

A New Spirit in Dutch Architecture: The 1840s

The 1840s were to see more movement and more initiatives concerning the art of building than had the previous decades. Economic conditions in the Netherlands were gradually improving, as were the chances of new commissions for her architects. More important in this period were the changes in the cultural climate. With the abdication of Willem I in 1840 came the end of an autocratic centralist regime. During the short reign of Willem II (1840–9) centralism proved untenable, and gradually a more pluralist society came into being. Establishing the rights and responsibilities of the individual became a political and cultural ideal.

Unlike his father, Willem II was a lover and patron of the arts. However, the true reasons for the revival of architecture probably lay elsewhere. The Stadholder court in The Hague and the Amsterdam aristocracy were no longer the main forces behind developments in architecture. In the 1840s it was the upper middle class in Amsterdam that started to set the tone, and for a long while to come. The foundation of the Maatschappij tot Bevordering der Bouwkunst (the MBB, the Society for the Advancement of the Art of Building) in 1842 played an important role in this shift. This society and its journal *Bouwkundige Bijdragen* (Architectural Essays) had a national scope but were dominated by the Amsterdam scene; and the society's activities were centred in Amsterdam, where by establishing contact with prominent artists it became one of the driving forces behind the social rise of the profession of architect.[1]

Roots in a distant past

The most prominent dignitary to devote himself to the art of building was Daniël David Büchler (1787–1871), an insurance broker from Amsterdam. Büchler was one of the founders of the MBB and would remain a member of the board until 1862. In 1843, as his entry for a competition that the new society had organized, he wrote a treatise entitled *On the Art of Dutch Building*, which was published in 1845. The central theme of the competition was: 'What is the reason for our poor progress in architecture compared with foreign architecture, and what can we do to stimulate the process so as to equal the position we hold in the arts generally?[2] Büchler argued that the level at which the art of building was being practised in the Netherlands could only be raised if architects were able to give their profession a solid twofold foundation – scientific as well as artistic. By the latter he meant the realm of the imagination, individual freedom of expression, the cultivation of personal taste and feeling. The former referred to objective knowledge, rational thinking, verifiable decisions, the laws of aesthetics. Indeed, Bouterwek's book on aesthetics (1830, see pp. 8–9) proved that the theory of aesthetics should be considered a part of science. According to Büchler, the art of building was 'of all the forms of art, the least related to *inspiration* or to an innate talent; it is a form of science rather than an art. The architect is not born as such, but is formed in the process. He does not possess art, but acquires it after an arduous journey.'

By setting high standards for the profession, Büchler distinguished the architect from the craftsman; a hierarchic distinction was being made between the thinker and the doer, the designer and the artisan. In this way he was recording the end of the long national tradition of architecture as the domain of uneducated practitioners – designer-craftsmen, master carpenters, master bricklayers, sometimes even surveyors, builders of mills, and Public Works officials.

The course of history in the decades following 1840 would seem to prove Büchler right. The master bricklayers and the other craftsmen appeared to be making their exit as the main protagonists on the building scene, and designing became a specialism, even a profession in its own right. However, this picture gives us only the superficial view. In the 1870s and well into the 1890s, the designer-craftsmen were more prominent than ever before, as will be shown later. They dominated the building trade and marginalized the architect. In the decades following 1840 these professional designers of buildings did not have an easy time. They possessed only one trump card that might prove them superior to the craftsmen. This was not their technical know-how – for a long time the craftsmen's skills

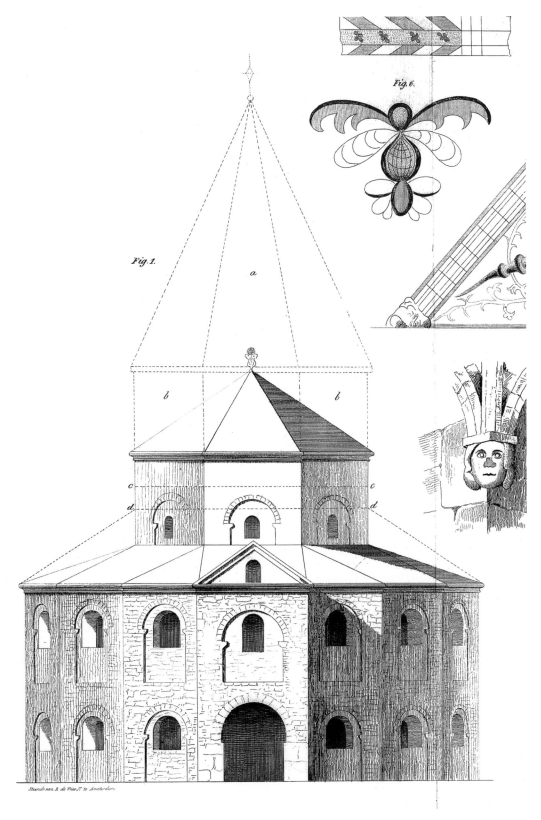

Fig.1.

Fig.6.

Fig.10
Details of the
drawings for the
reconstruction of the
Romanesque Chapel
of St Nicholas,
Nijmegen (1845), by
Alexander Oltmans
the younger,
published in
*Bouwkundige
Bijdragen* in 1846. Old
buildings no longer
functioned purely as
the site of historical
events, but were also
studied for their
architectural features,
becoming elements in
a gradually expanding
architectural history.

could hold their own against the architects' learning. Rather, the trump card was to be found in aesthetics and art. Architects started to conceive an art of building that complied with the rules they set themselves and which excluded the craftsmen's work as being non-art. The advancement of the art of building during the nineteenth century would thus be very closely connected with the protection of the professional status of the architect.

When, in the 1840s, supported by the MBB, the architects started to manifest themselves more emphatically as specialists, the time had come to play that trump card. The French and neoclassicist design concepts that had dominated the design process in the past decades were losing ground, resulting in a longing for change. Inspired by recent developments in German architectural theory and practice, a small group of young Dutch architects gave direction to that change, by starting critically to explore and analyse the foundations of the art of building. The time was ripe. Recent German research created a more multiform picture, in which art that according to that classicist standard could not have been recognized as such – for example, the art of the Middle Ages – was also given a place. Pioneering work in this field, carried out by the German art historian Franz Kugler, was published in his *Handbuch der Kunstgeschichte* (History of Art Handbook) (1841–2). The importance of this new version was soon recognized by the board of the MBB. From 1843 until 1851 the journal *Bouwkundige Bijdragen* published a serialized translation of texts from the *Handbuch*, which were devoted to architecture. Meanwhile, the editors also accepted for publication studies of monuments in the Netherlands.

During a meeting of the MBB in 1843, Büchler propounded the importance of the new vision. The new art-historical discoveries were 'an invaluable source of knowledge as well as a model, bequeathed to us by centuries gone by', and he further noted that 'the future revival of art has its roots in a distant past'.

These words attributed a meaning to the architecture of the past which throughout the nineteenth century would both stimulate and plague thinking about contemporary architecture. In 1843, the past still seemed full of promise for the future of architecture, but the intensifying scrutiny of the past would create increasing tension in the decades that followed. Architectural history would become a rich source of inspiration and research material, which would increase the understanding of the rules of the art of building. On the other hand, history would also tempt the searching nineteenth-century architect to cultivate the historical model indiscriminately, even to make it into an absolute, with servile imitation resulting. The dilemma

would become more and more evident: the contemporary art of building could not, it was clear, consist of repeating the steps that had been taken in the past: but, equally, originality not based on tradition was mere individualistic capriciousness and therefore could not be a basis for art. For the sine qua non of art was collective experiences laid down in *rules*. Complying with these rules implied an adherence to tradition, and to a collective and therefore more or less *objective* opinion. Büchler was among the many who, until the turn of the century, warned that the architect could not tear himself loose from the history of architecture without isolating himself creatively.

The view that the originality of an architectural design must be rooted in tradition if it was not to disqualify itself is interesting from the perspective of art theory. It differed from the Romantic ideal of the artist's individual personality that had been the stimulating force behind the visual arts and literature outside the Netherlands. Was the tendency to hold on to artistic conventions, and a collective ideal of aesthetics as advocated by Büchler, typically Dutch, in so far as the cult of genius was at odds with the Dutch cult of composure and moderation? Or was it simply typical of the art of building as opposed to painting and literature, in that architecture was heavily dependent on conventions in order to take material form?

The 1840s saw the beginning of the difficult process that nineteenth-century architecture apparently had to go through – namely, the beginning of the end of the belief that art is subject to objective laws, that process in which the pursuit of a collective ideal of beauty had to be abandoned and the dislike of individualism and multiformity overcome. That this process started as late as it did can be deduced from the new way in which the principles of the art of building were being openly discussed and described. The difference could be heard in the unprecedentedly strident tone that could now occasionally be witnessed in harsh architectural reviews, and in the increasingly sharp analysis of the possibilities and problems of contemporary architecture. There was a clear belief that an entirely contemporary architecture did not yet exist. The relative calm of the first decades of the nineteenth century were now making way for unrest, and the realization was sinking in that the key to a contemporary art of building had been lost and could only be retrieved by means of an assiduous search in many directions.

Attention was now directed not only towards the exterior manifestation of buildings, the form of the architectural design, but, just as importantly, towards the collective, social significance of the art of building, and

Fig.11
Jan David Zocher's Stock Exchange, Amsterdam (1840–5), the headquarters of the Dutch economic elite. The very image of conventional distinction? Depending on their position in the architectural debate of the time, insiders saw it as a sophisticated and fanciful use of architectural conventions, or as a flagrant violation of essential architectural values. The contractor for the building was Johannes van Straaten, the author of several books on architecture.

therefore towards the social significance of the architect. This significance did not centre on the art of building in general, but on a specific characteristic: *style*. Style, according to the popular viewpoint that was to remain in force for the decades post-1840, was an expression of the ethics, customs, characteristics and institutions of a nation. Therefore the nineteenth-century search for a contemporary style was in fact a search for society's identity – an identity which would prove to be increasingly diverse and therefore increasingly elusive. 'Style' was the link between contemporary architecture and society: the search for this style was arduous and sometimes even led to despondency – to give up on it would irrevocably place architecture outside society, resulting in its bankruptcy. Style was thus far more than an interrelated system of forms. Style represented integrity – 'truth' – and character, often with political or religious connotations. These principles of the art of building were now being propounded in an ever-increasing exchange of ideas, in journals, pamphlets and books.

Character, Vitruvius, and Zocher's Stock Exchange
The first public debate on the principles of the art of building that demonstrated the new, more critical and polemical, approach, was provoked by Jan David Zocher's design for the new Amsterdam Stock Exchange in 1840.

The most vehement and detailed criticism came from Isaäc Warnsinck (1811–57), a young architect from Amsterdam who in 1842 was to be a co-founder and director of the MBB. Warnsinck demonstrated, among other things, that this classicist building did not meet the necessary requirement of beauty which, since Vitruvius, had been considered necessary – that is, the requirement of *decor*, or the correct appearance of a building. The building as a whole, did not express its function. The closed façades gave no indication of the construction and layout of the interior, nor of its functions; moreover, they had been divided up, with recesses that looked like doors, which they in fact were not. And the portico lacked a fronton, as if to deny that it was part of the building.[3] Its Ionic columns suggested a museum, or a hall of science.

By the end of 1840, it became apparent that the criticism of the design of the new Stock Exchange was not an isolated phenomenon. A review published by the *Utrechtsche Provinciale en Stads-Courant* (*Utrecht Courier*) of the recently completed church of St Augustin, built by Zocher's younger brother Karel George (1797–1863), demonstrated in its detailed criticism that in many ways the architect had not strictly followed the classical rules.[4] Although this criticism may be interpreted as a delayed neoclassicist reaction once again proclaiming obedience to the original principles of the art of building, it is rather dubious whether as late as 1840 it could be interpreted as a plea for a purely neoclassicist way of building. Feeling that neoclassicism was no longer appropriate for Dutch architecture, Warnsinck was already drawing on contemporary German architecture for new inspiration. It could be argued, in fact, that he felt that, in 1840, neoclassicism as a 'style' was no longer suitable as a means of representing Dutch culture or the Dutch nation. Perhaps, given its claim that as a design concept it was universally suited to all places and times, classicism was by definition unable to express the specific qualities of contemporary place and time (as was neoclassicism). The growing need for an art of building expressing the nation's own culture and character is perhaps a more convincing explanation for the disappearance of classicism as a form concept in these years than the notion frequently suggested that it had reached the point of exhaustion. Warnsinck's criticism of Zocher was not a plea in favour of the classical art of building per se; it was, rather, a plea for the application of the rules of art. In other words, if one opted for neoclassicism, one had to comply with the rules associated with it, because without them, without the rules of beauty, no work of art could be created. Thus Warnsinck foreshadowed what Büchler was to formulate a few years later: that the art of building was not a matter of personal freedom, but of *science*.

This brings us to the second aspect concerning the debate on Zocher's Stock Exchange. In view of the themes raised by Büchler, it is probable that the attack on Zocher – for that is what it was – could also be interpreted as a sign of the growing professionalization of the architect; those who saw themselves as architects contrasted their theoretical and historical knowledge of the art of building with the ineptitude of the mere 'practitioner'. Furthermore, the new, more critical culture of the 1840s was playing its part in promoting the architect's status, not least of all in the verbal punishment it inflicted in one instance on one such 'practitioner'. In 1845 the *Bouwkundige Bijdragen* published an article containing fierce criticism of the recently completed St Joseph's Church at Haarlem (1841–3), the main architectural work of the Public Works engineer Herman Hendrik Dansdorp (1788–1873). Not mincing his words, the author of the article argued that the church was a product of somebody who either did not know or did not understand the rules and conventions of the art of building.[5]

Despite the similarity with the criticism of the Stock Exchange, there was one big difference. Unlike his brother and unlike Dansdorp, Jan David Zocher was a man of great standing, entirely familiar with developments inside and outside his profession. Of course he was capable, had he wished, of applying the rules of classicism. And there was no doubt that his rejection of this option was deliberate. The Stock Exchange had been the most prestigious commission of the 1840s, located at a prime site, diagonally opposite the Royal Palace on Dam Square. It was therefore only natural that Zocher went out of his way to make his statement as an architect.

To assess the building itself, we first need to establish that Zocher had the courage under these circumstances to deconstruct the value of classicism as a theory of form and a canon of artistic conventions. His design for the Stock Exchange showed clearly that he had opted for the Romantic conception of art, while using classicist material as he thought proper. Nor was he alone in doing so. A number of prominent architects including John Nash and John Soane in London, Hippolyte Lebas, Félix Duban, Louis Duc and others in Paris, had done the same. His artistic independence set Zocher at odds with the view held by Büchler and many others, that art would not tolerate an architect breaking loose from tradition in order to follow his own course. The Stock Exchange expressed better than Zocher ever could have done in words his reaction to Warnsinck: that he was interested not in 'scientific' neoclassicist grammar and vocabulary, but, rather, in more fundamental architectural phenomena, independent of style. By combining in stark simplicity height with depth, enclosure with openness, compression with width, mass with emptiness, and construction with decoration, Zocher was exploring spatial and psychological effects. The surviving illustrations of the building show that in it he created, with classicist fragments that no longer bore their conventional meaning here, a new architectural reality that was an exemplary expression of the theory of character. Other works of Zocher's also show the low priority that he gave to historical accuracy, or 'style'.

We must bear in mind that Zocher, renowned for his garden and park designs, was probably, unlike any other Dutch architect, familiar with the theory and practicalities of 'character'. English landscape garden design, his speciality, stood more or less at the root of character aesthetics and of the inherent manipulation of feelings through spatial design. The small temples that were erected in English gardens, evoking 'the sublime', ruins conjuring up eternity and mortality, hermitages and caves expressing loneliness and contemplation, small farms – all of these called on the noble simplicity of the observer's mind. Carefully arranged plantings, ponds and memorial stones evoked grace, gloom or joyfulness or the riches of history and civilization. Similarly, by the positioning of the floor above street level, Zocher ensured that his Stock Exchange represented loftiness and edification. The columns of the portico enhanced this effect by their relatively large number, their height and their fluting. The long exchange hall with its two Doric colonnades created an aura of stateliness and solidity.

Johannes Jacobus Penn and the German influence

In 1841, while the Stock Exchange was under construction, the *Handbook of the Fine Art of Building* was published. Written by the young Dutch architect Johannes Jacobus Penn (1812–49), it was based on the proposition that the art of building had to be learned by diligent study of the three Greek orders, 'for these contain all the artist will ever need; these are the only three pure sources the architect can draw on to acquire the necessary knowledge for his sublime profession'.[6] Penn then specified in the usual detail the original Greek – not the Roman – Doric, Ionic and Corinthian orders: the form and size of the column, the base, the capital, the entablature, the fronton and so on. By opting for the pure Greek system, he struck a different note: up till then, architectural education in the Netherlands had been dominated by the Roman orders.

Penn had studied at the Bauakademie in Berlin, where the elite among German architects and theorists, in particular Karl Friedrich Schinkel (1781–1841), set the curriculum. Penn was therefore the obvious architect to introduce the views of the modern 'German School' into Dutch architectural education. However, in his belief in the classical Greek approach as the only path to the fine art of building, a doctrine which had become somewhat dated abroad, he fulfilled this role only partially. The two options for a contemporary art of building which in Germany had received most attention since Hübsch's *In What Style Should We Build?* had appeared in 1828, the *Rundbogenstil* (the round-arch style) and the *Spitzbogenstil* (the pointed-arch style), were not considered by Penn appropriate alternatives, despite the fact that Schinkel had applied the two liberally in practice. Penn's theory on aesthetics was indeed, in essence, Vitruvianism brought up to date. He argued: 'Perfectly exquisite forms include: 1. the right proportions; 2. order; 3. harmony; 4. symmetry; 5. simplicity; 6. variety and additional beauty (ornamentation). The ancient Greek and Roman buildings must be considered as having an exemplary function.'[7]

This list can largely be reduced to the aesthetic elements used by Vitruvius to determine the concept of beauty, or *venustas*: *ordinatio* (proportionality), *dispositio* (disposition), *eurythmia* (harmony), *symmetria* (symmetry), *decor* (correctness) and *distributio* (proper distribution). Penn

defined the first four exclusively with the help of Vitruvius. To have the right proportions between the constituent parts of the building was essential; order meant that, to the eye, all parts were disposed in an orderly manner; harmony was the compatibility of all parts, the interior as well as the exterior of the building; and without symmetry, 'a building cannot become exquisite, and this would be a reason to think that the architect has not given his plan sufficient consideration'. However, Penn's concepts of simplicity and variety had no longer anything to do with *decor* and *distributio*. Simplicity meant choosing the decoration with taste and feeling, avoiding superfluity; variety meant varying the application of the preceding five elements so as to avoid monotony. By putting it this way, Penn introduced concepts belonging to eighteenth-century sensationalist aesthetics: beauty was not so much an objective fact governed by rules, but an experience of the observer.

Penn argued that 'character' was the very core of architectural aesthetics; the character of a building determined its aesthetic design:

Character in the art of building means that the exterior immediately announces the intentions of the architect to the public. Thus, a building must be given a sombre, stately, bright or charming exterior in accordance with its function; be it a prison, a church, a castle or a country estate, in order that the exterior may make a specific impression, stir our imagination, evoke a certain thought in our minds.

The required character could be expressed by three means: through the location of the building, through its form and, in particular, through the use of mouldings, 'since the perfect expression depends entirely on these'.[8]

We have already noted that the character theory had been known in the Netherlands since the late eighteenth century, and it is possible that it was more closely associated with architectural practice than we can know for sure. There are only a few written sources relating to the first decades of the nineteenth century that could provide a more decisive answer. However, the characteristics of the art of building were made public not only through lectures but also, and in particular, through the practice of designing and building itself. Zocher's œuvre is just such an example; like many other hardworking architects, he hardly ever published his ideas.

The novelty of Penn's *Handbook of the Fine Art of Building* was that in the Netherlands it was the first to formulate the character theory, the theory of *architecture parlante* – or, in Penn's words, 'architecture with a narrative exterior' – in terms of practical rules that could be passed on through education. Here he made use of the knowledge which in Germany had already for quite some time been systematically collected for educational purposes, for example in the anonymously published *Study of the Character of Buildings, of the Relationship between the Art of Building and the Fine Arts, and of the Effects to be Achieved* (1788).[9] The concept of character was also dealt with by C. M. Storm van 's Gravesande in his *Royal Academy Architectural Course on the Civil and Military Art of Building for cadets in military engineering* (1843, 1st edn), the second book on the subject to see the light in the 1840s. One of the major criteria applied by the MBB when holding competitions related to the way in which the character of a building had been expressed.[10] And character would continue to play an important role in architectural theory and criticism, further illustrating that subjective perceptions were incompatible with an objective theory. Character was a concept with a strong personal content, a concept that in the decades that followed would by its very nature signify many things.

The predilection for the Greek

Penn was not the only one to believe in the wholesome effect of the pure classical source. Büchler wasted no time in reviewing his *Handbook* in 1841, lavishing praise on it. Several years later Büchler wrote a treatise in which he referred to the 'clear dawn' that had broken in Prussia and Bavaria with the German architects Karl Friedrich Schinkel and Leo von Klenze (1784–1864), 'men steeped in the spirit of antiquity'. A Dutch edition of a biography of Schinkel appeared around 1846, presenting his body of work, erroneously, as if he had used almost exclusively the principles of Greek architecture and treating his Gothic designs as of far less importance.[11]

Outside the small circle of Dutch architects and architecture enthusiasts, similar views were discernible. On the Dutch literary scene, there had been for some years a conflict between what the critic Reinier Cornelis Bakhuizen van den Brink in 1838 referred to as the 'classical and Romantic schools'. Writers such as Jacob Geel, Bakhuizen and, somewhat later, Carel Vosmaer used the values derived from classical culture to oppose the influence of German Romanticism, in particular its idealization of the Middle Ages and its tendency to 'theologize' culture. Bakhuizen emphasized that, as far as opinions and culture were concerned, the modern era stood nearer to Greek antiquity than to the rather primitive and crude Middle Ages.[12] In 1844, an article in the *Kunstkronyk* (Art Chronicle) expressed an appreciation of Romantic art – its 'most beautiful aspect is its virtuousness' – but noted that:

at the same time it is true that in art the only thing that is flawlessly beautiful and immortal is that which is not specific to a particular era or country, but is of all times and of all peoples. Therefore the Greek style will always retain its elevated position as the leading light; because although it has the stamp of its creators' national character, and although it completely excludes the specific characteristics of Romantic beauty, it stands out above all through the universality of its truth ... The purely human was the the Greek artist's aim.[13]

In the Netherlands the love for Greek classicism does not appear to have had much to do with the philhellenism that flourished in various other parts of Western Europe as a result of the war of Greek independence (1821). In fact, this particular kind of philhellenism hardly existed in the Netherlands at all; the plea for Greek classicism heard in the 1840s relates to a specifically Dutch cultural concept. In 1844, reporting on a Greek artist, the *Kunstkronyk* stated: 'All extravagance and excess are counter to his most profound nature.' This is not far removed from the poet Jeronimo de Vries's definition in 1839 of the national character of Dutch poetry: 'Solidity, composure, piety, edification without excess – the basic characteristics of our true nature – these are what we must stand for and uphold; then and only then can we be and remain true patriots.' The Dutch cultural elite cultivated an image of itself that resembled its idealized image of the ancient Greeks – such as that same elite had done in the seventeenth and eighteenth centuries *vis-à-vis* the Batavians, the presumed ancestors of the Dutch people.[14]

These are indeed indications that there were several leaders of opinion who were more interested in the definition of 'the basic characteristics of our true nature' than in knowledge of classical culture. Interesting in this context is the study tour of Greece undertaken by the young architect Anthony Willem van Dam (1816–95), which ended in 1841. Some ninety years after the first English dilettanti he took measurements of temples and established that they did not comply with the rules of the orders.[15] At last, in the Netherlands, it had been empirically demonstrated that the old Vitruvianism no longer held. By that time it was too late for a 'second Renaissance' (back to antiquity, in this case Greek antiquity), as had occurred much earlier in Germany. The leading classicists in the Netherlands were averse to both archaeology and art history, subjects that flourished at the German universities.

Round or pointed arches?

Warnsinck had criticized Zocher in 1840 not just because of his casual way of dealing with the classical theory of architecture. He would also have preferred Zocher to have chosen 'Byzantine' architecture, the *round-arch style*, as his starting point instead of Greek. According to Warnsinck, the Dutch climate, Dutch social customs and needs, and Dutch building materials called for a contemporary and national architecture rather than one orientated towards ancient Greece.[16] These were the arguments that Heinrich Hübsch had published in 1828, but Warnsinck did not limit himself to theory. His own work showed a clear affinity with certain churches in Germany that had recently been designed in the *Rundbogenstil*, or round-arch style.

The round-arch style became particularly popular in and around Rotterdam. The municipal architect, Willem Nicolaas Rose (1801–77), used it for example for the façades of the Coolsingel Hospital (1839–40), in the 1840s the largest and, both technically and aesthetically, the most sophisticated building in the country. Many more examples of new buildings in the round-arch style were being published, in books such as the *Elemente des Rundbogenstiles* by K. Möllinger (Munich 1846), which was soon translated into Dutch as *Essays on the Knowledge of the Basic Principles and Components of the Byzantine, or Round-arch, Style* (1847–8, two volumes). In addition, Schinkel's work was admired in numerous Dutch publications; and a considerable number of both realized and unrealized designs demonstrated to those Dutch architects who were open to change that recent German architecture could provide the answer to the question of how architecture was to proceed now that it had become clear that classicism as a theory of design was no longer appropriate.

This seemed to signify the end of the influence of French architecture, which had been evident in the Netherlands for over half a century. All the same, we must not underestimate the continuing influence of the major pattern books and theoretical works, such as Durand's *Précis* (1802–5), Pierre-Jacques Goetghebuer's *Choix des monumens* (The Choice of Monuments, 1827) and Van Straaten's *Illustrations of Ancient and Modern Structures* (1828), all of which contained a considerable number of French models for buildings with round arches. In 1829 Jan David Zocher designed an extensive housing project for the city of Utrecht that clearly shows Durand's influence. The railway stations in Haarlem (1841) and Leiden (1842), designed by the engineer-architect Frederik Willem Conrad (1800–70), also point to Durand rather than Hübsch and his followers as their source.[17]

There were fundamental differences between Durand's and Hübsch's theories. Both understood that the nineteenth century, which was still young when they were writing, needed a new type of architecture that would meet the demands of austerity and functionality in the new

world of the Enlightenment and rationality. Durand elaborated on the theoretical Vitruvian tradition and reduced it, via geometrical forms and proportional schemes, to a system with a limited number of simple rules for the artistic aspects of architecture. Hübsch, on the other hand, was not interested in a design method. He wanted a *style*, an architecture that fitted the organization and nature of the nation in question, that met the requirements of climate, that suited the needs of the building trade and that was, above all, an architecture of truth.

Fig.13
Modern architecture
in the year 1850: the
Dutch Reformed
Church at
Gorinchem, near
Dordrecht (1849–51)
by Isaäc Warnsinck
and Abraham
Nicholaas Godefroy.
When the town's
most important
medieval church fell
into decay, restoration
was not an option. Its
high Gothic tower
remained, and behind
it the young architects
built a round-arched
basilica.

Fig. 14
Coolsingel Hospital,
Rotterdam (1839–49),
by Willem Nicolaas
Rose, the first hospital
in the Netherlands to
be built according to
the latest, mainly
German, medical and
technical innovations.
In the design of the
façade, 83 metres
wide and 25 high,
Rose aimed to give the
building a 'serious
and stately' character.
On the inside, the
'Moorish' hall
radiated a 'cheerful'
atmosphere for the
patients upon
entering the building.

In his *Handbook*, Johannes Jacobus Penn did not go into the possibilities of the modern round-arch style – a remarkable decision for a young architect who had only recently attended the Bauakademie. Neither did he choose to discuss the pointed-arch style, because although he considered the Gothic style 'wonderful and grand', it was 'the result of an era completely alien to us'. The second edition of Brade's *Theoretical and Practical Building* (1842) went further, contending that the Middle Ages ('centuries of darkness') produced a 'monstrous mixture of Greek and Gothic architecture, which before long resulted in the complete corruption of Gothic architecture. It has been correctly written that a building of the Gothic order is something of a puzzle to the eye beholding it, and the feelings are affected in a way similar to a confused poem'. Büchler, on the other hand, considered the Middle Ages quite instructive: 'one can learn from this tendency in art referred to as "the Romantic"; it contains a lesson and a warning'.[18]

In their enthusiasm for neoclassicism and their reticence concerning the round-arch and pointed-arch styles, Penn, Brade and Büchler demonstrated that they had no eye for

the spirit of the age. Classicism and neoclassicism as a tradition of form had had its day. The round-arch and pointed-arch styles both drew attention, and were put into practice in several instances with a great deal of verve. For example, between 1840 and 1849 (the year of his death) Willem II had various palaces constructed, mainly in The Hague, in the English pointed-arch style. As heir apparent he had become acquainted with 'medieval' country houses in England, which in 1840 had been in vogue for almost a century.

The buildings erected by Willem II – such as the Willemskerk and the 'Gothic Hall' in the Hague – may, as far as taste is concerned, have influenced the building plans of other aristocrats, such as De Schaffelaar country house in the province of Gelderland (1852), and Beverweerd and Sandenburg Castles in the province of Utrecht. However, it is questionable whether he increased the appreciation of the pointed-arch style in the small circle of prominent Dutch architects. Perhaps they hardly took the king's building campaign seriously at all. While the English and German royal courts made use of their most prominent architects – John Nash in England, Leo von Klenze,

Fig.15
Frederik Willem
Conrad's plans for
the Hollandsche
IJzeren Spoorweg-
Maatschappij
(HIJSM) railway
station, Haarlem
(built in 1841). Here
in the façade of the
main building and in
the side-entrance to
the platform railings
can be seen a railway
engineer's application
of the lessons of
Durand.

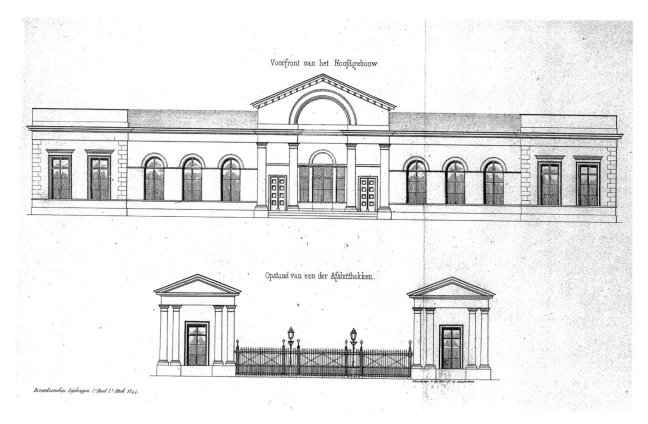

Friedrich von Gärtner (1791–1847) in Bavaria and Schinkel in Prussia – Willem II made no use of Zocher's talents or the design skills of Christiaan Kramm (1795–1875), the two Dutch architects who put into practice the possibilities of the English castellated country-house style. The king wanted to be his own architect. Terrible structural defects were the result.[19]

Apart from Willem II, in the 1840s enthusiasm in the Netherlands for the pointed-arch style appears to have been quite limited. This applies to both building practice and the development of theories. Abroad, the study of medieval architecture had contributed significantly to the architecture debate – we have only to mention Hübsch again – but in the Netherlands this debate had hardly begun, and only a very small number of books on the subject had been published. In 1838 the architect W. C. Timmerman's *Contribution to the History of Medieval Architecture; or Guide to the History of the Gothic Style of Architecture*,[20] which comprised mainly extracts from foreign studies, was published. In 1847 the painter Servaas de Jong published his *Contribution to the Knowledge of the Gothic, or Pointed-arch Style of Architecture in the Netherlands*, which claimed that the Gothic style was derived from freemasonry. Two years later the first serious

study of Dutch medieval architecture, written in accordance with the scientific rules already common practice abroad, was published. Called *Brief Survey of the Architectural Style of Medieval Churches in the Netherlands*, it was by the amateur archaeologist F. N. M. Eyck tot Zuylichem. But there is no indication that these historical studies, which focused on churches, influenced thinking on architecture at the time.

According to the contemporary view of aesthetics, religious thoughts and feelings were the highest man could achieve. Hence, buildings that were an expression of religion were considered the peak of achievement in the art of building. Friedrich Bouterwek stated in his *Principles* in 1830: 'Building temples is the most exalted and purest task to be desired of the art of building.' In 1841 Penn wrote in his *Handbook*:

What to man must be most venerable, his religion, ought also to produce the most sublime in art, and thus the churches have always occupied the most prominent position in architecture. These buildings display the most venerable, the most perfect and the purest character; it is their role to express exalted and serious notions. For this reason the rules of architectural truth and character must be adhered to more strictly than anywhere else.[21]

Penn sought these rules in the classical theory of the orders.

He did not for a moment consider recommending the pointed-arch style for the building of churches. Elsewhere, though, Schinkel and other foreign architects were using not only classical design in both theory and practice, but Gothic as well. Following eighteenth-century ideas, they chose the pointed arch to express the sublime and the infinite – two concepts that fit well with the nineteenth-century tendency towards a more personal and religious experience. In the Netherlands people were, of course, familiar with the specific symbolic value of the pointed arch, as shown in several churches with façades that did indeed combine classical composition and decoration with 'Gothic' windows. But we may assume that in these cases the pointed arch, as the symbol of Christian piety and devotion, was simply a symbol lacking in the classicist vocabulary.

The pointed-arch style in church building was an extension of the expressive repertoire of *character* in architecture, but in the 1850s it also became a means of publicly exemplifying, indeed became a central theme in, the Roman Catholic revival that started at that time in the Netherlands. From then on Gothic forms acquired a religious and specifically Catholic character – a significance rather different from that of the 1840s, when pointed arches, such as those of the railway station in Rotterdam (1846, Cornelius Outshoorn), could also echo modern industrial England.

Adherence to rules:
a mistaken interpretation of art?

In the late 1840s the latest French architecture occupied a very special position in the debate. After having set the standard for what was best in architecture for so long, to many architects it now came to exemplify everything that was wrong. French architecture now gained the reputation of being superficial and modish, a view propagated especially by those who considered the application of rules, and complying with them, to be of vital importance for the art of building. It is in his decade that, in response to public criticism of certain new works that denied the importance of such rules, the quest for new rules started. For instance, the reports of the adjudicators of the many competitions organized by the MBB for its members consistently denounced, as the next chapter will also show, the 'odd, indeed bizarre combinations, the ingenuity sometimes too sumptuous, so typical of the French Academy and its students'.[22] A design by Abraham Nicholaas Godefroy (1816–95) for a theatre, entered for a competition in 1849, came within the little appreciated category of 'currently fashionable in France'. He was among the architects who

took such 'curious combinations' quite seriously, and who deliberately distanced themselves from the debate on universal rules. These architects were not interested in any authority, whatever its theoretical or historical arguments, that claimed that contemporary architecture should adhere to specific standards. Perhaps this is what was really new: that there were now architects who openly doubted or even denied the existence of such an authority.

Men like Jan David Zocher and Godefroy showed this mainly through their designs. But the most interesting formulation of this doubt came not from a prominent architect such as these two, but from one Cornelis Zemel, who at that time was not a member of the tight little circle of opinion-leaders from Amsterdam and (to a lesser extent) Rotterdam. In his article 'What style shall I apply when building?' that appeared in *Bouwkundige Bijdragen* in 1847, Zemel introduced himself as 'an employee of the Royal Navy in Vlissingen and a member

Fig.16
The English Gothic Revival provided models for new Dutch churches, until, after about 1860, the Gothic Revival in the Netherlands became an exclusively Roman Catholic matter, taking medieval French architecture as its point of reference. N. Kamperdijk's Dutch Reformed Church, Zeist, near Utrecht (1841–3).

Fig.17
The Hollandsche
IJzeren Spoorweg-
Maatschappij railway
station by Cornelius
Outshoorn,
Rotterdam (1846),
side wall. English
castellated
architecture – an
almost frivolous
contrast with the
HIJSM railway
station at Haarlem
(Fig.15): possibly a
marketing ploy to
promote travelling
by train, in the
businesslike and
down-to-earth city of
Rotterdam, as fun.

OPPOSITE
Fig.18–19
Details of a project
for a theatre in a large
city (1849), front
façade and side wall.
This vibrant
watercolour design by
Abraham Nicolaas
Godefroy, in the latest
Parisian manner, was
entered for an
'unspecified'
competition organized
by the MBB (the
Society for the
Advancement of the
Art of Building). The
only purpose of such
a competition was to
challenge architects
freely to express their
professional skills and
creativity on paper.

of the Royal Academy of the Visual Arts in Amsterdam'. This is almost all that is known about his life. His article, whose title brings to mind Heinrich Hübsch, makes it clear that Zemel had a great interest in the recent foreign studies in the history and theory of architecture. He too admired the 'much praised works of the German architects'.[23]

Taking a view similar to that taken by Penn in his *Handbook* of 1841, Zemel argued that the discovery and study of classical Greek architecture had destroyed the authority of Vignola, Scamozzi, Palladio and Serlio. That this view was by no means generally accepted in the Netherlands is illustrated by the fact that the authority of these old masters was still unchallenged, as demonstrated by the new edition of Brade's *Theoretical and Practical Building* in 1842–4, the publication in 1848 of *The Rules of the Five Orders according to Vignola* by Martinus G. Tétar van Elven and in 1851 of the third edition of Van Straaten's *Vignola of Craftsmen*. But whereas Penn after his rejection of classicism found a new authority in neoclassicism, and the critics of the Zocher brothers in 1840 called upon the authority of fixed rules, Zemel believed that such certainties were built on quicksand.

He based his thesis on two considerations, the first of which stemmed from his knowledge of Greek architecture, which he had acquired from works by the German scholar J. M. Mauch,[24] amongst others. The 'incomparable forms, free, loose' of Greek architecture had demonstrated to him that a universal system after the manner of Vignola and his associates was impossible. 'Study of those admired works makes one realize that they were not designed according to any general standards, but according to the nature and the

circumstances of the individual building.' There would be no point, he continued, in drawing up a set of rules based on these specific values and to use them as design rules. Given their global nature, design rules based on general values would 'never entirely meet the requirements of a specific building' – opting for such rules would only demonstrate 'our impotence and a mistaken interpretation of art'.

The second consideration that made Zemel wary of making claims to a universal system of design was that he realized that there was no absolute authority able to devise and enforce such a system. And even if there had been, there would also have had to be experts capable of recognizing the general validity of such rules. But on the basis of which criteria, and according to whose authority? Nothing demonstrated better than classical buildings themselves that the predilection for uniformity and a systematic approach was pointless.

But Zemel did not see himself as an authority. On the contrary, he was merely addressing in an unassuming way 'a question that occurs to me frequently'; indeed, he hoped for 'admonitions from competent and meritorious men'. However, his article indicated the fundamental problem of choice resulting from the fact that classicism no longer held its supreme position.

One option was to create a new universal design system with objective rules and standards – an option that was already being propagated by Penn and others, with a variety of results. Zemel realized that any claim to universal validity could be nothing but fiction. The other option based a concept of architecture more on intuitive and perceptual grounds, in which the rules were no more than

indications, ordered into the categories suggested by the theory of 'character'. Zemel stated:

the guidelines for building are difficult to express in words. Nor can they be formulated in reasoning comparable to a mathematical concept. A general criterion is the following: Attempt to understand the purpose of the work to be built; become acquainted with the impression it is to convey; consider how this has been achieved in the past, and how it could be achieved now; attempt to order the building's appearance accordingly, and you will achieve this objective, and more, to the extent that both the nature and the aim of the work will be better understood.

Style as an orthodox, supra-personal system versus style as a heterodox, individual experience: the debate on architecture would gravitate between these two extremes in the nineteenth century.

Notes

1. Coert P. Krabbe 1998, ch. 4.
2. For Büchler, his activities in the field of art promotion and his treatise: Tiede J. Boersma, Coert P. Krabbe 1992.
3. A portico without a fronton was the architectural motif of the gateway or triumphal arch, as used for example for the Willemspoort, a neoclassical Amsterdam city gate (architect C. Alewijn, 1840). A summary of the polemic on the Stock Exchange: A. de Vries 1984.
4. The text of the criticism: Thomas H. von der Dunk 1994b. The nature of the criticism indicates that the critic was well acquainted with the relevant architectural theory.
5. Arjen J. Looijenga 1990.
6. J. J. Penn 1841, preface.
7. J. J. Penn 1841, 7.
8. J. J. Penn 1841, 9–11.
9. *Untersuchungen über den Charakter der Gebäude; über die Verbindung der Baukunst mit den Schönen Künsten und über die Wirkungen, welche durch dieselben hervorgebracht werden sollen.*
10. Examples of those competitions: Tiede J. Boersma 1993, 29–32.
11. Tiede J. Boersma 1989, 56–8.
12. Toos Streng 1988, 100–3.
13. B. 1844–13.
14. The *Kunstkronyk* (Art Chronicle): B. 1844, 13. Jeronymo de Vries: Toos Streng 1988, 103–4. The Batavians: Auke van der Woud 1998, ch. 1.
15. Tiede J. Boersma, Coert P. Krabbe 1992, 188–9. Van Dam studied in Paris, Italy and Athens from 1837 to 1841.
16. Warnsinck 1840, 23–5. On Warnsinck: Paul T. E. E. Rosenberg, Guido H. P. Steenmeijer 1995.
17. The Coolsingel Hospital: Hetty E. M. Berens 1999, 191–208. Zocher's project for Utrecht (1829–43): Peter Karstkarel 1988, 36–52, Constance D. H. Moes 1991, 32–5. Conrad's stations: H. Romers 1981, 16–20.
18. J. J. Penn 1841, 7; W. C. Brade 1842, 2nd edn, I, 7–8; Büchler: Tiede J. Boersma, Coert P. Krabbe 1992, 186.
19. A. J. Ubels 1966. For Zocher's 'English' designs: Constance D. H. Moes 1991, cat. nos 3–7, 16, 27–31, 37–8; for Kramm: Tiede J. Boersma 1989, 107–8.
20. *Bijdrage tot de geschiedenis van de bouwkunde der Middeleeuwen; of Handleiding tot de geschiedenis der Gothische bouworde.*
21. Friedrich Bouterwek 1830, 134; J. J. Penn 1841, 392–3. Also W. N. Rose 1858b, 266: 'The most outstanding products of art have always been the buildings dedicated to the worship of God.'
22. Cited by Karin M. Veenland-Heinemann 1985, 485.
23. Cornelis Zemel 1848, 307, 316.
24. J. M. Mauch 1832–9; J. M. Mauch 1845.

3

Post-classicism, and Classicism in Disguise: The 1850s

The diminishing authority of classicism

The debate on the essential nature of architecture that originated in the 1840s produced several fundamental views and questions which were further developed during the 50s. Classicism and neoclassicism were condemned to a marginal existence as far as architectural practice was concerned. They were occasionally still used for monumental commissions in the provinces, such as the Palace of Justice in Leeuwarden (1846–52, Thomas Romein), the New Church in Zierikzee (1848, Karel George Zocher), the main university building in Groningen (1846–50, Johannes Franciscus Scheepers) and the synagogue in Delft (1862, architect unknown). In the teaching of architecture the doctrine of the classical orders

remained part of the curriculum, although with a diminishing authority, but there was no generally accepted alternative. However, in the streets classicism still occupied a prominent position as a perfectly integrated part of middle-class culture, especially apparent in newly modernized shops and private houses. Their late-sixteenth- and seventeenth-century stepped gables were rebuilt with new, high windows and at the top a white horizontal wooden gutter-bearer, a remnant of the classical entablature. In 1852, when this aesthetic reconstruction of the inner cities got under way, the Maatschappij tot Bevordering der Bouwkunst (MBB, the Society for the Advancement of the Art of Building) published the first issues of its series, *Illustrations and Descriptions of Old*

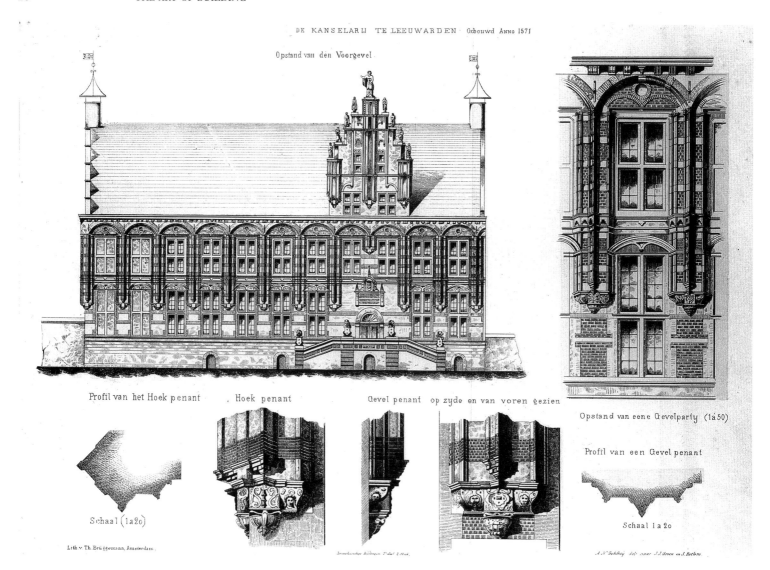

DE KANSELARIJ TE LEEUWARDEN · Gebouwd Anno 1571

Opstand van den Voorgevel

Profil van het Hoek penant

Hoek penant

Gevel penant op zyde en van voren gezien

Opstand van eene Gevelparty (1a 50)

Profil van een Gevel penant

Schaal (1a 2o)

Schaal 1a 2o

Lith. v. Th. Brüggemann, Amsterdam.

Fig.21
Sketches of the front façade and details of the sixteenth-century Chancellery in Leeuwarden (1850), by Abraham Nicholaas Godefroy, published in *Bouwkundige Bijdragen* in 1852. These drawings illustrate the earliest research into the historical roots of an assumed specifically Dutch national architecture.

Extant Buildings, focusing on noteworthy historic façades. These façades did not always meet the aesthetic demands made of contemporary architecture, but were appreciated for their historic value.

While classicism seemed gradually to be fading out, the questions that had been raised in the 1840s were still waiting to be answered. Did contemporary architecture demand a contemporary *style* – that is to say, a design system that would be a match for classicism, or did it demand freedom, an absence of style? And anyway, what *was* style? Was it a representation of the spirit of the age, or of the nation? And, in terms of the classic–romantic antithesis, was not all architecture that was not classicist or neoclassicist automatically romantic? These questions were answered in various ways by three eminent professionals of

the time: W. N. Rose, the Rotterdam city architect (after 1858 state architect in The Hague), Josephus Albertus Alberdingk Thijm (1820–89), Amsterdam merchant and author, and Johannes Hermanus Leliman (1828–1910), architect, also of Amsterdam.

The establishment in Amsterdam of the MBB in 1842 and of the architects' association Architectura et Amicitia in 1855 demonstrates the increasing need for an exchange of ideas on architectural practice. During the 1850s many meetings and lectures were held and publications proliferated, and Rose became prominent as a theorist.[1] He observed, in a more radical way than Zemel had done in 1847, that the era of the classical orders was over and that the resulting 'void' – his own term – called for new architectural principles. He was the first fundamentally to investigate the aesthetics of the post-classicist art of building.

In 1854 he published an article entitled 'On the general conditions that a beautiful work of architecture must meet'. His approach was very different from that adopted by Penn and Storm van 's Gravesande in their publications of 1841 and 1843 respectively. Rose linked his theory to everyday sensory perception, trying to convince his readers by means of elaborate argument instead of prescribing a set of concise rules, as Penn had done. This was another indication that times had changed.

Rose observed that he was living at the beginning of an important era, one marked by 'a confusion of styles' that was 'evidence of our quest and therefore shows that we are in a transitional stage'. For art theoretical reasons he saw no point in imitating styles from the past. 'The history of art is the history of human perception ... because we perceive in a different way from our ancestors, it is not possible to derive contemporary beauty from their art forms. Therefore we must concentrate on finding principles of a more general nature that apply to all styles.' He distinguished seven such principles: freedom, truth, unity, order, cohesion, harmony and proportion. Rose referred to the first three as the primary principles, because they were directly linked with realizing beauty. The other four principles were to a certain extent based on the first three, and therefore secondary. From his explanation it is apparent that order, unity, cohesion, harmony and proportion were new versions of the Vitruvian concepts *dispositio*, *eurythmia* and *ordinatio*.

But the importance of Rose's argument lay in the first two principles. It is worth noting that the term 'freedom' is mentioned first. Here we see architecture being included, for the first time in the Netherlands in a theoretical context, in the typically nineteenth-century Romantic concept of art. However, he referred to the second term, truth, as the most important and difficult of the seven: the building must express its function ('destination'). 'People are used to expressing this principle by means of the term *character*', he pointed out, 'but this is not entirely correct, as a building can have character without truth.' He defined 'character' in the same way as Penn had done earlier: as the 'expressive exterior, clearly conveying the client's aim'. But whereas Penn emphasized character as the key concept in aesthetics and left Hübsch's principle of truth unmentioned, Rose concurred with Hübsch's description of truth as 'the primary principle in art'. Moreover, he made character *a part* of truth. In other words: Rose extricated character from eighteenth-century, sensationalist aesthetics and

integrated it into the new, nineteenth-century aesthetics that focused on functionality, thereby demonstrating an interesting renewal – in the Netherlands – of Vitruvian *decor*: 'A building when observed from the exterior and the interior must impress us in a way that corresponds to the aim for which it was made.' If this is not the case, there is no truth, no beauty, and therefore no art of building.

Rose was attempting to follow the difficult path of understanding truth in terms of the contemporary theory that prevailed in the visual arts and in architecture. In these fields truth had been an issue for quite some time. The classical mimesis theory – that art develops in imitation of nature – was no longer regarded as self-evident, but Rose had come up with a proposition that appeared still to be generally valid: 'In fine art the following general rule applies: no beauty without truth: that is to say, there is nothing in art that is both beautiful *and* false.' A beautiful drawing of a landscape, for example, was worthless if the colours were not right. The criterion for the right colours, according to Rose, was that nature must be imitated accurately. However, architecture could not imitate nature, which made the distinction between good and bad very difficult to determine – 'the representation of truth in architecture is always to a certain extent of an abstract nature'.

This last observation seems more innocent than it actually is. In fact, it describes the separation – in artistic theory – of architecture from the other visual arts. Of course, it was well known that there were fundamental differences between architecture, the mother of all the arts, and her children. Penn had stated in 1841: 'The art of building is not an art of imitation, but the very creator of its works, contrary to the visual arts, which derive everything from nature.'[2] The neoclassicist Penn interpreted this to mean that the visual arts could imitate nature by using curved lines, while architecture could use only straight lines – for this reason architecture would never to able to imitate nature.

For Rose this issue was certainly not an academic problem of definition. His view was that the abstract nature of architecture created distance between architecture and its public. This confronted the architect with a special problem that the painter or sculptor did not have. While the 'imitative arts' could represent an 'inanimate' object, dead material, in a way that made it seem 'alive', a building could never convey this suggestion of a living being. How, then, could architecture, with its exclusively inanimate resources, ever convey to the observer emotions such as gravity, gaiety, dignity or sublimity? In the old days there had been rules for this. Now there were only subjective experiences. And

Fig.22–3
Lieven de Key's
Guild Hall, Haarlem
(1602–3). This colour
litho appeared in the
first edition of the
*Collection of
Illustrations and
Descriptions of Old
Existing Buildings*
published by the
MBB in 1852. In the
second half of the
nineteenth century
the Butchers' Guild
Hall became the
paradigm of the
Old Dutch brick
and sandstone
architecture, which
according to many
was the architectural
expression of the
Dutch national
indentity.

yet, 'the rules according to which we must judge a work of art must be objective'. With this contradiction Rose implied that for him the eighteenth-century theory of character belonged to the past. And as if the uncertainty resulting from this crumbling away of one of the pillars of aesthetics was not enough, he was forced to recognize that there were two very different types of beauty, 'classical beauty and romantic beauty, which both have their values and merits'.[3]

The spirit of the age: in search of a signpost

In 1856 or 57 Rose further elaborated on these questions, but now from a different angle. He dropped the Vitruvian method of defining beauty as a sum of 'principles'. Instead, he made an analysis of the classical and the romantic aspects contained in architecture, that is, the Greek and the Gothic, which he published as *On the Mythical and the Conventional in Architecture in relation to the Difference between the Classical and Romantic Styles*. He made no effort to explain this difference with the aid of the historical accounts in vogue at the time, but once again worked from the general theory of art and concentrated on architecture's position in it.[4] He warned that architectural styles of the past were to a great extent unfathomable. The world was interpreted, he said, against two types of background, the mythical and the conventional: the mythical consisted of our deepest feelings and 'edified ideas', the conventional of common assumptions and customs. These types of background were determined both culturally and temporally, making it almost impossible to understand anything about the style of a period or people with whose spirit we were not sufficiently familiar.

On the basis of this argument Rose concluded that it was incongruous to imitate Greek or Gothic examples in contemporary architecture, irrespective of the admiration these deserved. 'We are so far removed from the era of the Greeks that we think, feel and act completely differently.' But also, 'we are a different kind of citizen and Christian from those who lived in the Middle Ages. We are more civilized, more skilful, less prejudiced, more amicable and tolerant and, as a consequence, more virtuous than our ancestors who lived in the age of chivalry.'

Not long afterwards he was to present a more differentiated approach: the good qualities of, for example, the Gothic age could very well be applied, he declared, to everything that was being built.

We deem this to be quite possible and even very praiseworthy; this would move art forward, but it would of course no longer be a purely Gothic style, because the buildings would represent *our* ideas, which are far removed from medieval ideas. This would result in a new style that would be felt and understood by

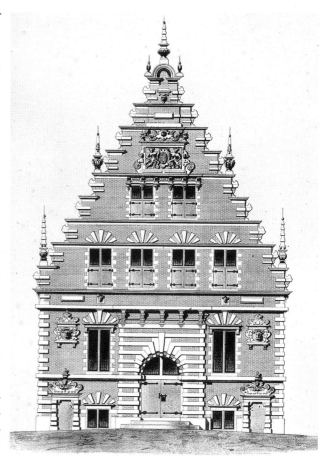

everyone. But for as long as we make no progress in this direction, for as long as it fails to become the aspiration of our feeling and our intellect combined, we will not produce any real works of art, and architecture will remain caught in a labyrinth of different styles, constantly in search of a signpost.[5]

In 1854 Rose had stated that the classical system of design had lost its meaning. Now he realized the consequences of this: architecture was lost in a labyrinth of problems and possibilities. The thing that had bothered him most was undoubtedly the Hegelian notion that art was an expression of 'the spirit of the age'. After all, if art wished to express that spirit, it was necessary to free oneself from the architecture of the past, because it expressed the spirit of an age that no longer existed. This implied that the problem of contemporary art could not be solved by the imitation or refinement of the works of our forefathers. Contemporary architecture could only develop if the architects had a clear image of the spirit of the modern age. But who was to define that spirit, who was to express it with authority in architectural forms? How could the spirit of the age be made recognizable through something as abstract

as 'inanimate architecture? These questions were all the more difficult because the public, as the MBB indicated in its report of 1858, showed little interest in architecture.[6]

It is not surprising that when the problems of the spirit of the age and of the indifferent attitude of the public were being aired, the question of a national style should also surface. It was in fact just another facet of that same attempt to define the 'idea' of one's own era and people in the hope that this idea could be made visible in architecture and would even create a *style*. In 1858 Rose was one of the group who were avidly discussing this subject in the MBB.[7] Taking a purely practical standpoint, he considered that the architect created a building that was the expression of his feelings: 'Now, these feelings can be nothing but the feelings of his era. And as they have developed here, they must necessarily be Dutch feelings.' Ideally, these were nurtured by a solid education in aesthetics, making the architect independent of all the old styles: 'Only aesthetics serves as his guide.' It is important to establish that, despite his belief in the Hegelian postulation that the national spirit was very much an expression of the time, Rose did not burden architecture with political, religious or ethnic ideologies or symbols. The architect, as far as he was concerned, was independent of these things. Aesthetics was indeed his only guide.

The logical Middle Ages: Alberdingk Thijm

Alberdingk Thijm was a merchant, but his passion was writing. Like Daniël Büchler he had no practical experience in the field of architecture. In 1850 he wrote favourably about the Zuiderkerk in Rotterdam, a newly built Protestant church in the pointed-arch style. He fervently hoped that the commission for a new Catholic church in the city would not be granted to the 'thoroughly pagan' classicist Tilleman François Suys (the architect of the Catholic Church of St Anthony of Padua in Amsterdam, 1837–41), but to one who understood that Christianity 'required a different art from the polytheism' of the ancient Greeks.[8] He thus linked Christianity to the pointed-arch style.

In 1853 the Pope decided to restore and reorganize the Catholic Church in the Netherlands, which had all but disappeared during the Reformation. The restoration was to take the form of the establishment of the archbishopric of Utrecht, with four dioceses, a move that aroused vehement political and anti-Catholic reactions. In the ensuing atmosphere of polarization, Thijm presented himself not as a man of reconciliation, but as a man not afraid of conflict. From now on he saw the Middle Ages as exemplifying an ideal unity of art and life, which had been destroyed by the Reformation. For Thijm, Protestantism had heralded a period of decline, and the present Catholic revival would regain this lost unity. This view became the basis of his controversial architectural mission, which was to last for almost forty years. He rapidly gained a reputation with his many opponents for being a fanatical Catholic. In 1858 he apparently set himself up as such an advocate of medieval art that he was accused of wanting to make everything Gothic. In an article that he wrote that year called 'Do we want only the Gothic style?' he explained that the issue for him was not the Gothic style itself, but 'logic': if this logic required the introduction of the Gothic style as the proper 'system of forms' for Dutch church building, this 'this system will have our support'. Thus Thijm acknowledged that he indeed wanted the Gothic style only.

And he was no longer speaking for himself only. Late in 1854 he had met the architect Petrus ('Pierre') Joseph Hubertus Cuypers (1827–1921), from Roermond, who would turn out to be a considerable ally. Cuypers had received his training in Antwerp, which was a centre of neo-Gothic church art and architecture, which was already flourishing at that time in Belgium.[9] In Cuypers' style of church building, based on the French Gothic, and also in his opinions, Thijm recognized the expression of the artistic and religious principles that he himself had come to espouse. Thijm's article was after all not about architecture as a whole, but focused on one aspect, the 'Gothic church style', which according to him was 'a natural realization of the rational principles that we have developed'. There were eighteen of these principles:

1. The exterior is never denied or contradicted by the interior.
2. The interior expresses itself in the exterior.
3. The part shows characteristics of the whole to which it belongs.
4. The whole neither hides nor exhibits its parts.
5. The material form contains a threefold spiritual core: the idea of functionality or convenience, of beauty, and of symbolic meaning.
6. This threefold nature shows that aesthetics cannot occur independently.
7. This form of art is not a duplicate of nature, but a representation of it.

The other eleven principles were based on these seven.

The first four rules, and the thesis that logic is the only issue, have in Dutch historiography served as proof that Cuypers' neo-Gothic style was 'rational', and they therefore became the basis on which Hendrik Petrus Berlage (1856–1934) and later the Nieuwe Zakelijkheid (New Realism) School were to build. It was widely noted that this rational aspect was derived from the views of the famous Parisian architect and expert on medieval architecture Eugène-Emmanuel Viollet-le-Duc (1814–79), with whom Cuypers had several discussions in 1854, which were reported invariably to have ended with the pronouncement that any architectural form not indicated by the structure of a building should be rejected.[10]

In 1858 Viollet-le-Duc's famous ten-volume *Dictionnaire raisonné de l'architecture française du XIe au XVIe siècle* was still in its early years (the first volume appeared in 1854, the last in 1868). It was an impressive acumulation of historical knowledge on the French Gothic style in all its aspects. Several of the articles in it (such as 'Style' and 'Construction') were historically based, but almost all the information contained in the ten volumes was of essentially practical use to restorers, archaeologists, and architects interested in building in the French Gothic style. This 'dictionary' was not intended as a textbook of contemporary nineteenth-century architecture. This role was filled by the first volume of Viollet-le-Duc's *Entretiens sur l'architecture* (Discourses on Architecture), published in 1863.

In the last chapter of that publication Viollet-le-Duc pointed at the Parisian École des Beaux-Arts, the influential state academy where the best students of France trained and that attracted young architects throughout Europe (the United States soon to follow). The École had been his employer for a very short time (becoming his scapegoat for a very long time). In his *Dictionnaire* Viollet-le-Duc cricitized its artistic poverty in falling back on the past, with its *néogrec*, *néoroman*, *néogothique* and hybrids of these. Originality, according to Viollet-le-Duc, was only possible if there was truth. In architecture there were two elements above all that required truth: the functional requirements of the given building, which had to be met exactly; and the substance and practice of building – the materials had to be used in accordance with their characteristics. He further developed this proposition by concluding: 'If we consider it important to have an architecture that belongs to our own age, we must first make an effort to make that architecture our own. This means that to find its form and structures, our architecture must search at the heart of our society, and nowhere else.'[11] These words, not least the requirement of truth, were in essence identical to what Rose had written in 1854 and 1857. And this is hardly surprising, since both Rose and Viollet-le-Duc echoed Hübsch's theory, which in turn had given a new meaning to several old Vitruvian concepts.

Thijm's first two principles – to do with the cohesion between the interior and the exterior – were also an expression of 'truth' in the sense attached to it by Hübsch and Rose, who had themselves derived them from the classical *decor*. Thijm's third and fourth principles – the cohesion of the whole and the parts – called *ordinatio* by Vitruvius, were defined by Penn in 1841 in his *Handbook* as 'proper proportion', and by Rose in 1854 as 'unity' and 'cohesion'. Even the fifth principle, the three elements of functionality, beauty and symbolic meaning, went back a long way. The classical traditon referred to the first two concepts as *utilitas* and *venustas*. The third, symbolism, which for Vitruvius was an aspect of *decor* and therefore subordinate to *venustas* (beauty), was given more prominence by Thijm – a logical consequence of his strong religious motivation.[12]

The debate about truth and character extended

Viollet-le-Duc's criticism of the École des Beaux-Arts can be interpreted as a controversy about what the leading principle in architecture should be: the German principle of truth, or the French theory of character. At the École during the 1850s, the borrowing of forms from past architecture developed into a design practice in which decorative motifs figured abundantly. By borrowing in this way, architects met their Second Empire clients' wishes for representativeness and ostentation. When Rose observed in 1854 that 'a building can have character without truth', it was to this trend in architecture that he was referring.

But despite the views that Rose, Viollet-le-Duc, Thijm and Cuypers shared on the priority of truth above character, there was one fundamental difference. Whereas Rose and Viollet-le-Duc advocated an original, contemporary style, Thijm and Cuypers wanted only the Gothic. Where Cuypers' work was concerned, Thijm had no problem with the contemporary spirit, but he disputed Rose's contention that it is practically impossible to really understand a historical style. For Thijm the Gothic style was ageless and universally applicable, a belief encapsulated in a statement of his of 1864 that 'nineteenth century art should not be entirely different from thirteenth century art'; after all, was not the Creator himself the same in 1860

as in 1360?[13] In 1858 Thijm rejected any suggestion that the nineteenth-century Gothic style was a 'hybrid' element in modern cities. Churches, for example, in Utrecht and Haarlem could be built, he said, 'in a truly Utrecht or Haarlem Gothic style'. When Cuypers built churches in Veghel, Wijk, Eindhoven and Alkmaar based on the French Gothic style, Thijm proved able to give this his own interpretation as well.[14] For him, the theory and criticism of architecture had become a means of Catholic propaganda.

In retrospect it can be noted that the position taken by Thijm and Cuypers, in the context of a Roman Catholic Church in the process of reorganizing itself, corresponded entirely with that adopted earlier by leaders of Catholic opinion in Belgium, northern France, England, the Rhineland and Westphalia. The idealization of the Middle Ages was apparent in the aesthetic manifestation of the modernization of the Church, and was promoted by its leadership. An example of the architectural manifestation of this approach is Cuypers' religious artefacts factory in Roermond, which was described as a 'medieval building workers' hut' by Thijm in 1855, but was in fact an ordinary modern company under the patronage of the Church authorities.[15] The immediate effect of Thijm's and Cuypers' success in this field was that neo-Gothic architecture, which in its pointed-arch form was generally Christian in nature, became increasingly the *corporate design* of the Catholic Church in the Netherlands.

From pointed arch to neo-Gothic

Indeed, it was in these years that the pointed-arch style became the neo-Gothic; the new French *néogothique* supplanted the old German *Spitzbogenstil* and the Dutch equivalent, the *spitsboogstijl*, which had been in use since the previous century. However, this did not mean that Dutch neo-Gothic was predominantly determined by French influence. The modernization, and Catholicization, of the pointed-arch style that took place in Germany had at least as great an influence in the Netherlands, perhaps even greater. The views that Thijm expounded in his article 'Do we want only the Gothic style?' reflected the ideas of the prominent German theorists of 'the Church Gothic style', such as August Reichensperger (1781–1848).[16] Reichensperger's much used *Fingerzeige auf dem Gebiete der Christlichen Kunst* (Pointers in the Field of Christian Art) (1854) linked together the issues of Gothic, nationality and Catholicism, and promoted the subservience of the arts to the Catholic Church. In this context he used many elements of Hübsch's theory, but disagreed with Hübsch in considering the Gothic style as the superior model for modern church building.

The change from 'pointed-arch style' to 'neo-Gothic' was more than a question of nomenclature. The new name belonged to a new phenomenon: in following medieval architecture, the accent shifted from character (as defined in the eighteenth century) to truth (as defined by Hübsch). This shift had immediate consequences, both for reputations and for livelihoods. The theory of character was in the mid-nineteenth century still strongly linked to the eighteenth-century building practice in which the carpenter, and especially the plasterer, were the most important producers of architectural beauty. The interest in truth, on the other hand, which had increased markedly in the 1850s, and the emphasis on architectural construction that went with it, resulted in a marginalization of the role of the plasterer and a growing appreciation of the bricklayer. Instead of carpentry and plastering it was now bricklaying that became the expression and the bearer of truth.

This change also had consequences for architects. In the name of truth, Thijm destroyed the reputations of the architects who had applied the theory of character to the building of Catholic churches. One of these architects was Theodorus Molkenboer (1796–1863), who built churches with plastered wooden arches and vaults in the Gothic style, which Thijm condemned as 'fake constructions'. Cuypers was fascinated by the architectural possibilities opened up by building with bricks. From a commercial point of view he benefited greatly from Thijm's philippic against the 'fake'. In 1856 Thijm started successfully to promote Cuypers, both in public and by means of personal contacts with the Catholic clergy.

Eclecticism: Johannes H. Leliman

Rose was in search of a contemporary style, but could see only a perplexing labyrinth. Thijm and Cuypers had found a style which appeared to them perfectly contemporary, objective and 'logical', even if its characteristics were four or five hundred years old. The third position in the architectural debate of the 1850s was represented by the young architect Johannes H. Leliman. In the 1860s and 70s he was to achieve a position of authority, based not so much on the quality of his designs and his buildings as on his knowledge and vision as regards both architecture itself and the profession. He propagated his ideas in a remarkable number of lectures and publications, and in his substantial administrative involvement in architectural organizations such as the MBB and Architectura et Amicitia (known as 'A et A') of which he was a co-founder.[17] Like Rose, he insisted that truth was an absolute requirement for architecture: 'the truth is the idol that we must always venerate,' he said

Fig.25
The 'eclectic' club and exhibition building of the artists' association, Arti et Amicitiae, Amsterdam (1855), by Johannes Hermanus Leliman. Eclecticism stated: the past is neither a point of reference nor a tool with which to style an assumed collective identity. History is pluperfect, and manifests itself in the present as a collection of fragments. What determines the point at which the fragments melt into one whole? – the individual taste or conviction of the client and his architect.

in 1871, a pronouncement typical of the many he made during those years. In 1860 he said: 'truth, combined with honest, meaningful architecture, means that a building is on the inside what it expresses on the outside, and vice versa'. Character was the impression that the 'aesthetically beautiful' made on the perceptions and the emotions, including those of the 'not architecturally trained, but nevertheless sensitive passer-by'.[18]

Leliman referred to himself as an *eclecticist*. When he received his first commission, he clarified his views not in words but through the structure in question itself: the 'Arti Building', the club and exhibition building of the artists' association Arti et Amicitiae in Amsterdam (1855). The design was not developed from one historical style, but demonstrated a free adaptation of forms taken from various building styles and periods. The past was not merely perpetuated or imitated, but transformed. The façade was

composed in the manner of a stately Amsterdam mansion; the decoration drew on examples from the past, but represented in such a way that, though remaining recognizable, they were utterly transformed. The main exterior forms of the building revealed the several functions of the interior, while the ornamentation showed the construction and the disposition.

Leliman studied in Paris during 1852–3. There he learned to freely interpret and use historic architectural types and to put into perspective the issue of a contemporary style. The free, styleless method of design was referred to in Paris as 'eclecticism'. In twentieth-century art history, with its markedly high regard for 'style', the term 'eclecticism' has often been used pejoratively. It meant lacking a sense of direction, artistic impotence, the low point of the nineteenth-century 'carnival of styles'. This negative image was confirmed by

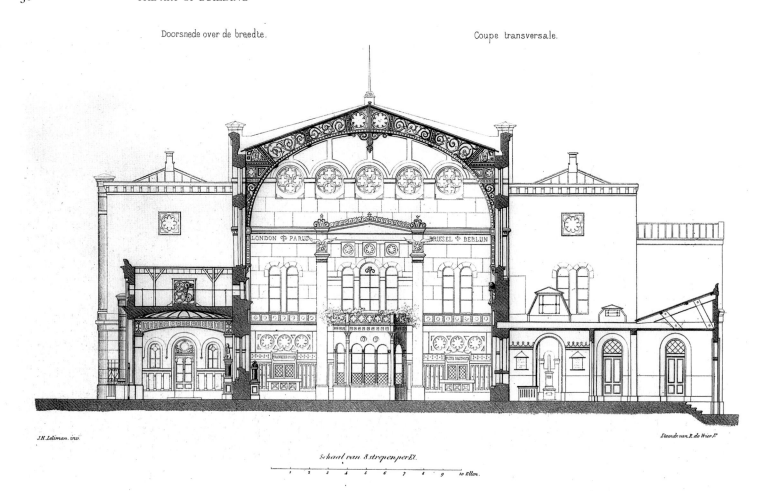

Doorsnede over de breedte.   Coupe transversale.

LONDON ✦ PARIS   BRUSEL ✦ BERLIN

J.H. Leliman. inv.   Steendr. van R. de Vries Jr.

Schaal van 8 strepen per El.

1   2   3   4   5   6   7   8   9   10 Ellen.

ABOVE AND OPPOSITE
Fig.26
J. H. Leliman's design
for a post office, an
award-winning
entry for another
'unspecified'
competition organized
by the MBB (1852),
cross-section. The
application of visible
iron trusses in an
important public
building and the
'styleless' detailing are
reminiscent of the
Bibliothèque Ste
Geneviève in Paris
(Henri Labrouste,
1838–50).

the way in which the architects of the time defined what they saw as a major issue, the matter to which the MBB devoted itself in 1856: 'To what extent, from an aesthetic point of view, is the combination of the principles of Gothic and Greek architecture possible and advisable?'[19]

In reality, the eclectics' ambition was not a style in the sense of an oppressive artistic orthodoxy; what they wanted was a recognizably contemporary architecture based on just one principle – the principle of individual artistic freedom.

Artistic freedom

The roots of eclecticism may be found in Paris around 1830. In the Salon of 1824 – a milestone in the history of the visual arts – Eugène Delacroix presented his painting *Scènes du massacre de Chios*, which was immediately dubbed a *massacre de la peinture*. But while this Romantic anti-academic rebellion in the visual arts has been given an important place in the history of art, a comparable rebellion in architecture has gained far less weight in historiography, although its

artistic consequences were equally fundamental. Four of the winners of the Grand Prix de Rome, the prestigious architectural prize awarded by the École des Beaux-Arts in Paris, caused a considerable stir in 1829 when their exhibits revealed that they had completely ignored the sacred authority of the École.[20] Their revolt against the École's classicist doctrines was by no means a battle of styles. On the contrary, they did not consider style to be a relevant factor in the search for a contemporary art of building, which in their view could be developed only by adhering to the new functional requirements for buildings that were dictated by modern times, and by taking advantage of the large number of new building materials and techniques. S.-C. Constant-Dufeux, one of the rebels, argued in 1830: 'Consider this: in order to produce good architecture, it is necessary first to visualize the spatial layout and the method of construction, without any preoccupation with style, but with a view only to the satisfaction of material and moral needs, as far as a prudent use of the means at our disposal will permit.'[21]

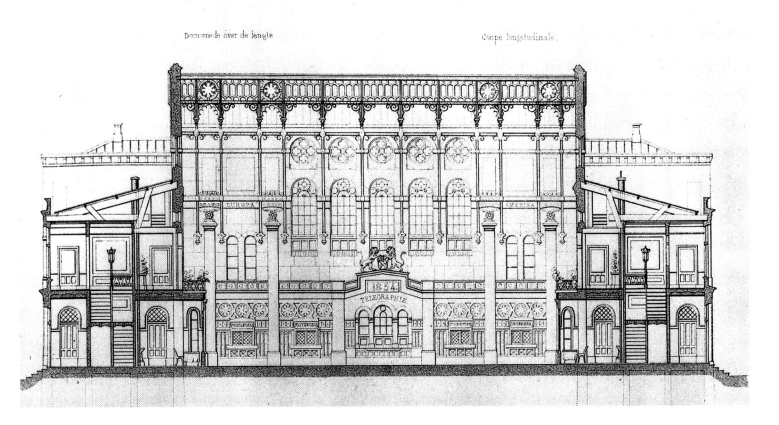

POSTKANTOOR.

BUREAU DE POSTES.

Doorsnede over de lengte   Coupe longitudinale.

Another rebel, the French architect Henri Labrouste (1801–75), opened an atelier in Paris in 1830 – it was in the atelier of an architectural practice that training usually took place. Labrouste's atelier was considered anarchistic, since he was keen on liberating his students from tradition.[22] In the 1840s and 50s his library, the Bibliothèque Ste-Geneviève (Paris 1838–50), was considered the foremost example of the new 'Romantic' French architecture. Whereas in his work on Greek architecture, *Die Tektonik der Hellenen* (1844–52), Karl Bötticher had introduced in Germany the concepts of *Kernform* ('core-form') and *Kunstform* ('art-form') in order to formulate the fundamental distinction between, on the one hand, the constructive and functional aspects of architecture and, on the other, its representational aspects, Labrouste at the same moment demonstrated with his library a similar example in material form. The spatial layout and construction were simple and striking, the interior displayed columns and iron girders – machine-made – and

the ornamentation, though based on the structure, left it visually intact. The main forms, the construction and the decoration in many ways harked back to buildings of the past, but without striving for an overall unity such as past styles had done. Via the many different historical references that it contained the building demonstrated that it did not conform to a specific tradition, and this, precisely, was what made it artistically modern and free.[23]

For a short while in the 1840s the new anti-traditional principles of the younger generation were partially adopted by the École. When, during the next decade, the Second Empire was proclaimed, the demand for architecture to be more representational increased, culminating in the excessively expensive Paris Opera (1861–74, Charles Garnier). The École des Beaux-Arts was now producing an elegant architecture in which the concept of character was given absolute priority. Composition and ornamentation were once again clearly following in the tradition of Louis XIV, XV and XVI, which the École had never ceased to uphold. With its new academicism, and its pragmatic adaptability as far as the market was concerned, the École, as mentioned earlier was attacked by Viollet-le-Duc for lacking truth. His response was in fact an attempt to bring French architecture back to the principles of the 'rationalist' Labrouste – the choice of adjective was Viollet-le-Duc's, who had a great affinity with Labrouste.

Events in Paris were significant for the Netherlands, because two of her young architects, Leliman and Anthony van Dam, mentioned in Chapter 2, had been students at Labrouste's revolutionary atelier. In addition, Egidius Stephanus Heynincx (1813–48), like Van Dam one of the founders of the MBB, had been a pupil of Félix Duban (1796–1871), another member of the rebellious Parisian quartet of 1829. Of these three students, Leliman was to become the most influential. Heynincx was regarded as promising, but died young, and Van Dam built up a large practice in Rotterdam of which very little is known. A fourth young architect also needs mentioning – Lucas H. Eberson (1822–89). From 1844 to 51 Eberson studied and worked in Paris, and in 1848 entered a competition organized by the MBB. His entry was a design for a theatre in the tradition of seventeenth- and eighteenth-century French classicism, which was held in high esteem at the École. He entered another MBB competition in 1850; this time the challenge was to design a Protestant church, and his entry clearly showed his switch to eclecticism. Various features of his design were appreciated by the adjudicators, but the 'odd, indeed bizarre, combinations, the ingenuity, sometimes too sumptuous, so typical of the French Academy and its students', were not.[24] This defensive reaction was one of many that would ensue in the second half of the nineteenth century from those Dutch architects who disapproved of the opulence and lack of sobriety of French architecture, which they deemed unsuitable for the 'uncomplicated and commonsensical' nature of the Dutch – notwithstanding that the Dutch were at the time abandoning themselves to French fashion and other novelties. It would time and again emerge that its focus on questions raised by the public and on contemporary issues, without bringing to bear preconceived ideas about style, nation or fatherland, was the very strength of eclecticism.

Unlike Leliman, Eberson avoided publicity, and during the 1850s he laid the foundations for a flourishing practice. Leliman was much more a theorist, even in his drawings. The extent to which he was influenced by the conceptual landslide initiated by Labrouste was apparent in the entry for an anti-academic competition for the design of a post office that Leliman sent to the MBB in 1852. In it, he made no attempt to associate himself with a historical style; the exterior made explicit the functions of the interior, the ornamentation accentuated the construction, and the entire building incorporated the new material, iron, in the large girders above the central hall.

In 1857, Leliman praised Viollet-le-Duc as a free and independent spirit. Coming from an eclecticist, this remark is interesting because it demonstrates again the monopoly over Viollet-le-Duc from the 1850s that would be exercised by some of the Dutch Gothic Revival architects and their circle, who annexed this atheistic and self-willed theorist as the spiritual mentor of their pre-eminently church-related art of building. The fact that Leliman praised him for his spiritual freedom and independence says much about Leliman himself. In the next three decades he would unflaggingly defend, in the public debate, the viewpoint that was completely at odds with that of Thijm and Cuypers: Leliman had no preoccupation with any particular style – the classical, the Gothic, and all the other styles were equally precious to him because of the pre-eminence he allotted to artistic freedom.

Leliman immediately received much praise for his Arti building. From the moment this young artists' association chose this latest ahistorical architectural concept for its public representation, eclecticism would play an important role in Dutch architectural practice. And it would maintain its position for a long time, even when by the end of the century the neo-Gothic and neo-Renaissance styles – 'building "in style"' – had become a thing of the past. Labrouste's and Leliman's indifference towards a collective style made their ahistorical concept of architecture essentially cosmopolitan and, through its individualism, ripped it in the direction of autonomy. This way of thinking heralded more architectural pluriformity, a development which after 1900 would prove unstoppable.

Classicism and Romanticism: European influences

In the 1850s the concept of truth became the sine qua non of building as an art for all serious architects. On other fundamental issues, however, opinions differed, as we have seen. These differences can be reduced to an essential dichotomy: the view that genuine architecture was the expression of a collective aspiration versus the view that it was the expression of the individual artist.

Rose understood the need for a contemporary collective style of building that was an expression of the spirit of the age and therefore could not be a repetition of the past. Because he could neither define that modern spirit nor express it in his designs, he created his own 'labyrinth'. Thijm defined the spirit of the age as the Catholic reconquest of the social and cultural positions that had

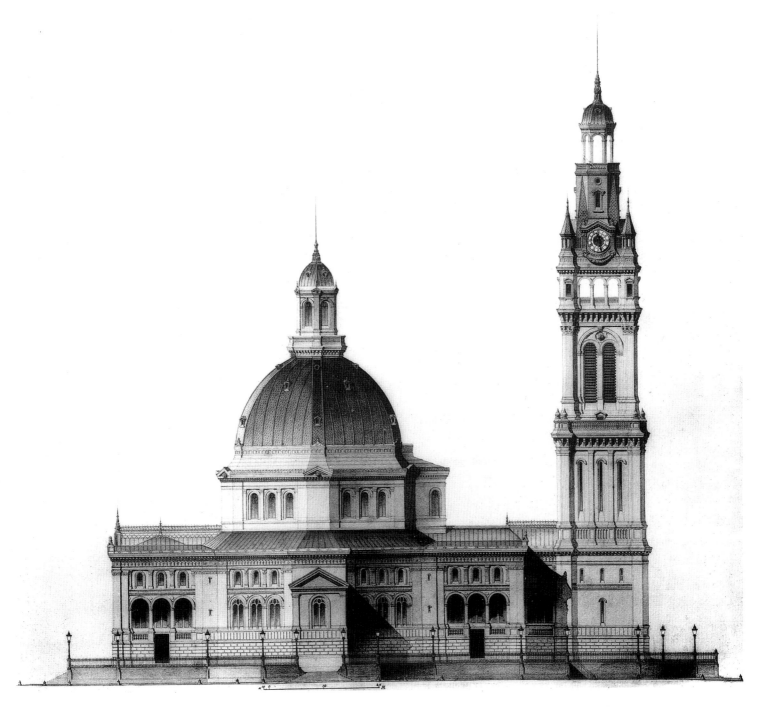

been lost since the Reformation; therefore contemporary architecture was, for him, the style of church building prevalent during the period that ended with the Reformation. Unlike Rose, Thijm did not perceive any difference between the requirements of contemporary architecture and those of architecture of the past. He argued that the more both the architects and the users of the buildings themselves identified with the spirit of the Middle Ages, the more 'rational' architecture would be.

Leliman rejected the axiom that post-classicist

architecture should have a style of its own, defining style as an amalgam of binding 'absolute principles'. The school of eclecticists that he reckoned himself part of had no specific responsibilities to the spirit of the age, he maintained, nor did it have any special relationship with a specific past era. It was untrue, however, that eclecticists had no responsibilities at all. Here Leliman dissociated himself from the 'dreamers and visionaries' who used all sorts of ideas from the most unlikely sources without checking whether the exterior of any given building expressed the function or met the other requirements dictated by common sense. These dreamers, Leliman argued, were not small in number, and they invariably avidly adopted ideas from others that they subsequently applied inadequately. Eclecticists, on the other hand,

[will never] apply randomly the most appropriate existing form simply according to the current fashion or the whim of the moment, but will, rather, according to the commission in question, carefully select or elaborate on those forms that unite functionalism with convenience. Common sense is the law they abide by. If circumstances so require, they will attempt to create new forms as well as adjusting existing forms with total freedom, always in order that these forms conform to the commission. They reject unconditional obedience or subjection to any rule whatsoever. Their principle is that any form can be useful, but that no particular form can be universally applied. The commission must not be adapted to the form: it must control the form, and as a result of this each commission will produce its own specific form.[25]

To Leliman, the need to create a contemporary architecture was above all the need to be free and original, with truth and character as guidelines and with a deliberate absence of style as a result. Rose, too, of all the seven requirements on his list – freedom, truth, unity, order, cohesion, harmony and proportion – attached the greatest value to freedom. As with his concept of the spirit of the age, his ideas on the primacy of freedom caused him to run into difficulty, because artistic liberty was essentially inconsistent with style in the sense of being an expression of collectivity. Thijm, however, encountered no such problem here. He rejected outright the liberty of the artist, arguing that art was at the service of the Church.

The issue here is always the individual architect's problem of trying to determine the extent to which the rules of art are collective, and where the individual artistic domain starts. We could also say that it is a matter of authority, and the extent to which this authority needs to be accepted. Elsewhere in Europe, this issue had been the subject of the extensive and heated debate concerning the classical versus the Romantic, but only later would this become a topical issue in the Netherlands. As we saw in the previous chapter, the ideal of culture held by the main leaders in Dutch opinion in the 1840s – 'edification without exaggeration' – had more affinity with the classical tradition than with the latest views of Romanticism. Their dislike for Romanticism implies a definition: everything that turns away from the classical tradition is Romanticism. It is not surprising, therefore, that in the second half of the nineteenth century neo-Gothic buildings were often labelled as Romantic and that Cuypers was seen as a representative of the Romantic movement. Furthermore, the German background to the classical–romantic antithesis (originating with Goethe, August Wilhelm Schlegel and Hegel) also associated the Romantic Movement with the medieval, the Christian and the non-Latin, which made the Romantic image of the Gothic Revival even more understandable.

Alongside this German background stood the French interpretation of Romantic architecture, which took shape in Labrouste's circle and had entirely different characteristics. French Romantics were also looking for an architecture different from classicism, but they opposed classicism only as a doctrine, as a monopoly, and in the notion that it was the sole revelation of eternal beauty. They had neither aversion nor preference for the forms that classicism had produced; they had merely decided to apply them henceforth at their discretion. Neither did they have any particular feelings of sympathy or antipathy towards the Middle Ages. Unlike many German Romanticists, the French displayed a more anticlerical attitude. The concept of Romanticism in nineteenth-century Dutch texts on architecture therefore needs to be carefully examined for the origins of their underlying ideas: were they French or German?

In addition, it is important to realize that the definition of the classical and the Romantic as formulated by Goethe, Schlegel and Hegel (and as propagated by Thijm in the Netherlands) conceived these two terms as opposites and so regarded daily architectural practice as a confrontation between two camps. This notion has not only clouded our understanding of individual events, but has also distorted the historical picture of post-classicist Dutch architecture. To remedy this we have to accept that we fail to understand the classical if we continue to define it in the old German tradition as the culture of the *Diesseits*, of the earthly and material side, as opposed to the *Jenseits*, the transcendental and spiritual characteristics typical of Romanticism. For the classical cultivated the material and spiritual aspects at the same time. Classicist architectural theory consisted of systematized aesthetics and a codified design method, an objective theory of harmony. Subjection to this structure, manifesting itself in ideal architectural types, resulted in practice in variants that had the ideal type as their basis, a 'unity in diversity', a *style*. Crucial in this was finding a rationale that would justify such a subjection, and in the classicist tradition this was the belief that the ideal form simultaneously represented the highest physical and metaphysical order. Pursuing this ideal therefore became the very essence of culture itself. The art of building (and art in general), according to this concept, was never an aim in itself but rather, an instrument, a means of achieving perfect harmony.

When classicism disappeared as a theory of design (as a system of columns and pediments), these characteristics of classicist architectural theory survived, and from then on they were frequently seen in the Netherlands in new architectural forms. They entered the pointed-arch style, which, as already observed, they transformed into the neo-Gothic. For when classicism disappeared the pointed-arch style, which since the eighteenth century had been a practice rather than a theory, was transformed into a doctrine of aesthetics anchored in an increasing knowledge of medieval architectural forms and techniques; and it was made visible through ideal types – in particular, thirteenth-century French Gothic – resulting in a style, while the pursuit of unity, the subjection to the higher order, was represented as an ideological necessity. Within neo-Gothic architecture, the art of building remained an instrument, a path to a higher transcendental reality and possessing beauty and truth of a divine origin. The whole subject was given an explicit Roman Catholic signature.

Opposite this classicist concept of architecture and its neo-Gothic metamorphosis stood the Romantic concept. The usual definition stipulates that it was with its focus on metaphysics and individual feelings that Romanticism distinguished itself from classicism. However, if this approach is applied to architecture it turns out to be as misleading as the traditional definition of classicism. In reality, classicism created a lot of space for metaphysics and for individual feelings; in the eighteenth century it was even embedded in a theoretical framework, the character theory, as we have seen. An orientation towards historical architecture has also been called one of the specific characteristics of Romanticism, while classicism itself showed a long tradition of modernization inspired by a new look at the past.

Probably the crucial difference between the classicist and Romantic concepts of architecture was individual artistic freedom. It was the central theme of Romantics; a freedom not formalized, let alone laid down in rules amounting to an objective for general system application. It

did not exist at the mercy of a benevolent authority; but was discovered or won by the individual artist and, as a consequence, was pre-eminently subjective in nature. So it could not lead to a style incorporating collective representations of the ideal, and it did not need to be protected or maintained by a collective ideology – except as it was conceived of in the new nineteenth-century ideology of individualism. The focus was indeed on the development of the individual. But even then art was not seen as an instrument, as a servant. It was an autonomous entity, with rules and with a beauty and truth that related to its own autonomous reality.

This approach sheds an altogether different light on the relation between classical and Romantic. Architects using classical forms in a subjective – recalcitrant – way, such as Zocher and Leliman, can be considered proponents of Romantic architecture. Thijm, the fierce apponent of 'pagan' classicism, was called a Romantic by the people who admired him for his passion and fanaticism. But he should be placed squarely in the classicist tradition of opinions on the social meaning and function of architecture.

The new dualism: spirit and matter

The contrast between an art of building conceived as a means towards a higher cause and an art of building for its own sake is part of a dualism in the theory of art which in the 1840s and 50s was discussed under different names; not only the established twin concepts of Romantic and classical, but also those of idealism and realism, spiritualism and formalism – or, more simply put, spirit and matter.[26] This polarization replaced the more or less homogeneous character of classicism with a new, bipolar artistic reality. For some time this dualism marked the transition to a theoretical development that tended more and more towards pluriformity.

It would be to grossly misrepresent the present understanding of historical events if we were to adopt the dualist way of thinking prevalent at the time, for so much was happening that could not be subsumed in either side. Thijm's views on art, for example, had become extremely spiritualized but were in no way unrelated to the material, formal characteristics of the artistic and architectural artefact. Rose considered the art of building to be an independent form of art, but at the same time did not regard it exclusively as an issue merely of material and technique. Despite being an engineer, in his essays he hardly touched on constructional and functional issues (*firmitas* and *utilitas*, in Vitruvian terms), confining himself almost exclusively to the conditions of *venustas*, or beauty, often in combination with explicit ideals of culture.

The debate did not focus entirely on visual beauty, for beauty had spiritual as well as material characteristics. The first lines of *A Study on Beauty and Art* (1856) by the young Dutch art critic Carel Vosmaer (1826–88) read: 'I will not argue for the great importance of *Beauty* and its exterior appearance and revelation, or for art and its moralizing and spiritualizing influence on mankind, but I will, rather, adopt these as truths that will no longer be disputed.'[27] Such conviction – or, rather, such certainty – also legitimized the importance attached to the concept of beauty in the theory of architecture. Beauty, materialized through art, could bring the individual to a morally and spiritually higher level, could *edify* him or her.

And thus the principal distinction made here between the concept of architecture as formulated by Thijm (*architecture as a means*) and by Rose (*architecture as an end*) seems to evaporate. For is it not true in both cases that it is architecture's task to edify people? It is not difficult to argue against this statement on the basis of the then current theory of art. Vosmaer's *Study* can be cited here too: following Kant, Vosmaer considered the domain of art and the domain of ethics as two areas that influenced each other but which were still independent of each other, each having 'its own cause, nature and laws'. 'In works of art it is not allowed to philosophize, to teach or to moralize with a specific purpose in mind, for the aesthetic principle must prevail and may not be hindered by any ulterior purpose whatsoever'; the purpose of art 'is not to be of use, but any usefulness may be the result of art, its possible outcome'. And the 'outcome' or effect of beauty was, according to Vosmaer, 'the edification of the soul'. He explained this by quoting Winckelmann's comment, in his *History of the Art of Antiquity*, that he would make sure he had an 'edified' attitude when contemplating a classical sculpture of Apollo in order to observe it 'with dignity'; Vosmaer also quoted Schiller, who had said that the 'moral spirit and joyfulness' that it aroused enabled him to gauge the aesthetic value of a work of art.[28]

Vosmaer, a lawyer from The Hague who in 1873 retired to live off his fortune, had a sharp pen and acquired thereby a prominent reputation as a commentator – in particular on the liberal *Nederlandsche Spectator* – and as a radical freethinker. In his aesthetics the Kantian concept of 'purposeless' beauty occupied the highest position. Medieval art, he wrote in 1856, had only limited value because 'its main purpose [was] the visual expression of religious doctrines and traditions', thus remaining a didactic form of art. It was no wonder that with these opinions and his talent for polemic he got on the wrong side of Thijm, who was six years his senior. They can be considered as antipodes, Thijm viewing art as subservient and Vosmaer seeing it as autonomous; Thijm modelled his cultural ideal on medieval art, whereas Vosmaer's cultural paradigm was Greek and Roman art. Thijm fought for an idealistic collective art, Vosmaer favoured an individualistic approach. Thijm respected most of all the spiritual in art, while Vosmaer protected the material and sensory values against an abundance of spirit.

And thus we return to the polarity in concepts of art around the middle of the nineteenth century, referred to above. Thijm and Vosmaer seem almost the personification of this polarity. But here too, the contrast is only relative. In reality things were more complicated than the rather black-and-white classification of idealist and realist, classicist and Romantic. Vosmaer also acknowledged for example, as did Thijm, that the spiritual in art was to be regarded as paramount. In 1856, Vosmaer argued: 'The spirit is certainly the first and foremost, the essence of art.' The difference between the two men is clear from these words of Vosmaer's: 'When its comes to the realization, the question is, *how* the spiritual is to be present in the work of art. Through contempt of the material world and of sensuality, through the expression of a mystical meaning? Or, rather, by edifying and spiritualizing the material and sensual?'[29]

A social function for architecture?

Beauty as spiritualizing and edifying the soul: this view gave an important impetus to the social meaning of architecture. The art of building could no longer be regarded as exclusively the domain of architects, their clients and the occasional well-to-do art lover. It also implied a social responsibility. Instead of a theoretical discussion, beauty became a public mission and would leave a prominent mark on the architectural debate until well into the twentieth century. In 1861, Vosmaer stated: 'The art of building, as has been shown many times, has provided the monuments in which the history, the spirit and the character of a nation live on recognizably; the art of building has the greatest influence on the formation, and, alas, also on the corruption, of the taste of the general public.[30]

The background to this social function was, in addition to the notion that art edified people, the theory of *character*. On account of its ethical connotations, *truth* was very suitable for the edification of the soul (as well as for the polemics centring on this subject), but it was clear that unity of form and construction could only be experienced by a select group that had some sort of technical understanding of building. Traditionally, character was the means through which a building was able to communicate with the general public, and had long been regarded as an instrument for edifying that public. The eighteenth-century *architecture parlante* could induce in the observer an edified attitude just as it could arouse gloom, gaiety, loneliness, grace or seriousness. It is not difficult to go one step further and to consider art as a way of educating the community as a whole. In Germany, too, it was accepted in the late eighteenth century that through its character architecture could have an edifying and ennobling effect.[31]

From the middle of the nineteenth century, Dutch society gradually divided into various ideologically defined religious and political groups. Architecture would play an important role here. It was helpful on the one hand in enabling a group to define itself and, on the other, in representing it to the outside world. In the same way as the Catholic Church came to use neo-Gothic architecture, so the 'official style' of new government buildings in the 1880s and 90s came to support the growing awareness of nationhood that took place under the guidance of the government. Similarly, the neo-Renaissance, based on the Dutch architecture of the seventeenth century, was to express the cultural aspiration of the upper middle class: its ideal of the Golden Age.

The new social responsibilities of architecture fitted the social ambitions of architects. As a member of the MBB and of the artists' association Arti et Amicitiae, the architect Isaäc Warnsinck had claimed in his discourse *Art as an Element of National Culture* in 1849: 'It is the artist's edifying mission to purify all earthly beauty and to separate it from the accidentally imperfect and less perfect, and to give the purified result back to the public.'[32] There is no doubt that amongst these artists with a mission to edify he was also including architects. The revered Karl Friedrich Schinkel had emphasized their important function: 'The architect is by definition the ennobler of all human relations.' Whereas Arti's annual report of 1853 stated that artists must shape their ideal beauty with perseverance and in solitude, sacrificing their own interests in the process, Rose argued in 1854 that the architect developed beauty 'in accordance with his own concepts', a process that took the form of a 'struggle, [of] the suffering of the artist, which no one can understand who has not experienced it himself'.[33]

The changes in the social position of artists and architects show remarkable similarities. The foundation of the MBB in 1842 had followed the foundation of Arti in 1839. Both were oriented towards increasing their members' status as well as the status of their work, by organizing lectures, publications and exhibitions, appointing famous people from abroad as honorary members and stimulating architectural and art reviews

respectively. Arti, established a distance between 'genuine' artists and amateurs or craftsmen, and MBB too created a hierarchy that separated the new 'scientifically' and aesthetically trained architects from the craftsmen – the practitioners who adhered to traditional methods – and the growing number of engineers. Prominent members of Arti were also members of the MBB and vice versa, underlining their identifical interests and social ambitions.

Notes

1. Jeroen Schilt, Jouke van der Werf 1992; Coert P. Krabbe 1998. Rose: Hetty E. M. Berens 1999.
2. J. J. Penn 1841, 7. Penn follows here almost literally the then still influential publication of Aloys Hirt (1809, 12): 'die Architektur ist keine nachahmende Kunst, wie die Mahlerey und die Skulptur, sie hat kein Vorbild in der Natur, sondern sie ist die eigenmachtige Schöpferin ihrer Werken.' On the self-representation of the art building: M. Olin 1986.
3. W. N. Rose 1854, 359–60.
4. W. N. Rose 1856–7, 54.
5. W. N. Rose 1858a, 184 (discourse published 1857).
6. Report of the general assembly, *Bouwkundige Bijdragen* XI (1860), 102–24.
7. W. N. Rose 1860b (discourse published in 1858).
8. M. [J. A. Alberdingk Thijm] 1850, 80–3.
9. For this Belgian context: Jan De Maeyer (ed.) 1988, *passim*.
10. This tradition was reported by Cuyper's patron Victor de Stuers (1897, 199). The statement 'Toute forme qui n'est pas indiquée par la structure doit être repoussée' ('every form that is not indicated by the construction should be rejected'), followed by 'V.L.D. [Viollet-le-Duc]') in 1863 served as Cuypers' slogan for his design for the Willem I Museum in Amsterdam, which was not executed.
11. Eugène-Emmanuel Viollet-le-Duc 1863–72, 451–77, 477: 'Si nous tenons à posséder une architecture de notre temps, faisons d'abord de sorte que cette architecture soit nôtre, et qu'elle n'aille point chercher partout ailleurs qu'au sein de notre société ses formes et ses dispositions.'
12. The enormous importance that symbolism in architecture had acquired for Alberdingk Thijm (as a means of communicating a theological message) is demonstrated most convincingly in his publication 1858c, to a great extent an imitation of J. M. Neale and B. Webb's English translation of the medieval bishop Durandus' *Rationale Divinorum Officiorum* (1843).
13. J. A. Alberdingk Thijm 1864, 104–5.
14. J. A. Alberdingk Thijm 1858b, 360: 'our' art profited from the most beautiful examples, so there was nothing wrong with borrowing these from 'our common Roman/German civilization'. It is often unclear what Thijm's use of 'our' refers to – the Dutch in general, or Catholics only.
15. Lidwien Schiphorst 1992. For Church policy and the idealization of the Middle Ages: Jan De Maeyer 1992.
16. Reichensperger: Michael J. Lewis 1993.
17. Marijke Estourgie-Beijer 1993, 53.
18. J. H. Leliman 1860c, 141.
19. Report of the general assembly 1856, *Bouwkundige Bijdragen* 10 (1858), 136–52.
20. David Van Zanten 1982; *idem* 1987, 2–43; Neil Levine 1977, 360–93.
21. S.-C. Constant-Dufeux, cited and translated by David Van Zanten 1982, 42–3.
22. Neil Levine 1977, 330. On the ateliers in general and their relation to the École des Beaux-Arts: Richard Chafee 1977, 77–97. For the design concepts common at the time: Louis Hautecœur 1955.

23. For illustrations, descriptions and analyses of the building: Neil Levine 1977, 333–57; *idem* 1982, 138–73; David Van Zanten 1982, 83–98.

24. Eberson: Karin M. Veenland-Heineman 1985; the jury: p. 485.

25. J. H. Leliman 1860e, 429.

26. Carel Vosmaer 1856 already points out the relationship between these pairs of concepts, the first three of which he mentions on p. 119, spirit and matter on pp. 142ff. On dualism between spirit and matter in the 1840s and 50s: Toos Streng 1992.

27. Carel Vosmaer 1856, v.

28. Carel Vosmaer 1856, 109–15; 49–50. Winckelmann (in his *Geschichte der Kunst des Altertums*): 'Ich nehme selbst einen erhabenen Stand an, um mit Würdigkeit anzuschauen.'

29. Carel Vosmaer 1856, 110.

30. Carel Vosmaer 1861a, 172.

31. Klaus Jan Philipp 1990.

32. Cited by M. Thijssen 1986, 45.

33. Schinkel: 'der Architekt ist seinem Begriff nach der Veredler aller menschlichen Verhältnisse' (H. Mackowsky [ed.] 1922, 192); W. N. Rose 1854, 357.

Part 2

Architecture and the World Outside:
The 1860s–1880s

4

The Rise of the Public

A technical revolution

For a long time now architects' discussions on contemporary architecture had shown a lively interest in foreign theories and practices. In the 1860s and onwards this increased – internal communication became more frequent and more intense. Ever more publications, including foreign ones, saw the light; foreign countries became less remote. In the 1850s, the Dutch national telegraph network was established, with connections to Belgium, Paris, Prussia and Hanover. The Railway Act of 1860 enabled more rapid and frequent railway connections, and with the increase in speed of sailing boats and steamships, Amsterdam and Rotterdam were able to maintain tight schedules with English, German and French, and later American, ports. The general need for knowledge and news also increased, as shown by the substantial growth of the importance of the printed word. The prominent French, German and English architectural journals circulated among Dutch architects through the libraries and subscriptions of the MBB and the other architectural organization, Architectura et Amicitia. Most authoritative of these were the *Revue générale de l'architecture et des travaux publics* (Paris), the *Allgemeine Bauzeitung* (Vienna), the *Deutsche Bauzeitung* (Berlin) and *The Builder* (London).

The two Dutch architectural magazines, *Bouwkundige Bijdragen* (Architectural Essays) and *De Opmerker* (The Observer), established in 1843 and 1866 respectively, reflected not only the international character of news-gathering but also the ever-increasing complexity of the building industry in all its facets. To mention just one aspect: due to Western European industrialization which exerted its influence in each and every field, the range of building materials expanded yearly with new inventions and applications – for example, new bricklaying techniques, new roofing materials, industrial processes for the preservation of wood, new types of paint, larger standard sizes for glass, and a stream of prefabricated ornaments. Most significant was the new industrial building material, iron, which the only professor of architecture in the Netherlands, Eugen Heinrich Gugel, in 1869 called 'the most important building material of our modern technology'.[1]

Architecture was more of a topic for public discussion in the 1860s than it had been in the previous decades. We have already noted the publication of professional reviews of designs and of buildings, as for example in the case of Zocher's Stock Exchange in 1840. Within the MBB the architectural review became, from 1842, a more or less set item on the agenda. Competitions were regularly held and entries critically adjudicated. The heated discussions that were sometimes published in the 1860s, however, indicate that the tactful comments typical of the 'artistic arena' of the MBB had been transformed into a much more passionate, and wider, public debate. Admittedly, it had always been clear that the art of building was a pre-eminently public art form, but it was now as if the social requirements applied to architecture had become both more specific and more varied, as if it were not sufficient to be merely contributing to the 'edification' of the public in a general sense. In the 1860s, the question was posed in the context of the Dutch state: who determines what is national, and what national architecture should look like?

Theory begins to decline

Concomitant with this new ideological dimension of the architectural review is an aspect that requires immediate consideration: the relationship between architectural criticism and architectural theory. Zocher's critics tested his Stock Exchange against the standards they derived from architectural theory. Their criticism can be seen as the application of a general theory, seen as an objective standard, to a specific case, in order to verify the quality of the result. This would change during the 1860s, when criticism sometimes showed that theory was losing ground. It was still helpful to erudite architects in their discussions of contemporary buildings, but it was gradually distancing itself from the changing world in which the art of building was to find its place. More specifically, architectural theory, long considered the template for architectural practice, started to lose its grip when, over a relatively short period, new circumstances were created by society. New types of building were required for new social and economic functions; and with new building materials and techniques, new ways of building and new finishes were created. The existing theories of architecture were illustrated exclusively by temples, churches and palaces. Railway stations, gasworks, shop fronts, working-class houses, iron girders or applications of Portland cement and other innovations were simply not referred to. In other words, the paradox of this day and age was that architectural theory, if its prominent function for the practice of design was to be maintained, would need to adapt to the ever-diversifying circumstances of that practice. In reality, this paradox created an unworkable situation, in which during the next decades architectural theory would increasingly lag behind, becoming more of a verbal phenomenon, a language deriving its main importance from the cultural added value it gave to the profession of architect. Before the end of the century architectural theory – even the concept of style – would be reduced to mere individual opinions and catch-phrases.

It lost ground in another area too, in a development that also had its origin in the changing society that was relentlessly advancing on the architectural world and forcing it to abandon its traditional ideas. This development related to the meaning that beauty held for society, interpreted according to the old tradition that art edifies society through its beauty. In 1867–8, Rose must have had an inkling of some fundamental change taking place when he wrote that the experience of beauty had no universal character. For, he argued, whereas the public usually assumed that beauty produced an agreeable experience, the expert, the architect, knew that beauty existed only if there was truth – and truth was not necessarily agreeable.[2]

This view encompassed two aspects that would become extremely important in the next decades. First, the notion that beauty, as an expression of truth, could be disagreeable. This made Rose the first author in the Netherlands to formulate the essence of Romantic art as it might apply to architecture; the notion had appeared at the beginning of the century in French literature and painting in the radical *le laid c'est le beau* – 'The ugly is the beautiful' – in which, in the name of truth, the artist had also to copy and represent nature's less sublime, even repellent, aspects. From the 1850s, this concept took concrete form in France in the school of *réalisme* in art; by the 1860s, it was as yet mainly in literary circles that this new 'ugly' beauty was discussed in the Netherlands.[3] When the idea of realism finally did reach the architectural world, it resulted in a complete repudiation of the new concept of beauty.

Neither did Rose accept the consequences of a 'realistic' aesthetics. In the following chapters, however, it will transpire that, despite the resistance of architects publishing and debating on the subject, this realism gained an increasingly strong hold on the practice of building. Here, too, practice proved more powerful than theory. The final chapter will show that, in order to practise their profession successfully, architects were compelled to focus on the 'realistic' beauty of everyday issues far removed from the sublime, such as comfort and functionality, while subordinating their own traditional ideals of beauty.

And this brings us to the second important aspect of Rose's remark on the experience of beauty. The choice of an artistic truth which in the name of art had to be accepted, no matter how disagreeable, implied a division between the artist and his public – ironically, during the very period when architects were preparing to put their art at the service of the new ideological movements that were manifesting themselves in society. The 1870s, 80s and 90s would increasingly and persistently demonstrate these two divisions: an ever more mature, multiform and demanding public and the growing ideologizing of architecture.

All these developments, that were radically to influence architecture in the next decades, were in the 1860s as inconspicuous as the seed that will grow into a tree. The conviction was still widespread that architectural theory would show how the art of building would rise ever higher; the present setbacks and malaise merely indicated that this was a transitional period, a temporary stop on the way up.

The architect and public taste

In 1857 the MBB invited its members to give their reactions to the question 'What rules should be adhered to when rejecting buildings?' Leliman argued that, when it came to the actual building, an architectural design was invariably adapted according to the ideas, interests and predispositions of officials, building workers, client – 'indeed, even family, friends and acquaintances of the client'. He believed the critic paid too little attention to this: 'Often it is not the architect but the client who ought to be assessed'.[4] In an article of 1863 Rose complained about the influence of money on architecture: 'Unlike painters, we cannot create a piece of art at relatively small cost. And those who are to provide the funds demand a control that can only be considered justified if their taste is rooted in a certain expertise.'[5] Such remarks illustrate that architects wanted critics to do more than just check whether or not the architectural theory had been applied properly – they wanted them to understand that architects were often powerless to apply that theory.

Fig.28
Willem Nicolaas
Rose's Ministry of
Colonial Affairs
Building, The Hague
(1859–61), side wall:
the first building in
the Netherlands to
manifest the typology
(and the 'character')
of the modern office
building as a specific
phenomenon.
Draconian cuts in
building budgets
reinforced Rose's
inclination to
substitute
conventional design
and building
techniques for risky
experimentation. In
the background to the
left is the façade of
the Ministry of
Justice Building
(Fig.48).

In 1861 strong public criticism of the new buildings for the Ministry of Colonial Affairs and of the Supreme Court in The Hague (1859–61) brought to light another indicator of the architect's vulnerability, architectural theories notwithstanding: the critic's subjective views. When Rose, the architect of these two buildings, expounded on the subject of architectural truths, that to the public might seem disagreeable, he was not far off the mark. The designs of both buildings were a public scandal. The Ministry Building had a cubic form with flat stuccoed façades painted terracotta. The windows had cast-iron frames, the almost flat zinc roof was supported by iron girders, and the floor's substructure consisted of iron beams; in the hall were iron columns displaying papyrus capitals.

Rose had demonstrated his interest in German architecture over many years, and here too he was making references to German prototypes such as work by Schinkel (the Bauakademie in Berlin, 1831–6, for the Ministry Building) and Hübsch (the façade of the Supreme Court). These two buildings had apparently helped him to find his own contemporary style, a style which, as the results showed, was modern in various ways: in its emphasis on the simplicity of both the main form and the details, in its emphasis on openness in both a literal and a figurative sense

(the unusually large windows), and in its use of new building techniques (the incorporation of iron). The cartoonist of *De Nederlandsche Spectator* caricatured the Ministry Building as an aviary and the Supreme Court as a dog kennel. Some time later the journal published an extensive critique by an anonymous observer, 'X', who all but demolished the buildings. He considered the windows of the ministry much too large and the entrance too small, the colour ridiculous, the façades too little articulated, and the capitals of the crude iron columns disagreeable – and, as with some of the ornaments, in violation of the concept of truth. To him, the overall look of the exterior together with the centrally located steam engine for heating and ventilation was more that of a factory than of a ministry building (and, therefore, in violation of the concept of character).[6]

Like Zocher in 1840, Rose did not try explicitly to defend his buildings against the criticism. Indeed, he is not recorded as having mentioned any criticism at all in his public pronouncements, but it must have played a role when six or seven years later he wrote an article about the art of reviewing entitled 'Is taste as it is understood in daily life suitable for judging the value of the fine arts?'[7] He made a distinction between the objective and subjective values of art. The objective, he said, expressed itself in the way truth was given shape, and he argued that in this context the representation of truth did not necessarily produce an agreeable result. The subjective value related to taste in the usual sense of the word. Contrary to what was often thought, taste and feeling, according to Rose, were insufficient as a means of judging art. 'Therefore, if we emphasize the importance of the knowledge of art acquired through training, this is not just in the interests of the individual, but of culture in general as well.' The fact that artistic knowledge of the art of building required a special study quite different from sculpture or painting he explained in a later article.[8]

The commotion that arose over these two buildings was in fact a confrontation between a contemporary architecture and a public asserting its taste without having the knowledge of art required to understand it. The criticism expressed by 'X' showed that there was something else, apart from subjective taste, that stood in the way of an appreciation of such an example of the contemporary mode: aesthetic conservatism. Just as Zocher in 1840 was blamed for the fact that his Stock Exchange did not meet the traditional neoclassicist laws that the critic considered valid, so the anonymous critic accused Rose of having given his Ministry Building a false character, that of a factory: 'It is a large factory, a factory for something requiring a lot of light. Manual work is performed in it because no steam chimney is visible. No one would ever think that this glass monstrosity might be a building housing a ministry.' What X had failed to realize, however, was that Rose had actually conceived the office building not as a distinguished ministerial palace such as the critic might have expected, but as a *work*place, and that he had tried to find a character to fit the purpose.

X also disliked the 'sparsity' and 'thinness' of the iron construction because, he thought, it made a proper balance and rhythm in the composition impossible. He and Rose were using identical aesthetic concepts and both were applying truth and character as a norm. X, however, attributed a meaning to these concepts befitting the architecture of past times with its traditional ideas on representation, functionality and construction, whereas Rose attempted to re-evaluate these concepts in accordance with the circumstances of the new age. X stated:

As regards the new style that this architect wants to develop out of the ruins of the past, we see that he instead derives his forms from the ancients themselves. The only new aspect is that he uses the forms in a way that contravenes their nature, in situations that their ancient creators would never have dared to contemplate because they are completely irrational.

The newcomer: iron

The tenuous connection between architectural theory and a changing building practice became clear in the 1860s in the way architects assessed the various possible applications of iron. The technical developments taking place in the field of iron construction were difficult to bring into line with the usual aesthetic conventions. Rose was not alone in this struggle. The aesthetic rule held that falsity was not allowed – meaning, in this context, that iron must look like iron. According to the MBB's verdict of 1849, 'Iron and other metals are still used to imitate stone or wood, whereas iron, in accordance with its specific characteristics, requires altogether different forms.'[9]

Problems would emerge later, but for the time being the conclusion was simple enough. The only iron design actually expressing its natural characteristics would be a relatively light construction for a relatively heavy load, or a relatively wide span with relatively few supports. The visual image and material characteristics of such constructions, however, were at odds with the aesthetic convention that what is heavy should appear heavy, and with the notion that the physical strength of a wide span must be demonstrated via sturdy girders and a visible distribution of the load. The Palace of National Industry (1858–64, Cornelis Outshoorn) was a construction which, according to Leliman, was unique in the Netherlands, and for this reason alone it should receive the public's close attention, but, like all other halls of iron construction, it was not a work of *architecture*. It headed the list 'of important industrial iron constructions of our century', he went on, but it did not meet the requirements set for monumental buildings 'because in our opinion iron as the main building material cannot be applied to the rigid, the unmoveable or the wide. Width, rigidity and immobility are requirements for monumental buildings that are destined like the Palace of National Industry to defy the test of time.'[10]

Leliman was not one to shut his eyes to innovation. When in 1869 the MBB was considering the contribution of the iron industry to the art of building with a view to a possible 'iron style', Leliman ventured that he considered the new Rhine bridge near Cologne and Les Halles, the Paris food market, to be among the wonders of his time. 'This summer I have spent hours admiring Les Halles, and I said to myself: here the architect has truly shown that he is an artist who is able to give a market hall or building a place alongside other creations of the art of architecture!'[11] And yet, 'Fine architecture uses stone; stone is firm and rigid, ageless, it has form, depth, relief, shadows; this is all lacking in iron. If this material [iron] is not *thin* and *lean*,

then the construction is poor.' The dilemma was clear. Iron failed to comply with one very basic requirement of the art of building, *firmitas* – firmness, durability. An iron construction, according to Leliman, called for continuous inspection to prevent rust. It also conflicted with the requirement considered sublime above all others, *venustas*; an iron construction was not beautiful, but thin and lean.

In the following years proof of the durability and beauty characteristic of large iron constructions accumulated in England, Germany and France. The constant attempts of the nineteenth century to harmonize the old traditions with the needs and possibilities of the time were doomed to fail unless the existing aesthetics were radically abandoned. But to many a serious architect, right up until the end of the

century, this was an absurd idea. As late as 1886 Berlage admitted that he knew of 'nothing more disquieting than the tangle of an iron construction.'[12] At that time the Eiffel Tower, the three-hundred-metre spectacle (1887–9), was soon to be built. The parallel between Berlage's statement and X's criticism of Rose is interesting. Not only the public, but architects themselves, sometimes shut themselves off from new trends because they still cherished their old aesthetic ideals.

Architectonic aesthetics was based on building with stone, to which all other materials were subordinate. The integration of iron into fine architecture would only be possible if it was accepted that iron should occupy second place, that it performed a subservient function, even though outside the domain of architecture it made possible what was previously thought impossible. As a consequence of the impossibility of changing the prevailing concept, a new type of architecture sprang up alongside he traditional art of building – this was a new art of building with its own aesthetic doctrine that was contradicting all the familiar tenets. Whereas 'stone architecture', in modelling the surface in a play of structure and texture, concentrated on the development of fixed forms, depth, relief and shadow, 'iron architecture' aspired to the opposite: immateriality, an almost indefinable space, extreme boundaries of thinness and leanness, a maximal result with minimal effort; in short, an aesthetics based on the technical paradigm that was to be referred to in the twentieth century as *less is more*.

The reasons why architects downplayed the role of iron in architecture were theoretical rather than practical. This may seem odd because, as we have already seen, the role that architectural theory played in practice was only minor anyway; how was it, then, that theory posed such a huge obstacle in this specific case? The paradox can be understood only if we realize that the acceptance of 'iron aesthetics' would have blown to smithereens the two basic principles of architecture: the conventions governing *truth* and *character*.

The gulf between practice and theory widens: Gottfried Semper and Viollet-le-Duc

In the domain of architectural theory, the 1860s produced the works of the German architect Gottfried Semper (1803–79) and his French colleague Viollet-le-Duc. Their books were to feed public opinion in the Netherlands for several decades. Semper's main work, *Style in the Technical and Structural Arts, or Practical Aesthetics. A Handbook for Engineers, Artists and Art Lovers*, was published in two volumes in 1860 and 1863. In the same year the first volume of Viollet-le-Duc's *Entretiens sur l'architecture* (Discourses on Architecture) was published, while the *Dictionnaire* was completed in 1868.

The fact that these works immediately gained authority seems difficult to reconcile with the fact that building practice was at this time undermining the relevance of theory. The inconsistency can, however, be explained if we take into account that, as we shall see later, architectural theory was increasingly becoming a subject in its own right: it may have been losing its connection with building practice, but it was considered important by those architects who were writing about it. And although most practising architects preferred to delete the problem from their consciousness, the phenomenon could no longer be ignored.

By the 1890s, it would no longer be possible to deny that architectural theory occupied a peripheral and isolated position. The journals would often refer to the theories of Viollet-le-Duc, but, as one critic succinctly put it in 1896: 'In general we can argue that the public is completely indifferent to the ideals that our architects aspire to, because it feels they have no value in real life. Who cares if his house has been built in accordance with the theory of Viollet-le-Duc, if he considers it sombre and cheerless?'[13] In the 90s the circumstances under which architecture developed would be completely different from those of the 60s. There would be no doubt in the 90s that public taste played an important, often decisive, economic role, and it would be accepted that the architectural profession was also a business.

In the 1860s, this understanding had not yet surfaced. Architects conceived of themselves as artists. To them it was unthinkable that their aesthetic theories should become relative, marginal. Semper's and Viollet-le-Duc's impressive contributions to the debate seemed to bring to many the possibility of a contemporary architectural style nearer than ever. For, using the most recent scientific methods, these two learned professionals were determining the laws from which the new architecture would arise and according to which its essential elements would relate to one another. Semper was relinquishing what he called 'pure aesthetics, or an abstract theory of aesthetics' – that is, the traditional method that used geometry to define harmony, proportion and symmetry and thereby determine what was beautiful and what was ugly. Instead he favoured a *reine Baulehre*, 'a pure building theory', a practical theory of aesthetics somewhere between abstract aesthetic theory based on unverified principles on the one hand, and technical considerations to do with materials and construction on the other.[14]

Semper's concept of style was based on the factors that underline architectural form but 'that have no form themselves' – factors such as the original idea, the natural forces, the materials and the technical resources.[15] It was practically oriented to the creative process in which an idea became form via the materials and the technique's used, and the forces of nature. He described the process using analogies from recent discoveries in biology and ethnography regarding the earliest stages in the development of civilization, and from this resulted his 'empirical theory of style'. Biology had provided him with the insight that it is the skeleton that determines the essential differences and similarities between the organisms and is the basis for their form and function.[16] Ethnography taught him that the primitive hut, which Vitruvius

OPPOSITE
Fig.29
Cornelis Outshoorn's Palace of National Industry, Amsterdam (1858–64). In the 1860s this was the largest building in the country (126 x 80 x 62 metres). Developed after the example of the famous Crystal Palace in London (1851), the Palace served as exhibition space for trade, industry and agriculture and for large cultural events. The conventional laws of architectural aesthetics prevented it from being regarded as architecture. Photo: Jacob Olie, 1892.

considered to be the architectural archetype, could not be the oldest type of dwelling – which was the tent, the dwelling used by nomads. Semper argued in 1860 that every primitive civilization started with spinning, weaving and sewing, then put up tents. The design used for a tent (a structural skeleton covered with cloth, which provided the basis for adornment) was essentially similar, he maintained, to the principles of the earliest types of architecture; both were equally 'natural'.[17] In this context it is important not to leave unmentioned Bötticher's work on Greek architecture, *Die Tektonik der Hellenen* (1844–52), in which he distinguished between the core-form and the art-form (see p. 37). Not much later, but probably independent of Bötticher, Semper formulated the fundamental difference between the structural core and its 'dressings'.[18]

In contrast to Semper, Viollet-le-Duc was still liberally propagating the rules of traditional aesthetics. He also used geometric figures, which he discussed in his *Discourses*, to demonstrate the rules of harmony, proportion and symmetry. New, however, was the way in which he sometimes gave these rules a technical basis: proper proportion was based on structural solidity, he stated. He defined and applied the term 'style' inconsistently, sometimes adding curiously fallacious propositions – for instance, that art in the style of Louis XV had no style. But the definition to which he gave most prominence – that style was 'natural': a leaf on a tree and an insect have style because they function according to 'very reliable laws' – was quite similar to Semper's, and not only because of the biological metaphors. As far as the ethnographical element was concerned, Viollet-le-Duc maintained that achieving style could be compared to making a cooking pot, the work of the potter being perhaps the oldest handicraft in human history because it is the most indispensable. The primitive pot had style, according to him, because it was formed in accordance with the material used and the technique applied, and because its form expressed its material and its function. The analogies with biology and anthropology and the references to applied art and to the expression of function, material and craft call to mind Semper's earlier publications. However, another definition of style, also found in the *Discourses*, referred directly to the old French aesthetic tradition: style as the expression of the character of a people and its circumstances. Three years later volume VIII of Viollet-le-Duc's *Dictionnaire* appeared, with yet more different definitions of style.[19]

The fundamentally new aspect in the concept of style as used by Bötticher and Semper and by Viollet-le-Duc in his Semperian concept was that style was interpreted as a characteristic inherent to architecture, and independent of the circumstances in which buildings are designed and constructed. This view was fundamentally different from definition of style used by Quatremère de Quincy in his *Encyclopédie Méthodique* (1788–1825) and by Hübsch, which stated that style was a contingent characteristic of architecture resulting from factors such as the nature of a people and the climate. It is conceivable that the new 'scientific', empirical concept of style solved for some people the theoretical impasse formulated by Rose, that if style was the expression of a people and of the spirit of a specific age, who was to determine what that expression looked like and who had the authority to attribute a general validity to it? After all, if style was an independent characteristic of architecture – the expression of the relation between construction and ornament – then the problem was more objective and more easily defined. Finding a solution then became a question of looking for the basic rules of art hidden in the connection between the idea (the concept), the natural forces, the building materials and the technical resources. This empirical approach required a knowledge and an understanding of architecture, not a speculative perception of society. However, this did not imply that the scientific definition of style would sever architecture from its societal implications. The emphasis on the representation of function guaranteed architecture's social relevance, in particular in the case of monumental architecture, which formed the setting in which the theatre of public life took place.

The ideological battle gathers momentum

It is conceivable that this supposedly objective foundation for style was responsible, both inside and outside the Netherlands, for the widespread submission of architects to historic stylistic types. The knowledge of the aesthetic rules and conventions governing historic architecture now increased sharply, and the result was demonstrated in numerous designs and buildings rivalling their historic models. Yet many Dutch architects were troubled by the feeling that these efforts, despite all the exertion and money involved, brought a style for the nineteenth century no closer. And criticism of the 'objective' imitation of historic architectural types came from the followers of that other old concept of style – style as the architectural expression of the spirit of the age, of the people, its culture, climate and geography. These two concepts of style would frequently clash with one another in the following decades. The real battle, however, was not so much architectural as ideological.

Bötticher's, Semper's and Viollet-le-Duc's publications did not go unnoticed in the Netherlands. Bötticher became an honorary member of the MBB. In 1863 the journal

THE RISE OF THE PUBLIC

53

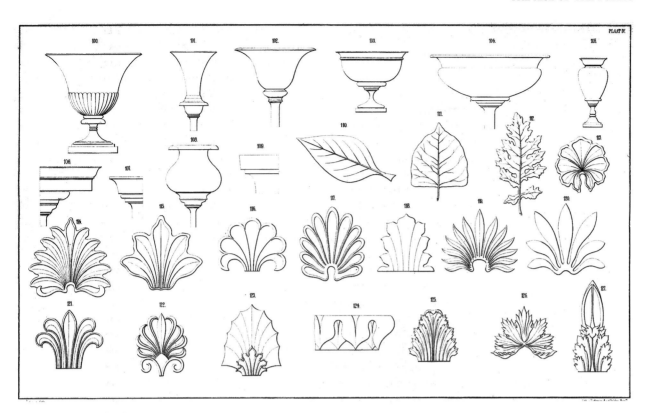

Fig.30
From W. N. Rose's
Theory of Ornament
(1863): illustration 4,
'Vase and leaf
patterns'.

Bouwkundige Bijdragen published a translation of Viollet-le-Duc's Semperian definition of style, and the first publication to refer to Semper's work appeared in 1864.[20] The chapter on the 1850s described how the ideas on truth in architecture, published by Viollet-le-Duc, had already been circulated in the Netherlands by W. N. Rose, claiming that they had become widely accepted among those who knew their Hübsch and Bötticher (we may assume that this applied to all the prominent members of the MBB). In 1863 Rose warned in a lecture against 'neglecting what constitutes the actual core of our art, namely the refinement and embellishment of forms, as derived from the construction. The Middle Ages and the Greeks set the right example, so why should we not follow it?'[21] For his study *The Theory of Ornament* (1863b), the first original Dutch work on the subject, Rose had made good use of Bötticher's *Tektonik der Hellenen*. Rose's book was not, as one might expect, a book of decorative patterns, but a contribution to the fundamental debate on the relation between the construction and its 'dressings'. In 1865, referring to the lessons taught by Bötticher and Viollet-le-Duc,[22] he once more emphasized that 'in addition to retaining the spirit of architecture, the use, embellishment and refinement of forms derived from the construction of the work to be built is a fundamental principle'.

It is remarkable that, although Semper's aesthetics had enormous influence in the Netherlands, in particular in the teaching of architecture and of arts and crafts, it is hardly mentioned in the arguments on architecture as published in journals and books. The situation with Viollet-le-Duc was very different – both the man and his views were frequently referred to. For example, an article by the French architect on taste published in the *Bouwkundige Bijdragen* in 1870 presented insights that were already familiar in the Netherlands. In the same year the preface to the *Discourses* of 1863 was translated and published.[23] Viollet-le-Duc was admired both by Rose, an architect oriented towards contemporary German architecture, and by Cuypers and his associates, supporters of the Gothic movement. He also enjoyed the approval of several prominent eclectics, such as Leliman and the architect Hugo Pieter Vogel (1833–86). In 1869, emphasizing the importance of the *Discourses* and of Viollet-le-Duc himself, Vogel stated: 'I have no doubt that every open-minded reader will feel a deep respect [for him].'[24] It was as if by 1870 Viollet-le-Duc had become an authority in the Netherlands whose views were always deemed relevant; he was honoured by all Dutch architects because he stood for their own standards and conventions. In France, however, his views were controversial. There he took issue with the 'untruth', as he saw it of the École des

Beaux-Arts and with his many more commercially inclined colleagues.

It is not clear why, for Semper, things were so different. Perhaps his publications were a little too theoretical, or perhaps the trouble lay with his practical work. Interestingly, his concept of form inspired by the Italian Renaissance of the fifteenth and sixteenth centuries, brought him success in Central Europe. As we shall see later, Dutch architects would become more interested in their Old Dutch 'Renaissance' architecture than in the Italian tradition. Also, the third part of Semper's book *Style in the Technical and Structural Arts* to be devoted to architecture, was never written, which meant that the application of his theory could only be studied in his buildings. In Viollet-le-Duc's case the situation was the other way around. His books showed extensive architectural applications, but these were not accompanied by a building practice that actually demonstrated how he wanted contemporary architecture to be. Aside from a few neo-Gothic churches, which remained almost unknown, he concentrated mainly on restoration work. What would have happened to Viollet-le-Duc's generally recognized authority in the Netherlands if he had built along the lines suggested in his entry for the design competition for the Opéra in Paris (1861) remains an open question. For the composition of the exterior was on some important points inconsistent with the layout of the interior, and the floor plan was ill-conceived in several essential respects. The façades were finished in the manner of the Italian Renaissance. This choice of design did not, incidentally, contradict the French architect's principles, for in his *Discourses* he emphasized that the issue was to have no specific artistic design prevail – 'for that is beyond our powers anyway'.[25]

A new voice: Eugen Heinrich Gugel

The view propagated by Bötticher, Semper and to a large extent by Viollet-le-Duc as well, that style is an inherent characteristic of architecture, took shape in the Netherlands in the form of a publication that for several generations of architects would remain a work of reference: *A History of Styles in the Main Architectural Periods* (1869), by Eugen Heinrich Gugel (1832–1905), a German who went to the Netherlands in 1864 on his appointment as professor of architecture at the Polytechnic School in Delft.[26]

His *History* was more a summary of authoritative views than an exposition of his own. In the preface Gugel stated that he had drawn extensively from the work of several German theorists, including Bötticher and Semper. The first chapter devoted almost forty pages to the 'fundamental principles of the aesthetics of architecture'. Gugel's book was not the first of its kind in the Netherlands; in 1865 *Aesthetics, or the Theory of Beauty* by the philosopher Johannes van Vloten (1818–83) was published, which also used the history of architecture as material for a system of aesthetics. The importance of Gugel's book lay mainly in the fact that it propounded the aesthetics of architecture in a way specifically directed at architects. Gugel, unlike Van Vloten, was not interested in philosophical theorizing but in contemporary building practice. He remained a professor for some thirty-five years; his book was reissued in 1886, and again in 1902, each time heavily revised.

The syncretic character of Gugel's aesthetics is apparent in the fact that he opted not only for Semper's empirical 'scientific' theory of style but also for the traditional principles of harmony, proportion and symmetry. This is also apparent from his definition of style, of which he offered three versions:

1. Style as the expression of the spirit of the age, the customs of a people and the natural circumstances of a country.
2. (Referring implicitly to Semper) style originating from the material and from the technique that is required for the working of that material (hence a stone style, an iron style, and so on)
3. Style as the term for a historical period showing a unity of artistic outlook.

In this context (point 3) Gugel used a metaphor to make the historical development of architecture more easily understandable: the idea that within an artistic era (a style) it is possible to distinguish a stage of ascendancy, an apogee and a decline. The idea had been long established, but had gained a new vitality via the recent emergence of natural science. It is interesting to note that Semper began his book *Style in the Technical and Structural Arts* with a description of the universe, in which the galaxies showed the stages of the eternal cycle of nature. Old matter was extinguished and turned to dust, but the dust was re-formed in order to give birth to the new. Semper was one of many who held on to such an idea in the hope that the artistic 'confusion' of the times was only a transitional phase, a period of re-formation in which the elements of the old were being rearranged in preparation for the new style.

This hope perhaps makes it easier to understand why so many architects committed themselves to a historical mode of architecture in the 1860s and later. The history of architectural styles as expounded by Gugel was not an assemblage of academic knowledge, but a necessary aid for understanding the essence of the art of building. Gugel's work was therefore not so much a small encyclopaedia of the past as a selection of historical material emphasizing what was still important. For example, he treated French architecture very differently from German architecture. For the foreseeable future he did not expect much good to come of the first. French neoclassicism was based on Roman examples, he wrote, and although this was all he said on the subject, the message must have come over loud and clear to the experts: the Roman source of inspiration meant a less sophisticated, less refined stage of development than the Greek, which had been the norm for Schinkel, for instance. After 1830 French architects, according to Gugel, had continued in the 'decorative' styles of the sixteenth, seventeenth and eighteenth centuries, 'using them with a rather uncritical attitude and without restraint'. Only a few architects, such as Labrouste, Félix-Louis-Jacques Duban (1797–1870) and Louis-Joseph Duc (1802–79), were able to break away from this and to strive for 'more severity and simplicity'. The massive demolition and reconstruction of Paris, in full swing since 1852, stood as monumental proof of the 'barrenness of our age' – no new ideas, everything according to the fashion of the sixteenth and seventeenth centuries. Then there was the 'Romantic school, which has the support of Viollet-le-Duc, the most eminent authority in Europe', but in France this school had achieved little more than the protection and restoration of medieval monuments.[27] Not only did Gugel allot six to seven times more pages to German architecture after 1800 than to French, but he discussed the subject with more affection and with far more subtle insights into the work of the most prominent architects. His stars were Schinkel, von Klenze, Friedrich von Gärtner (1792–1847) and Semper, and the 'almost unparalleled' new buildings in Vienna that had been built there after the demolition of the old city.

Architecture before 1800 was the main subject of Gugel's book. Part I covered Asian, Egyptian, Greek, Roman and medieval architecture, and Part II entitled 'Modern Architecture', covered the period starting around 1400 with the Renaissance and continuing up to the 1860s, a periodic division common in Germany since Franz Kugler's *Handbuch der Kunstgeschichte* (History of Art Handbook) (1841–56). Two things catch our attention here. The first is the fascinating fact that German theorists considered their own contemporary architecture to be linked via a continuous thread with the origins of 'modern architecture' in the Italian Renaissance. In the 1860s (as well as in the 70s and 80s) many seemed hardly aware of any discontinuity with the past, except for those such as Cuypers who viewed the Renaissance as an expulsion from the paradise of the Middle Ages, and the eclectics, who were convinced that the many revolutions of the nineteenth century constituted a fundamental break with the past. The majority of Dutch architects who contributed in the following decades to the public debate on architectural theory believed in a continuation of the Renaissance in a new, nineteenth-century, guise.

The second interesting aspect of Gugel's view of history is that it serves to justify his opinion of contemporary architecture. Italian fifteenth- and sixteenth-century architecture represented a period of high achievement, whereas the seventeenth and eighteenth centuries showed an increasing degree of decadence. This made it easier to understand the present situation: recent French architecture carried forward the tradition of a severely weakened, because superficially decorative, national architecture from the seventeenth and eighteenth centuries, whereas German architecture had developed after the example of its most flourishing period. In the 1869 edition (unlike the second edition of 1886) Gugel devoted fewer than ten lines to recent Dutch architecture – not because it had so little to offer, but because its diversity was simply too great, ran his courteous argument, and discussing the subject would require too much space: 'One could almost say that the entire range of historical building styles is currently being practised.' But from several other observations it can be inferred that he did not expect any good whatsoever to come of practising all those architectural styles together: 'irrespective of the number of new elements demonstrated in the styles being studied here, it is not possible for anyone to distinguish an independent, original architectural style from such a diverse assortment. In all honesty we must concede that in essence everything new [in contemporary Dutch architecture] is based merely on imitation of the preceding types of art'.[28]

The word 'merely' is proof of Gugel's dissatisfaction. He is also implying here that he regarded an 'independent, original architectural style', a style that would be just as independent as the main styles of the main eras treated in his book, as an assignment for the future. He was thus reformulating the dilemma that Rose had already faced in 1854: the contemporary style that must be developed can never be unrelated to history, but it must still be 'original'.[29]

The claims of history, the need for originality, and social relevance

This dilemma is revisited in the final paragraphs of Gugel's book, which further emphasize that he had two points of reference for his idea of a contemporary architecture. On one side of the divide was history, the inexhaustible supply of 'types of art', the perennial relevance of which was based on the insight that 'true progress is possible only by means of a rational connection with the past'. On the other side loomed the future, which was already becoming visible and which had nothing whatsoever to do with the past – although Gugel did not say so, but merely drew attention to the large railway buildings and the exhibition palaces, to iron, 'the most important building material of our modern technology', and to America: 'this is the country where the artistic forces are in a remarkable state of ferment; in particular we witness this in the enterprises being undertaken at the moment, which as far as pride and daring go are almost unparalleled'. But he drew no conclusions,[30] and in his chapter on the aesthetics of architecture made no reference to this dichotomy.

In the same chapter he drew a clear line between on the one hand architecture and on the other hand painting and sculpture: 'The difference between the two visual arts and their sister, architecture, is very substantial.' Nature offered no direct examples for its design, and 'therefore no art is more free and less imitative and more truly creative than the art of building'.[31] Fifteen years earlier Rose had had the same insight, but he had found no solution to the resulting circular argument. For if architecture could not imitate nature, it could only take itself as a model – so that its standards were to be found within itself, including the highest standard: truth. And this was the essence of the problem, because, as Rose had put it in 1854 with a certain understatement, 'the representation of truth in architecture is always rather abstract'.[32]

The solution that Gugel suggested was practical. 'The ideas that architecture must first and foremost express to us result from the construction itself, and are closely linked to the building materials that this form of art uses in order to create its works' – stone, wood, iron or other material. By means of 'idealized' forms architecture made visible the natural forces – gravity and the forces of traction and compression – which manifested themselves in the construction. In addition, he went on, architecture had a second 'ideal side', a second arena of possibilities for the artistic dimension: the expression of the function and social relevance of a building – a rich source of 'ethical considerations and edifying thoughts, the plastic transformation of which is the aim of the fine arts'. In both

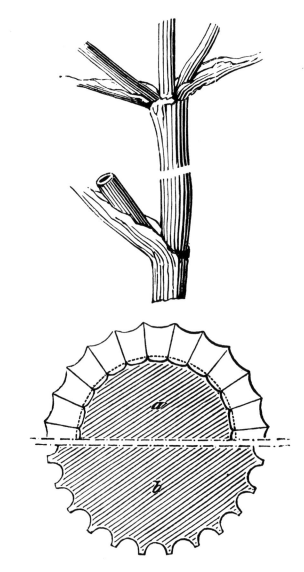

cases the designer must have 'a perfect technique' before the term 'practice of art' could be used, but not even a perfect technique or an inexhaustible source of ideas could make up for the lack of harmony that resulted if the objective and the subjective, or the interior and exterior, of a work of art were not in balance.[33]

This clearly demonstrates the effect of the practical aesthetics of Bötticher and Semper, who emphasized the relation between idea, material and technique. Gugel devoted a separate paragraph to the core-form (*Kernvorm*) and the art-form (*Kunstvorm*). Gugel also pointed out that the 'idealizing' – that is, the representing as an idea – of the natural forces inherent in construction and material would lead to architecture. Given that he was well versed in Semper's theories, it was not so strange that Gugel, following on from his observation that a contemporary original architecture had not yet been found pinpointed railway stations, exhibition halls and current American enterprises as three instances in which structural iron work was creating new architectural realities.[34] The path to beauty was still, in the terms used by Gugel, the path of truth and character. What Leliman, Rose and others had referred to from the 1850s onwards as truth was for Gugel one aspect of the art-form, the idealized core-form – the artistic representation of the construction and the materials. What Leliman referred to as character, Gugel referred to as 'the second ideal side' of the art-form – the representation of the building's function and social relevance.

With the introduction of the term 'social relevance' we encounter a totally different aspect of the architectural debate. It will have become clear from the above that architectural theory had become a complex matter. Is it then any wonder that most architects left the subject to a small number of enthusiasts and that most were satisfied with a few worn-out phrases? Indeed, there is no contradiction between the emergence of the monuments of architectural theory created by Semper and Viollet-le-Duc and the observation that the position of architectural theory was becoming increasingly weak in practice. However, something else was to take its place: theoretical reflection gave way to a stronger awareness of the concrete social task of architecture. Architects, critics and sometimes the commissioning agencies themselves, the clients, were increasingly able from the 1860s onwards to express this function. Gugel's *History of Styles* provides several examples of this change. Art must produce beauty, he wrote, and beauty, infinitely more even than science, contributes to 'the moral perfection of man'.[35] Here he was voicing a general wisdom or, if we prefer, a cliché.

Gugel was a practical person, not really a theorist, and certainly not an idealist or philosopher with a well considered cultural ideal such as the Amsterdam aesthetician Allard Pierson (1831–96) as he expressed himself in his book *Beauty and Wisdom* (1868). Gugel's book nevertheless displays a well entrenched cultural ideal for his own period, which explains his penchant for the Renaissance period. Reflection on contemporary culture in relation to the Renaissance was nurtured in Germany by the work of the Swiss art historian Jacob Burckhardt (1818–97). Burckhardt described the Italian Renaissance not as an artistic style, but as a comprehensive culture in which life itself became a work of art. After the darkness of the Middle Ages this culture avidly pursued rationality, individuality and humanism, and established a powerful bourgeoisie: what emerged from this was modern man.[36] This historical image coincided with the image that the bourgeoisie cultivated of itself. According to the bibliography in his book, Gugel, like every other member of the German educated classes, had read Burckhardt. His enthusiasm for Semper's work and for the 'unparalleled' building projects in Vienna also shows that he cherished this Renaissance cultural ideal: the ideal of a modern, civilized society, headed by a civil administration, where generous patronage was available – as in the sixteenth century when, according to Gugel, 'in the south of Europe the dawn of a new and glorious artistic era had arrived that before long, in the the north too, brought to a close the romantic twilight of the Middle Ages'.

This once again raises the antithesis of classicism versus romanticism. Gugel also discussed the antitheses of idealism versus realism and mind versus matter. The high points of medieval art were the result of the 'glorification of an idea', whereas in the Renaissance 'contemporary architecture was based on the necessary and useful works of public and private life'.[37] With this comment Gugel showed that he belonged to the camp of those who were convinced that architecture, understood as a style, originated in society.

A national architecture: a collective or an individualist vision?

When his *History of Styles* was published in 1869, Gugel had been living in the cultural climate of the Netherlands for five years. The historical image – especially from the architectural point of view – of the Renaissance, the growing self-awareness of the liberal citizen and the problem of a national art, were all-important influences in this context. The cultural ideal intrinsic to his German identity was not very different from the ideal that was dominant in the Netherlands; and similarly with the development of architecture, which relied so strongly on such an ideal. The following chapters will demonstrate time and again to what extent, structurally as well as in other ways, Dutch architecture was linked to foreign architecture. In the changes it underwent, Dutch society was part of the changing society of Western and Central Europe. The fact that the theme of a specifically national architecture became the vogue in the 1860s does not conflict with this – nationalism, including cultural nationalism, became a political phenomenon in many European states at this time.

The debate on national culture in general and national architecture in particular was a manifestation of the more prominent ideological profiles that society created for itself.

In view of the definition of style as an expression of the national character it is not surprising that this definition contained an ideological component. It is worth noting that this was also true of Semper's and Viollet-le-Duc's concepts of style, which saw style primarily as a characteristic of architecture itself and as the characteristic related to the idealized representation of concept, function and construction. In fact, the issue was the representation of truth in architecture as defined by Hübsch as far back as 1828 in his treatise *In What Style Should We Build?* After the 1860s the issue was ideologized first by Thijm and Cuypers, then by Berlage and all their supporters, who presented architectural truth as a representation of a metaphysical truth. The two ideologies strongly linked to the concept of style that will play a major role in the following chapter are *cultural nationalism* and *the ideology of Cuypers* and his circle. Both these ideologies idealized society as a homogeneous collective, a community in the fundamental sense of the word. But there was a third ideology as well. Unlike the other two, this one made hardly any effort to promote itself because its supporters increased in number as an automatic response to the spirit of the age. Perhaps we should call it the ideology of the modern age itself: the concept of *individualism*, of *idealist pluralism* and of *artistic liberty*. This concept did not see society as a collective entity, but as a collection of individuals with some basic collective interests. Whereas the two collective ideologies applied the concept of style so as to make manifest their collective ideals in an architectural way (with collective concepts of form and rules), the individualist ideology saw contemporary style as the necessary result of pluriformity. In a sense the contemporary style was a *lack of style*.

But all these views were no more than principles. In order for them to become architecture, concepts of form were necessary as well, concrete ideas of what a building should look like. As everywhere else in Western and Central Europe, the Dutch nationalist ideology used the concept of form of its own Renaissance, and the ideology of Cuypers and his circle, like their Catholic sympathizers abroad, used the Gothic concept of form. The third ideology, the individualist one, found expression in eclecticism. The first ideology was to become very popular in the 1870s and 80s, while the second would remain restricted to a small but very militant minority. The third ideology required no publicity and featured much less prominently in the architectural journals than the other two.

A contemporary national style with formal characteristics derived from a historical era: such conventional definitions of style continued to determine the way architects thought. Quatremère de Quincy wrote: 'the word "style" indicates ... that typical and characteristic form that leaves its very general mark on the products of the mind according to differences in climate ... customs and traditions, the acts of governments and of political and moral institutions'. Hübsch defined style also as an indication of a historical period with a characteristic concept in form, in the era in question the round-arch and the pointed-arch styles. The rise, in particular in Germany, of the discipline of architectural history refined the knowledge of styles as historical categories with more precise characteristics related to time and place. Thus the term 'style' referred increasingly to the concept of form of historic buildings. Rose was referring to this concept of style when in 1859 he spoke of the 'architect who has become independent of all styles'. Leliman did the same in 1860 when he described the eclectics as architects who did not 'restrict themselves to one particular style or period'.[38] During the 1850s, when hitherto unknown information on the history of Dutch architecture became available, the idea developed of a national Dutch style as a historical phenomenon. The Dutch art critic Carel Vosmaer stated in 1861: 'In the first years [of the sixteenth century] an entirely national, original style developed together with and alongside the Dutch Renaissance.'[39]

A few years later the idea of a national style – this time not in the form of a period from the past but of a contemporary ideal – acquired more prominence. Here we can observe an interesting conceptual shift. Ever since Hübsch the national aspect had been a characteristic of style: for instance, the Greek nation and the Greek climate generated a Greek style of architecture. In the 1860s this notion was also reversed: a specific set of architectural items (materials, colours, constructions, ornaments) was referred to as typical Dutch and could easily be proposed then as the representation of the Dutch nation, and as the expression of the Dutch character.

As a consequence, the debate on style changed – it became political. The assumption that the customs of a people determined its style was replaced by the adherents of the collective ideologies with the proposition that it was style that influenced customs and traditions. In addition to being the product of a nation, style became its 'producer'. Instead of being styled, it styled itself. Style, once the creation of the people, became the creation of architects; it became 'artificial'. Style became an instrument for propagating a social standpoint. It is clear that this political variant differed radically from the view formulated by Semper, in which style was understood to be an inherent characteristic of architecture. The national style that originated in the 1860s was, despite its general aspirations, like the neo-Gothic style, a *genre*.

The evolution towards the notion of style as a representation of the national, as a stylization of the people, originated not as profound armchair wisdom but as a consequence of social circumstances. The Dutch government did not yet play an active role in this process, as it would in the 1870s, but remained passive where the arts were concerned. In 1862, the liberal prime minister Johan Rudolph Thorbecke made a statement that was immediately summarized as 'art is not a government matter'. While in London, Paris, Berlin, Munich, Brussels and Vienna governments commissioned costly building assignments, the Dutch government demonstrated what Leliman in 1858 referred to as 'the peculiar reserve of the Dutch nature towards the fine arts'.

This particular manifestation of official reserve was not indifference but a consequence of the liberal politics that placed the responsibility for art with the citizen. In the Netherlands, the cultural nationalism that started to make itself felt in the 1850s and 60s and that expressed a growing national awareness, the notion of a society connected through language and art, was a culture of the middle classes rather than a state culture. The way in which this culture was to be represented was, therefore, a matter of opinion. Who determined the national character? The liberals, who since 1848 had regarded themselves as its guardians, or the Protestants, who were in favour of a revival of a lost national spirit, or the Catholics, who were working on their political comeback? But the situation was more complicated still. There were not just three standpoints: the liberals had an 'old' doctrinal and a 'new' young wing; the Catholics had a strong conservative and a colourful 'liberal' wing; and the Protestants had adherents and opponents of theological modernism, which also had social implications. The extreme Protestant and Catholic stands provoked conflicts, but thanks to their tolerant attitude the liberals could easily occupy a position above these two parties, act as conciliator and, moreover, set themselves up as the guardians of the most characteristic Dutch national quality valued by everyone: the spirit of freedom. The cultural self-image of the Dutch nation was also coloured by memories of the Golden Age of the seventeenth century. This had already been evoked in the 1840s, but now the effect was more powerful, partly as compensation for the rather insignificant position that the Netherlands had to accept among the great European powers, who were focusing on their own questions of nationality.

These diverging political and religious views were both attacked and defended in the increasing openness of Dutch society, and the discussions that went on contributed significantly to the ideologizing of that society. It appeared obvious that the issue of a national architecture would soon break out of the compound of architectural theory to become the plaything of the opposing parties in the debate. The art of building would become a public topic that far exceeded in scope and nature the architectural content of the issue.

What also became evident was the limited relevance of architectural theory for developing a national contemporary architecture. Of course, architects did not adopt a passive attitude in this respect; they had their own professional contribution to make, which may have had something to do with their attempts to strengthen the social prestige of their profession. Architects' desire to participate in the creation of a national identity was also a professional reaction to the fact that architecture received only very limited public support, as noted by the Society for the Advancement of the Art of Building (the MBB) in 1858. Leliman at the time also made a connection between the status of architecture, the social prestige of the architect and builder, and the cultural deficit that the Netherlands was building up compared with other countries: government ought to be creating more opportunities for architecture in order for the Netherlands to be able to 'raise its status in architectural matters in the eyes of other nations'.[40]

The search for new concepts of form

In their search for a new national architecture, architects came up with concepts of form from the past. This bore most of the signs of a collective behaviour that matched a trend observed throughout Western and Central Europe; the growing national awareness was founded on an ever-increasing bank of historical facts. In the eighteenth and early nineteenth centuries this 'history' had consisted of old documents such as deeds and charters. Then the historical interest began to concentrate on ancient buildings too, first only for reasons of a scientific nature but later, in the 1860s, so as to give shape to the concept of a national culture. Thanks to the link with the country's history, the concept of a national architecture became much more specific and dynamic in the Netherlands than it had hitherto been in the theoretical definitions of the subject. As we have seen, it was not yet easy to identify the national element in the young kingdom, but, clearly, the nation's past could help in determining the collective identity. It was in this context that historic architecture was given a

prominent role. Carel Vosmaer probably voiced a view held by many when in 1861 he wrote: 'Architecture provides the monuments in which the history, spirit and character of a nation continue to exist in a recognizable way.'[41]

The most powerful concepts of form for a contemporary national style were not developed through renewed study of the architecture of the Golden Age. This architecture was well known and admired in so far as it was classicist, Amsterdam Town Hall (1648–65) being the most striking example. The major impetus for a contemporary style, however, came when Dutch sixteenth-century architecture was 'discovered'. Previously because of its total lack of classical beauty, it had been as if aesthetically nonexistent. In the 1850s the first signs of change could be perceived. In 1852 the MBB published a survey of the Butchers' Guild

Hall in Haarlem (1602–3) and of the Chancellery in Leeuwarden (1566–71). Committee member and architect Isaäc Warnsinck had praised these buildings for the beautiful variety of their red brick and white sandstone, and their decorative profiles on the façades: these were the most outstanding examples of sixteenth-century Dutch architecture, he stated. He may have been familiar with the recently published pattern book of Georg Gottlob Ungewitter, *Vorlegblätter für Ziegel- und Steinarbeit* (Patterns of Brick and Stonework, 1849), which contained many examples of decorative brickwork of the Middle Ages. If so, was it this that had inspired him? Warnsinck's interest was mainly of a scholarly nature; as a young man he had shown interest in the 'national works of art of earlier periods'.[42] In 1859, his pupil Abraham Nicolaas Godefroy tentatively formulated the direction in which a new national architecture might be developed. Customs and traditions in the nineteenth century were becoming increasingly international, he argued, and were therefore unsuitable for determining a national style. The only option was to solve the problem in a purely architectural way by building with national building materials and techniques, 'taking careful account of what our forefathers have done in this respect. The most characteristic architecture for our country would seem to be the mixed brick and sandstone building technique of the early years of the seventeenth century; however, we fear that there would be many objections from clients if this style were to be reintroduced.'[43]

Godefroy considered extensive knowledge of international architecture, past or modern, a troublesome obstacle to the development of a national architecture. 'Really, it is very hard for the artist not to be inspired by the treasures of Rome, Athens, Memphis, the Byzantine Empire, Granada, et cetera which he knows so well, and to confine himself to the sound logic of what the sad climate and the unpretentious, if not artless, customs and traditions of his country require.' When the Old Dutch style became a fact in the next decades, this question of unpretentious Dutch customs would often be referred to, in keeping with the long Dutch tradition in which simplicity, serenity and balance were highly regarded, and fervour, passion and splendour were repressed.

The role of religion and politics

Thus politics came to interfere with the art of building. The second collective ideology that began to use architecture to represent itself – that of Cuypers and his circle, referred to earlier – came from Catholic quarters, occasionally giving rise to a suspicion of ultramontanism, an idea that in this period of searching for a national Dutch identity caused much tension. This intensified when in 1864 the papal encyclical *Quanta Cura* was published together with the *Syllabus Errorum*, the Enumeration of Errors. Not only did this denounce the separation of Church and state, but it also opposed liberalism, Protestantism and intellectual, cultural and religious freedom in general. Its intention was to have the Vatican acknowledged as the highest authority in matters concerning both state and Church. This confrontational policy pursued by Rome raised the question of whether or not Dutch Catholics could indeed be loyal to the idea of a modern Dutch state.

In this context, the activities of the merchant-polemicist Alberdingk Thijm were not always felicitous. For ten years he had been conducting a rather indiscreet crusade in the small world of the arts. The controversies he generated inevitably resulted in fierce public squabbles. It was evident that the extreme Catholic viewpoints that Thijm stood for were interpreted by the eclectic Leliman and his followers against the background of Vatican politics, which in many respects wanted to turn back the clock. Vosmaer condemned as reactionary and obscurantist Thijm's ideologizing of 'Germanic' medieval architecture and his rejection of the Renaissance as a period of decline.

Between the Middle Ages and our own time lie the art of printing, the revival of the study of classical literature, the Renaissance, as well as the works of Leonardo, Raphael, Michelangelo, Rembrandt, Shakespeare, Vondel, Spinoza and Kant; the French Revolution; Lessing and Goethe; many discoveries in the area of physics and astronomy; the critical and historical studies of the eighteenth and nineteenth centuries, and many small things we hold dear. We are separated from the Middle Ages by all these phenomena.[44]

The deep ideological contrast between the two camps would eventually develop into a public conflict. In 1863 ceremonies were organized to commemorate the restoration of Dutch sovereignty in 1813, and a contest was held for a national memorial in The Hague. The winning design, later executed, measured up to academic, and therefore classicist, aesthetics. The second prize went to a design by P. J. H. Cuypers, showing Willem I sitting enthroned under a neo-Gothic canopy; it resembled the Albert Memorial in London and raised many questions about its appropriateness. Cuypers' supporters started a fierce campaign to have his design executed, and were equally fiercely opposed by prominent members of cultural organizations, because, according to Leliman, 'medieval art should not influence contemporary art'.[45] Thijm considered this an expression of Protestant hatred towards Catholics and resistance against the 'logic' of the neo-Gothic style.

The conflict continued with another project for the commemoration of 1813, this time an international contest for a national Willem I Museum in Amsterdam, another private initiative. The museum was to exhibit Dutch treasures, particularly from the sixteenth and seventeenth centuries, and also to function as a national pantheon, for which a monumental space was required in which 'courageous and gifted Dutchmen' could be commemorated. In 1864 the entry from Ludwig and Emil Lange (Munich), designed in the classicist tradition, won first prize. Cuypers submitted two designs, one with neo-Gothic façades, the other with the formal characteristics of sixteenth-century Dutch architecture. The latter won him second prize, but only just. However, no entry met the

OPPOSITE
Fig.32
Jacob van Campen's Town Hall, Amsterdam (1648–65), the foremost example of seventeenth-century Dutch classicism – for many in the nineteenth century the ideal expression of Dutch monumental architecture. Since 1808, when it became the residence of King Louis Bonaparte, the building has been a royal palace. In the background to the right is the façade of the Main Post Office (Fig.93). Photo taken in 1938.

Fig.33
P.J.H. Cuypers'
unrealized design
(1863) for a
monument in
The Hague to
commemorate the
restoration of Dutch
sovereignty in 1813.
The design caused a
vehement polemic,
not only because it
was a remarkable
imitation of the
design for the Albert
Memorial in London
(Sir George Gilbert
Scott, 1863–72), but
in particular because
it now became clear
that neo-Gothic
design in the
Netherlands was
acquiring an
ideological significance.

requirements contained in the bill of quantities, and in 1867 the museum project petered out.[46]

Cuypers' neo-Gothic designs for the national monument and the museum were immediately regarded by his supporters as a heroic and admirable stand against classicism. This interpretation has generally been accepted without criticism, because this 'battle of the styles' seemed to illustrate perfectly that the great nineteenth-century conflict between classicism and Romanticism was being conducted in the Netherlands as elsewhere. But as we saw earlier, this conflict was conceived in 1800 in Germany and was declared logical and historically inevitable by Hegel.

This, of course, presents matters much too simply. Moreover, in this case the phrase 'battle of the styles' is inaccurate, because it creates the impression that the debate on the monument and the museum was of an artistic nature, whereas sources show that this was not the case. The differences of opinion did not centre on style as a concept of form, and neither did it centre on style in architecture as a general principle or on a national style in particular. The debate concerned the *character* of the

designs. Within the Dutch social context of 1863 the 'battle of the styles' was a political one, provoked by a small number of Catholic activists intent on staging an onslaught on the national character, which had mainly been determined by Protestant and liberal ideas. It may be that they were inspired by the success of the Gothic Revival in England. After all, there the contest for the most important political assignment of the century, the new Palace of Westminster, or Houses of Parliament in London, had been won with a neo-Gothic design, establishing the young Catholic church-builder Augustus Welby Northmore Pugin (1812–52) as an architect to be reckoned with. But whereas in London this choice of style was historically legitimate, this was not true of the Netherlands. As Leliman said on the subject of the national memorial 1813 to commemorate: 'Our civilization and the life of our people cannot be expressed by accepting a building style and social concepts that pre-date the year 1517. The history of a nation must be read from its monuments, and the monument to be erected in The Hague must immortalize the internal history of our social and moral being between 1813 and 1863.'[47]

There was never any criticism of the fact that the Catholics used the neo-Gothic style for their church-building, for it was pre-eminently suitable for expressing the character of a Catholic church. The great talents of Cuypers as a church builder were fully appreciated by his fellow architects. The neo-Gothic concept caused a stir only when it threatened to be applied outside Catholic circles. This was the inevitable consequence of the fact that in the 1850s the Catholic Church in the Netherlands had made the neo-Gothic concepts the basis of its corporate design.

Picturesque Old Dutch beauty

It is likely that the idea of the Old Dutch fondness for serenity and balance and the abhorrence of fervour, passion and splendour reached architecture via the art of painting. One painter in 1867 summarized the characteristics of the 'Old Dutch art of painting' thus. It displayed, he said,

no sense of the ideal and sublime, and hardly any talent for the so-called noble style. But it did exhibit a high degree of sensitivity to reality and the desire and power to represent it. And it was from a well developed feeling and love for the picturesque, for the magic powers of colour and of light effects, that all this was elevated and transformed into art. The same sense of the picturesque can be found in Old Dutch buildings, especially the private houses.[48]

The author of the discourse from which these words come

referred to Vosmaer, the art expert who in 1861 had noted that in the sixteenth century 'in addition to the Dutch Renaissance a completely new, original style' had evolved, with façades of red brick and white sandstone, ingenious brickwork bonds, leaded windows, shutters and semi-circular profiled arches with decorative stucco and sculpted ornaments. 'In this way,' concluded Vosmaer, 'these houses acquired an aura of beauty and extreme picturesqueness.'[49]

The first architect to follow the trail of Old Dutch beauty was the young Isaac Gosschalk (1838–1907) of Amsterdam. From 1858 to 1862 he trained as an architect in Munich and Zurich. In Zurich he pinpointed three tendencies that could be distinguished amongst architects. First, there were the advocates of the classicist tradition; second, the advocates of the neo-Gothic; and third, those 'attracted to the so-called picturesque, which I subscribe to'.[50] Between 1863 and 67 he travelled in the Netherlands and Belgium to study and to sketch examples of sixteenth- and early-seventeenth-century architecture. 'I became more and more convinced that we could find motifs that were flexible, easy to learn, simple and (what is particularly relevant) inexpensive.' But Gosschalk was not so much interested in new motifs as in an entirely new concept – a new vision, even – of architecture. This concept was 'the picturesque', which characterized Old Dutch architecture.

Vosmaer defined this picturesque national style as a phenomenon separate from 'Dutch Renaissance'. To Vosmaer, Dutch Renaissance was the classicism of Jacob van Campen (1596–1657), the architect of Amsterdam Town Hall, which was the most prominent example of Dutch assimilation of the Italian Renaissance. In the early 1860s the work of a second architect rose to prominence:

Hendrick de Keyser (1565–1621) of Amsterdam. His architecture embodied the transition from sixteenth-century Old Dutch to Van Campen's classicism. De Keyser's main work, the Westerkerk in Amsterdam (1620–31), was as late as 1860 still considered 'peculiar' because the classical orders seemed to have been applied, unlike the work of Van Campen, without understanding their nature and rules.[51] A few years later, however, Gosschalk was full of praise for the church. His experience of beauty was not based on reasoning but purely on observation: 'The beautifully proportioned chapels rise gravely up. The buttresses are decorated with stately columns. The high roof, covered with beautifully coloured slate, adds to the monumental impression, and the shadows cast upon it by the chapels make it look truly picturesque.'[52]

By emphasizing the impression that the building gave in terms of the psychology of observation, a new type of beauty was being expressed, a beauty that was unimaginable when judging the design solely on its theoretical accuracy. In proceeding in this direction Gosschalk was not alone, and in the circle of prominent architects of the 1860s the re-evaluation of De Keyser became widely accepted. Perhaps the most important point about the notion of the picturesque is that it introduced values that belonged to the concept of character – the visual characteristics of a building that move the observer. The eighteenth century had added the requirement that this should relate to the building's function, and in the 1850s the theory of character had been absorbed by the concept of truth: truth then implied character, meaning that a building showed its function.

The introduction of the picturesque was to a certain extent the return of the eighteenth-century picturesque of

Fig.34
Design for a national museum of fine arts, Amsterdam (1863), Lucas H. Eberson's entry for the proposed Museum Willem I (not realized). For the adjudicators the design was the least politically controversial, but this was not an advantage at a time when many thought it appropriate that architecture, the most public of all arts, should possess a political character.

the English landscape garden, which had been the cradle of the contemporary theory of character. Thus the visual and psychological characteristics of architecture were again being given a place along with the more cerebral elements of architectural truth, and from now on they were to retain their prominent position. Occasionally during the 1880s and 90s they would become more important than the requirement of truth, which for the generation of Rose, Leliman, Semper and Viollet-le-Duc had been the supreme law. Now, the visual observation and appreciation of a building tended progressively to be placed within the context of the Dutch townscape. The concept of the picturesque thus gained weight – which is hardly surprising, since in the past it had been employed precisely to make explicit the visual relationship between the building and its environment. But whereas in the

eighteenth century it described the relationship between architecture and nature, around 1860 and in the following decades it acquired an explicitly urban context. It gave shape to the rising interest in Old Dutch townscapes, which were also seen by travellers from abroad as the bearers par excellence of the Dutch cultural identity.

The shift in the balance between truth and character effected by the picturesque resulted in further loss of ground for the classical theory of architecture as the norm for actual practice, and in a territorial gain for the unregulated, more subjectively experienced visual qualities of a building. Unlike the old theory of character, the new visual concept knew no code or rulebook. It was a matter of 'feeling'.

New discoveries, new possibilities

The picturesque became a reality via the process of *observing* a building, not by a process of *understanding*. The picturesque manifested itself in the choice of material, details and forms, and in the silhouette a building produced; not in the notion of the coherence and accuracy of the plan, of the construction, or of the façade. Paying attention to the picturesque meant paying attention to colour, texture, visual harmony, contrast, volume, surface, light, dark, transparency and weight. The picturesque may have found its way from painting to architecture, as a concept and as an aesthetic ideal, but purely architectural elements were involved as well. The interest in colour, though, first appearing in the appreciation of the Old Dutch red façades with their white accents, was not restricted to the picturesque but belonged also to a much wider, international re-evaluation of colour in architecture. This re-evaluation had occurred in Paris around 1830 with the discovery that classical Greek architecture – which according to neoclassicist tradition was purely white – had in reality been polychrome; this resulted in new reconstructive drawings that replaced the monochrome image with a variety of colours. Later this revision (especially by the Parisian architect Jacques-Ignace Hittorff) led to the discovery of the use of colour in Gothic architecture and its introduction into church restoration and into the concept of the neo-Gothic. Already by the mid-nineteenth century the use of colour in French, German and English architecture rooted in the studies of prominent theorists,[53] had become a popular means of expression. In the Netherlands Rose, as we learned earlier, started a discussion on the colour of his government buildings at the Plein at The Hague (1859–61). And Cuypers put an end to the tradition of white plasterwork for the interiors of his new Catholic churches, replacing it with the rainbow spectacle of his detailing in red and yellow brick, sandstone, bluestone and terracotta, glazed tiles, stained-glass windows, wall paintings and polychrome church furniture.[54]

Another purely architectural element in the appreciation of the picturesque – an international trend as well as Dutch – was the increasing interest of architects in craftsmanship. In the 1860s factories were built in the Netherlands offering a wide range of ornaments: capitals, consoles, mouldings, decorative vases, reliefs in terracotta, zinc, cast iron or 'cast stone' (moulded cement). Improved means of bulk transport made it easier to import building materials from abroad, particularly natural stone, specific types of brick, and iron products. These materials widened the expressive and decorative possibilities of architecture and enhanced the visual opulence of architectural design – that is, if the architects were willing to take advantage of industrial mass production. Several comments made by architects in the 1860s, though, indicate that not everyone was happy with the industrialization of building. This was not only a matter of new materials, but also of the organization of the practice of building itself. An expanding Dutch economy and increasing prosperity encouraged building activity. At the same time old traditions were starting to be replaced by modern procedures: the public tender system (resulting in more competition), the first signs of mechanization on the building site itself (with semi-skilled and even unskilled workers), and the introduction of house building without a specific buyer – so-called speculative building.

As we saw earlier, in 1858 Leliman considered a better social position for the architect a precondition for the development of a national architecture. But while the structure of the building sector changed, the position of the architect remained marginal despite his growing ambition to wield the power in the building field. Gosschalk complained in 1867 that prominent European architects like Semper, Schinkel and Viollet-le-Duc 'study all their life and slave away, trying to penetrate the sacred and profound art of building', while being overshadowed by others who had achieved nothing.[55] Those not wholly unfamiliar with the architectural scene will have understood that the position of prominent Dutch architects was not much better. A year before, Gosschalk had lashed out at speculative building in new suburban developments in The Hague and in Amsterdam, painting a pretty picture indeed: 'someone piles together a stone wall of poor quality and adds some beams, the plasterer spreads a thin layer of plaster, the architect then buys some reproduction ornaments and fixes them to the façade with iron or copper wire. And that's it – the building is finished and the architect is applauded.'[56]

Apart from expressing his frustration that this increased activity in the building industry was especially benefiting the bungler, Gosschalk was keen to make two things clear. First, the true architect was a learned artist who closely studied the 'sacred and profound art of building' as scholarly architects had done since Alberti. His colleagues within the MBB shared this view. Second, he distinguished between architecture and non-architecture not by invoking the principle of truth but by starting from the practice of building itself – thereby demonstrating a whole new approach that might also be considered a symptom of the loss of ground of theoretical influence. Gosschalk's outburst against the 'architect' with his copper wire was the theme of the introduction to a treatise he wrote on building

OPPOSITE
Fig. 35
From J. L. Terwen's *Kingdom of the Netherlands, represented in a Series of Picturesque Drawings from Nature* (1858), p. 92: the town of Hoorn, seen from the Zuiderzee, an example of the 'picturesque' townscape with the 'Old Dutch' architecture of red brick accented with white sandstone. Such views were to strongly determine the aesthetics of the post-1860 decades.

with brick, on the decorative uses of brickwork bonds and on a series of brick-built Old Dutch arch constructions for windows. His article implied that in order to improve their situation architects would from then on be fighting on two fronts – that of the scholarly artist, and that of the superior craftsman, who through a thorough understanding of both materials and construction practices would surpass the building contractor when it came to expertise. At the end of his career Gosschalk described how, against the contractors' resistance, he had brought about constructional innovations derived from historical models.[57] The story of Gosschalk is not the only one portraying an innovative architect working within a somewhat rigid and conventional building profession. However, the architects' problem in the 1860s was not that the building profession

was conservative, but that it was changing so rapidly. So at a time when architects wanted to strengthen their position by emphasizing the craftsmanship and national characteristics of Old Dutch architecture, the building sector as a whole was turning to industrial products from home and abroad.

A Dutch national style in the making

The explanation of this paradox is to be found in the relationship between artistic beauty and traditional craftsmanship. The Great Exhibition in 1851, the first of its kind, brought to the attention of the international general public the fact that industrialization had permeated all aspects of life – including culture. In the 1860s this awareness also motivated the thoughts and acts of William

Fig. 36–7
The St Jacob
Institution,
Amsterdam (1866), by
Willem J. Offenberg, a
home for the elderly
Catholic infirm
located in a part of
the city that rapidly
developed into a
residential area for the
well-to-do. The
details of the façade
(Fig. 37, this page)
display an eclecticism
robustly
demonstrating
classical ornaments
such as acroteria and
palmettes as well as an
age-old repertoire of
other ornamental
masonry.

Morris (1834–96) and provided the seeds for the Arts and Crafts Movement. This movement, critical of industrial mass culture, attempted to provide an answer by encouraging designers to undertake a traditional training and, together with the craftsmen, to push out the frontiers of the trade. Their ideal was a culture that would escape from mechanical mass product to produce a class of craftsmen who, no longer reduced to the role of proletariat of the factories, would rise to professional eminence. Precisely these ideas are echoed in the article Gosschalk wrote in 1867 proclaiming that only highly professional craftsmen could save the art of building.

The link between artistic progress and socio-professional emancipation is expressed most clearly in Leliman's activities. His social commitment was neither theoretical nor utopian. He dedicated himself to the professional interests of architects and building workers and played a prominent role in the introduction of social housing projects for workers. In 1860 he noted, 'the crafts have almost been abolished and we are more likely to encounter the work of the craftsman in a museum or at an exhibition than in the places where such objects used to belong'.[58] He took the initiative of establishing the first technical school in the Netherlands – in Amsterdam in 1860.

The Dutch national style of the nineteenth century was in the making. It would involve a picturesque embellishment of the Dutch townscape and be a positive stimulus for a thoroughgoing overhaul of the building trade. It had become customary to refer to the time of the Eighty Years' War (1568–1646), the Dutch struggle for freedom in which the Republic of the Seven United Provinces liberated itself from Spanish supremacy, as 'a time that coincided with the forceful rise of the middle class and the establishment of the foundations of our independent existence as a nation'.[59] This precisely describes both the style of the rising middle-class culture of the 1860s and the ideal Dutch character: a love of freedom, independence and simplicity.

A description of the 1860s would not be complete without drawing attention to those Dutch architects who wanted to distance contemporary architecture from discourses on the country's history and national culture. When in 1859 the MBB convened to discuss the concept of a national architecture, A. N. Godefroy opened the meeting by stating that the main task of a work of architecture lay in its function. Its design would vary with 'the generations, the times, the countries and the peoples,' he said, implying an unbridgeable gap between the architecture of the past and the architecture of the present simply because in the

past the ushers of buildings had set lower requirements than their modern counterparts – 'people are even complaining of the cold air getting through the pores of windows'. So a past national architecture could never serve as a model for a contemporary national architecture. But the possibility of a contemporary national architecture depended anyway, he continued, on whether there were any specific national customs and traditions – for modern means of international communication tended to make them disappear. 'Language is the main thing that distinguishes us,' he concluded, 'ideas are becoming more or less the same anywhere.'[60] Godefroy's argument was typical of the eclectics, who on the basis of the eighteenth-century definition of style, and their individualistic interpretation of that definition, concluded that a collective and universal concept of form was impossible, whether national or not.

And not only because of modern manners and customs, as already suggested. Modern means of international communication affected the distribution of every sort of innovation, whether of a technical, functional or aesthetic nature. Rose wrote, 'Everything we approve or find better with foreigners, be it in construction, in the distribution of rooms, in forms or even in building materials, is promptly imitated.' Leliman ironically described the history of art as a continuous international exchange of ideas. If we go sufficiently far back in time, he commented, we Dutchmen, 'whether we adhere to the ancient, Gothic or Renaissance or whatever other style, are ultimately adulterated Egyptians'. And on a more serious note: 'because we, as a small people who have been long oppressed, have had to follow in the wake of the ever-expanding nations, each artistic movement – especially over the last six centuries – has been transplanted here or was transported to us on the wings of artistic theory'.[61]

The implications of modern times were formulated in Paris in 1867 by the editor-in-chief of the *Revue générale*, César Daly:

Today we have no typical building style, no building style founded entirely on fixed principles and acknowledged and accepted, to the exclusion of any other style, by both artists and the public, such as was the case in the great eras of the past. This lack of a building style that is exclusively ours is the major fact dominating the practice of contemporary architecture. Most architects acknowledge this *fact* with good sense and can live with it as the inevitable consequence of a set of moral, social and intellectual circumstances that have not been caused by them.[62]

A little earlier Daly had described the situation more explicitly. The eclectic architect, he wrote, was pre-eminently commercial and practical, neither mad about any particular historical period nor dreaming of an architecture of the future. He thought of architecture in very basic terms: good construction, meeting as well as possible the requirements of comfort, and harmonious design; and in particular; in terms of satisfying the client.[63] The St Jacob Institution, a home for infirm elderly persons designed by Willem Jacob Johan Offenberg (1812–73), is an example of this kind of 'styleless' architecture.

Needless to say, the eclectics viewed the growing enthusiasm for Old Dutch architecture with scepticism. Leliman was one of their spokesmen; it was hardly to be expected that he would be involved in the creation of a national architecture with party-political characteristics and design rules. In 1860 he drew attention to a series of Old Dutch houses in Amsterdam, pointing out the 'total disharmony' and 'untruthfulness' of the façades which in no way corresponded with the construction, function or layout of the interiors.[64] Should this architecture really be a source of inspiration for the modern age? he asked. But Leliman was hardly fighting a rearguard action – it was at precisely this moment that his criticism was boosted by Semper's and Viollet-le-Duc's theory of style.

Gosschalk's position is interesting in view of his role in the rediscovery of Old Dutch architecture. In 1864, concurring with Leliman, he rejected the idea that there had once been a national Dutch architecture. The architecture that passed for this represented the degeneration of a style, unsuitable for modern use, he confirmed. Having trained in Germany and Switzerland, Gosschalk was educated in the classicist theory of design, but he also succeeded in integrating the Old Dutch architecture into his work. 'Now that criticism and inquiry have purified our taste,' he said, 'we are able to avoid the mistakes and the corrupt and ugly forms of the past.'[65] The De Hooiberg Steam Brewery that he built in 1866–7 in Amsterdam for Heineken is an early example of the introduction of the Old Dutch manner into nineteenth-century architecture, as is the Henriëttehofje (Amsterdam 1868–9), a small apartment block for the elderly by Martinus Gerhard Tétar van Elven (1803–83). The composition and proportions of both buildings are academic and classicist, but the gable ends and the decorative masonry are Old Dutch. On the face of it this is an approach one would associate with Semper: fragments from a worn-out concept of architecture have been re-formed here according to the tenets of advanced contemporary aesthetics and made suitable for contemporary purposes.

The intricacies and pitfalls of terminology

In the competition of 1864 to design a national museum, what a contemporary national architecture might look like was not a consideration of any importance. Cuypers' award-winning Renaissance variants were as French as the Langes' award-winning design was German. The first attempts to make Old Dutch architecture suitable for contemporary requirements, building techniques and aesthetics were demonstrated by Gosschalk in 1866 with his De Hooiberg Brewery. Both Cuypers' adaptation of French architecture and Gosschalk's adaptation of Dutch are referred to in current Dutch specialist literature as 'neo-Renaissance', unlike the Langes' design. This use of the term is unfortunate. In the international literature 'Renaissance' refers to the Italian Renaissance and its immediate impact outside Italy. But the characteristics of Old Dutch architecture are more late-Gothic and Mannerist, and are both formally and conceptually very far removed from the Italian Renaissance. So in modern literature this group of Dutch (and Flemish) buildings is usually referred to as 'Dutch Mannerist'. Against this background the term 'neo-Renaissance' is indeed inadequate.

But the confusion becomes even greater. The meaning of the term as it is currently used in the Netherlands is somewhat haphazard and vague. In the nineteenth century it had a very precise, and moreover a very different, meaning. The term 'neo-Renaissance' was at the time restricted to architecture in the style of the Italian Renaissance and of the nineteenth-century French, German and Viennese interpretations of it. For example, the contemporary observer considered the exclusive and monumental Amstel Hotel in Amsterdam (1866–7, Cornelis Outshoorn) an example of neo-Renaissance architecture because it was a modern, French-oriented classicist design. In the 1860s and 70s linking the term 'Renaissance' to Italy was so automatic that it would have been ridiculous to use it for the Dutch architecture of the sixteenth century as well. Only in the 1880s did the term 'Old Dutch' disappear, to be replaced, as we shall see, by the term 'Dutch Renaissance'. In the 1870s the Old Dutch fashion began to be used on a broad scale. This meant that the 'national' picturesque architecture,

which was in its infancy, turned away from the Italian classicist Renaissance. Perhaps this is the true explanation for the relatively limited attention that Semper's architecture was given in the Netherlands.

But is it correct to give the impression that Dutch architects immersed themselves in the good points of Old Dutch architecture and the bad points of the Italian Renaissance in order to come to some sort of a decision? Or did they follow the taste of the public who, in no time at all, turned the Old Dutch style into a mass product? Even Gugel himself, as soon as he received a building assignment in the Netherlands, exchanged his preferred German-Italian classicist neo-Renaissance for a design mode that was more compatible with the new Old Dutch style.[66]

Notes

1. E. Gugel 1869, 563. For technical innovations in nineteenth-century Dutch building: W. R. F. van Leeuwen 1993.
2. W. N. Rose 1869a, 293, 296.
3. Toos Streng 1995, chs 5 and 6.
4. J. H. Leliman 1860a, 8–10.
5. W. N. Rose 1863a, 39.
6. The cartoon: *De Nederlandsche Spectator* 1861, opp. p.124. The review: X. 1761.
7. W. N. Rose 1869a, according to the note the article was written in 1867–8. Some of the viewpoints expressed in it come from a previous publication, W. N. Rose 1860a, 106–7, and from a translation of an article with similar ideas by Eugène-Emmanuel Viollet-le-Duc (1865, in particular 27–33).
8. W. N. Rose 1869b. In 1863 he pointed out that the importance attached to linking taste with value judgement had made architecture 'increasingly subjective' (W. N. Rose 1863a, 39).
9. *Bouwkundige Bijdragen* 5 (1849), 42. For iron constructions in buildings in the nineteenth-century in the Netherlands: J. Oosterhoff et al. 1988.

10. J. H. Leliman 1867, 13.
11. J. H. Leliman 1869, 137.
12. H. P. Berlage 1886, 204.
13. 'Nog eens speculatiebouw' ('Once again speculative building'), *De Opmerker* 31 (1896) no. 26, 204.
14. See for this a letter from Semper to Eduard Vieweg in 1843, published in H. Laudel 1991, 234–5.
15. Gottfried Semper 1860–3, I, viii.
16. Harry F. Mallgrave and W. Herrmann 1989, 29–40; Caroline van Eck 1994, 228–30; Harry F. Mallgrave 1996.
17. Gottfried Semper 1860–3, I, 227, 231.
18. For the relationship between the concepts of Bötticher and Semper: Wolfgang Herrmann 1984, ch. 3 and Harry F. Mallgrave 1996, 307.
19. The Semperian definition: Eugène-Emmanuel Viollet-le-Duc 1863–72 (1977), sixth Discourse, 179–93. The traditional definition, that style depends on the morals, customs and traditions of a people: Eugène-Emmanuel Viollet-le-Duc 1863–72, third Discourse, 99. The other definitions: Eugène-Emmanuel Viollet-le-Duc 1854–68, VIII, headword 'style' (where 'style relatif' seems a paraphrase of what Quatremère de Quincy called 'caractère', and 'style absolu' denotes the objective, universal style concept as defined earlier by Semper).
20. Bötticher's ideas were taught at the Hague Academy of the Visual Arts by the architect Vogel (cf. H. P. Vogel [1863, 1st edn]). The translation of Viollet-le-Duc: Eugène-Emmanuel Viollet-le-Duc 1863. The first reference to Semper: Adi Martis 1979, 110–12; M. Simon Thomas 1988, 36ff.; Titus Eliëns 1990, 92–3, 143 note 293.
21. W. N. Rose 1863a, 38.
22. W. N. Rose 1865, 6–8.
23. Eugène-Emmanuel Viollet-le-Duc 1870a and 1870b.
24. Report of the general assembly, *Bouwkundige Bijdragen* 16 (1869) appendix 1, 140.
25. Opéra: David van Zanten 1977, 282–5. Choice of design: Eugène-Emmanuel Viollet-le-Duc 1863–72, I, 147: 'Aujourd'hui, il ne s'agit pas de faire prévaloir une forme d'art sur une autre; nous n'en avons pas ce pouvoir.'
26. Dirk Baalman 1991, 43–6, 55–64.
27. E. Gugel 1869, 1st edn, 560–1.
28. E. Gugel 1869, 1st edn, 562.
29. W. N. Rose 1854.
30. E. Gugel 1869, 1st edn, 562–3.
31. E. Gugel 1869, 1st edn, 9.
32. W. N. Rose 1854, 359.
33. E. Gugel 1869, 1st edn, 9–13.
34. When Gugel wrote his book, in America only the *balloon* frame, the prefabricated timber construction with which buildings could be built very quickly and at low cost, was known. The steel skeleton construction that permitted the development of the skyscraper originated after the Great Fire of Chicago, 1871.
35. E. Gugel 1869, 1st edn, 2.
36. Jacob Burckhardt 1855, 1860, 1867. On the neo-Renaissance (German) art output: Petra Krutisch, Anke Hufschmidt (ed.) 1992.
37. E. Gugel 1869, 1st edn, 485.
38. W. N. Rose 1860b, 354; J. H. Leliman 1860e, 429.
39. Carel Vosmaer 1861a, 168.
40. J. H. Leliman 1860b, 121.
41. Carel Vosmaer 1861a, 172.
42. As is apparent from I. Warnsinck 1849.
43. A. N. Godefroy 1860, 360, 363–4. On Godefroy: Eveline Botman, Petra van den Heuvel 1989.
44. Carel Vosmaer 1864, 292.
45. J. H. Leliman 1864, 201.
46. Illustrations of the designs by the Langes, Cuypers and L. H. Eberson in Bernard Colenbrander (ed.) 1993, 145–51.
47. J. H. Leliman 1865, 182.
48. T. van Westrheene 1869, 15–16, discourse presented in 1867.
49. Carel Vosmaer 1861a, 168. For an excellent picture of the 'picturesque' sixteenth- and seventeenth-century architecture referred to, see R. Meischke et al. 1993–6.
50. I. Gosschalk 1899, 60. For Gosschalk: W. R. F. van Leeuwen 1987.
51. J. H. Leliman 1860e, 439.
52. I. Gosschalk 1864, 149.
53. The start of this development and its international dissemination: Robin Middleton 1984a, 2nd edn and David Van Zanten 1984, 2nd edn. Polychromy and Semper: Harry F. Mallgrave 1989, 2–16. With her study of Friedrich von Gärtner's work and its reception Kathleen Curran 1992 sheds new light on this matter because she demonstrates that the *Rundbogenstil* was already an important application of polychrome architecture.
54. Arjen J. Looijenga 1995; A. J. C. van Leeuwen 1995, 66–74.
55. I. Gosschalk 1868, 185 (written in 1867).
56. I. Gosschalk 1867, 174 (written in 1866).
57. I. Gosschalk 1899, 59.
58. J. H. Leliman 1860d, 380.
59. T. van Westrheene 1869, 16.
60. A. N. Godefroy 1860.
61. W. N. Rose 1860b, 352; J. H. Leliman 1860e, 426.
62. A. N. Godefroy 1867, 69–70. On César Daly and the *Revue générale de l'architecture et des travaux publics*: M. Saboya 1991.
63. 'L'architecte éclectique est l'homme positif et pratique par excellence; il ne s'enthousiasme pour aucune époque particulière du passé; il ne se plonge dans aucun rêve d'architecture à venir. Sa notion de l'architecture est le plus souvent toute matérielle: bien construire, réaliser de son mieux toutes les conditions de commodité et d'harmonie plastique, et avant tout satisfaire le client, c'est là à peu près toute sa doctrine' (César Daly, 'Ma nouvelle publication', 1863, cited by Manfred Bock 1983, 241).
64. J. H. Leliman 1860e.
65. I. Gosschalk 1864, 149.
66. Cf. his new design for the Parliament Building, The Hague and the students' society Minerva Club, Leiden (Dirk Baalman 1991, 46–52).

5
The Fall of Theory

A time of change for the profession

The stimulating climate of the 1860s had offered many new perspectives, to be followed in the 70s by feelings of depression, frustration and stagnation. This cyclical aspect was certainly the most prominent feature of the debates of the time. In fact, what was happening was not stagnation at all, but slow, fundamental changes that would become increasingly evident over the following decades. This is the point when architectural theory was finally to lose its central position in the development of architecture to building practice, and when that theory was to be reduced to the relatively simple – and materialistic – tenet that *construction is the quintessence of the art of building*. We could say that these changes represented the transition from the eighteenth-century to the twentieth-century concept of architecture.

Were these feelings of stagnation and depression due to the social circumstances in which architects had to struggle to establish themselves, or to the fact that the protagonists in the architectural debate were the same people who had figured in the 1860s, only ten years older? The answer is a matter of perspective. Be that as it may, the general mood was clear, and many architects were quite pessimistic. When in 1867 the Society for the Advancement of the Art of Building (the MBB) celebrated its twenty-fifth anniversary, the celebratory speaker briefly outlined the circumstances under which the architect had to work. The account makes gloomy reading: whimsical, demanding and ignorant clients, small budgets, and limited artistic freedom. 'I share your fears that you will have to give up many of your ideals and illusions,'[1] he concluded.

A diminished artistic authority

In the 1870s architects discovered that the art of building, with which they believed they had an exclusive relationship, was in reality everybody's friend. The weekly *De Opmerker* wrote in 1876: 'Architecture and style are discussed so frequently nowadays – not least amongst laymen – that it is becoming quite the fashion. So much so that the professional architect can only wonder what the future holds for the building profession in this country.'[2] In fact,

the professional architect had little new to say on either architecture or style. In 1870 the MBB once again cheerfully discussed the question of character in architecture; what was it and what rules did it follow? It was W. N. Rose, now almost seventy, who provided the answer: the definition of character was the same as it had been a hundred years ago.[3] The many articles on the concept of 'style' that were published at this time were also characterized by a repetition of earlier views and the continuing influence of Semper and Viollet-le-Duc. Similarly with the issue of a Dutch national style – in 1870 the whole idea was rejected by Leliman with equal fervour and the same arguments as he had used ten years earlier. When in 1878 the subject was raised in the MBB yet again, there would be no supporters, and Leliman would reject it for a third time.[4]

Absent from the debate this time was the view of the veteran who had been advocating the necessity of a contemporary, unhistorical architecture since the 1850s – Rose, who had died in the previous autumn. In 1872 he had published a summary of his aesthetic studies in a seventy-five-page article, 'On the aesthetics of the visual arts with particular reference to the fine art of building'. Rose's aesthetics was based on sensory and psychological perceptions, not on philosophical or transcendental theories. He was familiar with foreign literature on the subject, but his work consisted not of paraphrases of what he had read but adaptations, in the process of which he created something very much his own. He was the first and for many years the only theorist in the Netherlands to explore the psychological dimension of architecture (in Germany there was a much wider interest in the subject).[5]

Because Rose had realized that the issue of a contemporary style was not to be quickly resolved, he made an extensive study of the nature of architecture. Only from a deep insight into the subject could a new – contemporary – style emerge. This tendency towards theory was considered a weakness, because, then as now, the practical considerations of Dutch architecture were given a high priority. The special nature of Rose's approach is illuminated when it is compared, for instance, to Hugo

Fig.41
The royal stables, The Hague (1876–9), by Lucas H. Eberson and Hugo Pieter Vogel. Eberson (the king's architect since 1874) and Vogel designed here a building that was eclectic not only in its ornaments but also in its composition, which combines the monumental and the picturesque.

Vogel's *Fundamental Principles of the Art of Building: A Handbook for the Architect and a Guide to Teaching for Art Schools* (1872). Besides being an architect, Vogel was also senior lecturer at the Hague Academy of the Visual Arts. He had trained as a neoclassicist and in 1863 had published a *Guide to the Practice of Greek Architecture*. As a teacher, too, his attitude was that of a neoclassicist. To him, architecture was the application of indisputable rules, formulated by recognized authorities – a very conventional view compared with Rose's experimental and investigative approach, often based on individual experience. Vogel's 'fundamental principles' were polished propositions that were generally familiar. (He evidently thought it unnecessary to state their source, which were the works of Hübsch, Bötticher, Semper and Viollet-le-Duc.)

Intellectual overload: theory continues to lose ground

Perhaps because it constituted a convenient summary of conventional, authoritative views, Vogel's *Fundamental Principles* was very well received. However, in the following years it became less and less clear what the 'fundamental principles' actually were. Paradoxical as it might seem, this uncertainty was to a large extent caused by the ever-increasing flood of international publications. In contrast to the 1860s, Dutch architects were now publishing a stream of articles informing their colleagues of the many historical and theoretical works of architecture emanating from abroad. What started out as an exciting proliferation of ideas and opinions and an increasing amount of visual material, would turn into the beginnings of an intellectual and artistic surfeit. As early as 1860 Semper had shown a sharp eye for the changing situation: 'The material collected by science and research, which has been taken up by the large number, increasing daily, of publications (including illustrated works) on art and related matters, has long since become more than we can cope with, making it very difficult to orientate oneself and get one's bearings.'[6]

The widespread dissemination of ideas on architecture is only one aspect of this decade. The other, more hidden side was that, as already mentioned, architectural theory began to lose ground. The daily reality was that the art of building had to try to survive in a market economy that was developing into full-blown capitalism. As a teacher, Vogel was certainly not blind to this reality. In his book he had described eight 'rules' that architecture should comply with, but had concluded that it was becoming increasingly difficult to realize these rules and that they were usually disregarded – and this even applied to the principle of 'truth'.

It is worth reflecting on this last point for a moment, precisely because it plays such an important role in all European aesthetics, including Dutch. It is to be noted that even such an influential work as *Fundamental Principles* had to yield to practice – evidently Vogel had no choice. He had to acknowledge that architectural 'truth' was hardly known about outside the profession and that there were other great obstacles that were hampering the achievement of truth: fashion, the subordinate position of the architect, shortage of funds on the part of the commissioning agencies, and the locations of many of the construction sites. Immediately after the book's publication, *De Opmerker* remarked: 'Although we absolutely do not wish to reject truth in our buildings, we do believe that many people have an exaggerated and far-fetched impression of this concept.' Truth was a matter of common sense, of give and take. The main forms should result from the construction, good materials should be used, the rooms should have the required amount of light, air and space, and architects should 'try to apply the rules of symmetry'.[7]

Together with Vogel's remarks on the unruliness of the building sector, the laconic view of *De Opmerker* can be taken to show that the status of theory had sunk even further. In the 1860s, as we have seen, the art of building had become a subject of public debate, the increasing influence of the building industry had become apparent, and an appreciation of the – hardly theoretical – 'picturesque' had evolved. However, by emphasizing the essential meaning of theory, architects had managed to distinguish themselves from 'the unqualified', the contractors and master builders who called themselves architects. *De Opmerker* now challenged this view: amongst the architects themselves there were those who were openly questioning the necessity of architectural theory.

In the context of daily architectural practice, this was actually quite normal and natural. Of course there were architects who accepted commissions in a pragmatic and commercial way, architects who did not consider serving art as their highest responsibility. These were the ones who showed little interest in the architectural world outside their own practice or had little talent, the silent majority in the debate on the art of building. It is probable that this growing group – growing as well in the MBB with its one thousand members in the 1870s – contributed to the ever-decreasing importance attributed to architectural theory, making it into an increasing academic matter. Truth became to many a somewhat 'theoretical' – respectable but somewhat impractical – concept, as demonstrated by Vogel's observations and the position taken by *De Opmerker*. Unnamed colleagues confirmed that Vogel was right on this score – in 1876 the The Hague branch of the MBB debated the use of prefabricated cement components. It turned out that 'the general view was that "truth" cannot be absolutely maintained in the use of the material'.[8]

Another, directly related, structural change was revealed during this decade. In addition to the tendency to make theory an intellectual domain independent of practice, it became customary to use fragments of theory in a much simplified form and without any historical or architectural context.

Rose's *Discourses* (1872) were not only the final statement in a long life devoted to observation and reflection and the constant refining of ideas, but in a deeper sense were the swan-song of an era that had hoped to find the 'rules' of art through pure reason. This pattern of reasoning, which originated in the eighteenth century and became part of a generally respected intellectual tradition, changed into a more personal line of argument distinguished by categorical statements rather than careful

reasoning, its own individual sense of aesthetics and an apparent lack of awareness of all tradition. 'It is no longer exceptional', according to Leliman in 1868, 'to hear authors such as Goethe, Kant and Winckelmann, or Rousseau, Vasari and Victor Hugo, who were capable of edifying, even enthralling entire countries and peoples with their works on art, being described as "novelists"'[9] (it is worth nothing that in 1868 'novelist' appears to have been hardly an honourable title). Art theory had thus been reduced to a set of clever fabrications, to fiction, to something that had nothing to do with daily practice.

Take as an illustration of the simplification of theory the answer that the successful Dutch architect Johan Frederik Metzelaar (1818–97) gave at a meeting of the MBB in 1875 to the question 'How should we build?' He stated as the most important principle that a construction should comprise as few materials as possible, should provide the highest level of stability, and that it should be presented as simply and as beautifully as possible. He added, 'It is not the decoration or the dressings that make up a building style – this is achieved solely by the construction.' His argument for the primacy of the construction was that, 'just like the human skeleton', it determined the quality of the dressings.[10] This was an idea that belonged to Semper, reproduced without any reference to Semper, and without the accompanying reasoning.

Thus a theory was reduced to a slogan. And Metzelaar was not the only one to think in this way. For a hundred years or so Semper's easily reproducible 'theory' would be frequently repeated in this way – it was in fact the essence of the aesthetics of twentieth-century Modernism. In the context of 1875 it is especially the 'uncultured', 'technological' aspect of the answer that is notable. Metzelaar stripped the concept of truth of the artistic and moral connotations that it had possessed throughout the discussions of the previous twenty-five years. An intellectual and aesthetic theorem was thus very pragmatically dismantled, with only a simple maxim remaining.

The second illustration derives from a source that would still be much in evidence in the 1880s. In 1879 'Vox', whose real name has remained undiscovered, published eight articles entitled 'On Dutch architecture' in the *Nederlandsche Kunstbode* (Dutch Art Courier). Written in a personal, narrative style, the articles at first gave the impression of striking a different note. However, Vox's argument failed to turn up a single original thought. It was a rather individual 'theory' consisting of unconnected fragments from the work of Viollet-le-Duc and Hübsch, an inconsistent line of argument that apparently bothered

Fig.42
W. Doon's Hotel Central, The Hague (1879). Nowadays Doon would be described not only as an architect and builder, but also as a property developer. Here beside the administrative district, the Binnenhof, he realized a successful project which also included a shopping arcade, dwellings and a restaurant – the entire street unified on one side by a petrified avalanche of Old Dutch Renaissance forms.

neither the author nor the editor, which in itself is worth remarking on. In short, it was a fine example of the tendency to vulgarize architectural theory.

In 1870, in an article in *Bouwkundige Bijdragen*, Leliman attempted to encourage his colleagues not to abandon theory and to remain on course. But 'it appears that our era is not as disciplined as past centuries, which developed an artistic authority that could make even the soundest among our contemporaries jealous'.[11] Like Rose, Leliman as a theorist sometimes nurtured a future that already belonged to the past. The time of artistic authority was over.

Would building survive as an art?

In 1877 *De Opmerker* wrote about 'the unrelenting, unprecedented complaints about the tremendous opposition the building profession encounters nowadays'. The article mentioned no names, but concluded that 'a truly serious danger threatens the art of building'.[12] Apparently, no explanation was necessary. Intriguing words

indeed, that may have referred to the problem that kept surfacing throughout the 70s: could the art of building hold its own as an art, or would it become a matter of technology, science and commerce? The importance of the problem was enormous. If the art of building lost its status as an art and became mere building, it would have lost its main social function, its *raison d'être* – it would no longer be a means of 'edification', one of the higher manifestations of civilization.

This was not an academic point. Whether the art of building could survive as an art was highly uncertain in those years, when the economic growth in the building trade implicated more, clients without any feeling for art, an increasingly obtrusive and expanding industry, and more architects without any training. W. Doon, a contractor and property developer from The Hague, was one such successful 'architect' who received important commissions; 'architect' was an unprotected title and it was possible to make a good livelihood out of it. In 1876 *De Opmerker* noted that new buildings kept springing up with a 'complete lack of artistic character', built by folk who simply purchased some pattern books and 'proclaim themselves architects'.[13]

At the same time some of the institutions were posing a threat. In 1868, due to the reorganization of the Royal Academy (the later National Academy) of the Visual Arts in Amsterdam, the best tuition available in architecture was in danger of being transferred from Amsterdam to the Polytechnic in Delft. And in 1870 the government did indeed decide in favour of Delft, something that the MBB had resisted for years. Amsterdam was the cosmopolitan capital of the arts, Delft a provincial backwater. 'The architect must be fired with the ambition to make his art appreciated as the first among the fine arts', the MBB stated; 'This can hardly be accomplished in a deathly-quiet little town, with no major diversion, museums or libraries, and a dearth of fellow artists and patrons.' And, perhaps even worse, 'teaching in architecture at the Polytechnic is combined with the training for engineers and technicians'.[14]

The disappointment of the board of the MBB gives an interesting insight into the architect's perceptions of himself. An environment devoid of culture was suitable, apparently, for engineers, but not for architects. Behind this idea, though, there was the real fear that the art of building, if separated from its sister arts, would be reduced to technology.

Materialism, positivism, idealism

In another 'deathly-quiet' provincial town, Zwolle, in the north of the country, the relation between the art of building and the visual arts was redefined in a different, yet also very pragmatic, way. In 1876 the local branch of the MBB debated the question of whether the art of building belonged to the visual arts. A fundamental difference between the two was identified. The art of building cloaked the necessary and the useful in beauty, it was decided, a relationship in which the useful almost always took precedence. The other visual arts only produced beauty.[15]

Of course, this debate is no proof of a fundamental change in the theory of art, but by so strongly emphasizing the necessary and the useful it once more illustrated that architectural theory in the 1870s had started to assume a dual nature. It began to disappear from the heart of the art of building and to live on in two forms on the periphery, as an academic – non-practical – argument and in the vulgarized form of the slogan. The ideological and institutional weakening of the link between the art of building and the visual arts only went to show that architecture was to be increasingly led by technical considerations and social practice instead of theory.

This tendency can be interpreted as a Darwinian process, a necessary adaptation in order to survive in an inexorable economic reality. But these changes can also be considered as a component of a new *Weltanschauung* that was becoming influential internationally. In fact, it consisted of two philosophical concepts: materialism and positivism. For the materialist, matter is the only reality. As a contemporary put it: 'To the materialist the soul is the product of the body, the thought is an electrical spark, man is a galvanic battery, and the "master of creation" is a descendent of the ape.' The positivist 'attaches value only to facts, accepts nothing that is not proven'. Neither is interested in metaphysics, because this is an unprovable and therefore essentially nonexistent territory. Materialism and positivism could therefore both be seen as anti-idealist philosophies, unlike idealism, for which physical reality was a forever imperfect expression of a higher, ideal reality. Whereas the natural sciences and technical practice demonstrated the spectacular success of both materialism and positivism, idealism, which had formerly enjoyed a prominent cultural position, lost ground and increasingly became a morally edifying, but rather 'theoretical', way of thinking.

That these opposing philosophical views were considered relevant to the art of building is demonstrated by an article published in 1869 that also contained the above definitions of the materialist and the positivist. 'The lack of character and constructive beauty in current architectural style, which until recently was the reason why we expected – though in vain – that a new style would arise as a worthy representative of our times, cannot be seen as other than the result of materialism and of the state of ferment inherent in the period of transition that we are living in.'[16] The author of the article, the freethinker Sicco E. W. Roorda van Eysinga (1825–87), saw stimulating possibilities for a third way between materialism and idealism: 'the future is positivism'. After the Middle Ages, according to Roorda van Eysinga, the first signs became evident of a separation between Church and state, science and religion, belief and art, and man started work on a new ideal: the connection between science and humanity. They were now living, he said, in a transitional period, because religion was still not without influence and science was not yet wholeheartedly accepted. It was the artist's task to force a breakthrough and to bring truth, science and humanity in harmony with one another.

It fits well the positivist way of thinking that the concept of beauty, which occupied a central position in idealist aesthetics, was not considered so important, precisely because it was difficult to define it in an objective and factual way. When Metzelaar responded to the question 'How should we build?', he had little to say on aesthetic matters. He defined style as belonging to a technically perfect construction that should comprise a minimum of materials, and be presented as simply and beautifully as possible. As noted earlier, this answer exemplified the rise of a simplified, pragmatic theory. It can also be seen as an example of an emerging positivism: it reflected a total lack of idealistic theorizing, limited itself to the material core of the matter, the building's 'skeleton' – and when that was found to be satisfactory, there could be said to be style. In its conciseness and specificity this proposition is the opposite of the many attempts undertaken in the 1860s to define style in an immaterial, idealistic way, as Gosschalk had done in 1868: style, he said, was the expression of 'our times', or 'refined construction' – that is to say, 'construction governed by the laws of rhythm and harmony'. In 1871 he distinguished between architecture (that is, practical knowledge and science) and the art of building: art was a question of idealizing – the ordinary and everyday was at most a motive, but beauty was the aim.[17]

It was in the work of Semper and Viollet-le-Duc that the positivistic, factual current in architectural theory became inescapably clear. They freed themselves from traditional idealist aesthetics by designing an architectural theory similar to modern positivist science.[18] They rejected the notion that the principles of art can be inferred from a transcendent ideal that cannot be perceived by the senses. Viollet-le-Ducs *Dictionnaire* was indeed an impressive testament to the positivist method. While medieval architecture in France, Germany, England, Belgium and the Netherlands was idealized on a large scale in Catholic circles as the symbol of religiousness and morality, Viollet-le-Duc described it as a rational system without any metaphysical or symbolic content whatsoever. Proportions, in the Vitruvian tradition the basis of beauty, were to Viollet-le-Duc the 'logical, necessary links between the whole and its constituent parts'. True, they must be agreeable to the eye and the mind, but first they needed to obey the laws of stability which in turn were derived from geometry. This concept led Viollet-le-Duc to create an alternative to the classicist theory of proportion that was based on the cosmic harmonies of numerical proportions. He defined a formula, which had the level of abstraction of a law of nature, for the casual relationship between physical stability and proportion; the medieval cathedrals originated from the application of three types of triangle, he claimed.[19]

In 1872 Volume II of the *Discourses* was published, boosting Viollet-le-Duc's authority in the Netherlands.

Was its success attributable to the text being matter-of-factly concentrated on the nature of material and construction, and on the design process based on it? Or was it the technical feel to the illustrations and the attempt to integrate iron with architecture, no matter how unoriginal this latter may have seemed after Labrouste, the architect of the St-Geneviève Library and Baltard, the architect of *Les Halles*, both in Paris? In any event, the message of this publication was clear: architecture was pre-eminently a practical, modern science. And the message was objective, neutral, because it was 'scientific' enough to confer universal authority on Viollet-le-Duc's publications in the Netherlands, regardless of the reader's own doctrine. This was also the case even for those who attributed a metaphysical content to architecture, such as the religious idealist Cuypers who was soon to be presented by his adherents and advocates as the Dutch Viollet-le-Duc.

Architecture and the aesthetic ideal
The connection of architecture with an aesthetic ideal was still widely supported during these years. It was an old tradition interwoven with the generally accepted concept of civilization itself: art together with reason and morality formed the three sides of the pillar that gave man his position of supremacy in nature. Rose had been the person best suited to answer the question posed during a meeting in 1871, 'What are the advantages and disadvantages of an idealist school in architecture and its practice?'[20] As before, he argued that architecture had no examples of ideal beauty in nature to go by, as the 'imitative' arts had. In what direction should it develop in its pursuit of beauty, given the lack of rules as once furnished the classical order? Had Rose been a positivist, he would have been bound to answer: focus on the construction of the building. But since his thinking was idealist, he observed a 'spirit of progression' that had given rise to spectacular advances in the fields of the sciences, morals and technology. 'Everything is now developing as if there were an awakening, as if everything had suddenly started to bud and grow – there is a sense of progression. This spirit of progression seeks perfection.'

Beauty had a profound influence, argued Rose, on the development of the individual as well as on society as a whole. The psychological development of a child illustrated this: the perception of beauty, he said, developed before the sense of truth; the sense of beauty led to the sense of morality, which then aspired to a further edification of the soul. Society would have a bright future if only this were well understood; moral development was not founded on the dull teaching of ethics, but, rather, on the development of the perception of beauty, 'the most

Fig.43
Isaac Gosschalk's and
Herman Jan van den
Brink's De Groote
Club, Amsterdam
(1870–2): eclecticism
with a monumental
character, suitable for
the distinguished
men's club. The
building at the far
right is the Town Hall
by Jacob van Campen
(Fig.32).

agreeable that we know'.[21] These ideas may seem naive today, but one must realize that Rose was just one of many who adhered to the notion, supported by a philosophical tradition going back more than two millennia, that beauty, good and truth together formed a unity. Through beauty art edified the soul, and it was for the artist to lead the way.

During the 1870s these notions also served, as will become apparent later, to bolster the argument that the government should pursue an active art policy; by promoting the arts, the government would support the edification of the people, thus ensuring national prestige abroad. This edification did not always proceed smoothly, however. It was the inadequate artistic appreciation in the Netherlands that was the problem, as ever. The philosopher Van Vloten, author of *Aesthetics, or the Theory of Beauty* (1865, second edition 1871), thought that the churches were responsible for this; since the Reformation they had monopolized the moral development of the people. He called on the government to promote the teaching of aesthetics: 'Knowledge and appreciation of the arts must increasingly become a moral imperative of irresistible urgency for every Dutchman who claims to be a civilized person.'[22]

The public's scant interest in architecture was already evident in the 1850s and 60s as noted earlier with regard to the gulf that existed between architecture, the public art par excellence, and the public's totally uninformed attitude towards works of architecture. According to some, this problem was the main cause of the lack of a contemporary style originating in the people. Complaints about the social isolation of architecture grew more bitter during the 1870s, in particular because properly trained architects felt threatened by the commercial successes of the builders they viewed as little better than bunglers. And their expectations for the future were sombre indeed, 'as long as even the civilized upper middle class lack all taste for and appreciation of architecture and sculpture'.[23]

This was the demoralized view of a small group of architects in The Hague in 1878, but it was one of many examples illustrating the increasing distance in this decade between the ideal – edifying art – and reality, between theory and practice. Naturally, there was no one theory; there were some generally held viewpoints, as well as odd contributions such as an anonymous treatise on the relation between art and the level of civilization of a people, which saw the edifying function of art as quite problematical in view of the fact that so-called barbarians sometimes produced impressive works of art whereas the art of civilized Europe was currently in such great difficulty.[24] Another comment on the educative value of art came from the influential philosopher Cornelis Willem Opzoomer (1821–92), who in 1875 pointed out a recent tendency 'to glorify art and to make it the cornerstone of our moral life. However, in order to create a sound society, art itself must be sound in the first place.'[25]

Such conclusions put into perspective the optimism of idealist aesthetics which may sometimes have been excessive. Opzoomer represented in the Netherlands a philosophy based on a perceptible reality – we might call it the positivist movement within philosophy itself. He considered art to be a point of transition between the sensory and the spiritual. It is therefore not surprising that in 1875 he described the essence of art as the problem of how form turns into content and content turns into form. In his musings on this matter he used classical Greek art as a frame of reference. Allard Pierson (1831–96), who since 1877 had been professor of aesthetics and history of art at the University of Amsterdam, was strongly influenced by Opzoomer, and his book *On Style* (1863) was grounded in the Greek classics, especially Plato. In *Beauty and Wisdom* (1868) he criticized the new spirit of the time: 'Materialism, it is said, is increasing. Cultural life and the inner life are losing ground.' The development of the sense of beauty was therefore urgently needed. Beauty to Pierson meant serenity, order, harmony, good manners and respect for one another, as well as control, love, open-heartedness, generosity, cheerfulness and seriousness. 'The aesthetic? Is it not a reflection of the divine?', he remarked, then referred to Plato. It is not surprising that Pierson had an aversion for zealotry and intolerance in aesthetic matters. He categorically refused to be dragged into a debate on style: 'Don't take sides. You can have it all!' His aesthetic idealism was practically oriented, averse to anything transcendental: 'art especially must guard against metaphysics'.[26]

It would be wrong to regard the fact that authoritative writers such as Opzoomer, Pierson and Vosmaer based their views on Greek antiquity as an old-fashioned stance simply because classicism in architectural training had become so. True, in the 1870s it was established with some satisfaction that the time when the texts of Vignola and Bosboom were considered the ultimate in wisdom was long gone.[27] In the same decade *De Opmerker* regularly published articles on Greek architecture, but this was contemporary archaeological science. All the same, this focus on classical art theory proved how highly regarded Greek antiquity still was – not for scientific reasons, but as a civilizing influence in the present time. 'It is a peculiar phenomenon,' wrote Vosmaer in 1879, 'this unbreakable thread that ties us to antiquity; this strong, fine thread that runs through our entire civilization!'[28] The strength of Greek civilization, the edifying and moral power of art and the ideal unity of form and substance, were still repeatedly expressed by reference to Winckelmann, who had been forced by the sight of the statue of Apollo Belvedere in the Vatican Museum to take on a dignified posture himself in order to be able to observe it 'with dignity'.

Fig.44
The Hall of the Arts and Sciences, The Hague (1873–4), by Eugen Heinrich Gugel. This temple of the Muses could be described as 'a decorated shed', a definition coined by by the American Post-Modernist architect Robert Venturi. The very simple, almost utilitarian main forms achieve 'character' through the ornaments, which relate it to antiquity, the ideals of classical civilization and the Italian Renaissance.

Realism

The traditional pursuit of the ideal unity of beauty and truth was challenged in the 1870s by a new concept of art which in literature and painting was called 'realism'. This realism was developed about 1850 in French art, mainly by the painter Gustave Courbet and the writer Gustave Flaubert. In the Netherlands it was discussed in the 1860s, subsequently to be put into practice in the 70s by several writers. Like positivism in science, realism aimed to collect facts, and stated that these facts spoke for themselves. According to the nineteenth-century notion, the realist artist would represent what he saw, even if it was banal or unsightly. He would not intervene between nature – the visible reality that is to be imitated – and the observer. He would hold back, for the work of art, according to the realist viewpoint was a representation of material reality, not of an 'idea'. It may already be clear that realism had no ambition to edify the people through art.

The term 'realism' was mentioned briefly in Chapter 3 when the twin concept of realism-idealism was discussed. Vosmaer used 'realism' in 1856 to distinguish between Italian and Dutch painting of the seventeenth century. The latter he typified as realistic because it was a model of 'an open and receptive mind for the poetry of nature and of all aspects of life and reality'[29] – all aspects of reality, including the banal and the unsightly. But when the Old Dutch architecture was discovered in the 1850s and 60s it was not associated with the term 'realism', although this could easily have occurred by analogy with the Dutch painting of the same period. Arguments based on the nature of Old Dutch architecture itself could also easily have been summoned; for its distorted classical patterns and proportions, the inadequate 'truth' constituent, and its colourful, popular aesthetics implied that Old Dutch architecture – in the context of the 1850s–60s – did not aspire to an edifying 'idea'.

Fig.45
'Realist' utilitarian architecture, designed by a professor of construction at the Polytechnic School in Delft: Gerrit Jan Morre's bonded warehouse, De Vijf Werelddeelen (The Five Continents), Rotterdam (1879). The building incorporated a transport and distribution system operating between the harbour and the railway, and furthered Rotterdam's ambition to become, along with London and Hamburg, one of the world's largest and most modern harbours.

The term 'realism' was not applied, either, to the contemporary architecture of the 1860s–70s, although during the 70s and later many articles were published on modern realist novels and theatrical performances and on realist painting. Why, then, was the word taboo for architects writing about architecture? Perhaps the question should be formulated this way: Was realist architecture – architecture that was beautiful, but without 'idea', without substance – at all conceivable? The answer was no, according to the principles of the leading architects who presented themselves both in print and in person as the conscience of contemporary architecture. A form was only beautiful if it expressed its 'idea' well. The idea underlying an architectural form was a manifestation of truth and character. Without 'idea', the expression of truth and character, the architectural form was empty and therefore not beautiful, and the building would not be architecture. A realistic art of building was a contradiction in terms, a notion that by definition rendered itself impossible.

This reasoning and its conclusion have an idealist premise. It is for this reason alone that realist architecture was a contradiction, an absurd idea which could only much later, in the 1890s, be reassessed positively. Until that time architects in their publications and public debates remained dedicated to their idealist aesthetics (their motives for doing so will be explained in the next chapters). We can see once again that already during the 1870s idealist aesthetics were coming under pressure. Many buildings were erected that bore no marks of idealist aesthetics whatsoever, buildings that were strongly criticized in architectural journals as 'artless … without character, put up by those least qualified, architects unfamiliar with taste or art who produce buildings that are often overdecorated with a hotchpotch of ornaments, demonstrating a total lack of stylistic knowledge'. This referred not only to works of secondary importance, but also to projects that 'qualified' architects would count as their exclusive domain. 'Even the most important buildings [are assigned] to people without

any kind of art training, who draw on a few pattern books from some ornament factory or other.'[30] Was this a description of the realist architecture of the 70s? From the perspective of an idealist theory of art it was poor architecture indeed – empty even when considered as an 'idea'. With its attractive if trivial forms, it pleased the clients and the public in general, but to insiders it was an artless architecture without character.

In those days Amsterdam also had a 'realist' urban architecture, visible in the new housing estates that were built around the edges of the city. According to the comment of an architect who attended a meeting of the MBB in 1877, these new buildings had 'practical but boring passages', 'monotonous lines and monochrome façades'; 'on the drawing-table the ruler has prevailed' – the De Pijp district was 'drawn on graph paper'. Drawn on graph paper – a helpful tool when one was still learning to draw. The speaker would have preferred an artistic townscape, a picturesque landscape, perhaps.[31] He closed his eyes to the

artless aesthetics of the pragmatic, the utilitarian, the trivial – a foreshadowing of the realist aesthetics of the next century.

Fashion, and applied art

In the 1870s art and industry were still relatively unconnected concepts. In practice, they were only too frequently at odds. The nature of art, according to Jan Rudolf de Kruyff (1844–1923), an architect from Amsterdam, was that the fruits of our fantasy are provided with a cultivated form via our sense of beauty. Industry, on the other hand, produced merely so as to satisfy our daily needs. The applied arts, therefore, aimed at a synthesis: what resulted from that synthesis was aesthetically shaped appliances and utensils.[32]

In the Netherlands industrialization was slow to get going. Outside the Netherlands the issue of the applied arts had long since been dealt with and solved. The Great Exhibition in London (1851) had made the relationship

Fig. 46
Flats 'for the working classes', built in the 1880s in the Borgerstraat, Amsterdam, by unknown architects. This was commercial house-building for the masses realized by building companies who parcelled out the pastures on the outskirts of the city as efficiently as possible: filled ditches were turned into streets, making the new quarters highly reminiscent of the geometrical parcelling-out of the polders.

between the two very plain. Scientific discoveries and new technologies enabled industry to manufacture a huge range of new products and to modernize existing ones. It became possible with the aid of machines to apply production methods that previously had been considered almost unthinkable. It became as easy to saw porphyry and granite as it was to saw limestone and to polish it as smooth as glass. Ivory could be softened and pressed into moulds. Vulcanized rubber could be used for countless imitations of wooden, metal and stone sculptures. The galvanoplastic process gave a completely new dimension to the uses of metal.

Semper had analysed the products of all the industrialized countries that were represented at the Great Exhibition. He acknowledged the vast contribution to social progress collectively displayed there, but also tried to find an answer to the problem of how art could create order in this torrent of industrial design, this 'Tower of Babel' that might collapse under the weight of its almost unlimited possibilities. He published his thoughts in *Science, Industry and Art: Proposals for the Development of a National Taste in Art* (1852), in which he formulated the need for a practical, objective – 'scientific' – doctrine of aesthetics.[33] These ideas, together with his analysis of the crafts of the American Indians which were also exhibited in London, resulted in the concept that Semper would later present in more detail in his book *Style in the Technical and Structural Arts* (1860).

Semper had noted in 1852 that industrialization turned the 'order of things' upside down. It was not the consumer who created a demand for products, but the manufacturer. Unlike in the past, the manufacturer did not work for specific clients, but for a 'market' full of hypothetical customers, thus creating 'fashions'. All the most recent blessings, Semper wrote, were forced upon the public, as upon a Chinaman who is suddenly obliged to eat with a knife and fork. The manufacturer determined what the product would look like. The artist who did the design and the craftsman who converted it into an object were compelled to set aside the rules of their trade if the manufacturer so wished, with the degeneration of that trade the ultimate outcome.[34] In *Style* Semper indicted fierce competition and the division of labour in industry as the deeper causes. During the manufacturing stage, he stated, the technical and the artistic elements were separated. As a result, the relationship between function and form was not made visible and so was not understood. The social and professional position of the artist was poor: he was considered a nuisance by the manufacturer who saw himself as superior on the subject of aesthetics and who seldom rewarded the artist properly.[35]

The similarities with the Dutch building industry are striking. In 1867 Gosschalk criticized it harshly: the contribution of the architect was confined to showing the client an attractive drawing and finding a competent plasterer – the rest was none of his business.[36] As with many of the complaints from people belonging to the circle of the MBB, this one pertained to the speculative building by contractors who would tempt potential clients to commission buildings on the basis of an attractive sketch. Here, too, the order of things was reversed. Formerly the contractor would be involved only when he received the commission, but now he was the entrepreneur taking the initiative himself and employing the architect as he used to employ a carpenter or plasterer – as a subordinate who had to adapt to the contractor's commercial ideas and taste.

The similarities between what was happening in the applied arts and in architecture were not only to do with the social and economic positions of the protagonists. There were also parallels in the sphere of artistic theory between the two arts, one of which focused on usefulness and function while the other saw the relationship between form, function and construction as the core problem. As an architect, De Kruyff was closely involved in the promotion of the applied arts and he knew what he was talking about. He had received his training at the School of Applied Arts in Vienna, Europe's major centre for new ideas on the design of appliances and utensils and on interior decorating. He was now the driving force behind the School of Applied Arts in Amsterdam, of which he was to become the first director in 1881. In a book published in 1876 he analysed the miserable status of the applied arts in the Netherlands, and compared it to the situation in the rest of Europe. He identified six causes, three of which had long since wreaked their effect, including the abolition of the guilds around 1800 and the decline of the training in crafts that had ensued. The other three were the 'total decline of architecture', the encroachment of 'naturalism' in decorative art, and fashion – 'It is fashion and naturalism that are most responsible for the violation of our applied arts.'[37]

The first contemporary phenomenon that De Kruyff observed was the decline of architecture. In this he followed Semper, who in his foreword to *Style* argued that the problems in the applied arts and architecture stemmed from the same background. De Kruyff also shared Semper's view – which was now generally accepted – that the degradation of the 'true principles of art' had originated in France in the eighteenth century. 'The applied arts became detached from their mentor, architecture,' wrote De Kruyff, when during the reign of

Louis XV forms were corrupted by indiscriminate curves – corrupted, because they had nothing to do with architectural (that is, structural or functional) form. Through lack of education in art appreciation or of any sense of beauty, the public focused on the 'new'. 'This constant desire to create something new,' he concluded, 'numbed all artistic sense, and fashion thus forced its way in. A beautiful form was no longer important – what mattered was the "new idea", *la haute nouveauté*.'[38]

The novelties most in demand were examples of 'naturalism': true-to-life representations on objects, or transformations of objects, that from a functional or structural point of view had nothing to do with them: porcelain teacups in the form of wicker baskets, a cigar stand in the form of a locomotive, a carpet with hunting scenes: both Semper and William Morris's Arts and Crafts Movement condemned three-dimensional images on a solid two-dimensional surface because they suggested depth, and besides, it is simply not right to create the illusion that one can walk over hunters, dogs and horses – these were considered as violations of the law of 'truth'. De Kruyff's criticism of naturalism was similar to the architects' criticism of works produced by the 'unqualified', who with their aesthetic lies gave the public what they wanted. Here too he was following Semper. The applied arts and the visual arts, he warned, were separate categories because the idealization of nature called for entirely different sets of norms. 'Reason' was a matter of secondary importance in painting and sculpture, but in the applied arts it was the essence. He later explained that 'reason' implied a technical and functional logic involving the simplest design possible to express that essence.[39]

De Kruyff did battle with fashion and with the corrupted taste of the public that had addicted itself to naturalism. He did so in the first place in order to enhance the cultural level and prosperity of the people in general, but also to reinforce the position of the artist and designer. That high standards in the applied arts led to more prosperity had become an internationally and to some extent politically accepted conviction after the Great Exhibition. Semper had been one of the first to see that the increasing gap between the products of the mass market and what he referred to as the 'higher art' of the art schools could be bridged by developing a halfway house in which the artist and the craftsman could come together in knowledge and skill.[40] What this insight could mean in practice was demonstrated in Chapter 4 with Gosschalk's exploration of the aesthetic possibilities of plain brickwork in the early 1860s; he may have learned of Semper's views on the subject during his training in Zurich. It was similarly

demonstrated by Leliman, who around the same time was involved in the establishment of the first Dutch technical school. In 1869 Eugen Heinrich Gugel and his pupil Constantijn Muysken (1843–1922), also influenced by Semper's work, urged the need for education in the applied arts, which would lead the masses to knowledge of the beautiful'.[41]

Semper himself had examined the problem of the contemporary applied arts – including the art of building – in his book *Style*, under the heading of 'practical aesthetics'. He noted two recent phenomena that were impeding the search for a contemporary art. First there was the frantic instability in market supply resulting from the continual battle for the buyer's favour. 'What has only recently been introduced is already discarded as obsolete, even before its technical, let alone artistic, characteristics can have been accepted, because there is always something new – but not always better – to replace it.' The second stumbling-block, according to Semper, was the conceptual fragmentation of art itself emanating from the ever-increasing variety of theoretical specialisms and lines of approach in the theory of art and art history, and as found in practical books, especially in the field of architecture.[42] Semper's definition of the concept 'style' was fundamental precisely because it stood apart from the maelstrom of innovation and increasingly fragmentary knowledge, and focused on the immutable characteristics of each object – each object had a function, a construction and an external form. If there existed an unequivocal, rationally explicable, logical relationship between these three, then there was style.

In his essay *Science, Industry and Art* of 1852 Semper had devoted much attention to a fundamental overhaul of the problem of the applied arts from the perspective of both culture and national prosperity. His subtitle indicated as much: 'Proposals for the Development of a National Taste in Art'. These proposals included establishing art collections in the form of applied arts museums for the purpose of study, introducing formal education in the applied arts, and organizing competitions and exhibitions. Soon afterwards the South Kensington Museum (now the Victoria and Albert) was established in London. A series of similar museums and enterprises followed in Germany, Vienna, Paris and Italy. In 1876 De Kruyff noted that the Netherlands was the only country to show no sign of such activity and was therefore increasingly falling behind. He championed the establishment in his home country of an applied arts museum with a related training facility. In this context he considered the study of Old Dutch decorative art most useful, because its qualities were beyond all

Fig.47
P. J. H. Cuypers'
Rijksmuseum,
Amsterdam
(1876–85). This
national museum of
history and the fine
arts was criticized
because of its
'incorrect' character:
the main form (with
an arcaded street right
through the centre)
evoked an enormous
city gate rather than a
museum. Many critics
considered the details
and ornaments too
'medieval' to express
the Dutch Golden
Age.

suspicion. 'Old Dutch decorative art is *very highly* esteemed abroad, so much so that we have regularly encountered prominent artists who prefer an arts tour in the Netherlands to a study tour in Italy.'[43]

Art as a national concern
At the time De Kruyff wrote his plea, his wishes seemed set to be partly fulfilled. In 1872 the opinion had been expressed in the Lower House of the Dutch parliament that art should be treated as a national concern and should therefore become a government matter. In order to prevent this statement from coming to nothing, Victor E. L. de Stuers (1843–1916), a lawyer and art lover from The Hague, published the next year a philippic against the government's indifference towards the national heritage, consisting of architectural monuments as well as historical artefacts and documents. His treatise, *Holland at its Most Narrow-minded*, published in 1874, was followed by a second instalment, *Iteretur decoctum* (The Recipe is to be

Repeated). Both of these offerings were sharp and polemical, and focused on forcing the government by means of publicity to start treating art as a matter of public interest.

In that year, 1874, De Stuers achieved some results. The Minister of the Interior appointed a Government Advisory Council for Historic Monuments, which would advise government on the first stages of the preservation of monuments, the care of the – few – national museum collections, and the maintenance and establishment of government buildings. The Council had six members, including the art critic and Dutch history expert Carel Vosmaer and the architects E. H. Gugel and P. J. H. Cuypers. In 1875 Gugel resigned and was succeeded by Gosschalk. The secretary was De Stuers, who was also the driving force behind the Council's activities during the following years. In 1875 he once again courted publicity, this time with a little book called *Da Capo. Another Word on Government, Art and Historic Monuments*. In that year a

Fig.48
The Ministry of Justice Building, The Hague (1876), by Cornelis H. Peters. After the Rijksmuseum, the building was the next most ambitious and expensive example of the 'official style', launched by De Stuers in 1876. The architectural notion on which it was based related to De Stuers' 'favourite concept': the full reconstruction of the administrative district, the Binnenhof.

Department of Art and Science was established at the Ministry of the Interior, headed by De Stuers. From then on he was to report to the minister on matters concerning the arts. In fact, because of his great political talent and his flair for publicity, De Stuers held absolute sway over national policy matters pertaining to the arts until 1901. From the start, the promotion of architecture became one of his most important aims. But it quickly became apparent that he had a very special interpretation of architecture.

In order to realize his aim, De Stuers promoted Cuypers and made him his right-hand man; for a quarter of a century, he would be only too happy to be used in this way. The government commissions and the protection and preferential treatment he received from De Stuers gave him extensive power and influence, as well as ensuring a hefty income. In 1874 Cuypers started on his long and unstoppable climb to the top of the small world of Dutch architecture.

Officialdom takes control: Victor de Stuers

The publications with which De Stuers made his public entry into the art world made his motivation clear. In a stirring indictment he had confronted the government with its indifference and negligence in matters of art, arguing that this attitude had resulted in the cultural and economic deprivation of the Netherlands. In *Da Capo* (Another Word) he stated that his aim was 'the revival and appreciation of art in the Netherlands'. Although the general cultural indifference had been commented on by many others before, De Stuers was the first to propose a programme and a stringent strategy for improving the situation. He must have judged that the time was ripe. In the 1850s and 60s Rose and Leliman had still been able, in their little architectural circle, to dismiss the lack of public interest as a deplorable phenomenon. At that time Vosmaer was drawing wider attention to the problem through his publications. 'Art and the people have a strange relationship with one another in our country,' he said. 'Art is made and enjoyed by the few people with a noble mind, whereas the masses are almost devoid of all art.'[44] Now, in the 1870s, something else was emerging that would pose an immediate threat to the arts. The masses were able, for the first time in history, to choose from an ever-increasing supply of customer goods. And it opted overwhelmingly for fashion, superficiality and bad taste, leaving the artists alone on their Olympus.

De Stuers realized that the social and professional status of the art of building was in danger of sinking even further. And he had enough political sensitivity to understand that the effort that might be expected in this respect of the architectural community was lacking. Since the end of the 60s the architectural debate had stagnated; the most important things said and written about had been said and written about so often before. De Stuers broke the deadlock because he was able to take action. And the fact that he had the opportunity to do so resulted, of course, from his high rank and his influence behind the scenes, which enabled him actually to commission the Rijksmuseum in Amsterdam (1876–85), the Ministry of Justice Building in The Hague (1876–83), and a whole series of other new government buildings. He was also able to benefit from the political climate that had emerged after the laissez-faire of the 1860s – a climate that was characterized by a parliament that wanted more social and cultural guidance from the government.

To this was added another political factor – the question of whether the Netherlands actually had an identity of its own, an independent right to exist alongside the powerful German Empire, which was proclaimed in 1871. The emphasis that De Stuers placed after 1874 on the Old Dutch element in architecture, the outstandingly generous budgets that enabled him to build the Rijksmuseum and the Ministry of Justice, and the fact that he was able to maintain his influential position despite fierce criticism from the press and sometimes from the Lower House – all this had a political explanation, not just a cultural one. It was a matter of representing the state, of *raison d'état*.

It was no secret in the mid-1870s that the Netherlands was well behind in this field compared with neighbouring countries. An anonymous observer noted that the Dutchman could hardly fail to see all around anything but 'monstrous buildings', the result of the thriftiness of those who had commissioned them; often, for instance, the carpenter would be asked to draw up the plans in order to save on the architect's salary. Meanwhile, 'each year many Dutch tourists visit foreign capitals. Even the lower classes eagerly make cheap train trips abroad, and they can hardly fail to notice that everything they see there makes an immensely better impression than anything at home'.[45] In Germany, where the new empire required for its administration and representation many new public buildings, monumental architecture thrived as never before thanks to lavish government support; and with it, the applied arts necessary for the adornment and interior decoration of these buildings. Elsewhere, equally impressive large-scale modernizations had been in full swing for some fifteen or twenty years. In Victorian London, Second Empire Paris and Vienna, the capital of the Austro-Hungarian monarchy, the state had broken new ground with its commissions for monumental buildings.[46]

The passion for the past: an 'official style'

Let us return to the Netherlands. De Stuers now took advantage of the political climate to press for a strong representation, in the form of new buildings, of the modern state. It is notable that the aesthetic ideal and the aesthetic standards he aspired to evoked a distant past. He paid great attention to the preservation of monuments and historic buildings, which he saw as of national importance. The benefits were twofold, he wrote in *Another Word*: the taste of the people would be improved and the restoration of old buildings would be of 'incalculable' help to architects as a ready means of improving their taste and expanding their technical knowledge.[47] This line of reasoning was not new, and De Stuers was certainly not the only one to use it. For more than twenty years there had been ongoing discussions in the MBB on the edifying effects of the art of building and the importance of the works of their forefathers. But the focus of these discussions had always been the development of a *new* architecture, whereas De Stuers was focusing primarily on the preservation of venerable monuments. The arguments were similar, but the approach was quite different; and there was other evidence that De Stuers' ideas and activities were not aimed at promoting a contemporary architecture that would reflect the demands of a rapidly changing society. He preferred to recall cherished forms, images and working methods from an 'ancient past', a time when there had still been a collective aesthetic ideal to shape. According to De Stuers, the full flowering of the arts in the past had resulted from 'the appreciation of art and of the good taste of a government that almost instinctively demanded beauty as a necessary component of a building and its decoration, and that employed large numbers of artists'. This was the approach that the Dutch government should adopt today: the look of any new government building should reflect 'the desire to provide [it] with the aesthetic appearance to which it is entitled on the basis of its function, interior and location. This desire ought to be based not on the wish to provide artists with work or to artificially create some specific type of art, but on a natural desire for beauty.'[48]

This ideal, then, formulated by De Stuers in 1875, was an ideal that embraced a living past, a national appreciation of art, and a noble government that instinctively satisfied the people's natural desire for beauty. His activities the following year, mainly behind the scenes, demonstrated how he intended to give shape to this ideal: the government – in the person of De Stuers himself – would determine the form of beauty that would best satisfy the aesthetic needs of the people, and the kind of art – and of architects – that were best fitted to achieve this. Already in March 1876 De Opmerker warned that it seemed as if the minister was pursuing an 'official architecture'.[49]

Politically, the 1870s were a turbulent period. Tension was increasing because of a political and religious polarization. Germany was developing into the new centre of political and economic power in Europe. And domestic tension was also increasing because of a political and religious polarization. Needless to say, the architectural community was not impervious to these developments. When in 1871 Leliman called on his colleagues within the MBB to establish artistic principles and to uphold them, he anticipated conflicts between the basic principles of artistic freedom and those of artistic factions. 'The result ... will be a battle fought out before the public. It will be a bloody battle, but, provided it is fought with fair weapons, it will advance us as a profession and increase the influence of architecture,' he said.[50]

Leliman's prophecy came true, but in a different way than he had probably hoped. A bloody battle was indeed fought out before the public, but hardly with fair weapons; and whether architecture gained in influence was very doubtful. De Opmerker wrote in 1876: 'Dissension is becoming increasingly apparent. This can only have a very negative effect on art, and is the result of an exaggerated passion for the past.'[51]

But it was more than a passion for the past that was at issue. It was De Stuers' way of pursuing it, his very method of working, that was causing the great tension within the architectural community. His actions and the opposition he aroused were entirely in keeping with the climate of polarization and faction forming during this decade. De Stuers attempted to achieve his aims not by consensus, but by confrontation: by continually presenting people with faits accomplis through his use of budgets, political influence and tricks.

The events of 1876 bore witness to this. In the spring, Cuypers, who until then had built neo-Gothic churches almost exclusively, received the commission for the Central Station in Amsterdam, while his former employee and disciple Cornelis Hendrik Peters (1847–1932) was appointed architect to the Ministry of Finance with the task of building all the new post offices in the Netherlands. In the summer Cuypers was appointed architect of the Rijksmuseum, the most costly and probably most prestigious Dutch building commission of the entire nineteenth century. In this autumn his brother-in-law and propagandist Alberdingk Thijm was appointed to the National Academy of the Visual Arts in Amsterdam as professor of art history and aesthetics. This appointment flew in the face of the Supervisory Board of the National Academy which would have preferred either Vosmaer or Pierson for the job. At the same time the architect Vogel, who at government instruction was working on a building for the Ministry of Justice in The Hague, was replaced by Peters. At some point during these months the designer of the plans for the new university building in Leiden, Johan Frederik Metzelaar, was also pushed out to make way for a competition for the same commission, to be judged by an international panel of adjudicators consisting of Cuypers' supporters. In all these instances De Stuers was the driving force.[52]

The government's grip tightens

The reaction of the architectural community to all these events can be read in the columns of De Opmerker which, as a weekly, kept a close eye on what was happening and, after its initial expression of amazement at what it saw, developed into a highly critical commentator. In the summer of 1876 it emerged that Cuypers, in his capacity of government adviser, had been involved in the drawing up of the commission for the Rijksmuseum, and that he had subsequently become the winner by means of a secret procedure involving a jury of twenty laymen and one architect, the government adviser Gosschalk. The columns of De Opmerker were fuming for months; the whole episode was considered a flagrant insult to the architectural community.

Late the same year emotions were running high again when Cuypers' winning design for the Rijksmuseum was made public. What had been generally expected was now confirmed: his design was not a contemporary expression of the glorious Dutch seventeenth century, but an archaeological exercise, an anachronism. It was also clear that the already massive budget of one million guilders would be exceeded by at least a hundred per cent, mainly because a virtual street was planned to run right down the middle of the building and a tower at each side. It was rumoured that Thijm had thought this bit up, and indeed he wrote lyrically about the design as a symbolic new gate to the city of Amsterdam. *De Opmerker* was baffled that Cuypers had made this disputable symbolism the main point of his design, sacrificing a monumental exterior and a properly functional interior in the process. At precisely this time, another part of De Stuers' agenda was disclosed when Vosmaer published a sketch that his boss referred to as his 'favourite concept': the reconstruction in The Hague of the Binnenhof and the surrounding streets – the administrative district – in the Old Dutch image with strong medieval accents.

It now became only too clear what was happening behind the scenes. *De Opmerker* wrote that 'amateurs' were drawing up building plans that threatened to be executed by 'a few medieval zealots' who 'wrap art up in a shroud'.[53] The upheaval provoked by De Stuers was such that *De Opmerker* in 1877 talked of a revolution aimed at taking contemporary architecture back to the Middle Ages. The respected critic and man of letters Conrad Busken Huet also had De Stuers and Thijm in mind when he wrote that at present architectural know-nothings were realizing their own 'poor artistic concepts' in which they were assisted by a few architects who were being infinitely rewarded for their efforts, while 'art is buried in the process'.[54]

That a few architects did indeed receive quite a number of commissions had not gone unnoticed. It was Cuypers who was the main recipient, with the occasional titbit coming Gosschalk's way, as the other government adviser. The preservation of monuments and old buildings, the spearhead of De Stuers' policy, became in 1876 and for a long while afterwards the almost total monopoly of Cuypers. Meanwhile, it had also become public knowledge that the government advisers were using government funds to promote their own building plans and to finance commissions for their protégés. Hitherto, things had usually been arranged in a more subtle fashion, behind the scenes. At the applied arts exhibition of 1877 in Amsterdam Cuypers' medieval plastercasts were displayed as 'an example of the direction the government will prescribe for art education'. At the end of that year the Ministry of the Interior requested that the provincial authorities submit lists of the names of all the municipal architects; word had it that it was the intention to place them under government supervision. Early in 1878, when De Stuers' proposal to appoint Cuypers as state architect for all educational buildings was rejected, the young and inexperienced Jacob van Lokhorst (1844–1906) was chosen out of seventy-eight applicants for this prestigious position. Van Lokhorst was – of course, a supporter of Cuypers.[55]

At this time the Government Advisory Council for Historic Monuments, which had been in existence for just over three years, was wound up on account of internal conflicts that had hampered it almost since its inception. Vosmaer – one of the government advisers, it will be remembered – under the pen-name Flanor later published critical pieces on the activities of De Stuers and his friends in the columns of the *Nederlandsche Spectator.* Then, in July 1878 the chairman of the MBB wrote an open letter to the minister of the Interior making a passionate plea for artistic freedom:

In almost all the designs and government buildings under construction the 'archaeological school' is manifested in the universal application of a so-called Old Dutch building style, which is hardly fitting for our era and which, on the contrary, makes havoc of any development towards an independent, logical and viable art. Therefore in the true interests of art the MBB is making this serious protest against the one-sided and pernicious school of thought that has been applied in almost all new government building since 1876. In the interests of its architects the MBB makes a no less serious protest against certain actions of Your Excellency's Ministry that are denounced by the great majority of Dutch architects.

The society was referring here to the appointments and decisions that reinforced the 'archaeological school', and was drawing the minister's attention to the unremitting pressure that independent architects were being put under 'to apply its archaeological forms'.[56]

With his article 'An architectural ghost', published in 1877, De Stuers sought publicity for the fourth time. In it, he summarized the criticism of Cuypers and himself in the following way. 'We hear people saying that the government wants public buildings to be built in medieval or Old Dutch style with the secret aim of returning the Dutch people to the Roman Catholic Church, for the reason that the medieval, or Old Dutch, style of building is the style of ultramontanism.'[57] He then explained patiently that, first, there was a difference between medieval and Old Dutch; second, it was not correct to associate the neo-Gothic style with Catholic aspirations. He ended with a word on the present state of the art – which was, he said, abominable. 'The craftsmanship of our stonemasons, our carpenters our cabinetmakers, our smiths and our plumbers is *infinitely* inferior to that of their thirteenth-century predecessors.' This also applied in particular to 'our architects', who, he argued, failed to use building materials in accordance with their characteristics. They used wood to imitate stone and brick to imitate marble, and their buildings were bad. 'I could extend endlessly the list of mistakes that are made

Fig.49
Victor E. L. de
Stuers' sketch for the
reconstruction of the
Binnenhof in The
Hague (1876),
illustrating De Stuers'
dream and the
nightmare of many:
the representation of
the modern Dutch
state by the
ideological notions of
Cuypers and his
followers. The
buildings on the left
were to replace Rose's
Ministry of Colonial
Affairs (Fig.28), the
recurring scapegoat in
De Stuers' polemics.

every day in this respect – mistakes that could have been avoided had the architects concerned taken a carefully look at medieval buildings.' These latter contained 'sound, constructive lessons' and 'they teach us the principles that are still valuable today'. Why? 'Because,' De Stuers concluded, 'many of the circumstances under which architects in the period from the thirteenth to the fifteenth century had to work remain unaltered. The Dutch ground is still as swampy as it was then. The climate has not changed appreciably. Except for iron, the building materials we now have are the same that our ancestors had, and to many of the problems concerning stability and balance the subsequent centuries have provided no new solutions'.

In terms of theory, this argument followed the positivist view generally accepted since Semper and Viollet-le-Duc, the central theme being the construction of a building as the determinant of the architectural form. De Stuers was using the notion of the characteristics of the people, the climate and the soil as an argument for choosing a particular style, another line of reasoning that was not new either. His idea that medieval architecture was the only serious subject of study for a contemporary architecture had in Catholic circles a long-standing tradition going back many decades, both inside and outside the Netherlands.

But new in the article was the tone, the rhetoric reminiscent of the fact that in his earlier days De Stuers had been a lawyer. New also was the debating method, aimed not at convincing the opponent but rather at wrong-footing him, before dealing the knock-out blow. He did not consider seriously the criticism, that had now been voiced for a year and a half, concerning the government's incomprehensible partiality in the granting of commissions, its indifference towards the great majority of architects, its extravagant promotion of an architectural theory that cherished the distant past rather than trying to express the present. De Stuers drew up his own agenda. His first theme was a manoeuvre aimed at representing the criticism as an expression of anti-Catholicism and to subsequently expose it to ridicule: it is 'amusing to demonstrate the nonsense of the antipapists,' he remarked. His second theme was the decline of architecture, not so much the actual problem that everybody who was anybody in the architectural world was talking or writing about, but as a historical process that started immediately after the Middle Ages. His third theme was the most important, considering its far-reaching ramifications. This was De Stuer's cunning trick of reducing medieval architecture to a set of 'sound principles' and of totally avoiding any discussion about the way these principles had materialized.

True, the content of this polemic was far from new. It was precisely consistent with the way in which Thijm used to state his case twenty years earlier: criticism of neo-Gothic architecture was antipapism, therefore intolerant and improper. Moreover, Thijm had written in 1858, 'We Catholics are not concerned with neo-Gothic architecture at all. We want logic only.' And if this logic was found in the Gothic style, 'well, then we are in favour of the Gothic style'.[58]

'Sound principles'

It is certain that De Stuers, Cuypers and Thijm had coordinated their activities, and to many this came across as a Catholic offensive with an ultramontane inspiration. Immediately it became known that Cuypers had been commissioned to build the Rijksmuseum, memories were evoked of the vehement discussions held around 1863 concerning the national monument to 1813 planned for The Hague. The debate at that time had focused on the attempt by Cuypers and his associates to give the representation of the national a medieval – and therefore Catholic – accent. Since then Roman Catholics had intensified their efforts to add an explicit Catholic dimension to Dutch history. It is a fact that in the Netherlands Catholic leaders were true to the spirit of the *Syllabus Errorum* of 1864, adopting an anti-modern, anti-positivist and anti-liberal attitude.

De Stuers, however, was wrong in his assessment: neither his behaviour nor that of Thijm and Cuypers was criticized as a Catholic mission, at least not in public. For that matter, De Stuers' publications of the period reveal no indication of any religious motive. There is no reason to doubt the sincerity of his aims as formulated in *Another Word* – that his concern was to do with 'the revival of art and of the sense of art in the Netherlands'. And the serious architectural critics, for their part, tried their best to avoid any atmosphere of religious dispute. Although Thijm wrote in 1877 that 'the gentlemen of *De Opmerker* contend that the Gothic style coincides with Jesuitism',[59] the frequent and fierce attacks by the journal in fact contained no allusions to the religious denomination that counted De Stuers, Thijm and Cuypers among its members. The truth of the situation, however, was that the Catholics had indeed made medieval architecture Catholic. In 1868 in Utrecht the St Bernulphus Guild, with the archbishop as its patron, had been established in order to 'attain a profound knowledge of the true principles of religious art'. In practice, this study meant a promotion of neo-Gothic architecture that was also publicly proclaimed as a reorientation on the past: 'Archaism is not in violation of the true fundamentals of art, but is *useful* and *necessary*.'[60]

In Germany neo-Gothic architecture had already permeated politics. August Reichensperger, member of parliament and theorist of neo-Gothic Catholic church building, campaigned relentlessly from 1872 and with some success for the application of neo-Gothic architecture in government building.[61]

In other words, it would have been absurd around 1875 not to associate neo-Gothic architecture in the Netherlands with Catholicism. This holds true particularly for Cuypers' work. There was only a negligible fraction of it that had no specific Catholic function. Since the 1850s Thijm had tirelessly propagandized for Cuypers' work because it so emphatically presented the Catholic case to the public. De Stuers, however, with his article 'An architectural ghost', chose a strategy that he would adhere to for decades and that was the opposite of what Thijm had so carefully built up: he decatholicized Cuypers' reputation. He extended his medieval-architecture concept to the sixteenth and early-seventeenth century ('Old Dutch Renaissance'), transformed it into a plea for 'sound principles', and pretended that these were objectively necessary to stop the 'decline' in contemporary architecture.

Truth in architecture for both Thijm and De Stuers was a key concept, but unlike Thijm De Stuers never formulated it in moralistic or idealist terms, but always positivistically: 'The biggest mistake of the period from the beginning of the sixteenth to the nineteenth century was to repudiate the truth that architecture is first and foremost construction, and that any form or ornamentation that cannot be explained by the construction, or is incompatible with proper construction, ought to be condemned' – Viollet-le-Duc's words,[62] the last part of the proposition having been Cuypers' slogan for his entry for the Willem I Museum competition in 1864. With hindsight it may be noted that Cuypers had already started to get across to the public the notion that he was ideologically related to Viollet-le-Duc, and in doing so he also started to disguise his much stronger bonds with the Belgian, German and English Catholic neo-Gothic movements. De Stuers set out to perfect this image. The suggestion that Cuypers' 'sound principles' originated from the atheist Viollet-le-Duc supported his efforts to decatholicize Cuypers' work: 'However great the loathing for the Catholic religion, the partisan spirit should not intrude into matters concerning architecture and particularly those concerning construction itself – as Viollet-le-Duc says, who, please note, is himself most anticlerical.'[63]

The reference to Viollet-le-Duc presented yet another advantage. It gave Cuypers' 'sound principles' a status they would not have gained otherwise. For the suggestion that

he had been looking outside the Netherlands so as to add weight to his ideas implied that the Netherlands was an ideological desert when it came to architectural truth. It is worth noting that the reports of the adjudicators in all competitions that the MBB had organized in the 1840s prove that these sound principles were already being practised within the Dutch architectural community at a time when Viollet-le-Duc had yet to embark on his career and Cuypers was a mere schoolboy.

Both De Stuers and Thijm, then, put all emphasis on the principle of truth but is is not so clear what they, or Cuypers, had in mind with the principle of 'character'. Was it included in their concept of truth, as had been the case with Rose and Leliman? Those two had argued that a building could only be a work of art if it showed truth not just from the perspective of the construction and the layout of the interior and exterior, but also as an expression of its main function. Cuypers had no difficulty with the last aspect as far as his ecclesiastical work was concerned. But it was different with his secular work. This had already become apparent with his design for the national monument to 1813 to commemorate the birth of the modern Dutch state, modelled on the Albert Memorial, the London monument for the commemoration of a deceased prince. Cuypers' winning design for the Rijksmuseum had been harshly criticized because its references to a huge city gate gave a false suggestion of the building's function. In 'An architectural ghost' De Stuers recommended using medieval architecture to teach about structural truth. In so doing, however, he ignored the related questions concerning character. Presumably his main concern was not to argue the case for a sound architecture, but something else. In the late 1860s the idea had arisen that Old Dutch architecture could be used to represent the Dutch identity. Undoubtedly this must have been grist to De Stuers' mill. The design for the Rijksmuseum was the first step towards his 'national architecture': 'Cuypers' design is entirely in the style of the Dutch Renaissance of the late sixteenth and the beginning of the seventeenth century,'[64] he commented.

De Stuers, Thijm and Cuypers had reversed the line of reasoning they had previously followed – that style evolved from the people. They now saw style as something that could be imposed on people. They stressed that nothing had actually changed since the Middle Ages that should have resulted in a completely different architecture. In fact, they implied, the architectural style that they had imposed on the public was not their own discovery, but the restoration of a valuable communal possession that had been neglected out of ignorance. Thijm argued in 1876: 'This [old Dutch] concept … is so pre-eminently suitable for application to genuine Dutch brick building which puts roofs on top of houses, so necessary in our wet country.'[65] The artificiality of this style and character concept could not have been better demonstrated. The steep saddleback roofs of the Old Dutch style were justified by Thijm as a rational answer to the rainy Dutch climate, whereas the history of Dutch architecture proved that over the last few centuries roofs had become increasingly flat on rational – functional and technical – grounds. Equally artificial was Thijm's evocation of 'genuine Dutch' brick building, which around 1875 could only be realized if the required material could be obtained from abroad.

Critics of De Stuers and his acolytes considered character to be the most apposite expression of a building's main function and regarded as quite absurd the proposition that after the Middle Ages nothing had changed in building. On the contrary, they argued, much had changed, and architecture should reflect this. This, too, was a matter of character. *De Opmerker* wrote in 1877: 'Our contemporary men of letters write altogether differently from the medieval writers; our present doctors and lawyers are completely unlike their predecessors. Why, then, must architecture cultivate the Middle Ages and reject the contemporary?'[66]

The 'contemporary' in this context meant the *expression* of the contemporary, and 'character' referred to the creation of an image, the psychological dimension of design that imprints itself on the mind of the observer. The protest against Old Dutch architecture as an expression of the present is most poignantly highlighted by the adjective 'medieval' as used by many a critic of the time. This word often designated a type of behaviour that in the cultured and liberal nineteenth century appeared to be a thing of the past. The working method of De Stuers and his circle, for instance, was referred to as 'medieval oppression', 'medieval tyranny', 'medieval manoeuvring'. Publications appeared on 'the medieval state architecture' that was replete with old-fashioned forms inconsistent with a '*modern* design'.

The word 'medieval', however, could also have a scholarly meaning derived from stylistic analysis. While Old Dutch architecture was described as 'medieval' by some at this time, others called it 'Renaissance'. The background to this was the new direction that historical architectural research had recently taken in Germany. In 1871 the first edition of the nine-volume study by August Ortwein on the 'German Renaissance' was published. In

1872 Wilhelm Lübke's epoch-making book *The History of the German Renaissance*[67] was published, after which the term 'Renaissance' was no longer self-evidently the equivalent of 'Italian Renaissance'. Sixteenth- and seventeenth-century German and Austrian buildings demonstrating the influence of Italian prototypes were no longer regarded as failed attempts but, rather, as works in their own right, expressing their own national aesthetic.

It was only logical that those concerned in the Netherlands with Old Dutch architecture should adopt this view. A remark made by Gosschalk in 1875 illustrates the point. In the search for a contemporary architecture he advocated an alliance with Dutch 'Renaissance', referring here to the Chancellery in Leeuwarden (1566–71) and the Butchers Guild Hall in Haarlem (1602–3), two buildings that had previously been classified as 'Old Dutch'. Cuypers' design for the Rijksmuseum was considered by the jury to be 'entirely in harmony with the Dutch Renaissance of the late sixteenth and early seventeenth centuries', the period that until recently had been treated as the preserve of 'Old Dutch' architecture.[68] Naturally, De Stuers used to his advantage the fact that what had always been referred to as 'Old Dutch' could now be labelled 'Renaissance'. The message was that neither the government nor Cuypers had anything to do with the Middle Ages; they were promoting Dutch Renaissance architecture. De Stuers, an outstanding legal brain, knew the importance of the right formulation.

In 1878 *De Opmerker* reported that Cuypers allegedly redid his 'Dutch Renaissance' design for the Rijksmuseum in order to make it look 'medieval' – this is confirmed by surviving drawings, which show the application of ornamental masonry after medieval examples, and more verticals in the façade – characteristics that would remain in the final design (1880). The designs for the interior of this time also contained an abundance of medieval vaults (see Fig. 52).

An official smokescreen

The controversy over the government preferring Old Dutch architecture in general (or just Cuypers' architectural concept in particular) was in fact a dispute between two deaf parties. One emphasized the sound principles; the other, not wishing to discuss these principles since they seemed self-explanatory, criticized the historical forms that were their result. The weak point in the argument of the first party remained, however, that regardless of how logical the principles in themselves were, it could still not be logically explained why these principles had to result exclusively in medieval or sixteenth-century forms. Instead of

Fig.50
Eugen Heinrich
Gugel's students'
society Minerva Club,
Leiden (1874–5).
Unlike the Hall of the
Arts and Sciences at
The Hague (Fig.44),
here Gugel chose
the Old Dutch
interpretation of the
Renaissance, of which
a good example was
located near the Club
– Leiden Town Hall
(architect Lieven de
Key, 1594).

Fig.51
Oud-Wassenaar
Castle, Wassenaar
(1876–9), by
Constantijn Muysken:
a picturesque country
house on a vast estate
near The Hague. The
composition and
detailing show the
affluence of the
'national' architecture
of the Dutch Golden
Age as exemplified,
for instance, in the
Butchers' Guild Hall
at Haarlem (Figs 22
and 23).

explanations, De Stuers and Thijm resorted to statements without any proof. 'It is an all too familiar fact that the rational principles of architecture are preferably expressed in the exterior of the twelfth century, and this is confirmed by the buildings of many outstanding architects both outside and inside the Netherlands, including Mr Cuypers.'[69]

There was one outstanding architect from outside the Netherlands who produced many works on the basis of what could be called 'sound principles'. However, this expert was assiduously ignored by De Stuers and Thijm, perhaps on account of the fact that he reached the opposite conclusions from those same principles. His name was Gottfried Semper. Semper admired the Gothic style but considered it 'played out', 'finished', in the sense that all its possibilities had been endlessly investigated in the past and put into practice. He considered the neo-Gothic movement that revelled so passionately in the Middle Ages as *restorative*, and this was not intended as a compliment. The

word evoked a mentality, not unconnected with the somewhat regressive architectural ideology of De Stuers, Cuypers and Thijm, in particular their thinking about the present as a period of decline and the belief that the world would become a better place when the forms and symbols of a glorified past were once more accepted.

It may come as no surprise that De Stuers did not like the idea of becoming known as regressive, and therefore covered his tracks in advance. As a maxim for his article 'an architectural ghost' he quoted Viollet-le-Duc (in French): 'I am not one of those who despair of the present and are always looking back at the past. The past is gone, but it must be carefully and honestly investigated and heeded, not with the aim of reviving it but so as to get to know it in order to make use of it.'[70]

De Stuers and Thijm avoided stating in so many words that contemporary architecture and its design had to refer to the here and now rather than to a distant past. Instead,

Fig. 52
P. J. H. Cuypers'
Rijksmuseum,
Amsterdam. The first
impression that the
visitor gets of its
interior is the
fragmented space of
the main entrance; on
the left are the stairs
to the picture
galleries, on the right
the passage leading to
the print gallery and
the basement. Here
and in the rest of the
interior Cuypers
unreservedly showed
his love for medieval
architecture and
its inseparable
connotation: the unity
of Church and state.

they started a discussion about a nonexistent problem. They pretended architecture had two options: their 'sound principles', or exhausted classicism. They turned against imaginary opponents who, according to them, wanted to create a classicist architecture. It was urgent, De Stuers wrote, that 'our architects' take note of medieval architecture, because until recently architecture in the Netherlands had been 'so narrowly one-sided … , indeed, so bemused, so steeped in the misconception that there was nothing outside Vignola's five orders'.[71] It can hardly be imagined that De Stuers actually meant what he wrote. His claim, however, was no accident. His publications provide numerous comparable examples. And it is worth noting that in 1880 Cuypers put the final touches to the Roman Catholic Church of St Agatha and St Barbara in Oudenbosch (1867–80), a small copy of St Peter's in Rome, the greatest classicist building on earth.

It is remarkable, but from a psychological perspective perhaps not incomprehensible, that De Stuers and Thijm persisted in flogging the dead horse that classicism had become, rather than engaging in a polemic with the advocates of the liberal, contemporary, styleless architecture. They railed most vehemently against those features of classicism that were the essence of their own view, thereby distracting attention from it. However, they did not always succeed in this. It was not so long ago, wrote *De Opmerker* in 1876, that old architects adored Vignola – 'No matter the effort required, columns and pilasters simply had to be dragged in.' But, 'is it any different in our time with those to whom medieval architecture means everything?' Indeed it would seem that De Stuers, Thijm and Cuypers substituted the authority of the medieval church for the supremacy of the Greek temple, with Viollet-le-Duc's *Dictionnaire* as their Bible instead of the order books of Vignola. Already in 1858 Thijm had written, 'We totally reject any kind of Gothic style without rules. We

Fig. 53
Johan F. Metzelaar's District Court at Tiel (1879–82). Metzelaar, the state architect for the Ministry of Justice, was a prominent opponent of the 'official style'. In his designs for legal buildings, he sought a 'modern' – that is, eclectic – interpretation of the picturesque Old Dutch architecture.

recognize, respect, and will do our best to maintain no fewer than *three* complete systems of laws.'[72] He worked these out in the eighteen principles that were mentioned in Chapter 3.

The rules and systems, the orthodoxy of Thijm and De Stuers, became manifest in their propaganda and in the uniform opinions of Cuypers' supporters which his critics called 'one-sided'. Given these supporters and their one-sidedness, it is fascinating that De Stuers and Cuypers took Viollet-le-Duc for their model – a man who had spent his whole life fighting the École des Beaux-Arts' state monopoly of the arts, which deprived students of their artistic freedom and taught them to produce the

architecture that the authorities required.[73] And even worse, De Stuers' circle honoured Viollet-le-Duc for his resistance to state architecture in terms that would almost make one forget how dear the practice of state control was to themselves: 'He had to put up a fierce fight against the École and its supporters, the pillars of the classical and Italian style that has almost become official in France. Viollet-le-Duc's aspiration was to make clear that this stultifying school had to give way to the study of medieval architecture.'[74]

And so De Stuers, Thijm and Cuypers started to work on an architectural style for the Netherlands, an architecture with an artistic Bible, with a dogmatism, an orthodoxy and a following forever on the qui vive in a continuous fight against the 'decline'. In Chapter 3 the views of Cuypers and Thijm were seen as an offshoot of classicist architectural theory – not only because their ideas on neo-Gothic architecture possessed an objective aesthetics, but also because they implied that architecture was a means to a higher transcendental reality, the pursuit of an ideal beauty and truth embedded in metaphysics. And although these defendants of neo-Gothic architecture turned against the classicist (that is, the Italian Renaissance) *concept of form*, it was from classicism that they took their views of the role of architecture in society and the doctrinal nature of architectural theory, giving it a vigorous new life.

This ambiguity may explain why De Stuers and Thijm turned so violently against classicism while ignoring eclecticism, the one architectural concept that did not regard 'style' as a real problem and that considered architecture autonomous, not means to a higher goal but an expression of individual freedom and creativity. The fight that De Stuers, Thijm and Cuypers engaged in was not a fight against the totally unknown. On one level it was an Oedipus conflict – a fight to kill the father in order to gain the mother – architecture – and control.

Notes

1. T. van Westrheene 1869, 11 (speech delivered in 1867).
2. 'Onze oudheid-manie' ('Our passion for antiquity'), *De Opmerker* 11 no. 30, 23.7.1876.
3. W. N. Rose 1871a, 75.
4. J. H. Leliman 1871, 1860a.
5. Germany: Harry F. Mallgrave, Eleftherios Ikonomou 1994, 1–85.
6. Gottfried Semper 1860–3, I, xiv–xv.
7. H. P. Vogel 1872, my citation from the second edition (1888), 153 (truth in theory) 12 (truth in practice). Reaction: 'Architectonische waarheid' ('Architectural truth'), *De Opmerker* 7 no. 31, 3.8.1872.
8. *De Opmerker* 11 no. 16, 16.4.1876.
9. J. H. Leliman 1870a, 72.
10. *De Opmerker* 10 no. 10, 7.3.1875.
11. J. H. Leliman 1871, 91–2.
12. 'Een vraagbaak' ('An encyclopedia'), *De Opmerker* 12 no. 38, 23.9.1877.
13. 'Hedendaagsche bouwkunst' ('Contemporary architecture'), *De Opmerker* 11 no. 15, 9.4.1876.
14. J. H. Leliman 1870b.
15. *De Opmerker* 11 no. 8, 20.2.1876.
16. S. E. W. Roorda van Eysinga 1869.
17. I. Gosschalk 1868, 182; I. Gosschalk 1871, 173 and 163.
18. Nicolaus Pevsner 1972, 265 already pointed out that although Semper was often referred to as a materialist, his categorical denial in *Style in the Technical and Structural Arts* II, 249 ('the writer fundamentally disagrees with modern materialism in art') speaks against this. Harry F. Mallgrave and Eleftherios Ikonomou 1994, 32 also consider the view that Semper's theory is a positivist theory to be a misconception. For an extensive discussion on this matter: Harry F. Mallgrave 1996, 370–81.
19. Eugène-Emmanuel Viollet-le-Duc 1854–68, headword 'proportion': 'les rapports entre le tout et les parties, rapports logiques,

nécessaires, et tels qu'ils satisfassent en même temps la raison et les yeux'. See also Eugène-Emmanuel Viollet-le-Duc 1863–72, ninth Discourse.
20. W. N. Rose 1871b.
21. W. N. Rose 1871c, 77–8.
22. J. van Vloten 1871, 2nd edn, vi.
23. Müller et al. 1878, 139.
24. Anonymous 1870.
25. C. W. Opzoomer 1875, 34.
26. Allard Pierson 1868, 9, 32, 49, 55, 56.
27. For example, by J. W. Schaap 1877.
28. Carel Vosmaer 1879, 232 ('Faust and Helena').
29. Carel Vosmaer 1856, 141.
30. Müller et al. 1878, 139.
31. 'Het vijf en twintigjarig bestaan der afdeeling Amsterdam van de Maatschappij tot Bevordering der Bouwkunst' ('The twenty-fifth anniversary of the Amsterdam branch of the Maatschappij tot Bevordering der Bouwkunst', *De Opmerker* 12 no. 33, 19.8.1877.
32. J. R. de Kruyff 1876, 3.
33. Gottfried Semper 1966 (reprint of 1852 edn). The English annotated translation: Harry F. Mallgrave, Wolfgang Herrmann 1989.
34. Gottfried Semper 1966, 33–4; Harry F. Mallgrave, Wolfgang Herrmann 1989, 135–6.
35. According to the second edition, Gottfried Semper 1878–9, I, xiii; the passage in the 1860–3 edn (I, xii) is less sharp in tone.
36. I. Gosschalk 1867, 174.
37. J. R. de Kruyff 1876, 25.
38. J. R. de Kruyff 1876, 30. Applied arts becoming detached from architecture: Gottfried Semper 1860–3, II, 344–5.
39. J. R. de Kruyff 1876, 44; 54–5; 57–9.
40. Gottfried Semper 1860–3, I, xiii.
41. Adi Martis 1990, 107.
42. Gottfried Semper 1860–3, I, xii–xiv.
43. J. R. de Kruyff 1876, 48.
44. Carel Vosmaer 1861b, 7.
45. 'Iets over bouwkunst. I' ('A word about architecture. I') *De Opmerker* 10 no. 29, 18.7.1875, and part II in *De Opmerker* 10 no. 31, 1.8.1875.
46. State building campaigns in Paris: David Van Zanten 1994; in London: M. H. Port 1995; the Vienna Ringstrasse: R. Wagner-Rieger (ed.) 1969–81.
47. Victor de Stuers 1875, 69.
48. Victor de Stuers 1875, 45, 42.
49. 'Onze bouwkunst and de Rijkscommissie van adviseurs voor historische gebouwen' ('Our architecture and the Government Advisory Council for Historic Monuments'), *De Opmerker* 11 no. 13, 26.3.1876.
50. J. H. Leliman 1871, 92.
51. 'De prijsvraag van het nieuwe Rijksmuseum' ('The contest for the new Rijksmuseum'), *De Opmerker* 11 no. 31, 30.7.1876.
52. Central Station: Aart Oxenaar 1989. The commission and building of the Rijksmuseum: Thomas H. von der Dunk 1994a.
53. 'Het nieuwe Justitie-gebouw en verdere staatsgebouwen te 's-Hage' ('The New Ministry of Justice Building and other government buildings in The Hague'), *De Opmerker* 12 no. 11, 18.3.1877.
54. 'Logica' ('Logic'), *De Opmerker* 12 no. 45, 11.11.1877.
55. For Jacob van Lokhorst: Paul T. E. E. Rosenberg 1995a.
56. 'Amsterdam', *De Opmerker* 13 no. 29, 20.7.1878.
57. Victor de Stuers 1877, 539.
58. J. A. Alberdingk Thijm 1858a, 180.
59. Hein Strijder 1877.
60. *Het Gildeboek* I (1873), 158.
61. Michael J. Lewis 1993, 6 and 246–52; C. Bernheiden 1992, 227–8.
62. Victor de Stuers 1877, 539.
63. Victor de Stuers 1877, 548.

64. 'Rapport over de plannen voor een Rijks Museumgebouw' ('Report on the plans for a National Museum'), *Nederlandsche Kunstbode* 4 no. 8, 25.4.1877, 62.

65. A. Th. 1876, 601.

66. *De Opmerker* 12 no. 5, 4.2.1877.

67. For the nineteenth-century re-evaluation of the German Renaissance: G. Ulrich Grossmann 1992.

68. I. Gosschalk 1876 (written in May 1875), 147–8 and 'Rapport over de plannen voor een Rijks Museumgebouw' ('Report on the plans for a new National Museum'), *Nederlandsche Kunstbode* 4 no. 8, 25.4.1877, 62.

69. Th. van Herstelle [J. A. Alberdingk Thijm] 1869, 386.

70. Victor de Stuers 1877, 521: 'Je ne suis pas de ceux qui désespèrent du présent et jettent un regard vers le passé. Le passé est passé, mais il faut le fouiller avec soin, avec sincérité, s'attacher non pas à la faire revivre, mais à la connaître, pour s'en servir. Viollet-le-Duc'.

71. Victor de Stuers 1877, 541.

72. J. A. Alberdingk Thijm 1858a, 179.

73. See, for example, Eugène-Emmanuel Viollet-le-Duc 1863–72, II, 164 and 213.

74. *Nederlandsche Kunstbode* 1 no. 32, 25.10.1879, 255.

6

The Rules of Art in the Market-place

An 'official style' by stealth

Compared with the previous decade the 1870s were, on the face of it, a period of decline and stagnation in Dutch architectural theory; a period in which, for the architect, the world was changing rapidly and profoundly, while no theoretical renewal took place and artistic authority within and outside of the profession was rapidly being eroded. As we have seen, it became customary to reduce architectural theory to slogans and to give up long-held intellectual traditions. The 70s turned out to be, beneath the surface, the transition from eighteenth-century to twentieth-century conceptions of architecture, thus preparing for Modernism, which would see the building's construction as the core of its style, in which functionality and rationality in design were the main determinants of beauty. With hindsight we can pinpoint this shift. But in the 1870s it was hardly noticeable; for the architect, this subtle yet fundamental change was overshadowed by the everyday hustle and bustle, by the success of the numerous 'unqualified' persons posing as architects, and by the government's disregard for real architects and its introduction, by means of tricks and machinations, of a very particular 'official style'. The idyll of a united architectural fraternity – if it had ever existed – was over.

The small group dedicated to creating the official style aroused frustration and rancour, resulting in violent arguments in the 80s as well, as we shall see. In consequence, this decade has been portrayed in recent Dutch historiography as a period of faction, of conflict between Cuypers' party, with their 'sound principles', and the rest. What has happened here is that this historiography has adopted the conflict model of De Stuers. But no bipolar argument will be found in the following chapters, for there are too many facts, too many details, that do not fit that pattern.

By the beginning of the 80s *De Opmerker* had accepted the by then strong position of Cuypers as a fait accompli and now refrained from the kind of blistering tirade that it had published so often over the past years. In 1882 De Stuers and Thijm, with 'the loud applause' of those present, were appointed honorary members of the other prestigious architectural organization, Architectura et Amicitia, that had been established in order to give its young members more room for manoeuvre than they would have been permitted by the MBB. Cuypers had been a committee member of the MBB since 1870, and an honorary member of A et A since 1876. In 1881 he also joined the editorial staff of the *Bouwkundig Weekblad* (Architectural Weekly), the journal established that year by the MBB. All this hardly gives the impression of an irreconcilable conflict between Cuypers and the rest, but, rather, of a certain tolerance, a willingness to accommodate the various ideas and views, no matter how extreme. Cuypers was now receiving the respect he deserved on the basis of his talent and success as demonstrated in the many Catholic churches he had designed.

This recognition, however, did not include much appreciation of his *views* on architecture, which were sometimes rejected outright. But neither did this imply a split, or conflict, between two parties. On the contrary, there was a wide variety of views on architecture – which, as one Rotterdam architect interpreted it, was merely a reflection of the spirit of the times: 'A period such as we are living in, one of transition and conflict over material matters, and which in every part of society is characterized by turbulence, friction and opposition, cannot but manifest itself as turbulent in architecture too.'[1] Architectural criticism reflected this same diversity. The literary journal *De Portefeuille* (The Portfolio), in an article called 'Art and criticism', stated in 1889: 'among architects themselves, there are opposing views on the direction in which architecture is going. Furthermore, we must recognize that it is very difficult, when so many are involved, to achieve general acceptance of one set of opinions regarding their art.'[2] Indeed, it was only in the small circle around Cuypers that the pursuit of uniform views was cultivated.

Architectural colleges maintained a certain degree of neutrality, which meant that they represented the voice of the vast majority. In 1880 Gugel, then a professor at Delft Polytechnic, introduced his four-volume *Architectural Morphology* (1880–8). It included, he announced, as well as examples from the Renaissance – 'the style that is acknowledged and praised almost universally as the foundation of our contemporary architecture and of our industrial art' – characteristic elements from the 'medieval-romantic style … In choosing his examples, the author has tried to be as objective as possible and, in order to avoid any one-sided scholastic doctrine, has taken care to represent all the widely varying types and characteristics.' In the second, much enlarged, edition of his *History of Styles in the Main Architectural Periods* (1886), he emphasized his respect for the artistic skills of Cuypers, 'who, as the recognized head of the romantic school, has for a long time exerted a far-reaching influence. Endowed as he is with many outstanding talents … Cuypers has undeniably acquired a place of honour among the contemporary representatives of the Gothic style.'[3]

In his final paragraphs, Gugel ventured a few remarks on the government's architecture policy. Here, too, he tried to remain objective and to voice the general professional opinion. Official architecture, he wrote, had been met with little sympathy or interest: 'Received with limited enthusiasm, attacked and condemned by many for being religious, or realistic and coarse, its works have not exerted the influence on architects or on the general public that might have been expected had the contrast with the general view been less glaring.' 'The general view' was the mainstream of the 80s, the architecture that sought alliance with the Dutch Renaissance.

In 1886 it was indeed possible for Gugel and his contemporaries to reassess the 'official style'. The first major projects that had started in the 70s had now been completed – the Ministry of Justice Building, the Rijksmuseum, Van Lokhorst's first works. As we shall see later, Gugel was right: the results did not accord with the high aspirations with which the projects had been executed. They did not exert the 'sound', rejuvenating influence on Dutch architecture that De Stuers had so fervently predicted. After the opening of the Rijksmusem in 1885, it was clear that the 'official style' existed only because it was so heavily protected and subsidized. It was an artificial phenomenon and one that irritated many, but it was only one of a number of problems that architects had to face in the 80s.

Many minds, many views

The architect August van Delden's background helped him to put things in perspective. He had trained at the Polytechnic University of Zürich – the academic home base of Gottfried Semper – in Stuttgart and Berlin, and in Paris at the École des Beaux-Arts. In 1881 he published an article entitled 'An investigation into the causes of the struggle for

Dutch architecture', which gives us one of many indications that the central theme of those years was not some conflict between two parties. 'The fierce battle that we are now witnessing in the arena of our national architecture', said Van Delden, was a great intellectual struggle to create order in these hectic modern times; there was a sense of 'franticness now taking possession of everybody', in which everything, as soon as it was made, had immediately to be replaced by something new, in which merciless competition discouraged thoroughness in favour of skimping and in which 'inner truth must give way to outward appearances'. It was very difficult to establish 'truth' in these situations. 'Probably no other era has been as confusing. It would be hard to find two people who share the same fundamental principles on vital questions or on society.'

Van Delden suggested that the cause of this confusion was to be found in the great revolutions of the eighteenth century, breaking the continuity between past and present. It seemed to him that the nineteenth century had attempted artificially to restore this continuity through the concept of 'history'. In art, this resulted in a 'historical school' which was supported by a host of influential scholars. Far from taking topical issues as its starting point, this school wanted to force upon society the alien cultures and ways of thinking of the past – so it could not be expected to last long. The ideals on which the historical school was based were those of insiders 'who inhabit the higher spheres, far removed from where most of our present society live and feel'. This analysis was not unlike what Semper had written on the subject twenty years earlier.[4]

Van Delden, however, introduced a new element. He noted that any given view of history was bound to bear the stamp of the holder of that view. In other words, the historical school was not only regressive, it was essentially subjective. But if the past could not provide a useful source for the concept of contemporary beauty, what direction could beauty take? Van Delden provided only a few broad hints. Beauty could be conceived, he said, by adopting some aesthetic dogma or, alternatively, by studying the laws of nature. Here, too, Van Delden followed Semper, by choosing the second option, but once again he emphasized the subjective element. By studying nature, the artist would arrive at a personal solution to the question of how 'disparate reality can be united into one common picture'.

It is a pity that Van Delden did not develop his views any further – although he had announced his article as the first of a series, the rest failed to materialize. Perhaps his opinions on the historical school caused a clash with his then employer, Cuypers. The article shows a number of

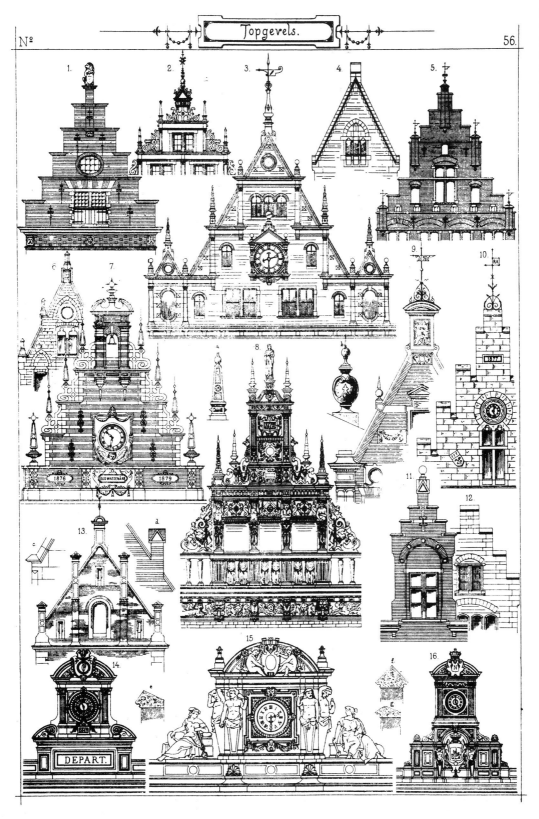

Fig. 54
'Gable-ends',
illustration 56 from
the first volume of
Gugel's *Architectural
Morphology* (1880–4),
an important
illustrated textbook.

interesting views that were to become important themes in Dutch art and culture of the 80s:

1. The essentially *subjective* aspect of architecture and architectonic beauty.
2. The notion that the historical school existed on a far higher plane than most of society – indeed, in the 90s, its artificiality would precipitate its end.
3. The notion that the artist was able to unite 'disparate reality' in one picture – an idea that evokes the process of *artistic abstraction* that was to develop immediately after the historical school's retreat, and with spectacular consequences.

In the eyes of their contemporaries, Dutch architects' views now started to diverge more than ever before. They also demonstrated remarkable contradictions. Many in the profession vehemently condemned the manifestations of contemporary architecture, while at least as many experienced this period as one of restoration and architectural prosperity. Adriaan Willem Weissman (1858–1923) belonged to the first category. In 1881 he wrote, 'our art of building is still so desperately *commonplace* that one comes across a decent example only sporadically'. However, 'fortunately in our country most buildings from the second half of the nineteenth century have been so badly built that subsequent generations will be forced to pull them down. Even though it may be possible to discern a better spirit at work in a number of more recent buildings, for the most part the field of architecture in the Netherlands still lies fallow.'[5] Harsh words, coming from a twenty-three-year-old, but they bear the freshness of a new generation that spoke plainly and that was to express itself emphatically in this decade. And Weissman was not alone in his opinion. In 1884, an Architectura et Amicitia member aired similar feelings, saying that the development of a new architecture was being cramped by the domination of historic architecture: 'Is this the consequence of our spiritual poverty, which renders us incapable of creating a nineteenth-century style?' he asked. Another wrote that he considered the inept knocking together of disparate themes as characteristic of a nineteenth-century building.[6]

Critical views such as these were based on the notion of style as defined by Quatremère de Quincy – that style reflected the character of a people, its customs and traditions, and its climate. Johannes J. van Nieukerken (1854–1913), for example, argued that the eighteenth and nineteenth centuries had produced more 'nonsense' in architecture than ever before, 'but no other era was so strongly characterized by vanity, weariness of life or excessive *joie de vivre*'. L. M. Moolenaar, a colleague from Groningen, commented that, just as many people talked of an ailing society, 'so our contemporary architecture is also ailing'. Why was it that the past century had produced no architecture of its own? Not because architects had spent too little time studying, but because society had no overarching ideal or uniform philosophy of life – 'almost any ideal or elevated emotion is frustrated as a result of vanity or material interest'. 'In past times there was a relative tranquillity due to which certain architectural forms were able to permeate everywhere, resulting in new stylistic periods,' noted the architect J. B. Jager. 'Now it is a different situation altogether.' A building that now required several years to materialize was old-fashioned before it was finished, so rapidly did architectural concepts change.[7]

Others found their own era problematical, but accepted it as an inevitable stage that heralded a new style. However, their notion of a 'transitional period' was not new. Already around 1845, when classicism was losing its artistic monopoly, the search for an alternative had started and architects had acknowledged that they were living in a transition. Now, in the 80s, there were signs that the new age was perhaps not so distant. Some young architects may have been infected by contemporaries of theirs – the '*Tachtigers*', or '80s' generation' – who had established a new literature course; and similarly in painting, there was now the Hague School (later in this chapter we shall investigate this issue in more detail). The architect Willem Kromhout (1864–1940), aged twenty-three, in 1887 referred obliquely to 'the forthcoming golden age' when it would be possible to speak of the age's 'own style'. How serious he was on this subject is not clear. The thirty-year-old Hendrik Petrus Berlage, still completely unaware of the future role he was to play, had been less optimistic the previous year: 'The modern age is still searching for its own style, and it will probably take another hundred years before a style has come into being that, from a historical perspective, can be greeted as an expression of the new civilization.'[8] And then there were those architects who just did not care whether or not there was a style, and who were interested in more earthly pursuits, such as success.

In the international competition for the new Stock Exchange in Amsterdam in 1884, the international panel of adjudicators judged the Dutch entrants favourably: 'the results of the competition have heartened many in that this demonstrates that Dutch architects measure up to their colleagues from neighbouring countries – and yet many feared they would not'.[9] Two years later, at the international Jubilee Exhibition in Berlin, the Dutch reporter was very confident: 'The many Amsterdam façades are getting a lot of

attention from colleagues, and all the entries show the sound ideas now being adopted in our country – that is to say, truth and honesty in the art of building, something that the Berlin architects might well learn from, with their façades covered from top to bottom with stucco ornaments.'

Subjectivity

Other voices expressing contentment and optimism about the present state of Dutch architecture confirmed that Van Delden was right; the past – in particular the recent past – was now viewed more subjectively. In many contemporary texts the 80s' architecture is described as having 'awakened from its sleep of death', or as in some other way resurrected. In earlier decades Rose, Vosmaer, Gugel and Leliman had also contended at one time or another that architecture was going through a period of revival; but now, the view that after a serious decline art was flourishing again became a commonplace.

Weissman, a great enthusiast for the Renaissance period, ascribed the new flowering to the new means of studying Renaissance buildings, which had greatly improved since 1875. Leliman attributed the 'resurrection' to the improved functionality of buildings, their improved appearance, and the increasing inventiveness of designers. He dated the start of this development (without explaining it) to around 1830 – the revolutionary year when Labrouste had opened his Paris atelier – and on another occasion to around 1850, the year he himself made his first appearance on the architectural scene. In 1882 the MBB celebrated its fortieth anniversary, claiming that it was the society itself that had put an end to mindless classicism and had initiated architecture's revival. In 1880 Architectura et Amicitia was twenty-five years old. One of its founders, Hugo Vogel, claimed that the formation of A et A was the real beginning of greater artistic freedom, of a new flourishing, and one that happened outside the confines of the MBB, whose

Fig.55
Nautical Training College, Amsterdam (1878–80), by Willem Springer and Jan L. Springer.

Fig. 56
Isaac Gosschalk's
Panorama Building,
Amsterdam (1880).
The design's
character exemplified
the international
vogue for modern
big-city
entertainment: cafés
and restaurants as
well as buildings
experimenting with
the new mass media –
as here, with the
panorama.

Fig. 56
Isaac Gosschalk's
Panorama Building,
Amsterdam (1880).
The design's
character exemplified
the international
vogue for modern
big-city
entertainment: cafés
and restaurants as
well as buildings
experimenting with
the new mass media –
as here, with the
panorama.

'senior members ... were still permeated with the classicist tradition'. Younger members of A et A were willing three years later to concede that already round about 1855 voices were 'occasionally heard trying to jolt the sleeping awake', but the real resurrection had started only recently, they insisted. In 1889, the members of the organization praised their popular chairman Jan Springer for having pioneered, with his young band, against enormous odds, the quest for the new Dutch architecture, when the art of architecture was just starting to emerge 'from the days of decline and bad taste'.

De Stuers, of course, attributed the 'resurrection' to himself alone. In 1877 in his article 'An architectural ghost', he had pointed out the terrible decline of contemporary architecture so as to legitimize the introduction of his own 'sound principles'. A kindred spirit described him four years later as a 'powerful champion of the appreciation of art, who has given it a new impetus' thanks to which there were now indications everywhere

'that our art has risen from its sleep'. Another claimed that the arts had been 'in the greatest danger' until De Stuers and the Government Advisory Council for Historic Monuments had come to the rescue in 1874.[10] Dormant art, bad taste – apparently, these were now things of the past. Classicism was the general designation for everything that architects were vigorously jettisoning: namely, lack of spirit, servility, *decline*.

A flourishing economy? The architect-businessman

The economic information available from the period demonstrates how precarious it is to ascribe the flourishing of architecture to individual actions or to a particular architects' association. The economic history of nineteenth-century Dutch housing shows a turbulent building trade, extremely sensitive to economic trends, and with frequent booms and depressions. The year 1859 had seen the beginning of a very sharp rise in production which lasted until 1863, to be followed by an even sharper fall.

Fig.57–8
A shopping arcade, The Hague (1882–5), by H. Wesstra and J. C. van der Wijk. Originally the arcade consisted of two covered shopping streets with a roundabout in the middle; in 1928 a third street was added. The architectural details, including motifs from the latest French Renaissance revival, gave it its international commercial character.

Four years later the low point was reached. Then came another high, which in 1873 again turned into a low. In 1876 – the year of triumph for Cuypers and the start of the young band of A et A – this low came to an end and another period of reflation started, to reach a higher peak than ever. Then, in 1882, the market collapsed. The recession lasted until 1886 when, as rapidly as before a new boom began which in 1889/90 created a new production record – to be followed immediately by a depression.

During these brief but frequent periods of boom and bust the number of skilled craftsmen in the specific building professions increased – by 40 per cent between 1859 and 1889 – despite the years of high unemployment.[11] Recent studies have also shown that purchasing power strongly increased in the mid-60s. This increase was a steady trend that disregarded the many highs and lows of the building trade, and it was also reflected in the continual rise of the average rental value of houses – substantial in the 50s and 60s, and booming in the 70s and 80s.[12] The

general trend was clear. If one looked back in 1889, despite the periods of unemployment one could see a growing upward movement over the past twenty-five years. There was more work, there were more workers, and wages had steadily increased. Here indeed, it seemed, was a flourishing economy.

But this prosperity also had its down side. As we saw in Chapter 5, opportunities for profit in the building trade attracted people who had never ventured there before, people for whom money came first, and who were not in any way interested in architecture. These were speculators, 'cowboys', suppliers of faulty and imitation building materials, moneylenders and adventurers, who passed on their risks to bona fide suppliers and buyers. Pleasure at the awakening of architecture from its deathlike sleep was marred by the presence of a permanent cloud – namely, the realization that all these upstart unqualified builders were calling the tune. In 1885 an anonymous commentator-architect described the building scene in The Hague, then

rapidly expanding, as rife with incompetent designers, barterers of inferior materials, moneylenders, speculators and their hangers-on, their fortunes gleaned from the bankruptcies of others. The real architect was the worst off of all in this arrangement. He had the option of holding on to his 'pure artistic attitude' – with predictable results – or of becoming a speculator-entrepreneur. 'In order to do this,' reported *De Opmerker*, 'he must leave his office and search high and low for what is said to be "lacking", devise projects for panoramas, shopping arcades, seaside hotels et cetera, for all of which it is essential to have a business sense, to be able to do the necessary financial calculations.' The profession of architect had thus reached a 'very dubious state'. 'It is no longer sufficient to be a competent artist, but one must be first and foremost a smart businessman, talker and writer.'[13] Could it be that the author was thinking of the contractor cum property developer cum architect W. Doon from The Hague, who in 1879 had developed and realized a very successful idea with his Hotel Central in that city?

It was essential to be a smart businessman. It is not sufficient to note this commercial element only in order to contrast to advantage the 'pure artistic attitude': the fact was that the need for the architect to be also an entrepreneur was to drastically influence the practical application of architectural theory. The commercialization of the architecture profession played a key role in the 80s – far more important than in the 70s – in issues concerning the nature and status of architecture. If the architects themselves did not always articulate this, there was always someone else who would. As Leliman wrote in 1884, 'The public is merciless, often severe in its judgement, slow to absorb information and, to cap it all, always tends to see the profession of architect as a commercial activity.[14]

In the architectural community itself, not everyone found this commercial aspect so objectionable. This became apparent, for example in 1882, when the Amsterdam branch of the Society for the Advancement of the Art of Building (the MBB) were discussing how to display their designs at the forthcoming Colonial Exhibition – with the

Fig.60
The Kurhaus,
Scheveningen
(1884–5, destroyed by
fire in 1886 and
rebuilt in 1887), by
Johann F. Henkenhaf
and Friedrich Ebert.
The two German
architect-
entrepreneurs built
this 'Grand Hotel'
with large party and
concert rooms to
appeal to the beau
monde, in the main
seaside resort of the
Netherlands, a suburb
of The Hague.

fine arts or with the commercial designs? Some were in favour of 'including architecture among the commodities'.[15] Six years later an architect in Groningen noted that, although architects were spending more time than ever studying their chosen subject, 'you notice that the products of architecture are increasingly regarded as a kind of commodity, and even among architects a certain business sense had developed'. In Arnhem, one observer concluded about the same time that young architects had no answer for 'a public that is imbued with the practical spirit of the age and is always asking, what good is it to me? Is it surprising that some younger people throw the excess artistic baggage overboard and become *businessmen*, and others, in order to satisfy their aspirations at least in part, merely follow architectural fashion?'[16]

But it was certainly not only the young who experienced the boundary between artistic calling and commerce as somewhat blurred. Older architects, in particular, were commercially active during the building booms. A motley assortment, they included people such as J. van Lith the younger (1835–88), 'architect and building entrepreneur in The Hague', and the Amsterdam architect-entrepreneur Jan de Haan (1845–1920), grey figures who were hardly ever in the public eye. Others, of course were very much in the limelight, such as the German architect Johann Friedrich Henkenhaf (1848–1908), one of the designers of the famous Kurhaus Hotel at Scheveningen (1884–7), who was to be the developer, the architect and the owner of the luxurious Victoria Hotel (1890) opposite the Central Station in Amsterdam. There were other prominent men, champions of the art of building, who were much involved in commerce, such as P. J. H. Cuypers himself who as a speculator was involved in the construction of mansions in Amsterdam's Vondelstraat.[17]

Fashion

The same observer from Arnhem bracketed business sense with fashion. L. M. Moolenaar, too, saw the commercial pull of fashion as a great threat to architecture. 'The amazing force of fashion, which generates more power than all the steam engines in the world put together, dominates every individual expression of artistic feeling and finds followers not least amongst architects. Some are even driven by this force without being aware of it.' An architect from Leiden observed in 1887 that three factors were changing the course of architecture: the widespread distribution of images of foreign architecture, the reduced price of certain building materials, and the extent to which authoritative architects were promoted as models. There was also a more subtle factor: 'The architect who resists the current trend risks being accused of a lack of taste.'[18]

Such comments illustrate how thoroughly ideas on architecture had changed over the last ten or fifteen years. Fashion, which in the 70s had still been regarded as the absolute opposite of art, in the 80s became the major determinant of architectural design for the great majority of architects. Fashion, for the contemporary architect, had a greater hold on his profession than individual practice and study – indeed, it began to parasitize and contaminate the art of building itself. An observer from Rotterdam in 1883 instanced speculative housing contractors making large-scale use of cheap imitations of Old Dutch façade motifs – the Old Dutch style had become the victim of mass consumption. And this fashion helped to precipitate amongst architects the passion for Dutch Renaissance – the 'new Old Dutch period, that we have rushed headlong into',[19] as the same observer put it.

The vogue for a colourful, picturesque architecture was not, however, a specifically Dutch phenomenon. In brick building, using motifs from sixteenth- and early-seventeenth-century architecture had become an international practice. Speculative housing in Antwerp at this time witnessed a change from white stucco to plain brick façades in the 'Old Flemish' style. In Berlin stucco-work remained in use for mass housing projects, but was strenuously discouraged in buildings that required an 'artistic' appearance. This was later replaced with plain brick building, or brick and sandstone combined.[20] In England, seventeenth-century Queen Anne with its red bricks was all the rage, reported *De Opmerker* in 1887, adding that the fashion even prescribed matching gardens and ladies' wear – something that can hardly have surprised the Netherlands: witness *De Portefeuille*, commenting in an article on Dutch taste in 1883, 'nothing is as new-fashioned (or as a cultured Dutchman might say, so *haute nouveauté* or *high fashion*) as the seventeenth century'. And at extravagant parties attendants would be dressed in seventeenth-century attire.[21] In fact, the manufacturing industries provided anything fashion required. 'Manufacturers are increasingly turning to the attractive forms of

the Renaissance', a Rotterdam architect wrote in 1882 'The choice is extensive. It is only a matter of making the *right* choice, one that does justice to the surroundings and blends in well. Studying abstract theories of laws of aesthetics et cetera is not required; in most cases an open eye and good taste will suffice.' One of his colleagues reported two years later that stucco was completely out of fashion: 'The use of artificial finishes has declined so much that you can no longer find even a speculative builder using stucco for his façades.[22]

Spectacular curiosities

Fashion entailed more than the commercial application of Renaissance forms; it still acknowledged some kind of edifying cultural idea, no matter how diluted. However, an architecture now emerged in which fashion demonstrated its true intent: the pursuit of the public's always fleeting attention, not in order to edify it, but to exploit it. That attention was captured by turning upside down the traditional rules and conventions of the art of building. In the United States, for instance, it was reported that at Coney Island, New York, a hotel was built in the shape of a gigantic elephant: in the Dutch dunes at Zandvoort appeared a beer house in the shape of a beer barrel, in Paris the highest tower in the world, a three-hundred-metre steel construction whose only function was to be spectacular.

That these constructions were built is relevant in the context of our narrative because they clashed with the culture of fine architecture. The architectural journals reported such curiosities as news items and described them sneeringly, sometimes even with grim concern. In the same way as incompetent builders and their work were used in the journals to sharpen ideas on the architect's status and expertise, this new and commercially successful category of anti-architecture was used to emphasize that architecture was a matter of culture. Of the American elephant: 'May this feeble effort act as a warning and go some way towards nipping in the bud this childish craving for the grotesque and sensational. Above all, it is necessary that men who devote themselves to art refrain from supporting or encouraging such pathetic, senseless trifles.' However, such a turn of events boded ill. The same voice was aware 'that the advertising disease has badly affected us too, and that it is all too clear that the public in [the Netherlands] shows worrying symptoms of susceptibility to this disease.[23]

In retrospect it is clear that this passionate appeal to curb the commercialization of architecture was no more than a lone voice crying in the wilderness. But would it not have been clear at the time that it could only be a rearguard action? The young architect A. W. Weissman wrote in 1881 that architects considered their profession too much as a livelihood, and that 'the enthusiasm that ought to inspire every real artist is all too often lacking'.[24] Thus the debate after 1880 no longer centred on the contrast between skilled architects and the 'unqualified'. New polarity was emerging, this time within the architectural community itself: between the businessman and the artist (with a broad hazy area in between). Weissman already anticipated the disappearance of the artist-architect: 'It may begin to sound incongruous to speak of artistic enthusiasm in the century of *Americanization*.'

Americanization in the 80s was synonymous with vulgar materialism, lack of culture, lack of taste, an obsession with success and with the anti-culture of the New World. With its thirst for action, its practical intelligence and its enormous prosperity, America was seen as the upstart that both irritated and fascinated the old 'civilized' nations. The country of unlimited opportunities produced an unlimited stream of superlatives and innovations, which also left their mark on the Dutch architectural journals. Because of its evident economic advantages the American cultivation of efficiency was bound to affect building practices in the Netherlands. Witness the fact that in 1881 on a major building project at the Binnenhof in the central administrative district of The Hague work continued throughout the night for three months thanks to the fact that electric lighting had been introduced on to the site. It was only a matter of time before architects, too, had to comply with the efficiency requirement. In this context it may be observed that the economic advantage provided by efficiency did not favour the labour-intensive, traditional 'historical school' – for this reason alone Van Delden's prediction in 1882 that its life expectancy was short was realistic.

The status of the architect plummets

When it became apparent that architects could no longer maintain their status as artists but would have to accept that they were just one factor among many in the building industry, the first attempts were made to bring their employment conditions into line with the new situation – another inevitable feature of the development of architecture as a commodity. Leliman, who from the 1860s had dedicated himself to bettering the social position of architects and building craftsmen, in 1884 redoubled his efforts: 'The architect must be acknowledged and properly paid for his work, in order for him to be able to live and study and advance his art.'[25] This message needed to be brought home, for when on one occasion a campaign was organized to obtain funds for a new church in Amsterdam,

several architects offered to provide a design free of charge. 'See how eager and ready to make sacrifices these people are,' scoffed a reporter.[26] Such incidents – or was this general practice, which only occasionally attracted publicity? – increased the demand for measures that would restrain the architect from turning his art into a commodity. Clearly, a binding, uniform system of remuneration was called for. The many publications on this subject in the 80s and later as well as, for instance, on the copyright of architectural designs, show that the Netherlands were no different in these respects from the rest of Europe, for precisely the same issues were being discussed in Germany, England and Belgium, and similar solutions being sought.

Publicity and self-promotion: the struggle to make a living

As commerce's grip on building practice tightened, public opinion started to weigh heavier on architects. In the 1850s and 60s, supported by the inspiring words of colleagues such as Rose and Leliman, they had still been able to aspire to an almost priest-like role in which they as servants of art could lead the people to a higher aesthetic and moral plane. Now they had to learn to accept that the public chose its own aesthetics and was inclined to ignore or forget the architect.

It therefore became vital for architects to convince the public of their importance. A sense of honour prevented most from extolling their work via advertisement. There were, in any case, other effective means of attracting attention, one of which was to have one's plans published in a newspaper. In view of the stiff competition among the growing number of architects, publicity-seeking became inescapable, especially during years of severe economic recession. The alternative, doing nothing, was risky. 'Our destiny almost always depends on one fortunate moment,' Leliman said in 1884, 'on a single whim, on one person, one building.' He too, was forced to acknowledge that public opinion was often decisive. The work of the poet and the painter was praised or forgotten, but the work of the architect, he said, was praised or denounced, for a building could not avoid being judged by the public. Therefore the role played by the press was crucial.

[If the architect] has the support of the press and someone gives him a push in the right direction, he is referred to as 'most competent' and fortune will smile upon him. But if he is not able to catch the attention of the press, or has no friends in high places, then his fate is far less enviable and in the eyes of the world he will never become a great man. He may be an artist through and through, be as virtuous as a saint, as busy as a bee, but it will be his fate to remain forgotten.[27]

In the architects' vehement reproaches to the press we repeatedly encounter the complaint that architecture was no longer appreciated because the public was ignorant and the press no more than the expression of that ignorance. It is characteristic of the 80s that even on this subject there was no consensus. One party would claim that the public took the prosaic view, that it was first and foremost practical and lacking in taste, and that it had turned away from architects because it believed that they could no longer function as 'leaders and masters of good taste'. Another party would protest that it could not accept such an evaluation, and summon up examples that supposedly demonstrated the contrary.[28]

The struggle to make a living was a struggle for publicity. Hence the 'usurped reputation', whereby an architect's fame became based on the work of nameless designers that he hired on a project basis. 'Our small country enjoys the advantage (?) of having many usurped reputations, who with the support of willing journals and thanks to an ignorant public pass for artists and who in the end themselves start to believe that they *are* artists. Their only "art" lies in the fact that they are sometimes able to choose excellent assistants, whom they keep as much as possible in the background, who may even be hidden in a closet or anteroom when the client turns up at the architect's office.'[29] These words were written in 1884 in response to a similar report in the German journal *Deutsche Bauzeitung* (German Builders' News). It was an international practice.

An ignorant public and willing journalists were the allies of the businessman-architect. The press saw every recently opened clothes shop as the eighth wonder of the world, complained one architect in 1886, and recorded everything the owner said. Recently they had reported the opening of a new linen shop built in the Louis XVI style, although there was nothing of any Louis style whatever to be seen there. Three years earlier *De Opmerker* had published a pastiche on such a newspaper story in a review of the new Amsterdam Park Theatre. The colours, the designs, the electric light, the beautiful ladies' dresses and the dazzling uniforms – all were truly magnificent on the opening night, it reported. The building's interior was outstanding; there was only one detail that seemed a little deficient: 'the proscenium, the consoles of which consist of leaping tigers, above which stands an Indian with one whole and one half-elephant on his head. We could have hoped for a little more opulence in the surrounding stage area too.'[30]

Criticism and architectural theory
Many architects who took the art of building seriously read

the press reports with horror. However, it was difficult to indicate the proper course to be taken. Should a critic be a specialist, or should he definitely not be? Should he be someone with a reputation, or might someone who had yet to prove himself as an architect pass criticism? More generally, should a critic be unassailable himself in respect of the mistakes he pointed out in others? Should a review be signed or should it be anonymous? Signing was the more honourable option, it was felt, but the disadvantage was that the reader took more notice of *who* was writing than of what was being written. Should a critic be knowledgeable about past building styles, or would this result in too antiquarian an appraisal? Many, many questions, but not even the beginnings of a consensus. There was no consensus on the critic's authority, nor on his reliability or intellectual status. The report of a talk given by the somewhat elderly Leliman in 1884 may serve as an example. In response to his emphasis on the need for integrity in the critic and in his reviews, the young Theodoor G. Schill (1852–1914) said that he did not feel strongly about the issue, considering it better to have a bad press than to be ignored completely.[31] To Schill architectural criticism meant publicity.

The disappearance of the intellectual meaning of criticism is interesting, because it implies that the intellectual relevance of architectural theory was diminishing even further, within architectural circles as well as outside of them. Schill was certainly not an insignificant architect – he was working at that moment on the new Amsterdam headquarters of the MBB (1884–5). The impoverishment of architectural criticism was apparent abroad as well. An article in the much read *Revue des Deux Mondes* stated that there had been a time when aesthetics functioned as a code via which the critic used to dispense some kind of justice, but that this time was long gone. 'Today there are no longer any generally accepted rules in art. Criticism is no longer founded on principles. The principles that are meaningful to one are contemptuously rejected by another.[32]

There had been for a long time many indications that theory was no longer the compulsory point of departure, the generally accepted system of rules representing the intrinsic qualities of architecture. In the 1880s, the numberless confrontations between the architects themselves, between artist-architects and businessmen-architects, and between architects and the increasingly independent-minded public, came very much to the fore. These public confrontations showed that architecture had become a matter of opinion.

Something new, something original

Such differences of opinion did not alter the fact that many architects experienced the same wide gap between the taste and the aesthetic judgements of their own professional circle on the one hand and the fickle taste of the public on the other. Perhaps it is incorrect to speak merely of a gap. The architects' reactions to the stories in the press often give the impression of a growing antagonism between good taste on the one hand and barbarism on the other. It is against this background that emerged the dangerous interaction between the artist and the public in which fashion played such an important role. Why, despite the enormous unprecedented possibilities offered by education was art now producing many styleless and ugly objects? The answer, of course, was that the public was always demanding something new, something original: 'the general public's craving for originality, all too easily resulting in the weird and wonderful, is the cause; the strangest, the most outlandish and ugly things often attract the most attention', commented one. He was in fact referring to Paris, but his observations could equally have been made in Amsterdam or The Hague.[33]

The gap between architecture and the public was no new phenomenon, as we have seen. This problem had occupied architects for decades – it had been one of the reasons for establishing the Society for the Advancement of the Art of Building (the MBB). But there was quite a difference between the ignorant public of 1860 and that of 1880. The public had become a demanding customer, and an increasing number of architects bade for its favour. Economic conditions had made the architect the servant of that public. The servant, however, also needed to obey his mistress Architecture. Between these two loyalties careful manoeuvring was called for. It was clear that, from the point of view of its attitude to architecture, there was no use waiting for the public to get itself an education in aesthetics. Architects knew that they must take command and engage in public relations exercises via the means available, such as by providing information and by advertising.

The campaign to educate the public: the supremacy of the visual image

This change took shape in 1881 through a redrafting of the MBB's constitution, which included the 'serious intent … to exert influence on the outside world using all available means; to help create a public taste for good architecture'. The MBB now employed a paid secretary, the architect C. T. J. Louis Rieber (1848–1908), and launched a new illustrated magazine, and in 1884 it established its own

premises in Amsterdam which were to become its new headquarters. The building was made accessible to the public: it had a library and a permanent exhibition, where individuals commissioning buildings could obtain information on materials, kinds of construction, and ornaments. Exhibitions where members could display their designs featured regularly. Its new weekly magazine, *Bouwkundig Weekblad* (Architectural Weekly), had to adapt itself to this 'wider need for information and advice'. It replaced the respectable *Bouwkundige Bijdragen*, which now appeared only occasionally and was consequently out of touch with new developments – and things were changing on the architectural front so much faster than had been the case ten years earlier. The Amsterdam architect Jan R. de Kruyff commented: 'What is exercising our minds now is sometimes forgotten after a couple of weeks. Polemic and the exchange of ideas are possible only in a weekly publication where government, municipal and private interests can be promoted'.[34] The MBB launched a second periodical in 1881, the *Bouwkundig Tijdschrift* (Architectural Journal), which was to appear several times a year. It contained illustrations of buildings and designs, with emphasis on the contemporary, neatly presented as plans, sections, elevations and details. The text consisted only of explanatory captions. The other architectural association Architectura et Amicitia, particularly after Jan Springer took over the chairmanship in 1878, had become very much the counterpart of the MBB. Following the example of that association, A et A changed its constitution in 1882, but did not aspire to a new building or a paid secretary. Neither did it have any need for its own weekly journal, because in 1883 it was to join forces with *De Opmerker*. A et A also issued a highly illustrated, low-text publication under the title *Verzameling van Bekroonde Ontwerpen* (Prize-winning Designs), which in 1885 was renamed *De Bouwmeester* (The Master Builder).

What made these new architectural magazines particularly novel was the fact that they were illustrated. Together with the architectural exhibitions, which rapidly gained in popularity, they were the ideal medium for informing the ignorant public and for generally extending the appreciation of architecture. In this respect, as in so many others, the Netherlands was following the international trend. In Brussels in 1883 an enormous exhibition of Belgian architecture was held, displaying some fourteen hundred drawings, engravings and pictures; five years later in Berlin an architectural museum was founded under the auspices of the Technical University. One critic, assessing the various architectural training institutes in Western Europe, reported that over the past

Fig.61
The MBB Building in
Amsterdam (1884–5),
designed by Theo
G. Schill and
D. H. Haverkamp.
Here an idealized
architectural
profession is
represented not via a
picturesque design,
but via a stately
classical Dutch
Renaissance design.
The tympanums
above the windows
show the portraits of
two famous architects
of the Dutch Golden
Age, Jacob van
Campen and Hendrik
de Keyser, and of the
great seventeenth-
century Dutch
sculptor Artus
Quellin.

Fig.62
The latest fashion – architecture with many turrets (on the right, the turret of the Oude Kerk) as an element of the picturesque townscape: Hendrik P. Berlage's entry for the second round of the Stock Exchange design competition, Amsterdam (1885). Here he used the latest presentation medium, a perspective drawing in watercolours.

few years immense progress had been made in England, 'to which undoubtedly the wide publicity afforded by publishing illustrations of modern buildings had substantially contributed'.[35]

In addition to being a tool for educating the public, at a somewhat more profound level these new magazines and exhibitions had another significance: they were an indication that communication between architect and public was changing. The rising interest in architectural images observed in this decade can be considered as an offshoot of the popularization of illustrated books, covering a wide range of subjects, that in the 70s had been available only in costly limited editions. This growing interest involving a shift from word to visual image, was to manifest itself emphatically, and no doubt marked a further decline in architectural theory – precisely because the visual had now superseded the verbal.

To the architect, then, the architectural drawing became more and more important as a means of communicating with the public. But the public had less interest in architectural pictures than in visual images of the other fine arts, because the layman often did not understand the technicalities of architectural drawing. (On the positive side it could be argued that the layman was hardly able, accordingly, to express any criticism and therefore could not force the architect to fulfil his every whim.) If architectural drawings could be read only by colleagues, that was good for architecture. 'Several architects, particularly younger ones,' stated *De Opmerker* 'have put more effort into their drawings lately and have used more colour and perspective. As long as this does not detract from representing the building in question, this striving for popularity, this willingness to make concessions, to the public, should not be condemned.'[36]

The new public-friendly approach entailed two risks, however, that were well recognized. First, the more artistic the presentation, the less the technical precision and the greater the risk of mistakes – or of deliberate manipulation or false promises. The point was not academic, since in Germany artists had specialized in presenting architecture with a very sophisticated drawing and painting technique, thus creating an image that, when the design was executed, proved 'often very disappointing'.[37] Second, the downgrading of the profession was a real threat here: it could become more important for an architect to produce flattering drawings to impress a client than to present a simple but accurate and reliable design. At the contest for the new Stock Exchange in Amsterdam in 1884, it turned out that for one of the prize-winning designs the architect in question had commissioned a landscape artist. An affluent architect could, apparently, 'buy' the talent of an artist without means in order to gloriously rake in the money afterwards.[38] In 1889 H. G. Jansen, a journalist on *De Opmerker*, took a stand against this practice. According to him, the awarding of honorary certificates and gold medals at international exhibitions had nothing to do with the quality of the designs. It was a form of fraud, of advertising under false pretenses – 'the scandal of the century,' he called it – performed by conniving adjudicators. It was all a matter of enhancing international political kudos – or bribery plain and simple.[39]

Architects were tempted during the 80s in other ways, too, as we shall see. They were well aware that the public favoured the architect who most pleased. Pleasing the public, however, would sooner or later mean the end of art. At the end of the decade Leliman would state that architecture had made important advances over the past twenty-five years, but that the moral stature of architects and their influence on society had not increased 'to the desired extent'. On the contrary, he would argue, in the past the architect had had a greater moral influence in cultural issues, and the social appreciation of his work had also been much greater.[40]

Amongst the members of Architectura et Amicitia too there were more rumblings of discontent. Vitruvius would be hard pressed to find anyone who could meet all the requirements that he had demanded of the architect, it was observed. Moreover, he would be surprised by the low moral standard of many in the profession.

Where are the architects who have even the slightest understanding of philosophy, who have acquired thereby a purity of soul and a degree of selflessness, he would have asked. What would he have said of the architects who approach the editorial offices of newspapers with their projects, in order to publicize the excellence of their plans? What would he have thought of the machinations so often employed today to obtain commissions? His judgement would have been severe indeed. The only thing we would be able to say in our defence is that the struggle to make a living is so much harder today than it was in his time.[41]

Notes

1.   *De Opmerker* 15 no. 22, 29.5.1880.
2.   'Kunst and critiek' ('Art and criticism'), *De Portefeuille* 11 (1889) no. 20, 246.
3.   E. Gugel 1880–1888, I, ii–iii, E. Gugel 1886, 2nd edn, 933.
4.   August van Delden 1881, 6; cf. Gottfried Semper 1860, xv.
5.   A. W. Weissman 1881, 370, 371.
6.   X. 1884a, 38; V. 1884, 80.
7.   J. J. van Nieukerken 1885, 40; L. M. Moolenaar 1885, 446–7; J. B. Jager 1886, 34.
8.   W. Kromhout 1888b, 9; H. P. Berlage 1886, 207.
9.   C. T. J. Louis Rieber 1885, 3.
10. Vox 1881a, 122; *Nederlandsche Kunstbode* 3 (1881) 26, 204–5.
11. G. E. Engberts 1977, 82; J. A. de Jonge 1976, 2nd edn, 501–3.
12. J. P. Smits 1995, 75; 338–9: the rental value of houses increased during the 1850s by 5 million guilders, during the 60s by 8.4 million and during the 70s and 80s by 19.5 and 18.9 million respectively.
13. *De Opmerker* 20 (1885) 33, 281–3.
14. J. H. Leliman 1884, 86.
15. *De Opmerker* 17 no. 49, 9.12.1882.
16. L. M. Moolenaar 1888, 400; P. H. Scheltema 1887, 80.
17. 'J. van Lith the younger', *Bouwkundig Weekblad* 8 (1888) 43, 265–6. De Haan: A. Dietze 1993. The Kurhaus: Willem Bruls, Dorothée van Hooff 1991, 152; the Victoria Hotel: Bert Vreeken, Ester Wouthuysen 1987, 137–44. Cuypers and the Vondelstraat: Aart Oxenaar 1993.
18. R. 1887, 428.
19. Flâneur 1883.
20. Antwerp: Lut Prims, Ronny De Meyer 1993, e.g. 138–42; Berlin: Hugo Licht 1884, 174.
21. 'Engelsche smaak' ('English taste'), *De Opmerker* 22 (1887) 36, 281–2; 'Nederland' ('The Netherlands'), *De Portefeuille* 5 no. 18, 4.8.1883.
22. Rotterdam architect: D. de Vries 1881. One of his colleagues: K. 1884, 298.
23. J. C. K. 1884, 299.
24. A. W. Weissman 1881, 370.
25. J. H. Leliman 1884, 86.
26. X. 1884b.
27. J. H. Leliman 1884, 88.
28. P. H. Scheltema 1887, 80; contra C. T. J. Louis Rieber 1887, 84.
29. Veritas 1884.
30. Linen shop: X. 1886, 377; 'De Parkschouwburg', *De Opmerker* 18 (1883) 18, 177.
31. *Bouwkundig Weekblad* 4 (1884) 52, 349.
32. R. v. E. [S. E. W. Roorda van Eysinga] 1884, 126.
33. E. J. Niermans 1886, 81.
34. J. R. de Kruyff 1881.
35. D. J. 1884, 232. The exhibition in Brussels: E. Allard 1883; Berlin: *Bouwkundig Weekblad* (1888) no. 31, 194.
36. *De Opmerker* 22 (1887) no. 9, 66.
37. Exponents of this technique were known as *Architekturmaler*. *De Opmerker* 21 (1886) no. 29, 232.
38. K. 1885, 218.
39. H. G. J. [H. G. Jansen] 1889, 328.
40. J. H. Leliman 1889, 167.
41. *De Opmerker* 21 (1886) 40, 320.

7

Fashion, Competition and Picturesque versus Monumental

The historical school: the neo-Gothic, Dutch Renaissance, and the 'official style'

To please the public would mean the end of art – but *not* pleasing the public could mean the end of the artist. This quandary was the crux of the problem faced by the architects who were trying to develop a contemporary style. The cultural relationship between the artist and his public was severed; they were on a different wavelength. And, of course, there was no such thing as *the architect*. The fact that architecture was frequently considered just another commodity illustrates the wide diversity of opinion within the profession. Who came off best, mattered: the 'real' architect with his aesthetic 'rules', or the public with its own standards. But there were still many architects who continued to idealize, verbally, their elevated artistic position, their 'aspiration and dedication to the beautiful, the sublime!' These architects also tended to foster a negative image of the public: 'the appreciation of art is not an innate trait of the practical Dutchman; so those who teach aesthetics have to face fierce resistance'.[1] In this respect the artist and the public were poles apart, and any encounter might precipitate a fierce battle.

This viewpoint was most vehemently voiced by the advocates of what many, Gottfried Semper among them, called 'the historical school'. In the Netherlands, the three main manifestations of this school during the 1880s were, as already mentioned, *neo-Gothic architecture*, the *Dutch Renaissance* revival, and the fusion of these two – the '*official style*'. What the three had in common was that they were all based on the study of architectural history, the fruits of which became the standard for their design. Whereas the historical school defended itself on the social plane with its claims to national tradition, the actual projects of the school could only be devised and judged by specialists. That was the problem that Van Delden perceived in 1881 when he predicted that the historical school would be granted only a short life. But many architects would simply have laughed off this prognosis at the time. And these architects, representing the vast majority, dominated the architectural debate with their belief that contemporary architecture could not exist without a strong link with history. This idea brought with it the notion that architects who had a profound knowledge of architectural history such as Gugel, Cuypers, Gosschalk, Muysken and De Kruyff were the authorities in their profession. Knowledge of history – and history was a very topical subject – earned them respect in discussions on contemporary architecture.

In practice, however, such knowledge was not invariably accompanied by the same significance and status. The status of the Middle Ages was lowest: knowledge of this period served in particular Catholic church building, to which the 'official style' was somewhat peripheral. The neo-Gothic design concept was almost nonexistent in the public debate, and the pretensions of the 'official style' were disposed of as absurd. Knowledge of classical antiquity, on the other hand, was still highly esteemed. As we saw in the previous chapter, the art scholars of the old school such as Vosmaer and Pierson regarded the values and standards of classical art as retaining a pre-eminent cultural importance. The same was true of architects themselves. This is shown, for example in the fact that Vogel's *Guide to the Practice of Greek Architecture* of 1863 was republished twenty-five years later. 'Greek architecture … was always dear to the author,' Vogel's obituary read in 1886.[2] He had died at the age of fifty-two. But what did age matter when it came to the appreciation of classicism? The young architect Jacob F. Klinkhamer (1854–1928) visited Vienna in 1881 and admired, like anybody else, the magnificent neo-Renaissance architecture of the new Ringstrasse, but he had no less admiration for the newly built neoclassicist parliament building. Jan Springer in 1882 had his audience at his feet and received 'loud ovations', when he gave a lecture on Greek temple building. Hendrik Petrus Berlage, visiting the international exhibition on architecture in Berlin in 1886, delivered a long, balanced commentary on the classical Greek, classicist and neoclassicist items on display. The twenty-four-year-old Willem Kromhout in 1889 considered Palladio 'well worth studying on account of his monumental compositions', even though they did not convey the sombre spirit of the early Italian Renaissance and already showed signs of the 'so called baroque style'.[3]

The Dutch Renaissance revival

There was no doubt that, of the various strands that made up the historical school, knowledge of Dutch sixteenth- and seventeenth-century architecture ranked highest. Its application, as we shall see later, functioned within a cultural ideal that was widely recognized both socially and politically. The success of the revival of Dutch sixteenth- and seventeenth-century architecture might seem to contradict the notion that the historical school was remote from the public, but the paradox is solved if we acknowledge that while the *form* of this type of architecture was very popular, the cultural and political contents was rather an elitist affair.

Dutch Renaissance architecture became a subject of specialist knowledge that grew considerably in the course of this decade. In the 70s the illustrated books by August Ortwein and the study by Wilhelm Lübke on the subject had broken new ground, to be followed in the 80s by studies that mapped Renaissance architecture in its international variety in an increasingly more detailed way. A. Schoy, the Belgian author of a book on seventeenth-century Dutch architecture (1878), published a study the next year on the influence of the Italian Renaissance on the architectural development of the Low Countries. Between 1880 and 1889 his fellow countryman J. J. van IJssendijck published a survey of architecture in the Netherlands since the early Middle Ages in which the sixteenth and seventeenth centuries featured prominently. In 1882 the Frenchman E. Rouyer published a survey of French Renaissance architecture, and the new edition of Lübke's *History of the German Renaissance* appeared.

German studies became very influential as far as the new national Dutch architecture was concerned. Immediately after publication in 1882, *The Renaissance in the Netherlands treated in its Historical Development* by Georg Galland was described by the *Bouwkundig Weekblad* as a book 'that may truly no longer be absent from any Dutch architect's library'.[4] It contained two new elements. First, unlike the usual studies on specific building types such as churches, town halls and castles, Galland made urban middle-class housing the main subject of his architectural history. Second, he was the first to note a regional differentiation: Renaissance architecture in the province of Overijssel, for instance, had formal characteristics that were different from those in Zuid-Holland or Friesland. In 1883 the first of the illustrated series *The Renaissance in Belgium and the Netherlands* by Fritz Ewerbeck was published, the result of study trips that Ewerbeck, professor at the Technical University in Aachen, had made in the Netherlands with his students. In late 1889 Galland's work appeared in a second, larger edition under the title of *A History of Dutch Architecture and Visual Arts during the Renaissance, the National Golden Age and Classicism.* Cornelius Gurlitt travelled through Germany, Austria, Switzerland, Italy, France, Belgium, the Netherlands and even Poland to collect data for his *History of the Baroque, Rococo and Classicism*, which, appearing in instalments between 1886 and 1888, reassessed positively style periods that had long been execrated.

All these studies were the work of experts, a new type of researcher working with modern positivist methods, collecting *facts* from sources that had not been examined before. Ewerbeck, Galland and Gurlitt performed fieldwork in the Netherlands; they examined buildings and searched archives for historical data. The scholarly curiosity and lack of inhibition of these three Germans enabled them to discover facts about Dutch architecture that their predecessors – Dutch architects – would perhaps for aesthetic reasons not have permitted into their historiography. When they began to manifest themselves, these new scholarly architectural historians were seen as rivals by Dutch architects such as Gosschalk, who, in the 1860s was one of the first to study the national architecture of the past. In 1871 Gosschalk wrote 'Do you know who it is who is emasculating art?' 'Art historians such as the eloquent Kugler and his pupil Lübke, who seek their salvation in numerous classifications and arbitrary subclassifications – the inventors of who knows how many styles. Their books are unfortunate, half-hearted creations, midway between popular archaeologies and illustrated catalogues.'[5]

However, in the 1870s and 1880s the new discoveries and concepts in the field of architectural history that were really influential came from these academic specialists. Their work made the many essays on architectural history by Gosschalk's compatriots seem increasingly amateurish and subjective, often written in the style of a travel brochure or as compilations of facts and observations. Everything indicated that for their knowledge of history Dutch architects had become dependent on academic researchers. In particular, those 'catalogues' so despised by Gosschalk now appeared to be widely used by architects to satisfy their need for interesting 'national' material. 'National architecture' was a fashion that would exploit historical research to the point of exhaustion.

The Dutch response to an international phenomenon

Wilhelm Lübke's *History of the German Renaissance*, published in 1872, was the first of many publications to appear in the Netherlands that illustrated the national, regional and local variants of Renaissance architecture at home and abroad. The major building programmes being undertaken in Berlin, Vienna, Antwerp, London, Paris and the Netherlands were evidence of the huge public support for the exploration of this architectural period. It is notable that in each country this fascination for the Renaissance had its own nationalist motives, which were recognized as such at the time. Since France's traditional dominance in Europe in political, scientific, social and artistic matters had dissolved during the first half of the century, wrote the *Bouwkundig Weekblad* in 1882,

there has been a return in almost all countries in the second half ... towards the historical and national artistic art styles of the sixteenth and seventeenth centuries, in order to lay the foundation for a more independent development of national art and industry. The power of the nationalist passions that have inspired our century and that now appear to redouble their control ... has now already unmistakably exerted its influence in the field of art as well.[6]

We perceive here a relationship between the international interest in the Renaissance and political and economic nationalism. The connection with the middle-class ideal of culture, however, was equally important. As we have seen, this theme had already been explored in the course of the previous decades, and it remained of great topical interest in the 80s. 'The architecture of the Renaissance is also our architecture, because it is the architectonic *expression of a civilization* that is the best we have ever achieved in the way of a universal solution to the problem of mankind,' wrote one observer in 1881.[7] It was nevertheless obvious that the nationalist aspects evoked the strongest emotions. Political, economic and cultural developments in Germany gave rise at this time to suspicious and protective Dutch reactions, in the field of architecture as elsewhere. The great achievements of the German architectural historians irritated Dutch architects not only because they saw them as intruders, but simply because they were German. Compared with theirs the Dutch architects' knowledge of history was rather amateurish, but that did not inhibit them from joining battle on the grounds that the German Renaissance had originated from the Dutch Renaissance. This argument had no historical basis, but relied on aesthetic judgements only. De Kruyff, for example, argued in 1885 that the Butchers' Guild Hall in Haarlem was proof that the Dutch Renaissance came first: 'This cannot be disputed if one compares the beautiful, rational composition of all its details with the often coarse and ill-considered treatment of

similar details in Germany.'[8] A year later, addressing the *Deutsche Bauzeitung* (the German Builders' News), which had written that the Dutch Renaissance could confidently be considered a part of the German Renaissance, *De Opmerker* responded with a terse denial. The Renaissance had been brought to northern Germany from the Netherlands, and besides, 'the output of Dutch sixteenth-century art in general ranks much higher than that of German art'.[9]

Historical correctness was not at the heart of this debate. *De Opmerker* drew attention in its article to the 'sense of kinship with the Dutch people, which the Germans express more frequently than we would like'. Indeed, historical research in this period was far from apolitical. The sleeping giant that was Germany seemed, after many centuries, to have awakened, and its enormous physical and intellectual vigour, along with its interest in its neighbours, increased by the day. The short and victorious Prussian-French war (1870–1) had shown its astonishing power; a few days before the war ended, Prime Minister Otto von Bismarck proclaimed the German Empire, which was to change the face of Europe. The Netherlands felt uncomfortable, since it was far from certain that these ideas of kinship would not result in annexation. The Frenchman Henry Havard, writing about his travels in the Netherlands, already in 1875 noted that he had spotted a German textbook on geography that on geographical and historical grounds considered the Netherlands, Belgium, Luxembourg and Denmark to be part of Germany.[10] Clearly, views on the Dutch Renaissance were not purely a matter of architectural theory.

The growing German influence, and the role of competition

But just as one person considered architecture to be a fine art while another saw it as a mere commodity, the German publications on the subject were regarded either as respected organs of scholarship or as an expanding reservoir of architectural attractions. Germany was creating an international market for its splendidly illustrated books on both ancient and contemporary architecture, using increasingly sophisticated reproduction techniques such as photolithography. The Dutch architect Jonas Ingenohl (1855–1925) was amongst many who noticed the influx: 'our country is flooded in a terrifying way by foreign, especially German, illustrated books on architecture'.[11] These publications, he maintained, were a source of inspiration not only to 'incompetents' and other 'unqualified persons', but to properly trained architects too, who were using them extensively. The minutes of A et A and MBB meetings demonstrate that members were taking their newly purchased books there and circulating them. Designs of theirs that were entered for exhibitions and competitions at this time show the results of their interest. The international competition for the new Stock Exchange in Amsterdam in 1884 produced 199 entries showing a comprehensive assortment of designs for that important public building. There were variations on Dutch, Flemish, French, German, Italian and Viennese Renaissance of the sixteenth, seventeenth and nineteenth centuries, including combinations on these themes, as well as examples of Henri Labrouste's restrained eclecticism and of the more luxurious 'Second Empire' of the École des Beaux-Arts, and classicist and neo-Gothic too.

Competitions and exhibitions were important indicators of the way ideas were conceived in architectural circles, for they enabled designers to express their work with fewer inhibitions and more idealism, and to forget for one moment daily torments such as self-willed clients, tight budgets and craftsmen devoid of talent. L. M. Cordonnier's design for the Stock Exchange won him first prize, but it was obvious that it was not feasible because it far exceeded the available budget. Conversely, the press had little to say in favour of the design by Berlage and Theodoor Sanders (Berlage eventually would build the new Stock Exchange) because it had 'suffered considerably' from attempts to keep within the budget.[12] The careless attitude towards the set limit for building costs may possibly be explained by the fact that, in order to focus exclusively on the role of imagination and art, in the competitions organized by the MBB since the 1840s budget restrictions had never been set and the society had never held out the prospect of commissions. It remained an open question whether in this difficult period with such carelessness architects would manage to strengthen their competitive position in relation to the commercially oriented, unqualified builders. On a more positive note, there was the occasional client who would provide the architect with liberal means to carry out his ideas and test the possibilities that Renaissance revival architecture offered as against the practice of the modern age. Important projects in this category included Oud-Wassenaar Castle near The Hague (designed by Constantijn Muysken, 1876–9), the Ministry of Justice Building, also in The Hague (Cornelis H. Peters, 1876–80); and in Amsterdam, the Rijksmuseum (1876–85), the Central Station (1882–9), the Wester Gasfabriek (gasworks, by Isaac Gosschalk, 1883–5), the Church of St Nicholas (Adrien C. Bleys, 1885–7) and the Residence at 380–2 Herengracht (Abraham Salm, 1890).

To say that there was no lack of suitable models or incentives for the design of buildings would be an understatement, for they were countless. The essential problem was the reasoning behind the idea for the new building in question, the motivation, the choices to be made and the question of how the meaning of the design was to be interpreted. It was all to do with representation. There was no longer a generally accepted definition of character and style, the two concepts in terms of which the issue of representation was discussed, although some definitions may have been used more frequently than others. In this area as well, the effects of the decline in knowledge about the origin and meaning of theoretical key concepts made themselves felt; a more personal approach had replaced them. In 1885 the critic Carel Vosmaer observed that the younger generation no longer knew its classics, nor did it any longer read the works of the older generations who had been trained in the classics: 'Nowadays it is necessary to defend what in the past never had to be defended: to uphold that form and content are one, and that these words imply a match between a building's character and its purpose.'[13]

Changes in semantics: truth, character, style

In a relatively short time the architectural profession had increased considerably, and the loss of ground of traditional values can be attributed to the entry into it of many architects for whom tradition meant little. But even for those who were familiar with tradition and respected it, the meaning of the old concepts also changed. The concept of character illustrates this. Since the 1850s character had led a somewhat submerged existence because it had been included, by Rose and Leliman among others, in the all-embracing requirement of truth; truth implied character – that is, a proper expression of function and construction. We could call this the 'objective' aspect of character. Thirty years later the more subjective, psychological aspect – the impression a building made on one's feelings – once again came to the fore. This distinction between the 'objective' and the 'subjective' is relevant because the concept of style was also defined in such an 'objective' and 'subjective' way. The multiple meanings of these key concepts make the interpretation of texts of the 80s a difficult matter. The old, familiar words were used, but their connotations were changing.

This growing semantic indistinctness particularly affected the term 'style'. An article of 1888 entitled 'Style and character' assigned to the term 'character' the content that Ingenohl had defined that same year as 'truth'. Five years earlier F. J. Nieuwenhuis, an architect from Utrecht, had maintained that style, by which he meant something like artistic originality, was primarily the result of lack of character.[14] There were more such individual ideas on style, but it can none the less be established that in the 80s the concept incorporated both definitions that had been witnessed in the earlier decades: *style as an objective and universal system of design*, and *style as the specific expression of the national character and the spirit of the times*. Now a third definition came to the fore: *style as an art-historical category*, as a system of formal visual characteristics. 'In our times, buildings are constructed in every conceivable style,' a certain K. wrote in 1884. The future of architecture seemed promising, because 'the architects' knowledge of style is gradually becoming more profound'. In the commercial and fashion-sensitive building sector this third, art-historical definition of style undoubtedly became the most important, because the indication of the 'style' of a building was the easiest, most concise expression of all of its aspects.

The serious architects remembered, however, that the historical styles were not to be used merely because of their beauty. They were primarily a means of expressing the 'idea', the *character* of the building. However, it became increasingly difficult to meet this requirement. One of the people who pondered on this problem was a writer who in 1883 chose the pseudonym Il Puttino. 'Style is character,' he wrote, and the expression of character was the highest aim the artist could aspire to. There were two possibilities. The character created by the artist coincided with the national character, in which case the style he created was also the national style. Or the two did not coincide, in which case the character he created was of a personal nature. This did not exclude the possibility of followers, but together these did not make up a style, but a 'school'. For instance, the Dutch Renaissance in the sixteenth and seventeenth centuries was a national style 'because it expressed the character of the people'. What passed for Dutch Renaissance now belonged only to the 'resurrectionists' and so it was not a style but a school.[15] For Il Puttino it was clear that only an artist 'of sheer genius' would succeed in creating a style with a universal power of expression.

The notion that it would be practically impossible to create a style of and for the people did not appear out of thin air; the study of architectural history had put an end to the innocent optimism that the early nineteenth century had demonstrated on this point. The observation of the architect Henri J. Evers (1855–1929) that architectural styles, like languages, could not be invented on the spur of the moment but needed hundreds of years to develop, accorded well with the latest historical insights. In addition, the truth of the 1850s argument, that the national character of modern times was so radically different that it could not possibly be represented by a historical style, had become increasingly evident.

This was the theory. But everyday practice made the possibility of a new national architecture no less doubtful, in particular because of the ever-increasing international traffic. J. R. de Kruyff observed, 'Rapid transport contributes to a wiping out of all that is idiosyncratic about a country and its people; for the same reason so much is disappearing, never to return. This is happening not only here, but everywhere'. 'Why does one desire a separate style for the Netherlands, as for other countries? If borders are increasingly disappearing, what will happen to all these styles?' wrote H. P. Vogel.[16]

But however fundamental the problem of style may have been, it did not prevent the imitation and adaptation of historical styles from flourishing in the 80s as never before. This applied not only to commercial architecture, but also to the work of the most prominent architects – yet more proof that practice prevailed over theory and that theory had become an exalted but academic issue. Of course there were men with ideals who opposed this state of affairs. At a time when French fashion and French knick-knacks were all the rage with the Dutch public, De Kruyff warned that Dutchmen active in the industrial arts should not go to Paris for their schooling, because of the 'infinite' difference between the French and Dutch national characters.[17]

The 'official style': C. H. Peters and J. van Lokhorst
Historical research has shown that everywhere in Western and Central Europe the national character was being 'invented' by the political and culture elite. This was reinforced by new 'rituals', and 'traditions' and public ceremonies.[18] The debates on a national Dutch architecture fit into this picture, but at the time a clear distinction was made between the representation of the Dutch national character by the Dutch Renaissance style, which was generally accepted despite its artificiality, and on the other hand the pretensions of the 'official style' to be its purest representation, which were widely rejected.

From the quantitative point of view the 'official style' of the 80s was a major success, particularly because of the output of the state architects Cornelis Hendrik Peters and Jacob van Lokhorst. Mastermind De Stuers enabled both architects to build up an elaborate official practice (in the end Van Lokhorst employed no fewer than seventy-five people) that for approximately twenty-five years was to produce a steady stream of government buildings across the country. Their output ranged from post offices, land registry offices and schools to national archives, laboratories, and a considerable number of national monuments restored to their 'original splendour'. The architectural qualities of the 'official style' first became

Fig.63
Cornelis H. Peters'
Post, Telephone and
Telegraph Office,
Arnhem (1889). For
Cuypers' circle it
represented rational,
'logical' architecture;
for the critics of the
'official style' it was a
bizarre mistake to
present a modern
public service, a
centre for
state-of-the-art
communication, as a
medieval chancellery.

OPPOSITE
Fig.64
The Central Station,
Amsterdam (1881–9),
designed by
P. J. H. Cuypers and
Adolf L. van Gendt.
It is generally
accepted that
De Stuers was
responsible for the
fact that Cuypers
was the building's
designer. After the
Rijksmuseum, this
was the second state
commission that
permitted Cuypers
to realize an
exceptionally
expensive building.
Photo: Jacob Olie.

visible when Peters completed the Ministry of Justice Building in 1883. The *Nederlandsche Kunstbode* (Dutch Art Courier, a journal well disposed towards De Stuers), De Stuers and especially Peters himself expounded at length on the building, but otherwise the response was limited. The year 1885 saw the opening of the real touchstone for the 'official style', the Rijksmuseum, which owed its existence to an unparalleled expenditure. According to the laws of aesthetics, the architectural press observed, the building could only be regarded as a failure. In 1888 a retrospective was organized of the work of Van Lokhorst. Joseph Theodoor Johannes ('Jos') Cuypers (1861–1949), the son and associate of P.J.H. Cuypers, wrote a very favourable review with many well-worn remarks on

'decline' and 'sound principles': 'The retrospective can in our opinion be considered a vigorous sign of life of the progressive spirit in architecture,' he concluded. Then the *Bouwkundig Weekblad* and *De Opmerker* entered the fray, reciting all the professional objections of the past fifteen years against the 'official style'.[19] When, the next year, the elder Cuypers' Central Station in Amsterdam was opened to the public, the architectural press confined himself to noting the fact.

Such a minimal response was not the sole indication that the 'official style' had only limited powers of persuasion. The many exhibitions and competitions that constantly demonstrated the enormous architectural diversity available confirmed that there was no support outside its own small circle. Interestingly, of the 199 entries for the Stock Exchange competition there was only one design that showed the influence the Rijksmuseum.[20]

It was in the area of truth, and even more in the area of character, that the 'official style' was found most wanting, as will become clear later. Peters' Ministry of Justice Building had been a foretaste of what the Rijksmuseum made perfectly clear in 1885: that the 'official style' offered an absurd representation of the contemporary national character. The museum's vaulted ceilings, the profuse multicoloured neo-Gothic that competed with the exhibits themselves, the chapel proclaiming 'Sanctus, Sanctus, Sanctus Deus Sabaoth, benedictus qui venit in nomine Dei', were all in perfect harmony with the other 'sermons' in stone. The national museum, far from conveying a national symbolic value, was a shrine to Catholicism. The architectural journals paid little attention to this aspect, but the rest of the press stirred up a storm of criticism, making it clear once more that the national character as they perceived it had everything to do with the cultural ideals of the bourgeoisie that had taken lead of the country in 1848, the year of the new 'liberal' Dutch Constitution. These ideals referred to the tradition of the Renaissance and were opposed to the 'dark' and theocratic Middle Ages as represented by the new national museum.

A contemporary national architecture: picturesque or monumental?

As noted in Chapter 4, in the 1860s the Dutch national character was related to one specific architectural image – that of the newly discovered Old Dutch brick and sandstone architecture, to be covered by the term 'Dutch Renaissance' in the 1870s. From the moment of its discovery Old Dutch was appreciated for its picturesque beauty, and when the sensibility for the picturesque increased the appreciation of Old Dutch architecture was soon followed by the discovery of the 'typical' picturesque Old Dutch townscape. In the 1880s, one of the most important debates on the art of building was the question of whether a contemporary, national architecture should have a picturesque or a monumental character. In the light of the views that had held sway since the 1860s, cultivating Old Dutch architecture and townscape, it seemed obvious that there would be a preference for the picturesque. But there was a problem: aesthetics as conventionally understood demanded that an important public building, because of its function and status, should have a monumental character.

The fact that this was a dilemma, albeit theoretical, implies that the status of the picturesque had improved after the 60s. Whereas it had then been a novel aesthetic experience and one of the first experiments in the work of the pioneering Gosschalk, twenty years later it had become a universally recognized, even prominent, architectural mode. This may have been brought about by three developments in particular:

1. The much increased knowledge of European architectural history in the Netherlands, which made it possible to regard Dutch 'national' architecture as essentially picturesque in order to distinguish it from foreign monumental architecture.
2. The tremendous expansion of the commercial building market, which because of the demolition of old buildings and the construction of new urban areas encouraged an appreciation of Old Dutch townscapes.
3. The increasing importance of visual appearance in architecture.

The first two developments have already been discussed, in a different context. The third was touched on in connection with the changing relationship between architects and the public – in particular, the introduction of the architectural exhibition, of the illustrated architectural journal and of lavishly illustrated books. To this can now be added another development relevant to the picturesque townscape – sketching from nature. There were frequent reports of young architects who, no longer satisfied with knowledge obtained from books, were now taking their sketchbooks outside. This was nothing new – in the 60s Gosschalk, for instance, had studied in this way – but now for architectural students it became one of their favourite exercises (with possible unorthodox artistic experiences). For once again the picturesque proved to be the breeding ground for a kind of creativity that evolved outside of theoretical, objective conventions. In art and architectural theory beauty is a matter of rules, but in the open air it is something that strikes the eye and appeals to the emotions. The advantage of sketching out of doors is that 'to many it makes clear for the first time what is beautiful and what is not. Many a late Gothic archway or late Renaissance detail, in the past branded as hideous by bookish scholars, is only appreciated as beautiful once it has been sketched, and can therefore be studied in great detail.'[21]

Clearly, during these years the picturesque Dutch townscape had no treatises on its aesthetics, nor any theory or academic convention. Architectural theory and aesthetics were related to the design of individual buildings, not to architecture in its urban context and certainly not to urban design. It would seem that in the 80s

the skills and aesthetic conventions that were needed for designing architecture in its picturesque urban context were developed by frequent sketching and observing in the open air, without any obligation to boil down its results to aesthetic theory. Just as in the 60s, the picturesque became a reality via the process of *observing*, not by a process of *understanding*. Architectura et Amicitia introduced a sketch club under the chairmanship of Jan Springer, which made field trips to picturesque towns such as Edam and Haarlem where its members would focus on interesting archways and façades. In 1884 a certain 'W' (Adriaan Weissman?)

from Amsterdam published an account of an 'exploratory walk' through a labyrinth of unfamiliar streets and alleys in the heart of Amsterdam, full of Old Dutch architectural remnants. In 1887–8 another young architect, Willem Kromhout, spent time in Flanders and along the Loire sketching picturesque objects. After he had finished his training, Willem Cornelis Bauer (1862–1904) took a trip across Europe and published sketches of Rouen and Nuremberg.[22] Bauer formulated very precisely his discovery of this new, unothodox beauty, and although his work also refers to other European locations, it shows a way

Fig.66
Willem Kromhout's
sketches from his
study tour along the
Loire. In 1888 the
twenty-four-year-old
Kromhout was as
fascinated by the
sophisticated,
picturesque French
Renaissance as were
his older colleagues,
but three years later
he was to become the
spokesman for the
young architects who
wanted to develop an
architecture without a
history.

Photolith.van G.J.Thieme, Arnhem.

Bijvoegsel van DE OPMERKER 1888, N° **43**.

Fig.67
Travel sketches of
Nuremberg by
Willem C. Bauer,
published in *De
Opmerker* in 1888.

of observing that is also compatible with the concept of the picturesque as a reflection of the Dutch national character. In Bauer's opinion an object did not always need to be of the calibre of a work of art in order to be able to beguile – in fact, he said, an object did not even have to be beautiful. Many old cities, for example, owed their importance to their picturesque character – or, to be more precise, to the appeal of their colours and the felicitous positioning of quite undistinguished houses. 'There is no greater pleasure than to wander through squares and streets, and to be enchanted by the most picturesque townscapes imaginable. Enhancing the picture are the many dormer windows, whose fanciful lines embellish the roofs, with their small, flat red tiles adding the finishing touch.'

Foreigners, too, noted the special visual qualities of the Dutch townscape, thereby further promoting the appreciation of the picturesque. Prominent among these were German Dutch Renaissance scholars such as Fritz Ewerbeck, author of *The Renaissance in Belgium and the Netherlands*, who in 1887 published an article entitled

'Dutch townscapes'. More important, in terms of their distribution and popularity, were the travel journals of the French writer Henry Havard, whose multivolume *La Hollande pittoresque* (The Picturesque Netherlands) (1874–7) and *La Hollande à vol d'oiseau* (The Netherlands as the Crow Flies, 1881) demonstrated the picturesque beauty of the Dutch provinces. In another splendid publication, *Amsterdam and Venice* (1876), he had used the townscapes of these cities as a backdrop against which to describe the inhabitants' often no less picturesque lives.

Picturesque buildings, picturesque townscape

From the more conscious observation of town or city as an aesthetic entity it was only a small step to relate the design of a new building to its urban context. It is difficult to establish what came first – the demand for picturesque buildings or the discovery of the picturesque townscape – but it is clear that the two were inextricably linked. In Chapter 4 it was noted that the roots of the picturesque architectural design are to be found in the English

Fig.68
The Oudezijds
Achterburgwal, one of
the numerous small
Amsterdam canals,
around 1896. This
picturesque
townscape of the
'Venice of the North'
was one of several
hundred photographs
of Amsterdam taken
by the impressionist
painter Georg
Hendrik Breitner.

Fig.68
The Oudezijds
Achterburgwal, one of
the numerous small
Amsterdam canals,
around 1896. This
picturesque
townscape of the
'Venice of the North'
was one of several
hundred photographs
of Amsterdam taken
by the impressionist
painter Georg
Hendrik Breitner.

landscape gardens of the eighteenth century. It seems plausible to trace the link between those gardens and the picturesque townscape to the new design concepts of Dutch villas. Constantijn Muysken's description of his design for a large country house on the rural estate of Oud-Wassenaar near The Hague contains all the elements relevant to designing in a picturesque context. The surroundings had been his starting point, he wrote. The status and the history of the location demanded a grand design, the majestic trees and the landscape called for harmonizing shapes and colours. Thus he arrived at the character ('or, if one prefers, style,' he added) and the trademarks of the 'heyday of Dutch Renaissance'. 'Do not our seventeenth-century Dutch cities owe their attractiveness precisely to the alternating bricks and cut stone used in most of the buildings?'[23] Muysken asked.

In 1885 plans were drawn up in Amsterdam for the demolition and reconstruction of a boarding house near the picturesque Mint Tower. When the citizens objected to the plans it was suggested that some idea of the proposed building's appearance should be offered them, by means of a rough wooden framework, to enable them to reach a better judgement. This itself is an indication of a new, more conscious perception of the townscape. Perhaps surprisingly, once the demolition process was under way, requests came from all sides to preserve the newly visible sky, the 'opened up view'.[24] This public reaction, echoed by the city council, showed that the picturesque townscape was more than a matter of façades; it was a also a matter of light, of 'opening up', and therefore of *space* – a quality hitherto absent from building theory. Such ideas on the picturesque townscape and their implementation marked the beginning of town planning as an architectural discipline and as a profession. The construction and reconstruction of cities had hitherto been mainly determined by civil engineering and commerce; the projects that Rose had designed for Rotterdam around 1850 remained, with their social and aesthetic dimension in so far as they had been executed, major exceptions.[25] In the 80s the 'form' of the city became an explicitly aesthetic architectural issue, not only for the experts but also for the general public.

The new buildings demonstrated what the architects were capable of. Whereas the Central Station, in the opinion of many Amsterdam citizens, had resulted in the disappearance of one of the city's most picturesque townscapes – the wide view over the IJ, a small bay on the Zuiderzee, with behind it the meadows and wide skies of North Holland – these new houses in the Dutch Renaissance style were creating a new picturesque. 'With no small amount of satisfaction' *De Portefeuille* recorded in 1886 that 'an abundance of attractive, delicate façades is springing up [in Amsterdam], inspired by seventeenth-century examples', which 'give the streets a lively, picturesque appearance'.

However, the townscape did not consist entirely of beautiful details and attractive façades, old and new. There was also the occasional large public building, which precisely because of its grandeur attracted attention. It was these buildings that had sparked the controversy between the picturesque and the monumental in the first place. The problem was not that there was widespread support for the idea of a monumental townscape during these years – there was not – but that the appreciation of the picturesque townscape conflicted with the time-honoured assumption that public buildings ought to be monumental. The contrast between the two design concepts is conveyed in the words of Vogel, who in 1885 argued for upholding 'our perennially serene and dignified monumental art' in the tradition of the classical Italian Renaissance. He regarded the appreciation of the picturesque as tantamount to the art of architecture conceding ground to the art of painting.[26] In this he was not alone. In 1881 an Architectura et Amicitia committee judged that the 'so-called Old Dutch style can hardly be used for a monumental building because of its lack of linear simplicity'. If one were to insist on using the Dutch Renaissance, it declared, the first half of the seventeenth century would be an option, 'because it was not as over-ornate then as in earlier periods'. The architect Juriaan Kok observed in 1884 that a magnificent monumental building in the 'style of our ancestors' had never been attempted, and, he added, 'with good reason, because such a style was neither intended nor suitable for such a purpose'.[27] The Rijksmuseum proved that the monumentality required for the building's function was almost impossible to combine with the picturesqueness that the townscape demanded. The Rijksmuseum's immense 'city gate', the virtual street running through it with its two massive adjacent towers, did have a certain quality both picturesque and monumental, but this had nothing to do with the character of the building itself, which demanded a monumental expression of its exalted purpose.

Fig.69
Picturesque 'Dutch Renaissance': an effective design mode for the visual and cultural integration of a large modern industrial complex in the city: Isaac Gosschalk's Wester Gasfabriek (gasworks), Amsterdam (1883–5).

In search of a picturesque monumentality: height and space

The designs for the Amsterdam Stock Exchange had shown the multitude of variations available on the theme of picturesque versus monumental. But the panel of adjudicators put aside all entries there were not in the Old Dutch fashion because, it argued, the design should not contradict the 'typical' picturesque spectacle that was Amsterdam. Many competitors, including the authors of several winning designs, acknowledged the inconsistency between the picturesque townscape to be preserved and the monumental assignment by providing their designs with a very high tower and very steep roofs (up to forty metres high), and high gables to match gigantic cross beams. The search for a picturesque monumentality resulted in the increase of the only dimension that classical monumentality had used with great constraint: *height*.

The possibilities of height were already being exploited internationally. The world record in this decade would, of course, be held by the Eiffel Tower, completed in 1889. Meanwhile Dutch architectural journals regularly published articles on the American skyscrapers that had started to go up. Inspired by his stay in the United States, the Dutch hotelier and architect C. A. A. Steinigeweg, in collaboration with the architect Ed Cuypers, a nephew of the architect of the Rijksmuseum, in 1883 designed the seven-storey American Hotel on the Leidseplein in Amsterdam, which had been equipped with the city's very first lift. On the terrace floor there was a belvedere with buffets from which one had a magnificent view of the city and its surroundings.[28]

It was modern technology that permitted the full exploitation of this third dimension, and the new possibilities were indeed sensational. The Amsterdam belvedere became a top attraction, but equally striking were other new phenomena such as the often picturesque water towers that sprang up on the skylines of cities and which – especially from a distance – demonstrated progress in a spectacular way.[29] Perhaps less spectacular, but soon widespread, was the preference for modern picturesque villas, such as could be found in England, with bays, loggias, sun rooms and even winter gardens – plus an abundance of turrets. In 1882 Vosmaer saw to his displeasure that the 'bugs of the turret disease' had blown over from The Hague to the neighbouring seaside resort of Scheveningen: the 'peculiar' villas that were being built there for the rich and famous, 'inspired by a carpenter-bricklayer imagination', showed turrets to be the latest

Fig.72
The Concertgebouw (Concert Hall), Amsterdam (1883–6), by Adolf L. van Gendt, Jan L. and Jan B. Springer, built no more than a few hundred metres to the rear of the Rijksmuseum (Fig.52). Like the City Theatre in Rotterdam, the Concertgebouw was a new challenge for 'our always calm and stately monumental art' in the tradition of the classical Italian Renaissance.

fashion. Several months later he observed that the 'turret disease' had also infected villa building in Haarlem. 'Turrets everywhere, real turret madness,' he protested, including the 'official style' in his abhorrence of the things.[30] And on the south side of Amsterdam on the banks of the former moat, a variation on the picturesque urban villa was soon to be seen: a luxurious apartment building – with a turret.

In 1883 Berlage articulated his thoughts on the problem of monumentality and picturesque in the townscape in his extensive article, 'Amsterdam and Venice'. Apparently, the reference to Havard's book, noted earlier, was so obvious that he found it unnecessary to mention it. Berlage noted that Venice had a variety of monumental and picturesque townscapes, whereas historic Amsterdam had only picturesque. He described as barbaric the filling in of canals and the destruction of bridges that was going on at several places in Amsterdam. He advocated the establishment of a committee of architects that would supervise from an aesthetic and architectural perspective the inevitable encroachments on to the 'peculiar beauties' of the old city, and that would also be responsible for drawing up an attractive plan, on monumental lines, for the expansion of the city, in order to avoid the monotony so characteristic of recently built districts. And so Berlage cleverly solved the contradiction of the monumental and the picturesque in town planning by geographically separating the two – but at the same time evading the question of how to tackle the sometimes unavoidable eventuality of having to situate a monumental building in a picturesque location.

Berlage's article only confirmed the dilemma caused by the incompatibility of the two aesthetic concepts. Although he demonstrated his loyalty to the classical tradition by emphasizing that the highest form of architecture was the monumental, he was more interested in the characteristics of the picturesque: 'Maintaining the beautiful works originating from that era of splendour is a national concern, universally recognized. And Amsterdam must recognize it too! If we are not vigilant, the loss of the picturesque beauties of our capital will be regretted too late.'

In 1889 the first book on the aesthetics of contemporary urban design was published, *Der Städtebau nach seinen künstlerischen Grundsätzen* (Town Planning according to its Artistic Principles) by the Viennese architect Camillo Sitte (1843–1903). It was based on extensive empirical research into the visual characteristics of picturesque and monumental townscapes. Sitte argued that modern cities required monumental urban design for practical reasons; picturesque urban design was uneconomical for logistical

reasons as well as inconvenient for traffic. However, he worked out proposals for embellishing monumental urban design with the visual and psychological features of the picturesque as embodied in Europe's medieval cities, and in the same year an enthusiastic summary of his plan appeared in *Bouwkundig Weekblad*. Three years later Berlage published a comprehensive article on contemporary town planning, largely plagiarized from Sitte but with his own views on planning issues as they related to Amsterdam.[31] While it is quite clear that Berlage agreed with Sitte's analyses of picturesque urban design, there is nothing to indicate that he was aware of the fact that Sitte was simultaneously working out the theoretical and practical details of two fundamentally new themes. One was the squaring of the circle in urban design: *picturesque monumentality*.[32] The other was the new dimension in the aesthetics of architecture: *urban space*.

Space was a subject that had hitherto received little attention from architects. Back in 1881, August van Delden in his article 'An investigation into the cause of the struggle for Dutch architecture' had considered the question in his discussion of how 'disparate reality can be united into one common picture'. His elaboration of this notion was fascinating: unlike all the other theorists, he made no mention of construction or ornament as the foundation of architecture, but referred to *space* – space as analogous to time in its function of structuring dimension to music. If only for this aspect of his theory, Van Delden proved to have an unusual view of architecture. Among the many thoughts put down on paper by Dutch architects in the 1880s, space did not appear to be a subject of reflection in itself. It must be noted, however, that in this respect they were not in a position to benefit from the views that evolved in Germany. There the strong ascendancy of the psychology of perception awarded the new science an important position in aesthetics and in art and architectural theory. In the last quarter of the century, the results were incorporated in an aesthetic that produced a vast amount of literature on such subjects as the creation of architectural space and the sensation of architectural space. However, hardly any interest in these views can be demonstrated in the Netherlands during this decade.[33] Even urban space was considered in terms of a visual image rather than as space in its own right.

Truth and character, idealism and idealization

Discussions on character and truth were no less central to the debate than they had ever been, the first focusing on the visual and psychological effects of buildings on the public, and the second on the problem of the right kind of

construction and the ornament that went with it. And although the debate was an internal one, taking place within the architectural profession itself, it had a universal relevance, an explicit cultural idealism, even though such idealism was becoming increasingly abstract.

Architecture was still regarded as the most public of all arts and of tremendous potential value as a means of civilizing society. What E. H. Gugel had written on the subject in 1869 in *The History of Styles in the Main Architectural Periods* still held true in 1886 when his book was reprinted: 'There can be no denying that all aspects of architecture ... need to be given a more ideal, a more moral character. If art elevates the coarse, inanimate mass of building materials and, so to say, gives life to them, then it should be instrumental in creating an environment for man that accords with his spiritual development, an environment in which his higher moral sensibility and his desire for artistic satisfaction can be gratified.'[34] The elevation of the coarse mass – formulated in this way,

architectural design itself was an expression of the civilization process. Just as aesthetics and ethics were related to one another, so architectural 'elevation' was also a matter of aesthetics. In other words, lack of architectural truth could never result in architecture, because untruth and civilization were mutually exclusive. This relationship was rarely explicitly referred to – it was manifest.

There was another, very practical reason why architects scrutinized one another on the subject of architectural truth. Truth was the best objective indicator for distinguishing the real architect from the incompetent. Being vigilant in the area of truth, not least in respect of the work of their colleagues, architects kept a keen eye not only on their professional standards but also on their profession itself. Self-regulation was paramount. When, in 1887, Johannes van Nieukerken noticed Adriaan Weissman had camouflaged an iron I-beam above a shop window with an 'impossible' flat brick arch,[35] he remarked that architecture was not 'a matter of tricks and subterfuges'. The basis of

Fig. 73
Ed Cuypers' and C. A. A. Steinigeweg's American Hotel on the Leidseplein in Amsterdam (1879–83). On the left is the Police Headquarters built by Willem Springer (1881). With its six floors and the belvedere on the roof (plus the novelty of a lift), the hotel illustrated the beginnings of the exploitation of height, after American examples, in commercial architecture.

Fig.74
A residential building at 10–14 Weteringschans, Amsterdam (1882), by J. Daverman: a variation on the urban villa – three residences in one tall picturesque Old Dutch building, then at the edge of the city.

the architectural profession was truth. According to Gugel, 'The ideas that architecture wants above all to express result from the construction, and are closely related to the building materials that it employs for the creation of its works.'[36]

These words had force of law – not because they featured in Gugel's book, but because they had been generally accepted for some time. This did not alter the fact that results could vary substantially. Efficiency and good construction were not immutable; they varied at any one time according to the social demands being made on architecture in respect of functionality and comfort, and also according to the technical innovations in the building trade. The work of the older, successful, architects illustrated this variability. Johan Metzelaar was such an architect. During his career, which had spanned forty years he retired in 1886, he had built mansions, villas and factories as well as banks, a swimming pool, shops, offices, prisons and courthouses. His work was characterized by all the new materials and construction methods that had been introduced in his time, whether it be white stuccoed walls or large glass and iron domes. It went without saying, therefore, that the basic building plans had evolved too.[37] Efficiency and good construction were concepts that were always defined in accordance with place, time, the client and the budget.

The plea for good construction and efficiency as essential architectural requirements was in fact nothing other than an echo of Vitruvius' *firmitas* (strength in the context of balance, construction and materials) and *utilitas*.

Fig.75
Johan F. and Willem
C. Metzelaar's State
Prison, Breda
(1883–6).
Commissioned by the
Ministry of Justice,
Metzelaar father and
son built into the
large new Dutch
prisons the modern
penitentiary views
incorporating single
cells and central
surveillance.

Fig.76
The central hall
of J. F. and
W. C. Metzelaar's
State Prison, Breda.
Four tiers of cells
surround the hall,
with surveillance
located in the central
pavilion. The iron
dome construction
has a span of 63
metres.

(successful use and functioning). In the hierarchy of architectural values, which had never been contested, these two led directly to the highest, all-embracing characteristic of architecture – *venustas*, beauty. According to Gugel, 'The beautiful form is always derived from the technical requirements of a building and its function, and is developed in accordance with these. There can never be beauty if efficiency or good construction have not been achieved.' Therefore the skill of the architect focused on the transition from good construction and functionality to beauty: precisely in this transition lay the mystery of architecture. And the transformation from skill to art was theoretically effected via the notion of 'idealization', the expression of the 'idea' of the construction. This idealization manifested itself in details, in particular in the ornamentation – during the 1880s, more important than ever before. There was now more money available, and clients favoured representational decoration more than they had in the past. The building industry supplied an increasing range of ornaments and decorative building materials, as noted earlier, and architectural training attached ever more importance to studying and drawing ornaments. It is important to realize that ornament meant more than superficial decoration. For aesthetics stipulated that ornament with its 'adaptability' reacted to the 'rigid' and 'permanent' aspects of the construction and reinforced the expression of the 'idea' of the building and its constituent parts – the physical 'ideas' such as the laws of statics as well as the 'moral' idea.[38]

Ornament was extremely important to architects during the 1880s. This was apparent from their designs, their buildings and the popularity of the picturesque, which relied on pre-eminently decorative effects. In the architectural journals the subject of ornamentation was covered more frequently than ever before, and this coincided with the equally unbridled enthusiasm for the large variety of historical styles. The differences between the Flemish, German, French, Italian and Dutch Renaissance and the 'official style' were not found in the efficiency or the construction of buildings, but in their ornament.

Stopping the 'decline': medievalism as rationalism

Like all other parts of a building, ornament had to comply with the requirement of truth. In the 60s this convention became accepted as a basic theory, and since that time had been firmly anchored in architectural education. Most relevant here were the concepts of Gottfried Semper and Karl Bötticher concerning the relationship between form, function and construction – the 'core-form' (*Kernform*), the 'art-form' (*Kunstform*) and the concept of 'dressings' (*Bekleidung*). Viollet-le-Duc's statement, 'every form that is not indicated by the construction should be rejected' formulated a little later, amounted to the same. In the 80s Viollet-le-Duc was proclaimed the only true protagonist of architectural truth; serious study was again giving way to slogans, and soon a word that in the context of Dutch architecture would sound very modern indeed would enter the debate: 'rationalism'.

It has already been pointed out that the old theoretical concepts retained their names during this period, while their contents changed. The opposite was also witnessed. 'Rationalism' was a new term with an old content. When it first appeared in the Dutch journals it was put between inverted commas or prefixed with 'so-called' – apparently, it was perceived as a fashionable new French term. This circumspect approach to the word can be explained by the fact that it expressed something for which there had been a Dutch equivalent for quite a while, namely *redegevend* (as the *Bouwkundige Bijdragen* commented at the time, this term had been in frequent use since the 40s). Forms and constructions were said to be *redegevend* if they were logical from the technical and functional point of view; in fact, the word referred to what Heinrich Hübsch had described as 'truth'. The new term made the old Dutch word obsolete within a matter of years.

Immediately after its introduction into the Netherlands, this new French word, *le rationalisme*, was associated with the elder Cuypers' architecture. It remains unclear whether Cuypers and his associates actually encouraged its use, but it is evident that they showed no restraint in using it themselves. The term fitted the strategy that De Stuers had practised since 1874 – namely, concealing his preference for medieval forms and his own ideology behind his 'sound principles', which he attributed exclusively to Viollet-le-Duc. Many examples could be cited to illustrate that this strategy continued to be successful during the 80s, the period when serious study gave way to the frenzy of individual opinions and emotions that we have already encountered. De Stuers' propaganda gained ground, in particular, among the many newcomers to the architectural profession.

'Flâneur', the pseudonym of an architect from Rotterdam, was among those unfamiliar with the traditions of the profession when in 1883 he observed that 'the movement to introduce *truth* into architecture came into existence several years ago'. Another, 'Spectator', wrote the next year that the Renaissance revival coincided with the practice of Viollet-le-Duc's 'rational theory of architecture': 'It is undeniable that the sound theory of Viollet-le-Duc has substantially advanced our national architecture, and that the strict way in which the rational doctrines have been applied have turned out to be a remedy for the many ailments that Dutch architecture has suffered from.' Spectator pointed out that 'only the first Dutch Renaissance period, which was still dominated by medieval construction methods, fitted into the framework of the rational theory of architecture.' This was the very period on which the 'official style' was based. In 1885–6 Cuypers' work was explicitly referred to for the first time as an example of the 'rational style', the style whose maxim was 'every form that is not indicated by the construction should be rejected' (another reference to Viollet-le-Duc, of course).[39] Over the following years, through endless repetitions, the concept of 'rational' would become an exclusive characteristic of Cuypers' work and crucial to his reputation.

It is interesting that this bit of manipulation – which could equally be considered as public relations or propaganda – was not an isolated Dutch affair. It is not dissimilar to what happened in France with Viollet-le-Duc. At the International Conference of Architects in Paris in 1889, one of his disciples fiercely defended the Frenchman's 'rationalist theory of architecture' while at the same time strongly criticizing the education provided by the École des Beaux-Arts. The speaker subsequently

Fig.77
P. J. H. Cuypers'
Central Station,
Amsterdam (1881–9):
entrance to the royal
waiting-room. This
manifestation of
anti-Renaissance
architecture illustrates
the repeated plea for
the restoration of
'permanent' medieval
universal values.
According to
Cuypers' followers,
the maxim for the
'rational style' was:
'every form that is not
indicated by the
construction should
be rejected'.

used the 'rational principles' of Viollet-le-Duc to promote the imitation of medieval architecture.[40]

The similarities with the Netherlands experience are striking. Viollet-le-Duc's theory of medieval architecture and Cuypers' repertoire were presented as purely rational and as the only feasible option to end the architectural decline. It is worth noting that the old feud between Viollet-le-Duc and the École des Beaux-Arts over his unsuccessful professorship in 1864 could still fuel the rhetorics of 1889 – worth noting, because as early as 1864 it had been clear that there were not a single party that could claim a monopoly over 'rationalism'. The influential French critic César Daly wrote that rationalism meant the same to all French architects – classicists, neo-Gothicists and eclectics alike – namely, that architecture consisted of ornamented construction and that architectural design must be based on rational grounds.[41] That the 'rational' contradicted only superficially the education of the École was well known in the Netherlands – and not only to those who were familiar with Parisian architectural practice such as Leliman, Eberson and Gerlof B. and Abraham Salm, father and son, but also to all readers of *Bouwkundig Weekblad*, which in 1885 published an article by Paul Sédille (1836–1900), famous Parisian architect, honorary member of the MBB and friend of Leliman, claiming that so-called rationalism was applied by every serious architect.[42]

No sooner had the adherents of the neo-Gothic and the 'official' style started to appropriate Viollet-le-Duc's theories on medieval architecture than some of their critics, in response, appointed Gottfried Semper as their leader. An article of 1885 recommended studying Semper's works as an antidote to the 'official artistic trend' which 'appears to know only Viollet-le-Duc's theory of utility'. In 1886 a brief outline was published of the basic ideas of Semper's *Style in the Technical and Structural Arts*; it included the subject of 'dressings', and concluded: 'In particular, now, when we are all too frequently required to believe that there is no artistic mode other than that of the late Middle Ages worth our serious study, the time has come to read Semper again.' Berlage too, educated as he had been at Semper's Zürich University from 1875 to 1878, joined in the international veneration of the great man. In an article that he wrote on Semper in 1884 he devoted not one single word to Viollet-le-Duc. The article was a confirmation, in the usual vein of the enlightened liberal and popular culture that chose the Renaissance as its source of inspiration. That Berlage took Semper's side became clear once again three years later when he gave a lecture in the spirit of his book *Style*: 'There is probably no chapter in the history of art

that is more important than that of dressings [*Bekleidung*], for dressings are the basis of all civilization.'[43]

These positions accorded well enough with the jousting that was going on among the few but powerful protagonists of the 'official style', and the rest; it was a debate not so much about the characteristics of architecture itself as about the ideological principles that could be manifested *through* architecture. The contrast created between Viollet-le-Duc and Semper was mainly a matter of semantics.

Realism: a concept appropriate to architecture?

A building becomes architecture when the construction, the floor plan and the elevation take such a shape that they express truth and character. The expression of these ideas is accomplished when the architect 'idealizes' the originally coarse mass of materials. The discussion of this subject cannot end without introducing the counterpart of idealism, realism. As mentioned earlier, the term was quite often encountered in relation to Dutch painting and literature of the 1860s and 70s. 'Realism' meant reflecting reality as it 'really was'. The artist did not *choose* which elements to represent, but respected what manifested itself visually, even if it was not attractive; nor did he have any intention of 'edifying' the observer. In other words, the foremost responsibility of a work of art was not to express some high idea. The literary representation of the commonplace, the 'ordinary', including the use of coarse language and 'banalities', made realism popular with the public – to the great displeasure of the conventional purveyors of culture. 'It is a dangerous phenomenon that the modern artist is ruled by the public at large, thus becoming its slave, whereas it is his duty to civilize and edify the public through his art.'[44]

However, at the time, the concept of realism was rarely associated with architecture. Indeed, as noted in Chapter 5, idealism was so fused with architecture that there was no room for realism. But the term was sometimes used during the 80s in the context of Cuypers' works. Referring to the interior of the Rijksmuseum, Adriaan Weissman wrote in 1885: 'Realism has ... already begun to invade architecture. "Truth above all things" is now here, too, the foremost requirement, and this truth is shown in its full nakedness: inner walls expose their coarse bricks, and rivets are gilded so as to demonstrate the architect's technical knowledge to the public.' Gugel noted another application of the word: the 'official style', he remarked, was considered 'realistic and vulgar' by many.[45]

There can be no doubt that Cuypers was an idealist and that his critics were fully aware of the fact; each detail of his œuvre was designed to make it possible to experience an ideal or thought of a higher reality. 'Exaltation' was Cuypers' highest aim. When critics pointed to examples of 'coarse realism' in his work, this was because they were looking for a synonym for 'poor execution'. The educational institutes designed by Van Lokhorst – a kindred spirit – had plain brick interiors; their heavy brick arches and flights of stairs, their brick vaulting and doorways, 'evoke thoughts of a state prison more than of a school that should excite feelings of joy'.[46] Cuypers' and Van Lokhorst's choice for such interior was subjective, a matter of taste, which by appealing to the precepts of Viollet-le-Duc acquired an appearance of objectiveness. Yet again the problem was something that the creators of the 'official style' were not able to bring off: achieving a character that suited a building's function. It would seem that the rhetoric of Cuypers and his associates themselves, that truth was the only important consideration, was responsible for the criticism of 'coarse realism'; after all, the realistic reflected nothing but the truth, however unattractive.

Apart from this play on words there was still, essentially, no room for the concept of realism in architecture. The relevance of this observation is not solely theoretical. Concepts reflect a way of thinking, but are also related to a way of acting, of doing things. The absence of realism in architecture in the 1880s implies that it was not considered possible to incorporate a touch of 'the commonplace' into it, in the sense of the popular, the 'ordinary', applied for its own sake and not as the expression of architectural laws, or truth. Realism took shape, as noted in Chapter 5, in a kind of architectural counterculture, visible mainly in large-scale city expansion. This counterculture, in fact, did reflect the real situation: the reality of commercial 'art' designed for a public that was being given what it wanted and that had no need for any expression of 'higher values'.

During the 80s the vast majority of 'real' architects still showed no trace of understanding, or indeed of tolerating, the new 'realism'. They egged each other on in their contempt for this ever-growing trend in building. 'No one would claim that the last ten or fifteen years, in which house building has reached an all-time peak, has been particularly instrumental in promoting national architecture – quite the contrary, in fact,' wrote one architect in 1886. 'What predominate are absence of character and the pursuit of profit.'[47] This bitterness was possibly motivated by envy, but even then it remains unclear why the qualified architects concentrated so exclusively on historic houses and picturesque townscapes derived from a distant past, while ignoring contemporary mass housing.

The only explanation seems to be that they were holding

one another hostage with their ideas on the art of building, with their notions of truth and character and their idealization of coarse materials. Haggling over these rules would, in the end, ring the death knell for their artistic calling. Most architects probably still agreed with the philosopher Johanns van Vloten's dictum that mass housing was by definition unsuitable for art, because it was 'exclusively intended for practical use, for farmers or manual workers'. However attractive such a house might be, it could not be 'beautiful in a higher sense', because this

presupposed that the architecture was expressing in the wood and stone an artistic idea. 'Of course this is far more difficult to realize in ordinary buildings than in temples or churches, for example, the spiritual dimension of which directly results in beautiful proportions.'[48]

Thus mass housing came into being in a climate which, according to the rules of art, permitted it no part in the art of building. Those who wished to hold on to the rules viewed this development in a sad light – witness a remark by one observer about a building project started in 1886 by an Amsterdam housing corporation: 'It is inexplicable to us how anyone can find the patience and stamina to draw hundreds of squares of identical shape and size on a piece of paper a metre wide and call this a façade.'[49]

To many architects in the 1880s it seemed as if architecture had been resurrected or awakened from a deep sleep. There were now so many clients, commissions and building activities. However, the public was more demanding than before. As a consequence, architects had

strong reasons to believe that architecture became a commodity, guided by publicity and fashion. In this atmosphere, it was only natural that the subjective basis of architectural beauty became more prominent, favouring the picturesque. In the late eighteenth century the picturesque had manifested itself in the design of beautiful landscape gardens; now it took shape in a new sense of urban space, in more discussion on the aesthetics of architecture in its urban context, in the appreciation of height and of richly ornamented façades. For all these new aspects, the Dutch Renaissance proved to be the ideal concept of form.

In the meantime architects continued their debates on what they saw as the art of building's essential issues – such as their expression of the elevating 'idea', or the creation of a 'national' style. Just like it had done in the 70s, the campaign of the 'official style' positioned itself in the focus of many a professional debate; new energy and new emotions were now being activated by the introduction of the term 'rationalism'. All these issues, fundamental as they

Fig.80
One hundred and forty-four flats designed by W. and P. J. Hamer in the Van Woustraat – 2de Jan van der Heydenstraat – Hemonystraat block, Amsterdam (1888), commissioned by the Association for the Working Classes. Hamer father and son were among the few architects who frequently took on social housing, with a realist aesthetic that included façades with 'hundreds of small squares of identical shapes and sizes'.

might have seemed in the 80s, were however very soon to become highly abstract, and peripheral.

Notes

1. Aspiration and dedication: the director of the 200-year-old Hague Academy of the Visual Arts, J. Ph. Koelman, cited by Flanor 1882, 185. Fierce resistance: A. W. Weissman 1882.
2. 'Hugo Pieter Vogel', *De Opmerker* 21 (1886) no. 2, 9–10.
3. J. F. Klinkhamer 1881; *De Opmerker* 17 no. 10, 11.3.1882; H. P. Berlage 1886; W. Kromhout 1889.
4. *Bouwkundig Weekblad* 2 (1882) no. 15, 269.
5. I. Gosschalk 1871, 169.
6. *Bouwkundig Weekblad* 2 (1882) no. 15, 269.
7. Y. 1881.
8. J. R. de Kruyff 1885, 78.
9. *De Opmerker* 21 (1886) no. 37, 296.
10. Henry Havard 1874–7, in 2nd edn of vol. 2, 3–4.
11. J. Ingenohl 1891, 19. Developments in photography and lithography: Ronald Stenvert 1995, 115–16. J. R. de Kruyff 1885, 104 had already pointed out that the Dutch book market was being flooded from Germany.
12. *De Portefeuille* 7 (1885) no. 11, 173.
13. Carel Vosmaer 1885, 263.
14. E. Rittner Bos 1888; J. Nieuwenhuis 1883, 450.
15. *Il Puttino* 1883, 72.
16. J. R. de Kruyff 1885, 104; H. P. Vogel [1888, 2nd edn], 152.
17. J. R. de Kruff 1876, 41.
18. E. J. Hobsbawm, Terence Ranger (ed.) 1983. For the Netherlands: J. Th. M. Bank 1990.
19. J. Th. J. Cuypers 1888; F. J. Nieuwenhuis 1888; 'De officieele richting tentoongesteld' ('The official style exhibited'), *De Opmerker* 23 (1888) no. 51, 408–9; no. 52, 415–16.
20. C. T. J. Louis Rieber 1884, 324.
21. A. W. Weissman 1883.
22. Sketch club: *De Opmerker* 18 (1883) no. 25, 245; W. 1884; W. Kromhout 1887 and 1888a; W. C. Bauer 1888.
23. C. Muysken 1881.
24. *De Opmerker* 20 (1885) no. 20, 173.
25. Hetty E. M. Berens 1999, chs 2 and 3.
26. H. P. Vogel 1885, 343, 345.
27. A et A: *De Opmerker* 16 no. 53, 31.12.1881. J. Kok 1884, 339.
28. Bert Vreeken, Ester Wouthuysen 1987, 113–18. The hotel was demolished in 1900 to make way for the present building with the same name. The main attraction of the lift was that there were only five other lifts at that time in the whole of the Netherlands: four in the Rotterdam hospital and one in the Diaconessen Hospital in Arnhem ('Hydraulic lifts', *Vademecum der Bouwvakken* 4 (1889), 14).
29. Water towers: Pauline Houwink 1973.

30. Jannes de Haan 1986, chs 4 and 5 for picturesque villa development in England and its influence in the Netherlands. Vosmaer: Flanor 1882, 86–7 and 346.

31. S. 1889; H. P. Berlage 1892a.

32. On the initial handling of Sitte by Berlage: Manfred Bock 1983, 104–20, in which Bock implicitly allied himself with the tradition in which Sitte's argument is considered (quite wrongly) a pure defence of the picturesque. On this tradition: Camillo Sitte 1991, afterword.

33. A bibliographical overview of developments in Germany: Harry F. Mallgrave, Eleftherios Ikonomou 1994 (introduction); this collection also contains several translations of relevant texts. For a few rare examples of Dutch texts: H. L. Berckenhoff 1875, 29, in a review of L. Noiré 1874: 'fine architecture is based in particular on specific dimensions of space'. H. W. A. Croiset van Uchelen 1887 reviewed F. Luthmer, *Malerische Innenräume moderner Wohnungen* (Picturesque Interiors of Modern Houses) (1885), in which the spatial effects of proportion, light and colour were mentioned. August van Delden 1881, 10 postulated that the perceptible world manifests itself in space and time; the eye produces an image of space which is itself invisible; 'space is the basis of architecture'.

34. E. Gugel 1869, 1st edn, 26; and 1886, 2nd edn, 25.

35. J. J. van Nieukerken 1887.

36. E. Gugel 1886, 2nd edn, 9.

37. A brief and incomplete overview of his work in C. T. J. Louis Rieber 1897; for work of his commissioned by the state: Paul T. E. E. Rosenberg 1995b, 301–13.

38. E. Gugel 1886, 2nd edn, 23–4 (technical requirements); 40 (ornament).

39. Flâneur 1883; Spectator 1884; Cuypers: A. Reyding 1885 and 1886, 46.

40. *De Opmerker* 24 (1889) no. 29, 243–4.

41. Cited by Peter Collins 1971, 3rd edn, 198. This statement from Daly is the beginning of Collins' chapter on rationalism, which despite Daly's multiform definition links rationalism almost exclusively to neo-Gothic architecture.

42. Paul Sédille 1885.

43. Antidote: *De Opmerker* 20 (1885) no. 1, 4–5. Brief outline: *De Opmerker* 21 (1886) no. 49, 393–4; no. 50, 401–2. H. P. Berlage 1884, 142; H. P. Berlage 1889, 23. For the influence of Semper's ideas on Berlage: Pieter Singelenberg 1976. Also illuminating, the analysis of Iain Boyd Whyte 1993, who compares the influence of Semper on Otto Wagner and Berlage.

44. Enrichetta (pseud.) 1883, 429.

45. A. W. Weissman 1885, 402; E. Gugel 1886, 2nd edn, 946.

46. A. B. J. Sterck 1889, 27.

47. W. J. de Groot 1886, 66.

48. J. van Vloten 1871, 2nd edn, 171.

49. R. 1886. For mass housing in Amsterdam: Carol Schade 1981; a typology of nineteenth-century Dutch housing: Niels L. Park 1991, chs 2 and 3.

8

On the Brink of Change

The relationship between the arts

Architecture is the mother of the visual arts, because prehistoric man first built a shelter and then decorated it with the first manifestations of sculpture and painting. Thus ran the old Vitruvian view that was maintained well into the nineteenth century. In this century architecture was also referred to as the sister of the arts, an expression that fits well with the democratizing tendencies of the times. After Semper's *Style in the Technical and Structural Arts*, room was also found for a radically different vision: the notion that architecture did not develop until relatively late in the evolution of the arts. On anthropological and archaeological grounds Semper had evolution start with the household goods of the nomads, their pottery and fabrics. It was therefore logical that his theory of art should start with these artefacts and that the art of building should make up the third and final part of his book (the part that remained unwritten). Semper's academic theory of art gave a tremendous boost to the social status of the decorative arts, and especially industrial art, as witnessed in the final decades of the century. What this emancipation ultimately implied would be explained much later, around 1925, by the artist and theorist Theo van Doesburg (1883–1931) when he proclaimed in the periodical *De Stijl* an art of painting that 'deconstructed' architecture by 'dissolving' buildings in colour – painting that made architecture disappear.

The emancipation of the decorative arts did not mean that their relationship with the art of building was a neutral one. On the contrary, the process that started in the nineteenth century made it necessary to develop anew the relationship between the arts. This new rapport is conveyed in a word that appears regularly in texts of the 1880s: 'cooperation'. One of these texts is Weissman's essay of 1886, 'The relationship between the arts'. Here he analysed the artistic flowering of the visual arts, architecture, music, opera, the theatre and belles-lettres, concluding that the revival of sculpture and painting in relation to architecture had started around 1870. This had come about, he said, as a result of the study of the Italian Renaissance, in which pioneering work had been done, especially in Germany, and good use made of education in the industrial arts. Although

Semper's name was not mentioned in the article, it is clear that he was the driving force behind the 'giant steps' that, in Weissman's view, industrial art had recently taken.

It is worth noting that Weissman did not include the neo-Gothic movement and the resulting 'official style' in this development – and this was all the more remarkable because Catholic church building throughout Western Europe had shown a strong partiality for the synthesis of the arts as exemplified in the neo-Gothic. All the same, as far as the Netherlands was concerned, Weissman's analysis seems reasonable. In relation to the vast span of the European Renaissance, the Dutch neo-Gothic movement was too specific and marginal to be considered the driving force behind the new rapport between the arts. The same could not be said of the 'official style', mainly because De Stuers spared no effort in promoting state architecture as the driving force behind both industrial art and the cooperation between the arts. Jos Cuypers touched on this with reference to the exhibition of Van Lokhorst's designs of 1888.

Today in particular many buildings show no sign of that intrinsic connection and collaboration required between the architect and sculptor involved in the same project. Both parties should venture on to one another's territory so as to gain a complete understanding of each other's work. All too few artists nowadays share this aim, to which they should now resolutely direct their efforts. The turmoil of artistic life is such that only a few reach a common level that permits them to share a common horizon. There will be a good chance for that rapport to come about when the architect is able to support and guide his fellow artists, the painter and the sculptor.[1]

This aptly illustrates the conservative route that the 'official style' was taking: the modern art world was in such a turbulent state, apparently, that some kind of authority was required to control it. This view cultivated the image of building as the most prominent of the visual arts – and therefore the image of the architect as the most prominent artist. By 1890 this image would be unrealistic and old-fashioned, because it denied the growing collaboration between the arts, which was based on equality. Jos Cuypers was in fact describing the practice of his father, who had demonstrated clearly enough with the Rijksmuseum what he understood by collaboration between the arts. The artists with whom the elder Cuypers worked were, with a few exceptions, not artists in the traditional sense but faceless employees, craftsmen who exercised minimal artistic freedom and whom the painter Anton B. J. Sterck in 1889 referred to as 'machines, with no will of their own'.[2] The idea of the architect's primacy over his fellow artists led the 'official style' to propagate a collaboration between the arts that was already past history.

The relationship with technology

While architecture was involved from the artistic point of view in a process that had started in the decorative arts, it now became involved in another identity crisis, this time concerning its relation to the technical sciences, which were developing rapidly. But was the problem here the social position of the architect, or architecture itself? The professionalization of the architect had over the past decades distanced him from the incompetents and the designer-craftsmen by emphasizing that the architectural profession comprised both art and science; and architects monitored developments in building techniques as well as those of the art world. The ever-increasing stream of information on new building methods that the journals produced illustrated the growing importance of the technical aspects of architectural practice.

In the 80s, even more than in the 60s, innovations in building techniques undermined architectural theory and made it increasingly obsolete. Take, for instance, the status of iron. In architectural theory there was still no clear concept of building with iron. While year by year the engineers were constantly expanding its possibilities, architects were fighting a rearguard action on the question of whether clad steel constructions should be regarded as an 'artistic lie'. The 1880s also witnessed the first experiments in building with concrete. While the architectural journals described the characteristics of the material and its applications, the artistic possibilities of concrete were not the subject of public discussion, it would seem, because aesthetics offered no framework in which to discuss it. Similarly with the latest inventions for the lighting and heating of buildings and in sanitary fittings and communication. Technical wonders from the United States, on the other hand, were reported with a degree of disbelief, frequently accompanied by a suggestion of artistic superiority. While the building sector witnessed an international revolution that would change for ever the nature of *firmitas* and *utilitas* in the art of building, the Netherlands refrained from any theoretical reflection on the consequences for *venustas*.

This is illustrated by architects' ambivalent attitude towards Delft Polytechnic. The tendency to criticize the school for its limited artistic curriculum, while showing no appreciation for its technical expertise, so important at this juncture, raises several questions. Was it that the architects, whether aware of it or not, were using the strategy they had adopted against the incompetent builders – that of idealizing their profession as art – against the engineers as well? For what other profession than that of the artist could claim to stand at the vanguard of civilization, the first in the field to attempt to edify the ordinary masses? Or was it that most architects were reluctant to adopt the new technology because it was creating a new world that they were not yet ready to get to grips with, caught up as they were in the familiar confines of the sixteenth and early seventeenth centuries? Or – yet another possibility – had the cultural gulf between art and science already become too great? The unprecedented success of the sciences in the nineteenth century did indeed result in a far-reaching cultural change – one in which the technical would supplant the artistic in its usefulness to society.

For the time being, we can only speculate on why architects were so ambivalent towards the technical sciences, which manifested themselves so powerfully in the field of architecture. It is understandable that they should have sought a way to remain in charge of their own discipline. Perhaps their ideal is expressed in Delft engineer and architect Posthumus Meyjes' enthusiastic description in 1885 of the new Palace of Justice in Brussels (1866–83), the Herculean work of the Belgian architect Joseph Poelaert. During the design stage Poelaert had been assisted by engineers, who had served to make the artist's talent shine even brighter. 'While the architect together with his young assistants was now able to concentrate on the artistic solutions and to make a thorough study of those aspects, the engineers and their technical assistants were busy realizing by means of ingenious constructions and elaborate calculations the ideas dictated by the artist. This meant that some people had to play a seemingly unrewarding role and to give a low profile to their own originality and personality, but it was the overriding intention of all concerned to help achieve the master's aim.'[3]

The decline of the historical school

While the past was a source of unlimited inspiration, at the same time it presented an enormous intellectual obstacle. This dichotomy was not new – the only new factor was that so many architects in the 1880s saw themselves confronted with it. There was such a vast reservoir both of historical knowledge and of architectural types to be followed, and yet so little time for reflection and so little intellectual consistency. In the 60s there had been relatively little knowledge of architectural history and relatively few architects, but these few had been fully convinced that history would turn out to be a source of knowledge for the future. Rose wrote in 1865: 'We know more, and there are more means available to us. It is easier than ever before to report on what is happening in even the most remote countries … There is a positive aspect to this because it brings us further, with less effort and in a shorter time, than at any other time.[4] By the 80s this optimism was on the wane. History had become as complex as the present, with an ever-diminishing ability to point to the future. Architects were in universal agreement on one issue only: making new copies of old types of building had nothing to do with art.

Adriaan Weissman was one of those who warned architects not to become archaeologists, not to select their models on the grounds of age but on the grounds of beauty, and to leave the rest to the 'professional antiquarians'. In reply, the young Henri Evers defended his profession against the reproaches 'which are heaped upon us almost daily by art critics, art lovers and laymen', that architects no longer designed, but copied, and had become scholars or archaeologists rather than artists. In 1887 one author, repudiating 'the desire to look for the historical background of everything', stated: 'our architects are no longer architects, they have become Viollet-le-Ducs – or, rather, that is who they all *want* to become'. Such reactions against the influence of history were the first signs that the end of the historical school was approaching. In 1888 L. M. Moolenaar wrote that the public regarded architecture in the 'so-called styles' as 'stuff to be got from the grocer's'. But, 'fortunately for that same public, and perhaps also for the art of building, we shall soon, unless I am mistaken, be relieved of these so-called Old Dutch and Old German façades and scrollwork. There are several indications that this is happening already in Germany.'[5]

The most severe criticism of historical architecture was the accusation that its artistic manifestations were not 'original'. Its advocates would unrelentingly emphasize that they did not imitate – let alone copy – historic examples, but, rather, studied them in order to apply their aesthetic 'rules'. But the critics argued that the results were hardly any different from the originals. Everything revolved around the meaning of the term 'imitation'. Just as previous generations imitated Vignola or Jan Willem Bosboom's five orders in an attempt to bring them back to life for each new commission, in the 80s many architects studied lavishly illustrated books such as Gugel's *Architectural Morphology*.

Yet there was an important difference between this and the earlier classicist practice. In their abstract perfection the five orders represented the very essence of architecture – were so abstract, indeed, as to exclude the possibility of imitation. The books of orders were little more than grammar books, the formal rules of an architectural 'language'. Did Dutch Renaissance have such a succinct formula, such an abstract set of rules? The answer, of course, was no. The nineteenth-century image of Dutch Renaissance had no abstract core, no matter how assiduously one was sought. The image was, rather, a sum of formal elements, an inventory of construction and ornament from the past which the study of architectural history caused to continually expand and diversify. Whereas classicism had its own 'grammar', Dutch Renaissance had only an ever-expanding dictionary.

In view of the proliferation of 'imitations' of one sort or another, the unwavering expectation of the 1880s that contemporary building style would develop shortly was remarkable. The often expressed view, mentioned earlier, that after a period of decline architecture was again thriving, reinforced the idea that a contemporary style would soon be forthcoming. What is odd is that this idea was current then, for it had already become clear that architecture was in no state to produce a new style in the sense of a generally and artistically applicable one. Heinrich Hübsch had realized as early as 1847 that the enormous versatility and volatility of commercial aesthetics made it impossible for a new building style to develop unless it was accepted that a new 'style' would spring up every few years.[6] But despite the fact that building experience itself had proved Hübsch right for forty years, this insight had been widely ignored. As the status of the architecture profession had eroded – at least, in the opinion of many architects – their optimism concerning a contemporary style, in the sense of a universal art form, only increased.

Imitation: a feasible alternative?

In retrospect it would be all too simple to characterize the aspiration of those architects who sought a universal contemporary art form as an illusion. The reality was that from the perspective of many in the 80s eclecticism was a capitulation to the superficial commercial spirit of the century and 'style' in the sense of one universally accepted convention was interpreted as the most natural, pure manifestation of architecture. To such people, renouncing this idea, this ideal, would have meant a step into the professional wilderness. In the transition from the 1880s to the 1890s, this tormenting problem would be gradually solved, as the idea began to dawn that a contemporary architecture could not derive from a past architecture. As soon as the notions of 'contemporary' and 'original' were linked, a new concept was born that was to have a powerful cultural impact. This new concept, which would come to full maturity in the 90s, allowed no room for the historical school. The historical school had claimed to be contemporary and original, but its imitation of the past, practised more intensely in the 1880s than ever before, made this claim unworthy of belief.

'Imitation' had already been the basis of art since antiquity, and because it was closely related to the artist's desire to surpass the original, the imitation of art also implied its progress. It would seem obvious, however, that the abundance of historic architectural types that study had revealed, particularly since the 1870s, rendered the principle of imitation unworkable – the amount of material available for study had simply expanded beyond control. What Hübsch and, later, Semper had established for the Gothic style – namely, that its medieval practitioners had explored all conceivable possibilities and thus exhausted it – was *mutatis mutandis* increasingly applicable to Dutch Renaissance. No matter how great the effort nineteenth-century architects made to study Dutch Renaissance, they could not surpass it, and this became more and more evident as new material became available for study.

As historical knowledge continued to expand beyond all imagining, the historical style slowly but surely became the victim of its own success. It then transpired that there was only one way forward: there had to be a contemporary originality that was separate from the past. Several articles, published at the time, illustrate this dawning realization. The first, which appeared anonymously in *De Opmerker* in 1883, described originality as pre-eminently a character of nineteenth-century art, but warned against excess and wild, individual fancy. To prevent this, the writer set this originality within the conventional context of emulation and imitation: 'It is better to follow good examples than to give life to original yet imperfect creations. To focus on originality is only permitted if the rules of aesthetics are duly observed.'[7]

A few years later the concept of originality would acquire a somewhat different meaning; here, the competition for the Amsterdam Stock Exchange in 1885 appears to have played the role of catalyst. The many entries for the competition were evidence of the strong position of the historical style in its many variants. However, they also posed a problem for the architectural community, especially those familiar with architectural history: namely, the limited scope of historical types for the purposes of competition: 'No architect can nowadays be found in this world who is able to design a monument that meets today's demands (in this case, a Stock Exchange) or that can outshine a single historic monument.' Proof of the truth of this claim, surprisingly enough, was delivered by the winning entry. It caused a stir because the French architect, L. M. Cordonnier, who had imitated a number of historical types in his entry, was accused of having committed plagiarism.[8] The debate that followed in the journals illustrated how open to question the usual assumption of emulation and imitation had become and how difficult it proved to be to defend at that time. When, a year after the Stock Exchange competition, a critic using historical examples as criteria took exception to the ornamentation of the architect A. C. Bleys' Church of St Nicholas in Amsterdam (1885–7) as lacking in taste, Bleys replied: 'We live at a time in which slavish imitation is so commonly accepted that people dare to copy anything and everything, even entire buildings. As a consequence, some of my details, which have nothing to do with copying, are criticized as being strange.'[9] The past contained the ideal that was to be imitated, but imitating bordered on copying, while free interpretation was likely to pale into insignificance compared with the historical example. This dilemma could not be allowed to paralyse the architectural world: completely new ways had to be explored.

Imitation or originality: the eclectics

This chapter and the previous two have focused a fair amount of attention on the ideas of the historical school, whose advocates set the agenda for the professional discussions that took place. But in the practice of architecture there was still more than enough room for that other design concept: *eclecticism*, with its conscious lack of style. J. H. Leliman and his friends, such as Lucas Eberson and the young virtuoso Abraham ('Bram') Salm (1857–1915), made a no less thorough study of historic architecture than their colleagues who built 'in style', but they felt no inclination to put all their money on one specific style.[10] As already noted, designing was for them the realization of the maximum of artistic freedom with regard to the past. The difficulty that presents itself in recording the history of eclecticism is that, because of its pragmatic and freedom-loving attitude, it resulted neither in the development of a theory nor in fierce controversies in defence of its own position. Therefore, there is little documentary evidence. Eclecticism had little to explain, except that the artist, provided he upheld the laws of truth and character, must be artistically free. The only possible

polemic contained in this view was the question of whether, given his role in the modelling of the modern nineteenth century, the architect was not *obliged* to depart from history.

It can be established without much difficulty that eclecticism played a much more limited role in determining the architectural debate in the 80s than the historical school did. The eclectics' limited inclination to develop a theory is certainly not the only explanation. Another lies in the character and performance of Leliman, who for years had been the champion of artistic freedom. He was still much respected by his colleagues, but as an architect he had failed to set an inspiring example – his œuvre had remained very limited, not least, perhaps, because from an early age he had been able to live on a private income. His entry for the international Jubilee Exhibition in Berlin in 1886 was in fact the old design that he had produced for the Arti et Amicitiae club and exhibition building at his debut in 1855. He was still much respected as a speaker – in 1888 he was reported as delivering his 'hundred and umpteenth' lecture[11] – but his words on architectural theory gradually became little more than eloquent entertainment. The other architects who worked successfully in the eclectic mode were neither speakers nor authors – they were simply too busy with building.

Perhaps it was not surprising, then, that the supporters of the historical school hardly ever referred to eclecticism. It may be an exaggeration to say that they followed a say-nothing policy, but their silence was nevertheless pretty stubborn. Intellectually, as we have seen, the historical school occupied a totally different world, in which people dreamed of a style, a collective and universal architectural concept, that gave no primacy – if it acknowledged it at all – to individual artistic freedom. But perhaps its supporters sometimes also had less worthy motives, such as a certain envy of the pragmatism and flexibility with which the eclectic architects complied with their clients' wishes. In practice the architecture of eclecticism was no more a 'commodity' than was that of the historical school; the difference lay in the fact that eclecticism accepted the commercial aspects of architecture as a condition of the modern age, whereas the historical school denied them, or – in theory, at least – rejected them.

The advance of commercial architecture which started in the Netherlands in the 1870s resulted for both the historical school and eclecticism in the vulgarization and mass production of the architectural repertoire. Here eclecticism turned out to be vulnerable to the criticism, and in some cases, envy, of its opponents. Whereas the 'real' eclectic architects based their work on a thorough study of architectural history, the incompetents made 'collages'

Fig.81
The Natura Artis Magistra Zoological Museum, Amsterdam (1879–82), by Gerlof Bart and Abraham Salm. Renaissance motifs from Italy and France are seen here in an eclectic arrangement: Salm father and son shared a love for the concepts of form of the École des Beaux-Arts in Paris, where the younger Salm was a student around 1880.

from the many illustrated books and building industry catalogues. The dividing line between the two was visible only to insiders: the criterion was, as ever, whether the buildings contained truth, in the sense in which it had ceaselessly been propounded by Leliman and many others.

The issue is illustrated by a rare example of eclectic 'architectural theorizing' that was published by *Bouwkundig Weekblad* in 1885. This was the article by Paul Sédille, mentioned earlier, cited in relation to his comments on 'rationalism'. Sédille's international reputation was based, among other things, on the sophisticated Au Printemps department store (1882–9) on the boulevard Haussman in Paris. In the article he refuted the 'trite reproach' that eclecticism had gone under in the maelstrom 'of eclectic taste, typical of modern times' by stating that the principles governing modern Parisian architecture were the very same that had been developed by great architects such as Labrouste, Duban, Duc and Vaudoyer, namely:

1. A building's layout must first and foremost take into account its function(s).
2. The function(s) and the layout of the interior must be made clear by the building's exterior.
3. The construction must use to advantage modern building techniques and be rationally geared to the nature and characteristics of the building materials.
4. The design and ornamentation of the building must accord with its function and character.

Sédille concluded that modern aesthetics had derived these rules from the architecture of all periods. They represented the conditions for truth in architecture; and because truth demanded that buildings with different functions should have different appearances, the image of variety complied perfectly with the nineteenth-century diversity of building types. Therefore truth implied that an architectural style in the traditional, historic sense – embodying a uniform and universally applicable concept of form – was impossible for the modern era.[12]

However, it is not impossible that, precisely because of its success in Paris, eclecticism was not as well regarded among architects in the Netherlands. As we have seen, Paris was considered the epitome of what a modish and fickle public could achieve.

The subjective gains ground
Eclecticism may not have had a significant role in the debates of the 80s, but, all the same, its position was a strong one, as contemporary originality manifested itself as the only possible alternative to the advent, uncertain as that

would be, of a new style based on historical examples. Within a few years there would be no doubt about it that contemporary originality would mean architecture *without style*. This was not a theoretical proposition, but a logical deduction based on practice. A building took several years to complete and had dated before it was finished, wrote one architect in 1886, 'showing how rapidly ideas in architecture change'.[13] A better way of expressing the uselessness of trying to envisage a contemporary style for this period would be hard to imagine. It was no longer possible to deny the fact that views on architecture were becoming more individual and more subjective. Furthermore, for some architects emotions were replacing reason as the guide to good architecture – during the 80s these formed a small minority, but they heralded a tendency that would make itself felt in the 90s. In 1885 Moolenaar wrote: 'As soon as cold reasoning becomes susceptible to the increasingly exalting effects of emotion, the foundation will have been laid for an architectural work of art.'[14]

The increased importance of the emotions had already manifested itself in the success of the picturesque; for, as already discussed, the picturesque emphasized the sensory and individual experience while attaching less value to the rational, or to what is open to objectification. It had only a few fixed rules, and it developed less from a design theory than from individual practice – in this it contrasted with monumental art, which held on to the canon of classicism. Take, for example, the application of one of the oldest and most basic rules of composition – the rule of symmetry. In monumental architecture, the image of a building is exactly mirrored on both sides of the central axis. Only in exceptional cases, such as with a graceful building in a wooded landscape, could the principle of symmetry be replaced by 'proportionality', or what the French called *la pondérabilité*: in this arrangement, the volumes on either side of the central axis would be roughly equal, but the two forms would differ strikingly.[15] In picturesque architecture, this traditional exception to the rule became the main rule. But balancing this deliberate asymmetry was more a matter of artistic intuition than of the ruler, and favourite compositional options such as turrets and steep trusses were sometimes far from rational as far as *utilitas* was concerned.

The fact that rationality lost ground is also evident in the fact that ornament, ideally the expression of the significance of a building in terms of truth and character, started to lose its *raison d'être*. This became apparent from the growing independence of the decorative arts, which started in art education and was to continue in practice into the next decade. This decline was also illustrated by the

Fig.82
Jacob Nienhuys'
Residence, 380–2
Herengracht,
Amsterdam
(1888–90), by
Abraham Salm. The
building demonstrates
the Renaissance style
in a refined
expression of
affluence – the client
was an extremely
wealthy tobacco
planter –
simultaneously
referring to the
elegant François I
style and the world-
famous 'billonaire's
residence' of William
K. Vanderbilt on Fifth
Avenue, New York
(1879–81, by Richard
Morris Hunt).

interest in non-Western ornaments, not with a view to discovering universal 'laws' but purely on account of their visual appeal. In 1885 it was observed, 'Recently young designers of ornament seem to have felt compelled to study in particular Japanese and Persian in order to create a kind of new, individual style.'[16]

Finally can be noted a new usage of language originated by architects writing on the subject of architecture. Their phraseology showed some similarity with contemporary literary criticism and with art reviews. This was a language produced by and for a cultural coterie, to do pre-eminently with the subjective formulation of a work of art, even if basic architectural themes which until then had always been associated with 'serious study' were its subject. Young Jan Ernst van der Pek (1865–1919) can be cited here: when in 1885 he drew a comparison between Belgian, German and Dutch Renaissance ornaments, he found the Dutch examples 'wittier and more sophisticated. In our country new ideas appear to have been expressed with more artistic feeling than in neighbouring countries'. The north German Renaissance, he continued, evolved a type of house with a 'deathlike' character resembling a 'mass of brickwork, dry in conception as well as in execution', which like the Belgian equivalents looked decidedly gloomy yet robust. He described the ornaments in a variety of ways – interesting, disturbing, anything but refreshing, a little messy, or downright atrocious.[17] Van der Pek was not exceptional in this respect: this was the way in which many of his colleagues described ornaments. In the late 80s, architecture became to many a matter of emotional response.

The pan-European generation

In 1885 Van der Pek was twenty years of age. He belonged to a new generation in their twenties and thirties who were well educated and who now had the opportunity to present themselves and their original ideas. They did not feel at ease in the ideological trenches in which the older generation was trapped, and were indifferent to their aesthetic conventions. What this younger generation could not find among their elders they looked for among their contemporaries, who would change the course of the visual arts and of literature, sometimes causing upheaval along the way. These young innovators included impressionist painters of the Hague School and the Amsterdam painter George Hendrik Breitner, sculptors such as Lambertus Zijl and Joseph Mendes de Costa, producers of realist 'monsters', and the *Tachtigers*, the '80s men' mentioned earlier, who were felt by some to be a threat to literature. The poet Albert Verwey was speaking for the *Tachtigers*

when he stated that around 1880 the imagination became the dominant and creative force in poetry, replacing reason. 'Reasoning' and 'ideas' were now replaced by an 'image of reality'. It was typical of this generation that its representatives were prepared to confront the established order of the older one. This was the generation that would prepare the ground for the radical changes in architecture that were to manifest themselves in the 1890s, and it seized its chance with the rise to prominence of the individual and the subjective.

The younger architects may have absorbed ideas and attitudes from abroad that would not have had any practical effect in this decade but which with hindsight would have played a role in the process. Both at home and abroad fundamental change was in the air. In England, influenced by the Arts and Crafts Movement, the value of the *vernacular*, the beauty of the ordinary dwelling, was discovered in architecture. In Germany, where for half a century great progress had been made in psychology, the first applications of the new science to architecture were published in the the form of studies of the effects of light, colour and space.[18] In France, the architectural eclecticism of men like Sédille was regarded as realism, to be transformed into *Sachlichkeit* – a major constituent of early Modernism – in the not too distant future via Viennese and German architects.[19] The German architect and theorist Adolf Göller caught the attention of Dutch architects with his *On the Aesthetics* (1887) and *The Origins of Architectural Style: A History of the Art of Building* (1888). This second book offered a new perspective on the origin and demise of architectural style – a vision that could offer an explanation as to why the years around 1890 were the closing phase of an era in Dutch architecture that would be transformed into something totally new.[20]

The totally new, however, often contains elements of the old. The time-honoured aesthetic principle – the classical principle of noble simplicity – that had been eclipsed by the picturesque had not disappeared altogether, and in the 90s it would re-emerge to dominate twentieth-century aesthetics for a long time to come. Carel Vosmaer, as always on the alert where classical standards and contemporary culture were concerned, was but a voice crying in the wilderness when in 1885 he warned against an art 'seeking its salvation in the restlessness of lines, in a bright confusion of colours and curlicues and little shapes, of gold and plush and velvet. Great architecture is pre-eminently the art of noble lines, pure forms and subtle relationships of forms.'[21] But times were about to change. Soon the Netherlands, like Germany, would seem to be a breeding ground for that blend of classical simplicity and a realism

Fig.83
The picturesque
townscape, artistically
snapped in the
impressionist manner:
a photograph by
G. H. Breitner, of the
Prinsengracht near
the Bloemstraat,
Amsterdam (around
1893).

seeking the cultural meaning of the ordinary – a union that shortly after 1900 would produce the concept of *Nieuwe Zakelijkheid* (New Realism) which was the early twentieth-century radicalization of *Sachlichkeit*.[22]

This new realism in architecture, presaging a new culture, perhaps even a new civilization, would contain the essence of the new century.

Notes

1. J. Th. J. Cuypers 1888, 308.
2. A. B. J. Sterck 1889, 20.
3. C. B. Posthumus Meyjes 1885, 78.
4. W. N. Rose 1865, 8.
5. A. W. Weissman 1881, 370; Henri Evers 1886, 411; X.X. 1887;
    L. M. Moolenaar 1888, 418.
6. Heinrich Hübsch 1847 (1992), 174.
7. *De Opmerker* 18 (1883) no. 9, 85–6; reactions from De M. 1883 and
    Il Puttino 1883.
8. No architect can nowadays be found: L. M. Moolenaar 1885, 447.
    The discussion on plagiarism: Guido Hoogewoud 1974, 315–20.
9. A. C. Bleys 1886a and 1886b.
10. On Eberson: Karin M. Veenland-Heineman 1985; On Salm: Jan
    Jaap Kuyt, Norbert Middelkoop, Auke van der Woud 1997.
11. J. H. Leliman 1888, 168.
12. Paul Sédille 1885, 209–11.
13. J. B. Jager 1886, 34.
14. L. M. Moolenaar 1885, 447.
15. A concise description of symmetry and proportionality: E. Gugel
    1869, 1st edn, 33–4 and 1886, 2nd edn, 38–40.
16. A. Reyding 1885, 557.
17. J. E. van der Pek 1889.
18. C. B. Posthumus Meyjes 1887, based partly on Richard Lucae 1869.
    For the development of psychology and the concept of space in
    Germany: introduction, Harry F. Mallgrave, Eleftherios Ikonomou
    1994.
19. On realism in France: A. Hofmann 1887; Harry F. Mallgrave (ed.)
    1993, 286. On the relationship between realism and *Sachlichkeit*:
    Harry F. Mallgrave 1993.
20. 'De toekomst der architectuur' ('The future of architecture'), *De
    Portefeuille* 10 (1888) no. 13, 173. An extensive review of Göller's
    Aesthetics of Architecture: J. R. de Kruyff 1888.
21. Carel Vosmaer 1885, 279.
22. *Nieuwe Zakelijkheid* is the Dutch equivalent of the German *Neue
    Sachlichkeit*. For a discussion on the *Neue Sachlichkeit* see
    Rosemarie Haag Bletter's introduction in Adolf Behne 1996;
    '*Sachlichkeit* is more properly translated as "the simple, practical,
    straightforward solution to a problem", as "matter-of-factness" and
    occasionally as "objectivity"' (p. 48). It is worth noticing that the
    original term and these translations reject the social idealism of
    which *Neue Sachlichkeit* was an expression.

Part 3

Style or No Style?
The 1890s and the New Movement

9

Image Building

The traditional view

At the end of the last chapter we touched on the young architects of the new generation. We must now redefine our terms, because the 1890s also witnessed the emergence of another generation of young people who would quickly assert themselves. The young architects of the 80s had secured major commissions for themselves, then in the 90s had occupied important teaching positions – sometimes both, at the same time. In the eyes of the 90s generation, most of these were already establishment figures. In 1890 Jan Springer had reached forty, Klinkhamer was thirty-six, Evers thirty-five, Berlage thirty-four, Bram Salm thirty-three, Weissman thirty-two. Posthumus Meyjes was thirty-one, as was the talented nephew of the elder Cuypers, Ed Cuypers, who was already the owner of a large architectural practice in Amsterdam. Jos Cuypers was a little younger than his cousin Ed; he was his father's right-hand man and partner, and therefore shared responsibility for a large organization. The only members of the 80s generation whose approach earned them a place in the 90s camp too were Willem Kromhout (twenty-six in 1890) and Willem C. Bauer (twenty-eight).

Berlage was a case apart. As *De Opmerker* wrote in 1898, 'he assumed the leadership of the "young architects"'[1] – Johannes Ludovicus Mattheus ('Mathieu') Lauweriks (1864–1932), Jan Ernst van der Pek, Karel Petrus Cornelis de Bazel (1869–1923) and Hermanus Joannes Maria Walenkamp (1871–1933). It was also *De Opmerker* that marked the activities of these three as the first indications of a 'new movement' in Dutch architecture – a movement that wanted to break with the past and to make a fresh start. A few years later, its most conspicuous manifestation was Berlage's new Stock Exchange, replacing Jan David Zocher's of 1840–5. According to the current historical view this 'new movement' was essentially Berlage's creation, having benefited from, as the art critic Jan Veth (1864–1925) claimed in 1900, a 'great master, his predecessor in Dutch architecture'.[2] This was, of course, the elder Cuypers, who was also recognized by the young architects of the 90s as their master. Thus it was established, about the turn of the century, how the

Netherlands had acquired its modern architecture: Cuypers' sound principles had inspired Berlage and the young generation to force a breakthrough, which had signalled the end, as far as the nineteenth century was concerned, of architecture 'in style'. This representation of events is still, broadly speaking, accepted today – one hundred years later.

For the purposes of this chapter, indeed of this book, it is impossible to dispose of this picture as a matter of minor importance, for it still largely determines our present ideas on the turbulent 1890s. The full reality of that representation becomes apparent when we examine the ideas and debates on the characteristics of architecture that flourished at the time. But the documentary evidence is not much help here, not least because the young architects' words and actions are fraught with contradictions. In this decade so open to change, old issues of architectural theory were raked up surprisingly often by architects both young and old. The standard of debate was often remarkably poor – the relevance of architectural theory seemed to have diminished even further. And if there had been consensus in previous years on the meaning of style, truth and character, there was now none at all.

The new subjectivity and the new mass culture

The 1890s had a cultural character and rhetoric that were entirely its own. Although the economic circumstances of the building sector remained unchanged, debates on architecture no longer focused on the tension between 'real' architects and the cowboys. Attention was now drawn to other developments, for example, the 'social issue' in its many guises, such as socialism, communism, anarchism, internationalism, pacifism, or the problem of public health; but also new spiritual movements such as theosophy, Rosicrucianism and oriental religions. These international phenomena proved rich sources of ideas which were disseminated through the press, specialist societies, meetings and courses, and rapidly assimilated in artistic circles. In 1888 the literary journal *De Nieuwe Gids* (The New Guide) launched a series of articles on 'Young Amsterdam': 'There exists a Young Amsterdam, of this

Fig.84
H. P. Berlage's
Stock Exchange,
Amsterdam
(1896–1903), façade
and side wall. On the
right is visible the side
of Zocher's old
Exchange (Fig.11)
which was demolished
in 1904. In the misty
background, middle
left, is the Central
Station (Fig.64).

there can no longer be any doubt. In politics, in literature and in art, especially painting, a movement is emerging that has been discernible for some years but is now not only increasing in strength by the day, but is showing all the signs of being a movement that will dominate the future.' This young Amsterdam was strongly committed socially, was open to religion and spirituality, and had a profound contempt for the old political and cultural establishment.[3] Young architects too joined this movement.

Apart from the abundance of impressions reaching the artistic world from outside, a change in the artist's mental and psychological attitude towards 'reality' can be discerned. Attention now shifted from the observed reality to the observing subject itself. Impressionism in painting had cleared the way for the interpretation of observed reality as a projection of the observer. It was but a small step from here to symbolism, in which aspects of the artist's own mind, including the metaphysical, became part of the subject. This shift towards a culturally accepted *subjectivity* led to an exploration of the boundaries of that subject – and finally to the overstepping of those boundaries, which in turn resulted in the extraordinary 'decadence' of the *fin de siècle*. Diametrically opposite to this – at least as far as intention was concerned – stood the orientation focused on 'the people'. This no longer referred only to the Dutch bourgeoisie or the Dutch nation as a whole, but particularly to the uncultured, poorly paid working classes who made up the majority of society. The discovery of the neglected masses and the new ideal of 'community art' brought the 'artist-architect' back to the realms of traditional art theory; now, again, he conceived himself as the peoples' guide, the one who would edify the people by means of beauty.

The irony of history was, however, that just when the common people, the uncultured masses, were being embraced by the artistic community, they were themselves set on developing their own 'depraved' mass culture. The sleazy popular clubs of the 90s formed the springboard for the triumphal progress of cabaret with its risqué songs, and variety theatre. It is significant that once the ideal of 'community-art' was formulated the word 'realism' was dropped from the vocabulary. Idealism in architecture once again prevailed. While painters such as Breitner and Toorop chose 'realistic' subjects such as prostitutes and sexual desire, and Lodewijk van Deyssel broke the sexual taboo in literature with his novel *A Love Affair* (1887), young architects were pursuing on paper lofty ideals for the edification of art and society. But their main source of income consisted, nevertheless, of 'realistic' commissions such as shop-front and café alterations, subjects on which the architectural community preferred to keep silent.

The cult of the genius
The specific character of the 1890s was the result of a long process, which around 1840 was already in its infancy. D. D. Büchler emphasized in his *On the Art of Dutch Building* that architecture was least of all the arts as a matter of inspiration; rather it was a 'science' with its own history and 'rules' that had to be studied and observed. An architect who ignored these would place himself and his work outside the tradition and turn himself into an outsider.

Whereas in 1840 being an exception to the rule, an eccentric, was a risky business, by the 90s it had become generally accepted, if only because of its commercial advantages (though it was not considered good form to discuss the commercial aspects of architecture). Originality was seen, rather, as a purely artistic phenomenon: this was of course understandable, since the concept of originality had its own strong cultural determinants in 1890 or 1900, just as it had in 1840. Büchler's words could be understood, then, as a warning against the romantic cult of the genius, which has secured a firm position in French, German and English belles-lettres, in the visual arts and in music. This cult assumed that the artist, through the gift of his highly developed 'feelings', was in close touch with a higher and more profound reality, that of the 'edified', and that through his art he was able to make others experience this reality.

In the 1890s the cult of the genius – and the related cult of the feelings – had at last made itself felt in Dutch architecture. The old idea that architecture, because it was based on an objective theory, was first and foremost a science, disappeared, to be replaced by the notion that architecture was an essentially subjective, irrational artistic reality, achieved through inspiration, not by study. Part of the Romantic concept of the genius that now became discernible in architecture was the idea that the architect worked as an autonomous artist. In this the art critic Jan Veth defended artistic freedom in the debate on Berlage's design for the Stock Exchange. According to Veth it was the artist-architect's 'indisputable right', once he had received the commission, 'to reckon, for the design, with nothing but his own inspiration'.[4] In 1900 there were probably no more than two architects capable of exercising the 'indisputable right' of self-expression that the critic referred to; these were the same duo who were also the focus of a certain cult of the genius – namely, the elder Cuypers and Berlage. Both were able to do so because they had clients who permitted them a large degree of artistic and financial freedom. However, the published writings and drawings of the young architects who did not enjoy these

Fig.85
Roelof Kuipers'
Nieuwe-Amstel Town
Hall (1889–92): the
love for Old Dutch
architecture – in this
case the inspiration
was the Town Hall of
the little town of
Bolsward in the north
of the country
(1613–17) – was still
insatiable around
1890. Or had it
become just a
convention?
Photograph: Jacob
Olie.

privileges also testify to the tendency to create architecture not from its 'rules', but from one's own inner self.

A new historiography?

The disappearance of the idea that architecture is foremost a science is also discernible in the entirely new attitude towards architectural history. Whereas the solution to the problem of style had formerly been sought in the study of the history and rules of architecture, this approach was questioned in the 8os and sharply rejected in the 90s because it was said to result in copying. This was to lead to the rejection of all historical building types (to be examined in more detail later), a most radical step to take and one that undermined the tradition that architecture was a 'science' based on an objective theory, while at the same time going some way towards subjectifying the architectural concept. The ultimate consequence was aptly expressed in 1890: the emptier the bookshelves of the young architects, the more original their work would be. Two years later Kromhout contended that 'we', the artists, 'are the feeling persons of our society, each shockwave that hits society leaves us quivering; each new movement has been sensed in advance by us, and it is solely by intuition that our works are in harmony with this society'. The view that the artist was able to discern the unconscious motives of society like a sensitive seismograph was certainly not new, belonging as it did to the old convention that art edifies society. Kromhout's conclusion, however, was anti-traditional; according to him, the contemporary architect's intuition determined that 'the forms that we should most vehemently call our own, cannot be found in any earlier period'. Even *De Opmerker*, hardly a mouthpiece for modernism, wrote in 1895 that the twentieth century would only be able to produce architecture if it stopped looking back to the past: 'it will have to stow away in the attic Viollet-le-Duc and Semper, Schinkel and Blondel, Vitruvius and Vignola, and devote itself entirely to its own inspiration, free from all ties with the past'.[5]

But once the bookshelves were empty, new ideas would compete to occupy the empty spaces. Did Berlage, for example, have a 'theory' in mind when he wrote his famous essay 'Bouwkunst en impressionisme' ('Architecture and impressionism') (1894; to be discussed later), which in the late twentieth century was construed as a 'theory of pre-modern Dutch architecture? This issue is not without importance, given that architectural practice did not, on the whole, take the slightest notice of architectural theory during this period. If the 'new movement' had come into being solely as a result of theoretical reflection, this could truly have been regarded as a miracle. But in view of the

tendency demonstrated over the previous years, it would seem more probable that it came about as a result of *imitation* – not of historical building types, but of contemporary ones. In the 8os architectural theory's declining position was increasingly compensated for by the ascendancy of visual representation. Debates on the characteristics and implications of the 'rules' were replaced by the persuasive force of the many illustrated catalogues and books that flooded the building market. In 1891 *De Opmerker* described the developments in architecture between 1875 and 1890 without making a single reference to theory; the illustrated publications and the new building materials were seen as the two driving forces of architectural design. A new book on the theoretical basis of architecture was greeted in 1895 with no trace of enthusiasm: 'so far the use of books on the nature of beauty seemed rather limited'. Some young architects, such as Kromhout and Van der Pek, were scornful of the rules of aesthetics. Van der Pek wrote in 1894:

Every artist hates philosophy. We who love life and attempt to convey life, hate the rules drawn up by philosophers for their archeological studies of the works of our predecessors. We know that expressing love has nothing to do with rules, and that we can do without 'aesthetics' … Such a word can safely disappear from the architectural vocabulary … Books on aesthetics were invented when people felt the need to discuss art because they were not able to produce it, and wished to explain away the deficiency … Art history is only of little help in these matters.[6]

Expressing the inexpressible: the new movement

Berlage's many publications, especially after 1900, seem to contradict this picture. He was fond of the broad brushstroke when referring to architectural history, often quoting from the works of the great theorists, poets and philosophers, from the recent foreign publications of aestheticians and prominent fellow architects. His texts seemed to vigorously refute the argument that around this time the relevance of the essay on architectural theory was diminishing still further. But once again we must ask whether these texts were having any effect at all on design practice now that it was dominated by visual representation and the possibilities offered by the new building techniques. Berlage wrote about architecture and society in general cultural terms, choosing the form that nowadays is referred to as a 'feature' or 'column' – personal opinions that were far removed from theory.

And the young architects themselves? J. L. M. Lauweriks wrote about theosophy in the journal *Architectura* and translated texts of Viollet-le-Duc into Dutch, but he abstained from articulating, however briefly, the aesthetics of the 'new movement'. Lauweriks was certainly not the only one to have problems with explaining what was new. An attempt made by a certain 'K' in 1895 is illustrative. According to him the 'new movement' could be characterized as 'seemingly lawless, yet its lawlessness is rooted in a very strong and elementary conviction, that is, however, difficult to describe'. This conviction and, as 'K' put it, the 'haze of intimate desire' – the word subconscious did not exist – drive the designer in a definite direction, but the nature of this direction is 'inexpressible' and known only to those who in the recent 'real works of art' could discern a 'universal principle'; one that was manifested in all countries and that they also adhere to, 'even if they are unaware of the fact'. Not until its results will have become more distinct, 'K' concluded, will one be able to qualify this 'new movement' in a more precise way. This attempt made by 'K' to characterize 'the new' was a relatively detailed one. Generally the architectural journals of the 90s confined themselves to an occasional qualification that soon became a cliché, such as that 'the new' stood for rejecting any kind of authority in art. In early 1894 *De Opmerker* had assumed that this phenomenon that was referred to as 'new' might even be the beginnings of the new style 'that has been so assiduously sought'.[7]

This assumption is just another indication of how fundamentally the term 'style' had changed. Obviously it still seemed a key concept of the art of building, but its characteristics had become inexpressible. However, there were architects who denied this reality and held on to tradition. Cornelis Hendrik Peters, one of Cuypers associates and a government architect, mentioned earlier, postulated in an article on Old Dutch brick building that a style was based on a single guiding principle and lasted for centuries – a view that at the time could easily be explained as that of a conservative who opposed the dynamics of modern times. Van der Pek and Berlage too, however, applied precisely the same definition of style, and it was precisely this definition that brought the latter in 1894 to the conclusion that, because individualism prevented the necessary unity of ideas, a new style was no longer an option. Interestingly, this view had already been expressed by Gugel in 1869 in the first edition of his *History of Styles* but had been cast aside during the 70s and especially the 80s in favour of the unifying potential of a national style. Now, in the 1890s, when the political situation was so different, when individualism was at last being recognized as a positive characteristic, it had to be admitted that the ideal of a national style was futile and it was time to face the consequences of Gugel's conclusion that a new style was indeed no longer an option. In the somewhat bitter words

of an author writing in 1894: 'the style of the nineteenth century is apparently a style of "one's own self" that no longer has any links with the principle of objectivity'. It was no longer regarded as absurd to refer to the 'style' of an individual architect, as when, for example, in the same year it was in all seriousness observed that 'the influence of Jan Springer's style is already making itself felt'.[8]

The 'inexpressibility' of the characteristics of the 'new movement' and the disappearance of objective, collective principles were two sides of the same picture. Berlage's new commercial buildings, the offices of De Algemeene (1893–4) and De Nederlanden (1894–5) insurance companies, both in Amsterdam, and the designs for the Stock Exchange (published in 1898) were seen as examples of the new movement, but any theoretical response was very slight and very subjective. Berlage's sympathizers never referred to architectural 'rules', but limited themselves to aesthetic qualifications such as 'essentially beautiful', individual responses without explanation. Neither did Berlage himself, despite his wide reading, attempt to arrive at an explanation of the new architecture from the point of view of architectural theory. When he presented his design for the Stock Exchange to his colleagues, he was very specific on the heating system he had chosen, but did not account for his reasons to design the façades without any trace of Dutch Renaissance or picturesque embellishment, saying that this was 'somewhat a matter of principle', without offering a clue as to which principle that might be. Another report of the presentation ran (again without explanation, as if it was perfectly normal): 'on the architectural aspect itself Mr Berlage was not prepared to say anything'.[9]

The old generation used its own explicit traditional standards to determine aesthetic 'errors' in the modern designs – which, given that these designs were to a large extent motivated by opposition to the old precepts and customs, were inevitably 'wrong' to those who still adhered to them and 'right' for those who rejected them. According to convention, the façade of the Algemeene Building should have had a moulding at the top left to indicate that the roof behind it was flat, but leaving it out, and thereby creating uncertainty, was apparently a manifestation of the new ideal. An interesting aspect of the new movement is that by means of innovations such as this façade with no moulding, it created new conventions that made it recognizable as a movement, but these were not conventions in the traditional sense.[10] Occasionally a more or less objective explanation was attached to them, as, for example, with Berlage's proposition in 1894 that certain economic and social conditions required the utmost simplicity of design. In this case, traditional theory would have demanded much more than a vague reference to social conditions: it would have demanded a systematic line of reasoning centring on its *own* requirements – namely, on the relation between physical solidity, functionality and aesthetics. According to the traditional train of thought, creating a new aesthetic ideal would have required redefining beauty in relation to solidity and functionality.

But the architects in the vanguard of the new movement were neither able nor willing to follow this tradition. As already noted, they developed a new aesthetic ideal without a corresponding theory; their ideal became 'inexpressible', but was wordlessly laid down in conventions and, as far as the older generation was concerned, precisely because these new conventions were irrational and lacked a theoretical basis they fell into the category that since the 70s and 80s had been the arch-enemy of architecture – that of aesthetic idleness, superficial splendour, commercial concession to fashion. In 1899 the architect Isaac Gosschalk remonstrated about 'buildings without mouldings, without definition at the top, this mad quest for newfangled things which nowadays is all the vogue'.[11] The aesthetics of the young architects did indeed appear to ignore the problems of construction and functionality while focusing on what had always been the major issue for the unqualified and incompetent: the visual effect. If there was any breakthrough in architecture during the 90s, this was it.

The supremacy of the subjective

The increasing subjectivity was a root-and-branch process, and the younger architects were accelerating it. W. N. Rose had memorably encapsulated the tradition in which their elders had been trained: music was the most subjective art, he said, because it appealed most directly to the senses. Architecture, on the other hand, was the most objective, because it forged a strong link with the objective laws of nature and the objective requirements of practicality – thus it was least well suited to conveying feelings.[12] It was precisely in this area that the younger architects were eager to take verbal risks that until recently had been inconceivable. Their high regard for 'feeling' enabled them to justify striking out, despite their lack of knowledge or expertise; they put themselves beyond the reach of rational counter-arguments. Inevitably, the standard of the debate reached a new low, and the emotional intensity of the situation promoted the formation of coteries. The verbal demolition in 1895 of the recently completed Stedelijk Museum in Amsterdam, the work of the architect Adriaan W. Weissman, by the young and inexperienced Van der Pek exemplifies the new attitude: Weissman's 'unconsecrated

hands', he said, had provided Lady Architecture with 'shabby togs' – and the cause of all this misery was 'that his feeling is poorly developed, so poorly in fact that his works will never be *works of art*'.[13]

This subjective, individualist aesthetics was discernible everywhere, and was confirmed from all sides by developments in the visual arts, belles-lettres and music. Empirical psychological research, especially in Germany, demonstrated that observation was a subjective matter. All that the supporters of objective aesthetics could set against this was a belief in a kind of Pythagorean harmony – beauty based on 'eternal' promotions – or in a metaphysical principle – beauty as a reflection of a supernatural reality – or in a synthesis of both. These beliefs were not infrequently encountered, and the paradox is that the belief in objective aesthetics had also to a certain extent become a personal and subjective matter – take, for example, amongst other esoteric ideas, 'designing by system' (see p. 209), which was in vogue for several years. But the earlier consensus that the beauty of architecture was based on 'science' continued to disintegrate.

This disintegration could be reversed in one way only – by denying it, by promoting the idea that there was a new aesthetics reflecting a higher reality, and that complying with its rules was a moral issue and, moreover, the only way to arrive at true architecture: true, *because* it was the expression of that higher reality. In the late 90s Berlage was the chief advocate of this idea. Beauty was a subjective matter, he had stated; in 1895 he referred to symbolism in architecture as an arbitrary, personal affair.[14] The mid-1890s witnessed his conversion to objective, 'pure principles' – principles which, as we shall see, he defined in a rather impure way, often by resorting to words such as 'simplicity' and 'construction', words that failed to define, but that were delivered in the tone of moral superiority appropriate to the pronouncement of 'pure principles'. 'We must extricate ourselves from all *direct* influences of the earlier styles,' Berlage wrote in 1896, 'and instead build in a simple way according to the structural principles of medieval art. For building in a style has been a plague on all our modern cities. It has been a repulsive, a really repulsive practice, because of the lies and the incredible ugliness, because it is not *felt*, because it cannot have been felt.' And in 1905 he proclaimed, 'Personally, I hold that the only proper principle for the present is honest construction in simplified form, according to which, I would say, architects should work as if following a formula.'

Words such as 'lies' and 'honesty', the moral concepts that replaced the old, neutral 'truth', would remain in use during the twentieth century for conducting architectural

Fig.86
The offices of the life insurance company De Algemeene, Amsterdam (1893–4) by H. P. Berlage. To Berlage's followers the building showed that he was the leader of the 'new movement', but critics observed that he 'was still caught up in the old manner'.

purges. Berlage's article 'Thoughts on style' concludes on a metaphysical note, articulating the conviction, borrowed from the German art historian Karl Scheffler, that the modern movement in architecture had an idealist, even religious, basis. According to Scheffler Christianity was indeed dead, but the modern pursuit of simplicity and functionality was fundamentally an 'idea of causality, and therefore a godlike idea'; attempts at bestowing on buildings and furniture a rational construction could be reduced to motives of a religious nature. If the principle of simple, 'rational' construction were applied generally, Berlage wrote, we would be standing at the gateway to a new art – at least, 'if the new world concept of the social equality of all people had manifested itself as well'. This 'new world' concept was for Berlage no ideal of the hereafter, but very much one to be realized on earth – the equality of all people. While he regarded this as the absolute goal of Christianity,[15] in his secularized version of the religious ideal Berlage saw the spiritual basis of the modern movement – the 'unity of wishing and feeling' without which no great art is possible. The ultimate aim, however, was even broader. Whereas in 1894 Berlage felt impelled to rule out, on grounds of individualism, the creation of a new style, after 1900 the *unity of wishing and feeling* in his 'new world' concept made the creation of a new style not only possible, but imperative.

Berlage would emerge as the guardian of an aesthetic that was the expression of a universal principle – but as with Cuypers, this would be an ideological, non-architectural principle in which architecture was at most a means, never the goal. Because of his success in assuming the role of father of modern Dutch architecture, this concept of objective (if tersely expressed) aesthetics was so acclaimed and taken for granted that the multiform subjective aesthetics that emerged in the 90s, and that has thrived ever since, became a stumbling-block to contemporaries and art historians alike. As soon as the way had been paved for the expression of a personal diversity and autonomy in architecture, this subjective aesthetics was vigorously contested by the supporters of the ideologically determined objective aesthetics. The reaction was immediate, insisting on adaptation, on subjection, on the suppression of artistic freedom. One of its advocates, art historian Jan Veth, again exemplified the prevailing view: 'The overconfident doctrine of an all-pervasive individualism will in the end result in a dispersive, fruitless and debilitating particularism', cutting off the broad traditions of our former artistic culture. If society were based on harmony instead of arbitrary social relationships, it would produce art that would not 'look for its roots in superficial particulars and transitory stimuli, but in the eternal'.[16]

This opposition to the multiformity of subjective, autonomous architecture had everything to do with the issue with which this chapter began: image building in the early days of modern architecture – the myth of the hero or heroes, upholders of all the architectural virtues, putting up a valiant fight against the forces of chaos and darkness.

'Everything into the sewer!': the rallying cry of the new eclecticism

Our investigation into the historiography of the architectural 'breakthrough' conceived as the achievement of one or two individuals must consider the chronology of facts. From the perspective of the contemporary it was not Berlage but the elder Cuypers who stood in the lime-light. During these years Cuypers could boast two different groups of influential admirers: first, the adherents of the 'official style' (still headed by Victor de Stuers), whose numbers, thank to De Stuers' policy on subsidies and appointments over the past fifteen or twenty years, had expanded considerably; the other group had begun with a few young people who met at Cuypers' practice.

It was not Berlage, either, who gave the signal for the ideological revolution of the 90s, but Willem Kromhout. In November 1891 he gave a splendid lecture for Architectura et Amicitia, full of irony, sarcasm, and idealism and entitled '*Tout à l'égout*' ('Everything into the sewer'):

I would love to make an ideal sewerage system that would drain off everything that we can do without; a sewer of gigantic dimensions constructed in such a way as to send everything thundering down to the wasteland where it would always be foggy and steaming, to be transformed into dust, to renew itself, and, after complete regeneration, to be channelled away along other routes. I would love to send all traditional art forms into this sewer – first, cartloads of orders, to be followed by whole series of capitals, whole entablatures – everything into the sewer. I would have gargoyles and masks meet one another in that wasteland, accompanied by whole series of style. I would have them consort with one another under an incessant stream of everyday waste. Old Dutch and new Old Dutch, all must be carried off via the sewer, including all products of imitation. Gothic as well as Renaissance, the Romanesque as well as Byzantine, Greek, Roman, Indonesian, Norse, Russian – everything into the sewer.

Kromhout spared nothing and no one. Neither the press, nor the architectural associations, the German architecture books, the 'official style', the state architects, Gugel and his educational models. Kromhout wanted to start afresh without 'statements on style, on classicism, on rationalism',

Fig.87
H. P. Berlage's offices
for the insurance
company De
Nederlanden on the
Muntplein,
Amsterdam (1894–5).
The building served
as a starting point for
the lobby that claimed
that Berlage was the
rescuer of Dutch
architecture, the
champion in the fight
against 'fake art'.

free from all conventions – 'We do *not* want to create new styles, we want only to be ourselves – that's all we want!' It was the rallying cry of the new eclecticism. The lecture was received with great acclaim. Had a genie been let out of the bottle?

In January 1892 a young and anonymous group of writers called 'Multiplex' started to publish a series of 'Fragments' in *De Opmerker* in which topical issues were ridiculed in student fashion and it was made quite clear that these young people were no longer prepared to follow in the steps of their elders. Then in July one of the members of Multiplex revealed himself as a follower of Cuypers, when he quashed a critic of the Rijksmuseum with the retort, 'If he had the tiniest understanding of art, he would have been grateful, to say the least, that Cuypers had put an end to the foolish stone monstrosities that before his time were forced upon us as products of architecture. He would acknowledge – just as we are now doing – that Cuypers' robust attitude has benefited our much valued contemporary architecture.'[17] Exactly how, he did not say. The Rijksmuseum 'may be improved on', he concluded, but it was nevertheless 'a magnificent expression of the individual concept of aesthetics, which earns our respect'.

P. J. H. Cuypers: 'the conquering hero battling against convention'

In 1893 the radical trend that had been marked by '*Tout à l'égout*', and which not only entailed the desire to clear the decks but also turned out to be a matter of young versus old, was still in evidence. The atmosphere of the young architects' association, A et A, appeared no longer compatible with the editorial atmosphere of *De Opmerker*, which for ten years had published Architectura et Amicitia's writings. At the end of 1892 the contract had expired, after which A et A established its own journal, *Architectura*. Kromhout became a member of the editorial staff, as did J. L. M. Lauweriks, who immediately exploited his position in an affair to do with a colleague, twenty-year-old H. W. Mol who, like himself, was a draughtsman at Cuypers' practice. Mol wrote articles for a newspaper in which he extolled Cuypers' 'bloody fine' architecture. *Architectura* too published an article of his, which Mol described as a 'philosophy of architecture' – in fact a rather muddled, conceited piece full of schoolboy wisdom apparently drawing on the ideas of his employer. Several architects, including Kromhout, were highly annoyed with young Mol's pedantry, but Lauweriks believed Mol was entitled to speak and stood up for him. *De Opmerker* considered it remarkable that Cuypers' views were now propagated by his younger assistants and supposed that

Cuypers himself would not appreciate the way in which this was being done.[18] However, the opposite may have been the case, because these very youngsters, through their loyalty, their indifference to established reputations and their eye for publicity, exercised a by no means negligible power – there was no other architect in the Netherlands with a comparable following. In December 1895 *De Opmerker* claimed that whereas in the past the 'official style' had followers who felt an affinity for the Middle Ages only for religious or related reasons, Cuypers had now, so to speak, bred missionaries who had infiltrated every government office and who converted even *Architectura*.[19]

This comment was not unfounded. In addition, via De Stuers, Cuypers had been teaching at the Art School and at the School of Applied Arts, both in Amsterdam. In May 1895, students and former students turned his leaving into a public display of loyalty and appreciation, organized by the art teacher J. H. de Groot (1865–1932) and H. W. Mol. De Groot ended his eulogy with the wish that 'the greatest Dutch architect of the century, indeed of all centuries, may remain with us for years to come'. De Stuers praised Cuypers' hard work, his modesty and his sincerity, and Cuypers in turn expressed his gratitude by modestly referring to the 'higher origin' of his contributions to architecture, gifts 'innate to us all through the hand of God, not created by artists or teachers, but eternally present'. *De Opmerker* added its note of dissent, stating that whereas Cuypers and his followers had always vigorously denied that their work had a spiritual nature, they now apparently felt powerful enough to admit openly that this was the case. *Architectura*, on the other hand, was not interested in such historical analyses but only in the here and now: 'The festival meeting must have struck a jubilant, victorious note, to *all* the students and guests, because Mr Cuypers is the conquering hero battling against convention.'[20] The art critic Jan Veth on this occasion praised Cuypers in *De Kroniek*, the 90s' leading cultural weekly, as 'the sage master builder'. This was nothing compared to the accolade published a week later by Alphons Diepenbrock, the Catholic classical scholar, composer and music editor of *De Kroniek* who also happened to be Cuypers' nephew. Here Cuypers was pictured as the 'man who has heralded the revival of architecture in Holland', as 'the only one among his contemporaries who together with Josef Alberdingk Thijm has understood the need for a monumental aesthetic culture in the midst of nineteenth-century Dutch decadence.' Diepenbrock heaped lavish praise, to the extent of conferring on him the royal capital: Cuypers had principles, he said, 'which to Him represented the truth and about which it was impossible to argue with Him'.[21]

In January the next year it was Berlage's turn to speak out. 'After long observation, and having made a strictly objective comparison of everything that architecture has produced here over the past twenty-five years, I have come to the conclusion that Cuypers' architecture is the only one worth our attention, simply because it *is* architecture; it is architecture of a classical, and therefore lasting, value.' It was to Cuypers' 'immortal merit', Berlage continued, that through 'a proper understanding' he had hauled architecture back out of the depths to which it had fallen. In September, Van der Pek acclaimed Berlage's newly completed office building on the Muntplein as marking the

end of the 'petty bourgeois, increasingly trivial pseudo-art'; the movement of Berlage and his followers was no longer dependent on balusters, capitals and other 'pointless, spiritless appurtenances,' but operated from an 'inner structural sense' and employed a method of working that 'is spiritually based on, and influenced by, the aspirations of no less a person than Mr Cuypers'. Within one week this provoked reactions from two different quarters. Weissman wrote in *De Kroniek* that Berlage had not borrowed his new forms from Cuypers' principles, but from illustrations of works by the American architect Henry Hobson Richardson (1838–86); Lauweriks argued that Berlage could not have been a follower of Cuypers because 'he had no understanding at all of Cuypers' spiritual grounding in Christian art'.[22]

In 1897 Cuypers, turned seventy, retired and moved from Amsterdam to his birthplace Roermond. In his honour festivities were organized, which lasted three days in Amsterdam and two in Roermond. Once again, it was as if a king was being honoured. *De Opmerker* and the *Bouwkundig Weekblad* covered events tersely, with a wry smile, and *Architectura* celebrated with a special festive issue. De Stuers published a forty-page biography of Cuypers, in which he painted a detailed portrait of his protégé as the brilliant and self-sacrificing prophet who had joined battle with 'the carpenters and the plasterers' and made a firm stand against the jealous anti-Catholic opposition of the incompetent who taunted his works of art. As for the Rijksmuseum, Berlage described it as 'the Master's full confession of faith', 'in its proclaiming of the structural principles of great medieval art, [it is] a glorious reaction against the prevailing insipid neoclassical style so utterly lacking in principles; a merciless corrective of the neo-Renaissance style flourishing alongside it'. And if the signs did not deceive us, he continued, Cuypers' art would 'represent the dawn of a new era in art – not because the questing young generation were imitating his art, directly or indirectly, but because they were applying its 'fundamental principles and the influence of its edifying culture'.[23]

Cuypers stood above all considerations of party, generation, and cultural stance. He was the hero of a weekly anti-establishment socialist magazine, became an honorary member of the conservative clerical St Bernulphus Guild, and an honorary member of the avant-garde Hague Art Circle. His work was considered to be virtually transcendental. It was inconceivable, someone declared, that the master had used medieval forms, because medieval principles did not allow this. André Jolles, a twenty-three-year-old working for *De Kroniek*, voiced an opposing view which in no way prevented him from idolizing Cuypers. The Rijksmuseum, he mused, as he made his way to one of the festivities, had not escaped the spirit of the time, which had been able to produce only a 'non-innate beauty' – but that was *our* fault, not Cuypers', 'who truly cannot help our wretchedness'.[24]

The national need for a saviour
The canonization of Cuypers lends itself to description. To explain it, however, is quite another matter. We can begin by saying that in the unsettled architectural climate of the 90s there appears to have been a general need, amid all the

individualism and dissension, for a symbol of professional and human integrity that stood above all parties, a symbol of the higher values of an ideal art of building and of its significance for society. It seems that Cuypers and his work fulfilled this symbolic function admirably. But any attempt to explain the rapid rise of his reputation should focus not on the person of Cuypers or on his work, but on the ideas that were projected on to him and on to his work by others. And this was all in relation not so much to his complete œuvre, but to one building – the Rijksmuseum.

These projections had an ideological and psychological as well as an architectural-theory dimension. The notion that Cuypers had saved Dutch architecture from decline became ever more prevalent during the 90s. Add to this that the idea commonly held during the 80s, that the nineteenth century was itself a period of decline, was for the first time included in historical research and given an official status in 1892 in an article by C. T. J. Louis Rieber, the secretary of the Society the Advancement of the Art of Building, the MBB, who published the article on the occasion of its fiftieth anniversary.[25] In it, Rieber rendered a lively description of architecture's 'sharp decline' before 1842 – we may assume that it was his intention to emphasize in this way the MBB's promotion of architecture in the years that followed. However, it is more likely that his historiography had the opposite effect. His account of the role of the founders of the MBB – for example, of the contractor-architect Van Straaten, the master-carpenter Gerrit Moele and the dilettante D. D. Büchler – is unlikely to have gone down well with the architects of the 90s, since they had great difficulty holding their own against the present generation of dilettantes and contractor-architects.

Rieber's MBB emerges as a society that wished to promote architecture by organizing meetings to discuss it, but this notion can have done nothing for the association's current image, since it was no secret that after spending a great deal of money on a new building in 1884 it had accomplished nothing of any significance. How vital, by contrast, was the image of Cuypers that De Stuers had been circulating for so long – the lone crusader refusing to compromise, who had saved architecture from the hands of the contractor-architects and the plasterer-carpenters and made it pure again; who on his own initiative had established training courses in the applied art for craftsmen and architects so as to introduce 'sound principles' there too.

The architects of the 90s were no historians. Unlike their predecessors, Rose and Leliman, they did not browse through piles of old issues of the *Bouwkundige Bijdragen* before rendering their opinion on the past. And it is not surprising that the historical picture De Stuers had propounded so vigorously for the past twenty years – an emotional narrative redolent with self-sacrifice, envy, conflict, high principles and Dutch common sense – was more attractive than Rieber's dry account with its drab protagonists. Architects like Leliman, Gosschalk, Godefroy, Johan Metzelaar, Gugel and others who, from their personal experience, were in a position to correct this one-sided picture, kept silent, even when Lauweriks, Mol, Diepenbrock, Van der Pek and other young architects, and Berlage, appeared to be propagating an image of nineteenth-century architecture that was no different from De Stuers'. Certainly, any resistance would have been considered biased. Thus, youngsters without any historical awareness whatsoever felt more inclined to regard the sewers as the proper place for the views of the older architects, while awarding Cuypers the historical significance that he and his conservative lobby had been claiming for some twenty years. But precisely because history was not this younger generation's strong point, Cuypers' historical role cannot have been the main source of their admiration. So what was it? We shall return to this subject in a moment, but first let us consider the generation gap as it generally manifested itself.

A generation conflict that Cuypers escaped?

The age difference between Cuypers and his admirers was striking. These young men so resented other members of his generation that we may say there was a generation conflict. Although they were not the first group of young architects to dismiss an older generation, it is clear that the differences had become more evident and more entrenched. This merely reflected the rest of society. Political mores, for example, were hardly exemplary, and the precepts of decorum and mutual respect had given way under press campaigns that played on the public's sentiments. It paid off to carp at opponents or to arouse moral indignation. Abuse and insults in both cultural and political circles had now become routine.

Was this an international phenomenon? *De Opmerker* quoted a French source complaining about the 'reign of terror' of the 'moderns' who were in control of the media, and wistfully reflected on the good old days when architectural reviews could be counted on for their objectivity. Now everything revolved around personal and public relations. If the critic was sympathetic towards the artist, he would be full of praise; if he was not, he would display his disdain. In either case, substantive argument would be as good as absent. In 1894 C. W. Nijhoff, A et A's vice-chairman, protested to Lauweriks about the 'system of

abuse' applied by young architects with no achievements to their credit. Lauweriks, however, far from being impressed, even suggested to Nijhoff that he was 'an obscurantist'. Such conflicting values and standards of behaviour made the older architects feel less at home with A et A; they withdrew from the board and editorial staff and left the association to their younger colleagues.[26] And although Kromhout wrote in the first issue of *Architectura* that this new journal was opposed to clique and coterie, it soon transpired that the younger architects had their own coterie, as an expression not only of their resistance to the established architectural order but also of their attachment to their 'own clique'. In 1894 Kromhout wrote a weekly column in *De Kunstwereld* (Art World), in which he lauded Berlage, Bauer, De Bazel, Lauweriks and Walenkamp. Van der Pek and Berlage praised each other in *De Kroniek*. Lauweriks, Kromhout and later De Bazel devoted much space for themselves and their friends in *Architectura* and in the lavishly illustrated periodical *De Architect*. *De Opmerker* resentfully wrote about the '*admiration mutuelle*' of 'architects with no building experience' which, after the example of the literary journal *De Nieuwe Gids* (The New Guide), mouthpiece of the literary avant-garde, was widespread.[27]

Architects with no building experience: that they had to listen to these inexperienced youngsters – whether they were spouting fierce criticism or high praise – was probably the hardest thing for the older architects to swallow. *De Opmerker* which, after the establishment of *Architectura*, set itself up as the conscience of architecture, was teaching 'their' young architects many a lesson, it had no doubt. They drew beautifully, but oh, their practice! They knew nothing of building techniques and showed no interest in them – hence the leaky roofs, the sodden walls, and the chimneys that did not draw properly.[28]

It is difficult to say which young architects in particular *De Opmerker* was referring to here. Lauweriks and Walenkamp were 'decorative draughtsmen' at Cuypers' practice. The young De Bazel, on the other hand, already had a solid reputation; in 1892 at twenty-three he was appointed Cuypers' office manager. Until that year Kromhout had been manager of Jan Springer's office and he received his first commission as an independent architect in 1893. At that time Willem C. Bauer, aged thirty-one, had no building experience at all.[29] In other words, it is almost inconceivable that the leaks and badly performing chimneys had anything to do with the younger league at A et A and *Architectura*. So was the criticism empty rhetoric, perhaps, a platform on which the older architects could display their only advantage, practical

Fig.89
'Anarchy', a woodcut by Herman J. M. Walenkamp illustrating J. M. Mackay's *The Anarchists* published in the magazine *Licht en Waarheid* (Light and Truth), August 1894. The liberated human being rises, while Church and state, which have done their best to repress him, go under.

himself at dawn in front of a building that had recently been finished, ended in melancholy.[31] A second coincidence, sharply indicating the gap between the two generations, happened that year when Kromhout had delivered his '*Tout à l'égout*' article. As soon as the cheering had calmed down, old Leliman took the floor to preach about the thorough architectural training in times past. Leliman, the doyen of A et A, had wanted to tell the present generation about the 'thorny path' that he himself had trodden fifty years earlier while everyone knew that his private wealth had shielded him against the daily struggle.[32] But the battle between the enfeebled elders and the strong young males intent on taking over the leadership was as evident in everyday life as on the printed pages. In 1892 Kromhout engineered the departure, as chairman of A et A, of Jan Springer, who once had been its brightest light. In 1894 he demolished in a remarkable tirade Springer's main work, the Amsterdam City Theatre: 'here we see that Springer as an artist is finished'. The next year he himself became the chairman of A et A.[33] In 1893 Berlage and A. C. Bleys renovated the Arti building, Leliman's first commission (1855), without consulting Leliman and removing the old foundation stone, which they had delivered to Leliman's home. There can be no doubt that these acts were purposefully offensive.[34]

The prominent figures of the past were now fast disappearing from the architectural scene. De Kruyff retired in 1899, Gugel in 1902. Metzelaar Sr and Salm Sr both died in 1897, Godefroy in 1899, and Frederik Willem van Gendt (born in 1831), the founder and driving force of *De Opmerker*, in 1900. But whereas the *Bouwkundig Weekblad* published extensive obituaries, *Architectura* expended hardly any ink on these deaths – because 'people of our generation have hardly known Mr So-and-so'.

Seen in this light, the enthusiasm of the young for the elderly Cuypers, and the many printed words devoted to him, were all the more remarkable.

experience? They called their younger colleagues dreamers and denigrated the new movement, as Gosschalk did in 1900 when he referred to it as 'the sad product of spiritual poverty or aberration' to which a temple was currently being erected in Amsterdam – Berlage's Stock Exchange.[30] But they could muster no real defence against the young architects.

The generation gap revealed itself also in coincidences. In 1893 *Architectura* published a piece by Abraham Godefroy, now well over seventy, in which he offered a dull explanation of some designs he had done during the 60s, The same issue featured a poetic impression by Bauer on a spree (he was, as always, without work) that, as he found

An ambivalent relationship nonetheless: Cuypers and the younger set

Cuypers had not fallen victim to the young critics' 'system of abuse', neither was he renounced or challenged by some young aspiring leader. Rather the opposite was the case. Could one say that the eternal problem of the generations had no grip on him? Probably it did, but less visibly.

Cuypers' relationship with the younger generation was crammed with hidden meanings and hidden agendas. While accepting their tributes, of which he made optimal use, he rejected the essence of their artistic views. Like Gosschalk, he publicly denigrated Berlage's Stock Exchange as an example of impoverishing architecture. His relationship

Fig.90
P. J. H. Cuypers'
reconstruction of
De Haar Castle,
Haarzuilens, near
Utrecht (1891–1915),
the opulent residence
of a Dutch count who
married a daughter of
the Rothschild family.
Of the medieval castle
only fragments of the
walls remained when
Cuypers started the
project – one of his
many restorations
that was largely the
re-creation of
'history'.

Fig. 91
A woodcut by the theosophist-architect Karel P. C. de Bazel, entitled 'The natural development of man from the mineral, plant and animal world', reproduced in the March 1894 issue of the magazine *Licht en Waarheid*. In the theosophical view of evolution, matter becomes spirit.

with Bauer was probably nonexistent, since Bauer at a design competition in 1894 had confronted him with the slogan, 'No God, no master – anarchy is harmony, property is theft'; in the same year Walenkamp, too, openly avowed his anarchist sympathies. Cuypers' relationship with Kromhout became tense when the latter harshly criticized Cuypers' exorbitantly expensive reconstruction of the medieval De Haar Castle (Haarzuilens, 1891–1915), calling it a waste of time and money. His relationship with De Bazel ended when the younger man, together with Lauweriks, became a theosophist (he was also anticlerical and anticapitalist – two other characteristics that did not please Cuypers). Cuypers and Lauweriks, who was his foster child, entered a phase in their relationship in 1894 that bore a strong resemblance to an adolescent conflict (although Lauweriks was already thirty), characterized by a succession of provocations and expressions of loyalty from Lauweriks and admonitions and angry outbursts from Cuypers. Then in March 1895 Lauweriks published the translation of a theosophical discourse that sent Cuypers into a rage – Lauweriks' views were 'godless and insane … such people must learn to think before pretending to be philosophers!' When a month later Cuypers had been publicly honoured by his students, he warned them in his thank-you speech not to display arrogance, idleness or self-indulgence – which was immediately seen as a reprimand to Lauweriks and his friends.[35]

The young architects, for their part, made no secret of the fundamental differences between Cuypers and themselves. With their theosophy, Eastern ideas and anarchism, Lauweriks, De Bazel and Bauer found themselves in another ideological world. Van der Pek wrote in 1894 that there would never be another 'period of great Christian architecture', because Christians were hopelessly divided amongst themselves; and for architecture to flourish, uniformity in aim and vision was a prerequisite. When in 1896 it seemed that Berlage was being presented as Cuypers' successor, Lauweriks pointed out that the two men took entirely different approaches to their work. He was indirectly proved right when Berlage's kindred soul, the poet Albert Verwey, in a debate conducted in *De Kroniek* on 'The people and Catholicism', argued that Catholics cultivated the great tradition – that was to say, the past – whereas the 'people' focused on the future.

The differences between Cuypers and the younger men concerned not only philosophical issues, but also specific architectural matters. In 1894 Kromhout wrote that Cuypers' restoration methods were an expression of 'art-conservatism' and as such were impeding the development of a new art. The next year Berlage wrote in *De Kroniek*

that Cornelis Peters' recent design for the Amsterdam Main Post Office, a major work in the tradition of Cuypers, had 'disappointed him immensely' and proceeded to demolish the pretence that this was a work of rational architecture. *De Opmerker* observed in 1896 that the young architects, 'whose idol Mr Cuypers was, and no doubt about it', were taking a different course with their own work. Kromhout had indeed already established that Berlage, Lauweriks, De Bazel and Bauer 'express themselves differently, devoid of Mr Cuypers' influence, independent of government buildings'. As far as the 'official style' was concerned, Lauweriks observed in 1898 that he saw few positive effects from Cuypers' concept of architecture, which at least had not developed into a worthy new school. Cuypers' followers, according to Lauweriks, were mainly 'dead copyists', and the state architects had the 'barren, shrivelled spirit of the civil servant' of which architecture could expect nothing. Even Mol conceded, in 1900, that the buildings produced by state architects, even when some slight influence of rationality could be discerned, had little to do with art.[36]

So why *was* Cuypers so admired, given that the evidence demonstrates such great differences between him and his young admirers, some even going so far as to denounce his dearest beliefs? The explanation given by *De Opmerker* in 1896 – that the new A et A and its journal *Architectura* were in favour of Cuypers because he was a source of jobs – seems somewhat simplistic, although Kromhout observed as early as 1891 that the 'rationals' attracted many young people keen to find work.[37] Indeed, it would be naive to ignore the fact that the large, busy practices of Cuypers and of the state architects Peters and Van Lokhorst, not to mention De Stuers' power and Cuypers' vast social network and his membership of so many boards and committees, were very attractive to young architects looking for a job. None of this, though, can explain the fervour of the Cuypers cult, which contained a strong element of emotion, a deep psychological motivation. What was operating here, in fact, was a powerful symbiotic relationship. The young architects 'used' Cuypers as the subject on which to project their own aspirations, and Cuypers used their homage as confirmation of the supremacy of his curiously closed professional world view. And he, who had always been praised for his modesty, never objected to the picture of the nineteenth century as a period of darkness in which he himself was the only beacon.

Cuypers as catalyst

It would appear that this symbiosis was a vital element of the Dutch architectural scene of the 90s, but after the turn of the century only the husk of it remained; the homage paid to the old architect by the 90s generation, no longer so young themselves, became hollow phrases, formulas. Their publications show that they were projecting their resistance to the conventions on to Cuypers as the 'victorious fighter against conventionalism'. Aware that their own marginal position was due to their wilfulness, they viewed Cuypers as the outsider who, while maintaining his convictions, had fought his way to the top. While they themselves were struggling to develop an architectural concept out of a more personal perception, they worshipped him as the creator of a 'fresh' and 'living' architecture in an 'an era completely devoid of a sense of architecture'; as the prototype of the real artist whose being was 'entirely dedicated to his art' and whose work was the expression of 'passion' and 'love'. Those who risked their necks to express in their work their spiritual beliefs admired Cuypers for his profound religiosity. Other, perhaps more negative, motives can also be discerned. For instance, as long as the established order, as embodied in the MBB, the *Bouwkundig Weekblad* and *De Opmerker*, was negative towards Cuypers or critical of him, to publicly venerate him meant deliberately confronting that established order.[38]

All motives thus met in the one amorphous need for a

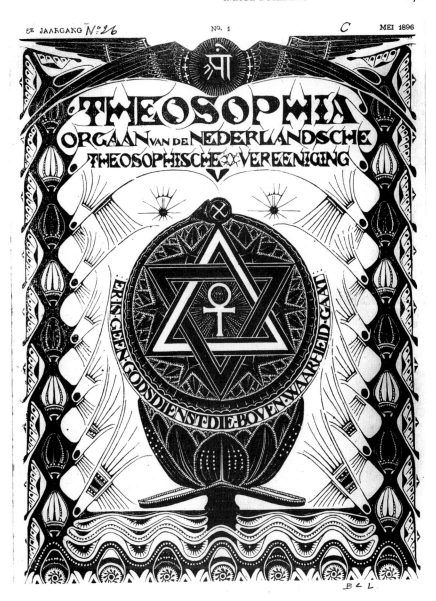

movement aware that it was embarking on something new without fully knowing what that new was, or even whether it really was the start of something new – inherent was the need for a past, for a father, for a pioneer. Finding a significant pioneer might be the solution because that pioneer would prove that the new had a *raison d'être* by the very fact that it had been initiated by someone entitled to speak for all. The personal prestige of such a pioneer was more important than any affinity with his work. This had already been demonstrated some years earlier when the young literary generation had chosen the acclaimed Conrad Busken Huet (1826–86) as their pioneer despite the fact that he was not attuned to their literary achievements.[39] For

Fig.92
J. L. 'Mathieu' Lauweriks' woodcut for the cover of *Theosophia* magazine (1896), the organ of the Dutch Theosophical Association. The motto around the sphere above the lotus reads, 'There is no religion above truth'.

the young architects of the 1890s the veneration of Cuypers seems to have been a *rite de passage*, petering out naturally by the end of the nineteenth century when each had found his own way.

The significance of the Cuypers cult

If we consider the elements of the Cuypers cult as just outlined as belonging to the secret agendas of those involved, we must mention the hidden meanings, the ambiguities in the way the veneration was expressed. These ambiguities – as they applied both to the reputation of the person of Cuypers and to that of his work – were so manifest that their denial by Cuypers' admirers suggests suppression, opportunism or cynicism. With his extensive

œuvre (including the most costly Dutch architectural enterprise of the century), his near-monopoly of the government-subsidized restorations and his business enterprises, Cuypers had acquired a prominent social position as well as, undoubtedly, a considerable fortune. In their tributes his admirers kept silent about this, drawing attention instead to his self-sacrifice and humility. Through his wealth, his position and De Stuers' very effective protection, Cuypers was able to exert his influence as probably no other Dutch architect could, but his admirers ignored this power and pointed only to his many opponents and his victimization.

Although for fifty years Cuypers had done what all his colleagues had done – namely, followed, in his work, the examples of architectural history – his followers made it appear as if his work was based not on historical forms, but on *principles*. Anyone who wished to see its forms 'had to free himself of all the preconceived theoretical subcategories and try to understand his work in the setting in which it had its being,' said H. W. Mol in 1900. 'It is understandable that in his work Cuypers tried to find a connection with the Middle Ages.'[40] But such an understanding was not bestowed on all of Cuypers' colleagues and contemporaries. While Cuypers' work was praised as the exemplary manifestation of the art of building, the 'official style' that was based on it was not taken seriously as an artistic phenomenon, although Cuypers' followers had for twenty years considered his 'school' as a unity. And despite the fact that it was the dozens of Catholic churches that he had built that constituted his life's work, in terms of both quality and numbers, they were ignored; while his Rijksmuseum – which, though a very important commission, was just one atypical item in his œuvre – was considered the very essence of his art. And there was also some ambiguity in the general veneration of the Rijksmuseum. It was praised as a masterwork even though everyone knew how ineffectively the building was functioning as a museum. Jan Veth, one of the admirers of the 'sage master builder', had in 1894 initiated the campaign of criticizing the interior.[41] At a more profound level these ambiguities touched on the changed meaning of architectural theory and of architectural reviews, which were no longer instruments in the quest for the essence of the art of building, but conscious or unconscious projections of one's own interests or prejudices, or expressions of one's predilection for one's own coterie.

The cult of personality, Berlage, and the Modern Movement

In the veneration of the Rijksmuseum, in addition to the ideological and psychological aspects, a third component of the Cuypers cult emerges: the element of architectural theory. (Because it is part of the main theme of this book it will be discussed more extensively later, but as part of the veneration of Cuypers it is appropriate to mention it here.) This theoretical aspect has three elements:

1. Cuypers' reputation profited from the growing interest in 'rationalism' in architecture, an interest fed, among other things, by the renewed interest in Viollet-le-Duc.
2. It also profited from the renewed interest in idealism in architecture, expressed in the notion that it was an art of and for society, the basis of a 'community art'. This idea,

first formulated and propagated in England by William Morris and John Ruskin, used medieval art and society as its point of reference, and spread in the 1890s to the rest of Western Europe.
3. Because of the narrowing of his œuvre to the Rijksmuseum, Cuypers' reputation profited from the renewed interest in monumentality and simplicity that was a reaction to the complexity of the picturesque, the ideal of the 80s.

The veneration of the Rijksmuseum was the Cuypers cult in a nutshell, full of ideological, psychological and aesthetic projections that had come into being without reference to contemporary history, and exemplified too by the suppression of contradictions in architectural theory. The 90s generation felt it was able to 'understand' and appreciate the Rijksmuseum, unlike the old guard who had abused it. Admiration for the museum was thus seen as a sign of a more profound understanding, of more 'feeling', of the further development and hence the superiority of the younger generation *vis-à-vis* the older. This view also implied that Cuypers, having been misunderstood earlier, had then been ahead of his time – his present admirers, therefore, had chosen the right side, that of the victor. As Kromhout observed in 1895, 'Cuypers' conception has been too deep to comprehend, but it is now completely understood'.[42]

The essence here is to see how the idea took shape that a few individuals created a 'new movement', that put an end to the artistic incapability of the nineteenth century, thus creating a contemporary style.

In 1895, shortly after Cuypers had been honoured by his students and by *Architectura*, Berlage acknowledged his own admiration for medieval architecture, in particular the relationship in it between ornament and construction: 'the ornamented construction as the real essence of architecture ought to be pure style'. Six months later he called Cuypers 'without any doubt the most competent architect in the Netherlands and one of the most competent of our time', the only architect whose work inspired hope in a new architecture, and who had only one fault: 'he has remained too much of a medievalist in his views and in his activities'. In September 1896 Van der Pek argued that Berlage's recent work – despite the fact that it looked totally different from Cuypers' – was 'spiritually based on it'; furthermore, the twenty-year-olds of today would continue the process of renewal.[43] These views almost immediately crystallized into what was to remain the prevailing historical interpretation of the origins of modern Dutch architecture.

According to this view only one architect could be

OPPOSITE
Fig.93
Cornelis H. Peters'
Main Post Office,
Amsterdam (1895–9).
To the younger
generation this was,
after the Amsterdam
City Theatre (Fig.95)
and the Stedelijk
Museum (Fig.88), the
third most annoying
manifestation from
the past. This model
of the 'official style'
which, twenty years of
protection
notwithstanding, had
never in fact become a
style, here excelled
itself in its useless
opulence of historical
detail.

important to Berlage, namely Cuypers, but, being too much of an 'archaeologist', a man of the past, this one exception was essentially not modern. The work of Berlage was, on the other hand, considered 'logical' and 'sound', not only thanks to Cuypers' influence but because it was also original – and therefore modern. In this interpretation of art history Berlage was given a more prominent position than the young architects of the 90s; already at the beginning of 1898 he was considered their leader, albeit on grounds that were never made clear. That he maintained this position can be attributed to the astonishing persistence with which he repeated his ideas on Cuypers over a span of some forty years (until his death in 1934), and to the ease with which others continued to accept and reproduce these views as authoritative. Immediately after Berlage's death, Cuypers was presented as the John the Baptist of Dutch modern architecture, and Berlage therefore as the Messiah (the word had already been used in 1898 to refer to Berlage).[44]

This personality-centred interpretation may seem naive nowadays, but the fact is that as historiography it was completely in line with the historiography of the international Modern Movement as a whole. The latter came about via architects such as Berlage who claimed for themselves a crucial role, assisted in this by historians who personally knew the 'pioneers of modern design'.[45] But these are observations made after the event – it would be rash to speculate that it was because he was already aware of his own position in history that Berlage had formulated such ideas on Cuypers in 1896. It is possible that they arose later, around 1900, when his Stock Exchange was described as the first modern architectural monument. In 1895–6 Berlage's overt admiration for Cuypers can be explained, as was the case with the younger generation in general, as the result of *projection*, as a means of representing oneself in another, and as the formulation of a stance on architectural theory; probably Berlage, too, had a hidden agenda. By choosing Cuypers as his model and by making skilful use of his choice, he took advantage of Cuypers' patriarchal status without any fear of competition from him – for 'the sage master-builder', as noted above, was too much of an 'archaeologist'. One way or another, Berlage's public image would increasingly resemble Cuypers': here was a patriarch, a master-builder, an honorary doctor, a genuine and modest human being – and all this was regularly underlined by public tributes (not least, the beautiful memorial book and other accolades that he received on his sixtieth birthday).[46] Berlage's choosing in favour of Cuypers in 1896 meant choosing not to go with the established order of the MBB and Dutch Renaissance. It also meant choosing in favour of the young architects of the day; 'it is the younger people, and not his contemporaries, who appreciate [Cuypers'] art,' Berlage wrote in January that year (thereby suggesting that he considered himself a member of the younger set too).

The way Berlage used Cuypers was loaded with ambiguity, too. Choosing not to go with the establishment (of which he himself had been a valued young member in the previous decade) meant also parting from some of the professional contacts who were no longer useful to him, as well as furnishing him with a well timed encounter with such newly prominent figures as the Amsterdam alderman M. W. F. Treub and poet Verwey, who would help him in his quest to become the leader of modern architecture (and in so doing, would also serve their own political and cultural interests). By claiming that Cuypers, and Cuypers alone, had been his exemplar, Berlage could pretend that he had developed his modern architectural theories himself, thereby successfully diverting attention away from his German, English, Belgian, American and Dutch sources. We should also bear in mind that around 1895 there was no consensus as to who was in fact the leader of the new movement. The younger generation had produced some impressive words and architectural fantasies to indicate generally what it wanted or not, but it had not had an opportunity yet to bring its ideas into architectural practice. It was only natural that now Berlage had recently associated himself with the 'new movement', his De Algemeene Building was regarded as its first achievement. Was it just gossip and slander, though, when in 1895 *De Opmerker* reported that insiders were whispering that Berlage 'still remained stuck in tradition'? Or was that really what they said? The building did indeed incorporate numerous references to historical style elements, and the interior looked very much as if inspired by the 'official style'. *De Opmerker* had earlier referred to the work of De Bazel and Lauweriks, when they were setting up their own practice, as the 'most modern art style' – work 'that did not, for a change, originate in the old-fashioned historical styles'.[47] The relevance here is that, in order to consolidate his position in modern architecture, it was very important for Berlage at this point to verbally erase his dependence on historical architectural types. By emphasizing only the *meaning* of medieval constructions and principles, he made it appear as if the 'new movement' owed its originality to a radically new understanding of building. In so doing, he diverted attention from the possibility that he had arrived at his design concepts through *visual imitation*.

Imitation, copying – these were the deadly sins of the old generations. Berlage's position as heir apparent to the

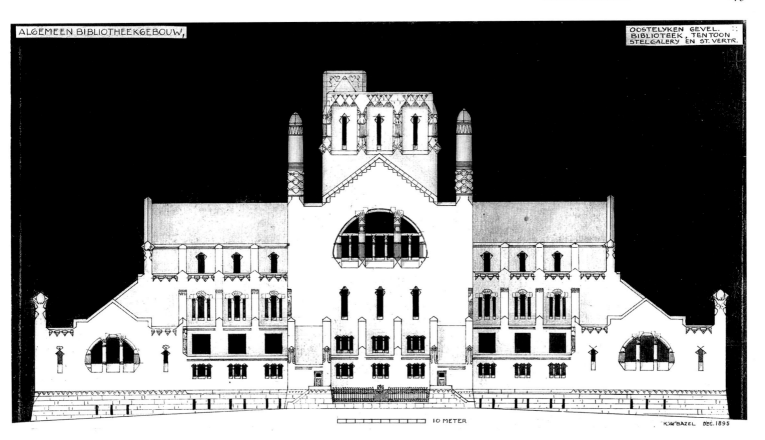

OOSTELYKEN GEVEL.
BIBLIOTEEK, TENTOON
STELGALERY EN ST. VERTR.

IO METER

K. de BAZEL DEC. 1895

forerunner of modern architecture was, indeed, ambiguous. Lauded in the 80s as 'promising' by young and old alike, now he was balancing like an acrobat above the chasm separating the parties. He could easily admire and criticize, all in the same breath, classical or medieval architecture, or Semper, Cuypers or Viollet-le-Duc, or refer to Cuypers' work as classical and to Semper's as rational – if necessary, all in the same article. Berlage was the anti-bourgeois middle-class man, socially committed, much too commonsensical for theosophy or mysticism, an advocate of passion and love in architecture and an adherent of the 'new world idea'. He was at one with the young generation, but at the same time completely different from them; he was not an anarchist like Bauer, nor a dreamer like Kromhout, nor a great architect like De Bazel; but he was a much better architect than Lauweriks, Walenkamp or Bauer; he was young but not *too* young, an architect who always put reason first. Above all, he knew exactly how and when to reconcile his conservative architectural principles with the aesthetics of the modern era.

Movements on the wane: the Renaissance out of favour, and the end of the neo-Gothic

We have touched on several psychological aspects of the emerging new movement, and we shall now apply a similar eye to its views on architecture. These were initially developed – and how could it have been otherwise? – by making choices from amongst the many ideas on offer around 1890: numerous adaptations of Renaissance architecture, styleless architecture (in other words, eclecticism, referred to in France as 'realism'); and, less important from the quantitative point of view, neo-Gothic architecture and the 'official' style. In the 80s it had become clear that the old tradition of studying architectural history was a dead end; by 1890 there was simply too much history, too much pointless studying. The present day, it was thought, required a different, non-traditional approach.

For this reason Kromhout's '*Tout à l'égout*' cannot have come entirely unexpected in 1891. Perhaps its success can be attributed especially to the unrelentingly radical way in which he expressed his discontent. The young architects were later frequently to reject the study and imitation of historical styles, and it is notable that the Renaissance was their particular scapegoat. Their aversion was probably not

Fig.94
A design by Karel P. C. de Bazel for a public library entered in a competition organized by Architectura et Amicitia in 1895. The adjudicators (Pierre Cuypers, Peters and Berlage) did not consider the design (here showing the east side) good enough for a prize – the monumentality was 'dubious'. This did not prevent Berlage from immediately adopting the aesthetic innovations for his Stock Exchange.

only a reaction to the fact that Renaissance architecture had recently been so widely adopted that it had in many cases become a cliché – the related semantics, too, must have played a role. The reaction to the 8os' celebration of the Renaissance as an expression of nationhood and bourgeois civilization necessarily called for the converse, some expression of 'the common people', the uncultured masses without power, property or prestige. Clearly, in this climate, Renaissance architecture conveyed precisely the wrong message. The new ideal required an expression of simplicity, collectivity, brotherhood, 'real life'. In 1896 Van der Pek welcomed Berlage's new office building at the Muntplein as true art that sprang from 'real life' and that stood for a departure from the 'petit bourgeois' 'fake art' exemplified by Jan Springer's new City Theatre.[48]

In 1894 Kromhout had used the City Theatre to criticize a very different aspect of the Renaissance. The building was a clever assembly of formal and compositional elements 'in the tradition of the classical method of design – and it most certainly *is* a method', he said, but at the same time it was a virtuoso manifestation of a movement past its prime, 'on the wane'.[49] Kromhout's remarks laid bare an essential point. The Renaissance, via the architectural training system (at Delft Polytechnic and elsewhere), had been compressed into a method - along the lines of the classical design method – undoubtedly with the corresponding objective rules, skills and tricks, and thus it stood for the opposite of the *subjective feeling* that the new movement chose as its guide.

This would explain the young architects' aversion to rational design methods, while confirming their marginal position in the building world. They could still afford to reject a building world that increasingly leaned towards rationalization as a consequence of industrialization, commercialization and the division of labour both in the architectural practice and on the building site; and they demonstrated the same lack of understanding of the buildings designed in the 'official style', which made frequent use of rationalized design methods. Hence Lauweriks' reference to the large practices of the state architects Van Lokhorst and Peters as 'dead copyists'. However, whereas the young architects associated the Renaissance, on account of its academic practice, with a strict adherence to a model – 'servile imitation' they called it – neither neo-Gothic design practice nor the 'official style' (which from a methodological point of view was hardly any different) gave them cause to campaign against Gothic architecture. It is worth noting here that despite their disapproval of the rationalized design method, except when it was based on the proportional systems of

Viollet-le-Duc and other non-Renaissance sources, they often expressed an appreciation of 'rationalism'.

Perhaps the vehemence of many of their attacks on the Renaissance style can be attributed to the fact that their stance forced all these new architects of the 90s to renounce both their training and in some cases their first practical experience as well. Van der Pek – the same Van der Pek who a few years later would campaign fiercely against 'petit bourgeois pseudo Renaissance art' – had studied with Gugel, and in 1890 had built shop premises in the Renaissance style.[50] Berlage turned out in this respect to be a master of the smokescreen, especially concerning his thoughts on the grand master of nineteenth-century Renaissance, Gottfried Semper. In 1884 he had honoured Semper as the 'leader of a new era of building that was of the very greatest importance to modern art'. During the 80s Berlage had done a lot of designing in the Old Dutch manner; in 1891 he commented on a splendid residence that Bram Salm had built in the French Renaissance style, saying that it was a pity that the architect had not studied Dutch art. He thus demonstrated – in the same year that '*Tout à l'égout*' was published – that he shared the way of thinking of the older architects; the young generation certainly no longer had any affinity with what Berlage admiringly referred to as a 'real piece of national art'. In 1892, again using terms that place him squarely in the 80s, he described Springer's design for the City Theatre as 'truly modern' because of its picturesque silhouette, and 'certainly very national' in so far as his treatment of the material was concerned. Only in 1893 did he concede the view that Kromhout had taken in '*Tout à l'égout*' – that the age of the 'schools' and of building in a particular style was over. But in that very same year he started on the renovation of the Arti et Amicitiae building – in the Renaissance style.[51]

In 1894, with the De Algemeene Building completed, it was clear that Berlage had left the Renaissance behind him. It was precisely at this time that he started to adopt a condescending attitude towards that period. When in 1895, before an audience of MBB members, Van der Pek took the view that the Renaissance could not be regarded as a period of art at all, Berlage supported him. And when several months later Van der Pek described the new Stedelijk Museum in Amsterdam as a total failure on the grounds of his 'feelings' about it, Berlage gave a repeat performance.[52] In the long article 'On architecture' that he wrote in 1895 he praised Semper highly, but added that his work was based on a misunderstanding: the Renaissance was based on Roman 'pseudo-art', the Roman 'dressings architecture' that had been decoratively applied to the 'splendid

structurally pure, column-based architecture of the Greeks'. This made Renaissance architecture very attractive, 'but [it] is not straightforward; it flirts gracefully, but does not tell the truth. In a word, it lacks earnestness'. Neo-Renaissance architecture had gained no standing at all in the Netherlands, he continued, so it was an ideal point of departure, on the solid foundation of Cuypers' work, from which to develop modern art. Cuypers' love, his passion, his dedicated art that has 'held out against the desperate jumble that the talentless Renaissance men have burdened us with, has demonstrated to us anew the lofty essence of architecture, at precisely the right moment, when the incompetents have been called to a halt'. Thus in 1895 Berlage renounced the environment that had both nurtured and cherished him. And he secured a role for himself

among the leaders of the new movement by paying tribute to its new idol – only to immediately render himself ineffectual – for Cuypers' art, 'with that one mistake for which it cannot be forgiven entirely, however modern its intentions, has nevertheless for our era remained much too medieval in character'.[53]

Although by calling his work and influence the result of a misunderstanding Berlage set himself above Semper, the next year he was designing furniture with structural innovations that Semper had published in his book *Style* as early as 1860. In the historic perspective that Berlage applied to the new movement after 1895, in which everything centred on the proper understanding of the architectural construction, Semper was hardly mentioned at all. But when in 1902 Berlage wrote a book on his own

Fig.95
Jan L. Springer's City Theatre, Amsterdam (1892–4): Dutch Renaissance at its peak, and a masterwork by a virtuoso designer that was built too late and which, for that reason, was the object of much criticism and referred to as an example of a 'movement on the wane'.

views on design, *On Style in Architecture and Furniture*, these views turned out to be permeated with Semper's ideas.[54] The spokesmen of the new movement used their criticism of all that was 'old' as a means of experiencing their feelings of novelty, of originality, and of displaying them to others. They were in fact, as intensely as possible whether they were aware of it or not, building an image.

Despite their expressions of loyalty to Cuypers, in practice neo-Gothic architecture was for the young architects as much a 'movement on the wane' as was the neo-Renaissance. Their aversion to neo-Gothic architecture did, however, leave room for positive feelings towards medieval art. These feelings were focused not so much on this art itself, as on several topical themes they thought they could discern in the Middle Ages. In a way, the Middle Ages was a mirror in which the young could discover aspects that they considered new and stimulating, whereas the Renaissance was a mirror that displayed only aspects of their own era that they wanted to get rid of. The two qualities that they projected on to the Middle Ages were 'rational' construction and the ideal of a humane, brotherly society. In this, the Netherlands proved once again that it was not an island: the international flourishing of neo-Renaissance architecture was followed all over Western and Central Europe by a new, international, anti-Renaissance movement that favoured principles of construction and social ideals that had come to be associated with the Middle Ages.

The exhibition of decorative and applied arts that took place in early 1896 in Haarlem comprised the usual mass-produced neo-Gothic articles intended for use in Catholic church services, along with articles flying the Renaissance banner. Apparently uninhibited by his recent publications on the Renaissance as a 'misunderstanding' and as pseudo-art, Berlage had entered a recent design for the interior of a café in Renaissance style.[55] For *De Opmerker*, the exhibition had one redeeming feature. 'It is a great relief', it wrote, 'after this exercise in raking up the past, to examine the entries of Mr De Bazel and Mr Lauweriks. It would seem to us that this very artistic duo stands at the moment in the vanguard of the young artists who have devoted themselves to the art of decoration. On the road to a new style, they have advanced the furthest.'

Rationalism: the dying echo of an era

In 1894 Kromhout considered it pointless to make rationalism into a particular current in architecture, for it was something that belonged, part and parcel, to the training of each individual architect.[56] He was proved right. Berlage, though, appeared to have a particularly keen eye

for the strategic meaning of the term 'rationalism', it offered a unique opportunity to pass judgement, both favourable and unfavourable. No other term was so useful for distinguishing his own 'logical' approach from the pseudo-architecture and 'pure ostentation' of colleagues of different persuasions. Again, this was about image, and in this theory-deficient decade there was one theorist whose work was still very frequently cited, often in connection with the term 'rationalism'. This was Viollet-le-Duc, the leader of the medieval school. Thus in the historiography of twentieth-century Dutch architecture the view arose that rationalism as practised by Viollet-le-Duc, Cuypers and Berlage was the main theme of the 1890s and the start of a modern Dutch architecture. However, all this concentration on Viollet-le-Duc probably requires a sociological explanation rather than one based on architectural theory. For it would be naive to assume that the many references to his *Dictionnaire* and to his *Discourses* emanated from a hunger for theoretical knowledge among the reading public. The articles on Viollet-le-Duc that appeared at this time were the dying echo of the era of great theories. As a historical monument his works were respected by every 'competent' Dutch architect, but that was as far as it went.

The young architects of the new movement used the term 'rationalism' anything but consistently. Their periodical *Architectura* promised from the start to employ 'artistic-rational' grounds for its reviews, but Kromhout – who had drafted this declaration of principles – was soon writing critical commentaries that were more like visual fine-art reviews. He described only his visual observations, to which biographical details of the designer were occasionally added. Many documents of the time demonstrate that it took more than elaborations on the relationship between design and construction to whip up the young set's enthusiasm. Their culture was primarily a visual one.

Their minimal interest in rationalism is demonstrated by their designs. The first impressive architectural images of the new movement were those submitted for competitions by De Bazel and Walenkamp in 1895. For these they used symmetrical floor plans in the way still taught by the École des Beaux-Arts in Paris, the institution held by many in the Netherlands to be the bastion of antirationalism. In these designs symmetry – the traditional classicist instrument – undoubtedly served to express monumentality. But to these young architects choosing symmetry was the equivalent of choosing a beautiful design rather than a 'rationalist' one. The aesthetic ideal of the 'profoundly flat' façades, also exhibited, constituted an

Fig.96
Herman
J. M. Walenkamp's
design for a public
library, entered in the
competition organized
by Architectura et
Amicitia in 1895,
showing the façade.
The design concept
has much affinity with
the façade of the
Ceres bread factory
(Fig.99). It is even
more 'primitive' than
De Bazel's public
library design (Fig.94)
entered in the same
competition, but at
the same time it is
much more abstract,
remaining closer to
the representation of
a principle than to
that of a potential
building.

even more resounding adieu to the rationalism of the older generation. As *De Opmerker* wrote in 1896, 'No façade is "beautiful" any more unless it is "profoundly flat"; Viollet-le-Duc's axiom, 'every form that is not indicated by the construction should be rejected', was apparently on the wane.[57] The young architects showed no liking either for using the projecting parts of the walls, brickwork and mouldings in a way that would make a building's interior arrangement visible on the outside – something that generations of architects before them, on the authority of all the German and French theorists since Hübsch, had always done. But given their aversion to the conventions of their elders, why should they make an exception for this sacrosanct principle of truth? Was not their lack of respect for truth the best demonstration of their independence?

Thus the 90s generation was questioning everything. An almost symbolic instance of the confrontation between old and new occurred when the elder Salm, the elder Cuypers and Henri J. Evers adjudicated over a design for an architectural competition entered by Bauer in 1891. Here were three older architects, representatives of eclectic, medieval and Renaissance architecture, respectively, against a young architect who wanted to strike a new note. But Bauer's design – for a theatre façade – was judged 'untrue' because it did not show how the interior was organized. The artistic but impractical Bauer was not the only architect to be treated in this way. Via the pages of *De Opmerker* Gosschalk advised Berlage to bring forward at certain points the Stock Exchange's long, flat Dam-side façade for the sake of better proportions – and because Viollet-le-Duc taught that the exterior must be visibly expressed in every part of a building.[58] But Gosschalk pleaded to no avail. In the new movement, art stood for 'feeling', even if the opposite was maintained on paper.

Fig.97
Walenkamp's plan of
the ground floor of
the public library
(Fig.96). His search
for an antipicturesque,
monumental
simplicity resulted in
an 'ideal' Beaux-Arts
floor plan.

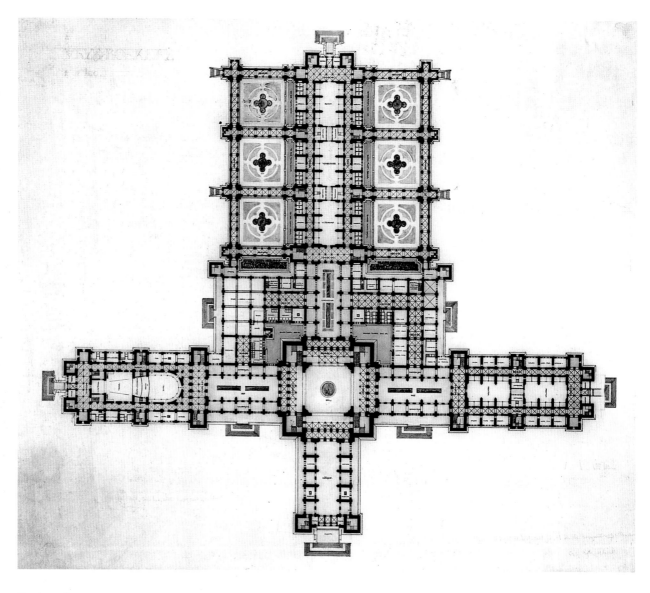

Rationalism and Berlage: an opportunistic interpretation

As we have seen, the young guard showed little appreciation of the 'official style'. A popular focus for criticism was the Main Post Office building in Amsterdam, which possessed, according to the man who designed it, Cornelis Peters, both rationality and functionality. The criticism fell into two categories. Lauweriks wrote disapprovingly about the 'unaesthetic form' and ornamentation of the façades, a judgement based on his subjective aesthetic feeling, and typical of the genre of critical observation that the young architects had introduced, focusing on the visual image without taking account of the rational, however that term might be defined. Berlage, on the other hand, condemned

the design because Peters had ignored the principle of rational building 'in the most flagrant way', for there was a lack of coherence, he claimed, between the exterior and the interior[59] – a criticism, clearly, that was more in line with the way of thinking of the older generation than with the 'feeling' of the young ones. For Berlage, rationalism appeared to be merely a question of rhetoric, just as it had always been for Cuypers and his followers. By emphasizing the rational construction, Berlage, too, made it appear as if the architectural form came into being spontaneously, as if the form was an independent emanation of a principle. His office building on the Muntplein, completed in 1896, displays unambiguously his opportunistic use of the rationalist creed: the façade shows protruding elements

PROJET D'UN THÉÂTRE

FAÇADE PRINCIPALE

applied for visual reasons only – something for which Berlage had fiercely criticized Peters' Post Office building.

In the crucial years between 1895 and 1900 Berlage's writings and designs showed much of the rhetoric of the new movement, but the patterns of thought of the old guard lingered on in his work – to become, after 1900, very explicit indeed. For instance, in 1895 he declared himself opposed to using an iron beam over a large shop window with a façade made of stone above it; iron, according to Berlage, was intrinsically 'thin' and therefore visually inappropriate to bear a mass of stone. Referring back to classical antiquity, he demonstrated that a building style did not emerge from the characteristics of the building materials, but that, on the contrary, style dictated the building materials that would be used and how they would be applied. With this historical 'evidence' he argued that it was impossible that iron – even when applied to American skyscrapers – would be able to dictate the architecture of the twentieth century. He acknowledged that the 'blatant presence of iron' was everywhere the order of the day, but was confident that 'something so utterly unsightly' could never have anything to do with style.[60]

These words contain several of the older generations'

ideas, which were hardly compatible with the younger mentality. These were:

1. Berlage's firm belief that a new architectural style, in the sense of an objective and universal aesthetic, would emerge.
2. Berlage's negative views on the use of iron, which had already been current for thirty years and which during that period had prevented the full integration of the material, and the constructions based on it, into the art of building.
3. His firm belief in traditional aesthetics. As he said, a wall resting on a shop window was 'something my eyes do not wish to get used to'.

Berlage's knowledge of historical theory convinced him that architectural practice did not create a style. He would continue to build according to traditional methods and would base his designs on a detailed expression of those methods, because the 'timeless', but in fact medieval constructions exemplified in these methods were the means by which he was able to give tangible form to his idealistic aesthetic. After the success of his Stock Exchange, this

Fig.98
Willem C. Bauer's design for a theatre, in a competition organized by the association Architectura et Amicitia in The Hague in 1891. To the old school, this was typical of the method of working of the young generation: 'highly artistic' it may have been, but 'careless drawing result[ed] in ill-considered designs and equally ill-considered constructions and realizations'.

aesthetic, which went back as far as the nineteenth century, would again in Berlage's circles purport to be valid both objectively and universally.

Even when, in the 90s, architectural theory had become obsolete, some remnants of it survived – not as a design guide, but in order to lend the architectural profession an air of cultural mission, with the aim of bringing culture and beauty into a world full of 'unsightliness and falsehood'.

A movement achieving fruition

The 1890s saw a widespread aversion to tradition, convention and of institutions, and at the same time the germination of something positive and vital that could not be described yet, and that was referred to as 'the new'. But was it essentially new? Willem Kromhout's call in 1891 for absolute artistic freedom, independent of all -isms and styles, heralding the 'new movement' of the 90s, was in fact the eclectic attitude. And what was new to the activities and ideas of Berlage? Only a few years after Kromhout's proclamation of individual freedom had broken ground, it was opposed by the campaign led by Berlage, that claimed to be a struggle to realize 'the new' but that really wanted to maintain and restore old traditions and old positions.

Be this as it may, the 90s undoubtedly had a sense of something definitely new. Around 1895 the nineteenth century was past history, and the new age had already begun.

Notes

1. *De Opmerker* 33 (1898) no. 18, 139.
2. Cited by *Architectura* 8 (1900) no. 16, 125.
3. An outline of that 'Young Amsterdam': Lieske Tibbe 1994, 15ff.
4. J. V. [Jan Veth] 1898.
5. Bookshelves: X. 1890, 194; also *De Opmerker* 26 (1891) no. 17, 139–40; W. Kromhout 1893, 6 (a speech from 1892). Viollet-le-Duc for the attic: *De Opmerker* 30 (1895) no. 17, 131.
6. For an overview of 1875–90: 'Oude en nieuwe kunst' ('Old and new art'), *De Opmerker* 26 (1891) no. 18, 146–8; a review devoted to L. M. Moolenaar 1895, in *De Opmerker* 30 (1895) no. 49, 389–90, reviewing L. M. Moolenaar 1895. Van der Pek: J. E. van der Pek 1894, 229–30.
7. K. 1895; striving in one particular direction, and the beginnings of the new style: *De Opmerker* 29 (1894) no. 5, 35.
8. C. H. Peters 1894, 62–3; J. E. van der Pek 1894, 225; H. P. Berlage 1894, 99; E. Gugel 1869, 1st edn, 20; a style of 'one's own self': H. C. J. M. van Nispen tot Sevenaer 1894, 14. Springer's style: *De Opmerker* 29 (1894) no. 46, 392.
9. *Architectura* 6 (1898) no. 17, 70 and R. [C. T. J. Louis Rieber] 1898, 111.
10. For example, a number of texts relating to the De Algemeene Building: Berlage's presentation of his designs, an article in *Architectura* 1 (1893) no. 43, 186–7, which, however, is very poor on theory. Reactions to the building: W. Kr. [W. Kromhout] 1894; *De Opmerker* 29 (1894) no. 15, 114, and no. 17, 129–30; J. Kok 1894. On Berlage's office building at the Muntplein: J. E. van der Pek

11. I. Gosschalk 1899, 58.
12. W. N. Rose 1860, 106.
13. J. E. van der Pek 1895.
14. *Bouwkundig Weekblad* 15 (1895) no. 32, 206. Berlage may have had pragmatic (and subjective) rather than philosophical motives for his viewpoint, given his attempt to express the character of the insurance company De Algemeene through symbols he had thought up himself (the results of which were ridiculed mercilessly by *De Opmerker* 29 [1894] no. 18, 138–9).
15. H. P. Berlage 1895–6, 224; H. P. Berlage 1905, 80–1.
16. Jan Veth in his introduction to Walter Crane 1894, v, reprinted in Jan Veth 1904, 35–6.
17. *De Opmerker* 27 (1892) no. 30, 241–2; no. 31, 249–51.
18. H. W. Mol 1894a. The reaction came in the form of letters to the editor by Lauweriks' editor colleague C. W. Nijhoff, *Architectura* 2 (1894) no. 41, 175–6, referring to the 'boundless self-satisfaction' of the young Mol, with a reply from Mol in no. 42, 179–80; Lauweriks' reaction in no. 43, 182–4.
19. *De Opmerker* 30 (1895) no. 50, 396.
20. *Architectura* 3 (1895) no. 20, 84; De Groot's speech in no. 21, 87–8; De Stuers' speech in no. 22, 90–1; the reply: P. J. H. Cuypers 1895. *De Opmerker*'s comment: 30 (1895) no. 20, 153–4.
21. V. [Jan Veth] 1895; Alphons Diepenbrock 1895, 169.
22. H. P. Berlage 1895–6, 216, 218; J. E. van der Pek 1896; the reaction of Weissman in *De Kroniek* 2 (1896), 235; J. L. M. Lauweriks 1896, 300.
23. The festive issue: *Architectura* 5 (1897) no. 20. The other publications: ('Dr. P. J. H. Cuypers 1827–16 May–1897'), *De Opmerker* 32 (1897) no. 20, 153–5 (with portrait); 'Het jubileum van Dr. P. J. H. Cuypers' ('The jubilee of Dr P. J. H. Cuypers'), no. 20, 155–8; 'Het feest van Dr. P. J. H. Cuypers' ('The celebrations for Dr. P. J. H. Cuypers'), no. 21, 163–6; 'Uit Amsterdam' ('From Amsterdam'), no. 23, 177 and 180; 'Het feest van Dr. P. J. H. Cuypers', *Bouwkundig Weekblad* 17 (1897) no. 21, 153–5; H. P. Berlage 1897b and Victor de Stuers 1897.
24. The honours and honorary memberships: *De Opmerker* 32 (1897) no. 21, 165–6. The socialist magazine: *De Kroniek* 3 (1897), 162–3; medieval forms: B. 1897a; the collective debt: André Jolles 1897.
25. C. T. J. Louis Rieber 1892a.
26. 'Schrikbewind' ('Reign of Terror'): *De Opmerker* 31 (1896) no. 51, 407–8. Sympathetic or not: 'Critiek over bouwkunst' ('Criticism on art'), *De Opmerker* 31 (1896) no. 35, 275–8. Nijhoff against Lauweriks: letter to the editor in *Architectura* 2 (1894) no. 44, 187.
27. Kromhout in *De Kunstwereld* 1 (1894) no. 7, 5; no. 16, 5 and no. 18, 3–4; J. E. van der Pek 1896 and H. P. Berlage 1896; 'admiration mutuelle': *De Opmerker* 29 (1894) no. 9, 66–7.
28. For example *De Opmerker* 28 (1893) no. 3, 18–19; no. 7, 55–6; no. 38, 306 and no. 42, 337.
29. Lauweriks and Walenkamp in 1893: Frans van Burkom, Marty Bax 1989, 9; De Bazel: A. W. Reinink 1965, 9–12; Kromhout: Ida Jager 1992, 137; Bauer: Manfred Bock 1975, 9–11.
30. Gosschalk cited by *De Opmerker* 35 (1900) no. 27, 212.
31. A. N. Godefroy 1893; W. C. Bauer 1893.
32. 'Degelijk onderwijs' ('proper education'): *De Opmerker* 26 (1891) no. 47, 377; 'doornige pad' ('thorny path'): *Architectura* 1 (1893) no. 2, 6.
33. W. Kromhout 1894a; Jeroen Schilt, Jouke van der Werf 1992, 70.
34. *De Bouwwereld* 9 (1910) no. 50, 402.
35. Cuypers' view of the Stock Exchange: *Architectura* 9 (1901), 234. Bauer and the design competition: Manfred Bock 1975, 11. Kromhout on the De Haar Castle reconstruction: W. Kromhout 1894b. Anticlerical behaviour of Lauweriks and De Bazel: A. W. Reinink 1965, 23–4, and p. 20 on their anarchistic and theosophical views (in 1895 they both left their employment with Cuypers to set up in business on their own). The relationship

1896; J. 1896.

between Cuyper and Lauweriks: Frans van Burkom, Marty Bax 1989, in which also 'godless and insane' (p. 14). Cuypers' thankyou speech in May 1895: P. J. H. Cuypers 1895. The interpretation of this as a reprimand: Alphons Diepenbrock 1895, 169; see also Frans van Burkom, Marty Bax 1989, 15.

36. The spiritual base of Berlage and Cuypers: J. L. M. Lauweriks 1896, 300. Christian architecture: J. E. van der Pek 1894, 225. Conservatism in art: W. Kromhout 1894b. Main Post Office: B. [H. P. Berlage] 1895, 251. The young architects and their 'idol': *De Opmerker* 31 (1896) no. 12, 91. Taking a different course: W. Kromhout 1894c no. 16, 5. 'Dead copyists': J. L. M. Lauweriks 1898b; H. W. M. [H. W. Mol] 1900, 356.

37. 'Architectura et Amicitia', *De Opmerker* 31 (1896) no. 3, 21 and no. 5, 36, with a contemptuous reply from *Architectura* 4 (1896) no. 4, 18 and no. 6, 36. Kromhout's observation: W. Kromhout 1891, 371.

38. Cuypers as an anti-conventionalist: *Architectura* 3 (1895) no. 28, 84; 'an era completely devoid of a sense of architecture': H. W. M. [H. W. Mol] 1900, 355; passion and love: H. P. Berlage 1895–6, 217.

39. O. Praamstra 1991, 340–8.

40. H. W. M. [H. W. Mol] 1900, 356.

41. In *De Amsterdammer* and Jan Veth 1894. J. Boomgaard 1984 describes the endless problems of the interior, in particular for the presentation of Rembrandt's *Night Watch*.

42. W. Kromhout 1895, 167.

43. H. P. Berlage 1895–6, 218–19; J. E. van der Pek 1896, 224.

44. The perception in 1898: put forward, for example, by the art historian A. Pit, cited by Daniel (pseud.) 1898, 93. Further: 'Ter overweging' ('To consider'), *De Opmerker* 33 (1898) no. 17, 130–1. Some examples of Berlage's repetition of his ideas on Cuypers: H. P. Berlage 1905, 18, again published in H. P. Berlage 1910a; H. P. Berlage 1935 (cited in Sergio Polano et al. 1988, 93; see also Berlage's last publication of 1934, cited by Manfred Bock 1975, 35). An outline of Berlage's position in the twentieth-century historiography of architecture: Manfred Bock 1983, 24–52. A comparison with John the Baptist made by Cuypers' pupil and Berlage's friend, the director of the furniture shop *'t Binnenhuis*, Jacob van den Bosch in a speech on the occasion of Berlage's death, cited by C. Schoemaker 1987, 44. 'Messiah' in 1898: 'Ter overweging' ('To consider'), *De Opmerker* 33 (1898) no. 17, 130.

45. Henry-Russell Hitchcock 1929; Nicholaus Pevsner 1936, 1st edn; Sigfried Giedion 1941, 1st edn; Henry-Russell Hitchcock 1958, 1st edn; including many reprints and new editions of the last three.

46. K. P. C. de Bazel et al. 1916; see also *Bouwkundig Weekblad* 34 (1916) nos 43–6, which contains many statements on Berlage's crucial importance for Dutch architecture.

47. Insiders: 'Nieuwe kunst' ('New Art'), *De Opmerker* 30 (1895) no. 40, 313. 'Most modern art style': *De Opmerker* 30 (1895) no. 29, 229–30.

48. J. E. van der Pek 1896, 224.

49. W. Kromhout 1894a.

50. Shop premises, Kalverstraat 28, Amsterdam: Carol Schade 1993.

51. He had honoured Semper: H. P. Berlage 1884, 142; splendid residence: H. P. Berlage 1891b, 830; Springer's design: H. P. Berlage 1892b; age of the 'schools' was over: H. P. Berlage 1894, 106.

52. Renaissance not a period of art: Ernst Branding 1895, in particular 40. The Stedelijk Museum a total failure: J. E. van der Pek 1895 and H. P. Berlage 1895a, 362. See also H. P. Berlage 1894, 95: 'het vonnis is geveld over alle moderne renaissance' ('the verdict on all modern Renaissance architecture has been pronounced') etc.

53. H. P. Berlage 1895–6, 425–6 and 202–22, in which all of his positive marks on the neo-Renaissance at home and abroad are immediately followed by criticism that sweeps it all away.

54. Berlage's Semper-like furniture has been the subject of many studies, e.g. Pieter Singelenberg 1972, 19–20 (for example, Berlage's furniture for Carel Henny, 1898), and Lieske Tibbe et al.

1987, 51–2. Sergio Polano et al. 1988, 253 mentions that Berlage wrote the text for *On Style in Architecture and Furniture* in 1902; the book was published in 1904.

55. *De Opmerker* 31 (1896) no. 5, 33–5. Berlage's design: S. Polano et al. 1988, 136.

56. W. K. Cz. [W. Kromhout] 1894 no. 14, 6.

57. *De Opmerker* 31 (1896) no. 49, 391.

58. Bauer's design: Manfred Bock 1975, 8; the Dam-side façade of the Stock Exchange: *De Opmerker* 33 (1898) no. 18, 139.

59. C. H. Peters on rational building: J. Tideman 1894, 3. Criticism: J. L. M. Lauweriks 1898b and B. [H. P. Berlage] 1895.

60. H. P. Berlage 1894, 95.

10

Concepts for a New Age: Sublime Beauty, Personal Taste, and the Importance of Quite Ordinary Things

A new movement, a new beauty

The new movement in Dutch architecture could not define itself by what it did *not* want; it had to have an idea of what it did want. The young set's growing desire for the new and their realization that the days of conventional architecture were over were shared by the older architects who were setting out afresh, such as Ed Cuypers, Jan de Kruyff, Frederik van Gendt of *De Opmerker*, Jacob Klinkhamer, G. van Arkel (1858–1918), J. Verheul and Bram Salm. All were aided by a tremendous creative energy that was generated both at home and abroad as hitherto unknown architectural realities were discovered, such as the vernacular in England, *le réalisme* in France and *die Sachlichkeit* in Germany and Vienna.

Was the new movement regarded by its creators and supporters as a new style, or as no style at all? In other words, was a new style being sought anyway? As will become apparent, there are indicators for both of these ideas. Much depends on what is understood by a 'style'. As mentioned earlier, there were three current definitions: two of them quite old – style as the expression of the nature of the people and the times, and style as an objective, universal artistic system; the third, art-historical definition became popular in the 80s. It is clear that aversion to building 'in style' relates in particular to this last. The other two definitions continued in use, as they had done for more than a hundred years, alongside or (sometimes) in opposition to one another.

The most important question remains. What was the new movement's deepest desire, deeper, possibly, than the desire to create a contemporary style? The answer is: a new kind of beauty. This answer may seem trivial, but creating a totally new kind of beauty is a most drastic affair, because its birth destroys the old kind of beauty. The birth of a new aesthetic can be painful, repellent and absurd – characteristics that, in the end, strengthen it. In such an event emerges a new, unsuspected aspect – 'the sublime', the category of beauty that by definition falls outside of conventional beauty and is therefore initially incomprehensible and absurd. These phenomena can be examined in the two age-old basic characteristics of

architecture, *truth* and *character*, as conceived and made concrete by the young generation of the 90s. Together these two made up the content, but we need now to obtain a clearer picture of the form. And the form that was sought after by the new movement was the materialization of an ideal – the ideal of *simplicity* and *independence of history*.

Noble simplicity and primitivism: a new vision

Although there are exceptions, such as Willem C. Bauer's designs, the new movement developed mainly by focusing on the absolute opposite of picturesque and neo-Renaissance design, and by experimenting with the greatest possible reduction in decorative elements and with façades that were 'profoundly flat'. This experiment could only succeed because there was sufficient economic and commercial support for it. That this 'profound flatness' became the latest architectural trend after the decorative abundance of the 80s was as much to do with businessmen wanting the latest shop-front design as architects embracing new artistic ideas. 'From the excessive, architects have now suddenly switched to an intentional austerity. One can already see white-stuccoed façades arising in several places in the capital,' observed *De Opmerker* in 1896.[1] It was around this time that De Bazel created his first, very original work of architecture with 'profoundly flat' façades.

The turn-around from decorative abundance to simplicity – sometimes even a decorative dearth – implied, though, far more than a new fashion or new tactics in the architect's daily struggle. In essence it concerned a new vision of architecture itself – a vision that was not, however, explained in terms of architectural theory. Kromhout's article '*Tout à l'égout*' (1891) and Berlage's 'Architecture and impressionism' (1894) each expressed this new vision in their own different ways, and both contained many polemical points that had much to say on contemporary building practice. Kromhout wanted the architects' minds to become *tabula rasa*, as a necessary step for making a new start. Berlage argued that social and economic reasons were forcing architects to become 'impressionists', by which he meant that they should give

Fig.99
Gerlof B. Salm's
Ceres bread and flour
factory (1891),
Amsterdam, its façade
clad with reinforced
concrete according to
the Monier system.
An early experiment
with the new
'realistic' beauty of
an ornamentless,
ahistorical
architecture, used for
an industrial building.

up their desire to make 'rich' designs – these days architecture needed simple forms and ornaments. Neither, however, can be regarded as a useful analysis or as a definition of aesthetic concepts. So the rise of a new vision has mainly to be inferred from the design aspect. Until the 90s ornament had been an inextricable component of architecture, the essential means whereby the bare, structural, functional elements of a building could become art and the source of artistic enjoyment. They were the means through which a building's 'character' could be established, through which the eternal laws of nature (for example, statics) could be represented, and the building made to suit its surroundings. These characteristics, laid down in theories, traditions and conventions, in principle made it possible to distinguish between art and non-art; the way in which the designer treated ornament showed whether or not he had understood the rules of truth and character. This would imply that the absence of ornament was tantamount to the absence of the art of building.

Although the 90s generation considered historical styles and the related decorative conventions as things of the past, they did not opt for an architecture totally devoid of ornament (this was to become the ideal of a later generation). Instead they sought an ornamentation of the greatest simplicity, that had nothing to do with any historical style. By rejecting tradition in this way, they also rejected the more or less objective criterion that the older generation had used to establish whether ornamentation had been properly 'understood' and thus to what extent a building was good art. The young generation went for an ornamentation without any doctrine, without rules requiring a rational approach; theirs was an ornamentation without any objective, 'correct' applications or criteria. Their concept or architecture was therefore, as has been observed earlier, essentially *subjective*; the distinction between art and non-art was made on the basis of 'feelings'. Everyone entertaining traditional views on style was despatched to the wasteland: 'I want to make them return to a primitive state,' said Kromhout in '*Tout à l'égout*', 'without their trousers, coat or waistcoats, so they will be no different from Malays, and with nothing with which to express themselves but their natural aesthetic sense, plus materials.'[2]

This metaphor introduces a new element that further specifies the new 'simplicity'. The sophisticated architecture of the 80s, brought to a standstill *because* of its sophistication, had to return to a primitive state in order to continue to grow. Compare the situation of a hundred years earlier, when the Romantic desire for a noble simplicity ended the rococo. In 1892 Kromhout had observed that the

beginning of the new art was discernible, because there was already a general tendency 'toward a simpler and more primitive conception of art'. Now, four years later, the first results of this could be seen. 'One of the peculiar aspects of our times is the sympathy for antique periods of art. The Golden Ages are becoming discredited; Greek, Gothic and Renaissance creations no longer appeal to us. We seek the primitive, the awkward – indeed, if possible, we will follow in its path.'[3]

In 1897 Bauer wrote that the 'beauty of simplicity' had degenerated into a superficial 'service to form'. Lauweriks supported this view: under the pretence of economic stringency, he said, buildings everywhere were being built accordingly to severe, stark designs, and decoration was being excluded as if it was 'harmful vermin'; and the background to all this was not so much artistic intention as a general spiritual poverty.[4] Thus the trend towards the primitive was rapidly winning ground and becoming fashionable; the new movement was a general one, it would seem, and its aesthetics was the expression of a more or less collective desire.

The search for new concepts of form: Art Nouveau and the Arts and Crafts Movement

Simplicity and primitivism were stimulating ideas, but in order to turn them into architecture *concepts of form* were required. Kromhout's parable ended with a *deus ex machina*: after all the architects had disappeared into the sewers, a mill builder emerged like a Noah after the Flood, an honest artisan completely oblivious to stylistic problems, and founded a new school of architecture. But such a noble savage did not in reality exist. The young generation could rebel against its training and environment, but it could not erase them. Besides, the young felt as great a need for illustrated books and periodicals and stimulating prototypes as previous generations had done – the only difference was that they did not choose the same ones. Nor was the young generation able to avoid making the choice that had had to be made in the 80s: namely, whether to design in a monumental or in a picturesque way. It is worth noting here that their aversion to piling one decorative form on top of another was closely related to the aesthetics of Vogel (De Bazel's teacher, incidentally) and of Vosmaer, who only a few years before had protested against the mania for gables and turrets, claiming it gave short shrift to architecture's noble simplicity. The prototypes with which De Bazel and Lauweriks set out on their quest for primitive simplicity (initially in typography and other applied arts) derived from the art of ancient Egypt, the Near and Far East. By 1895 their work had reached such a level of visual refinement that it was considered part of the international Art Nouveau movement.

Indeed, Belgian Art Nouveau buildings such as the Tassel House in Brussels (Victor Horta, 1893), of which an illustration was published in the Belgian journal *L'Émulation*, must have made a great impression because of their graceful simplicity and total independence of stylistic ornamentation. These buildings must also have focused attention in the Netherlands on the question of what form the new primitive simplicity would take in architecture. But any contribution that Art Nouveau may have made would seem to have been either invisible or negative; basing their criticism on a particular view of truth in architecture, Dutch critics often wrote very unfavourably about it. Perhaps their fierce criticism conceals the possibility that the visual innovations of the Belgian architects were more influential than the opinion leaders of the 1890s were willing to admit. In any event, the Belgian examples undoubtedly contributed to the increasing awareness that simplicity entailed a new kind of beauty.

A major element in the origin of Belgian Art Nouveau was the movement concerned with artistic reform that was going on in England at the time. Perhaps this also played a role in the feeling in the Netherlands towards Belgian Art Nouveau – the Dutch artists enjoyed the affinity they felt for their English colleagues, and liked to consider themselves unique in this respect.[5] Primarily to do with the applied and graphic arts, the reforms in England had been initiated by the work and the ideas of William Morris and Walter Crane (1845–1915) and their Arts and Crafts Movement, the design of whose products was oriented towards plant shapes and the 'nature' of the materials used. the effect that this new style had in Western and Central Europe, described by Herrmann Muthesius (1861–1927) – first between 1896 and 1903 when he was in London and later when he was the leader of the German applied-arts movement – was striking. England, wrote Muthesius, partly thanks to the success of journals such as *The Studio*, had become almost overnight an artistic authority – indeed, the leader who was determining the direction in which art was to go.

Within a few years and with surprising violence, the Arts and Crafts Movement had eliminated the influence of the historical styles.[6] Its own influence was strongly felt in both the fine-arts and the applied-arts institutions, and in the practice of the applied and graphic arts. Ahistorical, 'organic' ornaments were disseminated via pattern books and illustrated periodicals, as had been the case with the historical models. When, towards 1900, floral motifs seemed to have been exhausted, the amazing 'primitive'

beauty of micro-organism took their place.[7] It is in keeping with the hectic activity that characterized this decade that, only a few years after the English innovations, critics were already referring to the 'almost full-blown movement' that they had given rise to in the Netherlands. Then, in 1898, *De Opmerker* observed that the movement had lost its momentum. Until recently, the journal wrote, furniture designers from the Continent went to London every year, just as people from the fashion scene would go to Paris for the latest designs; but the developments in England had now come to a standstill.[8]

This was indeed the case as far as the applied arts were concerned, but Dutch architecture's connection with the new movement cannot have been entirely severed, even if writers on architecture hardly referred to the subject, let alone theorized on it. The fact that furniture designers went to England because that was where 'simplicity and construction held priority' points in that direction. Apart from the continued talk about Cuypers' value as trailblazer for the new movement, the Dutch architecture profession remained quiet, even about the English and Belgian innovations that had led to the liberation from the historical styles – something which several generations of Dutch architects had only been able to dream. The silence was broken now and then, but only by mention of matters that did not really touch on the core of the architectural issue – for example, it was noted that Berlage had recently been presenting his drawings according to 'the English style'.[9]

But scant attention was being devoted in the Netherlands to modern English house building, whereas the English journals showed a steady stream of illustrations that demonstrated a different concept of dwelling compared with the traditions connected with the traditional Dutch mansion. Architects such as Charles Francis Annesley Voysey (1857–1941) and M. H. Baillie Scott (1865–1945) introduced a new type of detached house, the proportions and composition of which, although based on considerations of function, were initially considered rather 'coarse' according to Dutch taste. The new aesthetics of the vernacular provided surprising materials and processing techniques: thatched roofs, white-stuccoed façades, 'natural', seemingly unprocessed materials for interiors – everything arranged from a perspective of functionality and pleasure in the beauty of simplicity. Art and extravagant decoration were often synonyms in the Netherlands, wrote *Architectura* in 1895 when discussing a design of Baille Scott's, and the most extravagantly splendoured house was considered the most artistic one: 'But we observe that the contrary is usually the case and that the artistic value of a house depends more on

188

Fig. 100
Henri J. Evers' and
J. P. Stok's Church of
the Remonstrance,
Rotterdam (1895–7),
one of the first
examples of the new
'noble simplicity'.
According to Evers
the design was
'inspired by the
church buldings in
the East of the first
centuries of
Christianity, simple
yet noble creations of
devout artistic
sensibility'.

OPPOSITE
Fig. 101
The Roman Catholic
Cathedral of St Bavo,
Haarlem (1895–8),
designed by Jos
Th. J. Cuypers. The
reproduced part of
the building dates
from 1895–8, the
transept, the central
tower and the nave
were built in 1902–30.
The lower course of
one of the two towers
on the west façade is
visible at the
building's right end.
Like Evers and Stok,
Jos Cuypers met the
new requirement of
simplicity by further
developing motifs
from Byzantine
church building.

carefully considered design than on the amount of ornamentation that has been added to it.'[10] It is remarkable that such views, which in fact mark a significant shift in traditional thinking, were not discussed more fully in the Dutch architectural world.

Romanesque, Byzantine, Early Christian, and the recurring question of imitation

There was another source from which the concept of simplicity drew its inspiration and which, similarly, was hardly ever discussed – though in this case silence was understandable since historical architecture was the issue. The architecture of the Romanesque, Early Christian and Byzantine periods had not been considered worthy of imitation since the *Rundbogenstil* of half a century earlier. Now, because of their 'archaic' character and ornamental simplicity, they became once more the object of much

international interest – though mainly in relation to church building, since these architectural periods offered mainly ecclesiastical models. That this old material still had the power to fascinate in the year 1891 is demonstrated by the reaction of the Dutch architect H. J. Jesse, devotee of the Renaissance, to the Sacré-Cœur in Paris (1876–1919, architect Paul Abadie). He may have reported that the building was too massive, too 'plain', without a single beautiful detail – it had more the look of a prison than of a church – but all the same he took the trouble to draw the Roman-Byzantine design in great detail, and publish it. Shortly afterwards, the first examples of the Romanesque in Dutch church building emerged, stimulated too by German examples such as the Catholic Church of the Sacred Heart in The Hague (architect Wilhelm Bernard van Liefland), built in the crucial years 1893–4 when the ideal of simplicity began to materialize. After 1895

Fig.102
Adriaan
W. Weissman's
'American-
Romanesque' design
for a cemetery
building near
Amsterdam (1892),
which was never
realized. Weissman
was one of the very
few who openly
admitted that he used
the world-famous
work of the American
architect Henry
Hobson Richardson
(as in this case) in
order to find a form
for this as yet
unknown new
architecture of
simple, 'primitive'
origin.

Lauweriks felt increasingly drawn to 'good Romanesque architecture' and less and less towards 'its bad twin sister, Gothic architecture'. In a text of 1897 he ranked Romanesque and Byzantine art with ancient Greek and Egyptian art – four 'primitive' art forms that stood close to the fountainhead of art and were therefore superior to Gothic.[11]

The fountainhead of art – despite the prevalent disdain for classicism, which was still seen as the epitome of base imitation and arid talent, the Greek and Roman classics were not yet forgotten by the young architects. The tradition of propagating the eminence of classical architecture by means of lectures and courses had not come to an end. In 1901 Lauweriks and De Groot published their proposal for a course at the National Academy of the Visual Arts, based partly on Vitruvius, that was later to be adopted by Kromhout.[12] At issue was not only theory, but also concepts of form. The aversion to the picturesque and a renewed interest in monumentality occasionally resulted in buildings displaying classical composition and ornament. And the current appreciation of a noble simplicity permitted a tentative reassessment of neoclassicism – tentative, because there had been nothing in the last decade that had been such a potent symbol of aridity and decline as neoclassicism.[13]

As already demonstrated, it took Berlage somewhat longer than the young generation to appreciate the new beauty. As late as 1895 he began a detailed analysis of Gothic architecture with some very conventional comments on the Romanesque, which, according to him, was bleak, severe and uncomfortable. It was only with the advent of the Gothic style that architecture 'soared', he said.[14] The praise he lavished on Cuypers after 1895 also leads one to suspect that he was interested in medieval architecture mainly on account of its use of the Gothic style. The curious thing, though, is that his design focused increasingly on the imitation of Romanesque simplicity – in particular, the Stock Exchange and the ANDB Building (the Dutch diamond-cutters union) in Amsterdam (1898–1900).[15] However, his imitation of the Romanesque was hardly ever, if at all, discussed in public. Only the occasional remark was made on the subject even by those architects who were familiar with the history of architecture – and this still applied to nearly all of them.

The explanation for this remarkable conspiracy of silence on the characteristics of a few buildings with a high public profile may lie in the fact that in this decade, unlike the previous one, it was considered inappropriate – taboo, even – to refer to 'imitation'. Seen in this light, it is not so strange that Berlage was always going on about 'sound principles', implying that architectural form was something that came about by itself. When the Catholic Cathedral of St Bavo in Haarlem (1895–1930), designed by Jos Cuypers, one of the leaders of A et A, turned out to contain many Romanesque-Byzantine and other stylistic components, the reviewer wrote that the building was 'thoroughly Dutch' and could definitely not be considered an example of building 'in style': 'it cannot be denied that this is clearly a case of carrying forward old principles in an original way'.[16]

The taboo surrounding imitation became quite apparent when Berlage completed his first experiments with the new movement. De Opmerker regularly commented that he had borrowed his new forms from recent American architecture, which itself was a startling adaptation of the Romanesque. Weissman, who had already discovered the expressive simplicity of 'American-Romanesque' architecture in 1891, was to badger Berlage for years with his refrain that the cradle of the new movement was to be found in the United States. Art-historical research of almost a century later has indeed confirmed that Berlage used recent American examples.[17] But he never responded to Weissman's or De Opmerker's comments on this score. Perhaps his friend Van der Pek was speaking for him when he rather testily wrote in 1895 that anybody claiming that Berlage was copying 'archaic-Romanesque' forms from America must be one of the old guard, who knew all about imitation. 'About finding one's own way and drawing on one's own resources as characteristics of Berlage's working method we read nothing,' he wrote.[18] Drawing on one's own resources was indeed the ideal of the new movement, ever since in 1891 Kromhout had declared that the architect, culturally naked as a primitive 'Malay', was to act on his own natural, aesthetic feelings. But, willingly or unwillingly, the new movement was part of a development that was taking place both nationally and internationally, and that development included a susceptibility to concepts of form from the New World.

Berlage, and the image of Germany on the Dutch architectural scene

The question of Germany, that powerful nation with a highly developed architectural culture that had served both as guide and as fount of knowledge and inspiration to the Netherlands for some sixty years, is an interesting one. From the beginning of the century Germany had been familiar with the same problems concerning the assimilation of the available historical examples and had looked for solutions in the same direction, but each time slightly earlier than the Netherlands – and had exerted more intellectual and artistic effort in the process and produced more results. It was to be expected that during this decade, which put such a high premium on drawing on one's own resources while turning a blind eye to the practice of imitation going on all around, relations with Germany started to show signs of stress. Little of this could have been detected in the Bouwkundig Weekblad, for instance, which paid considerable, but selective, attention to recent German architecture, creating the impression that Germany was still very much rooted in the Renaissance and other historical modes. The young architects and their journal Architectura ignored Germany altogether. Similarly, De Opmerker's coverage was insufficient to keep Dutch architects informed of the fundamental ideas being developed in Germany, such as Einfühlung (empathy), Raum (space), Raumgefühl (the perception of architectural space) and Sachlichkeit (realism).

In the creation of an image of Germany Berlage played a curious role. In his many publications, he delighted in denigrating German architecture. The Germans had no taste, he wrote; their buildings were coarse and ponderous. They were still obsessed with stuccoed façades and pseudo-architecture, and wine and beer taverns were the star turns in other repertoire. Only in 1910 did he venture that a certain sense of beauty was emerging in Germany – but with the warning that there was still much that was impure, coarse and repulsive about the present German contribution to European architecture.[19] Was he playing on supposed anti-German sentiments on the part of his readers? Or did he genuinely believe – a blinkered view indeed – that a century of German and Dutch architectural ingenuity, except for the work of two or three faithful followers who together with Cuypers had kept watch over the Grail, had been nothing but a misunderstanding? Or was it his habit to work his own way up by belittling the reputations of others?

There seems no doubt that Berlage was well informed on the developments taking place in Germany within the new movement and that he turned this to his advantage. Perhaps the negative picture he painted of Germany was only a smokescreen. It was recently discovered, for example, that the entirely new treatment that he came up with for the façade of his office building on the Muntplein

(1894–5) bore a strong affinity with the façade of a Berlin building of 1890 that appeared the next year in the *Deutsche Bauzeitung*. The simple brick façade of the German building, almost without ornament, displayed an aesthetic that was far removed from the academic convention of building 'in style'. The *Bauzeitung* connected this aesthetic, which it referred to as 'naturalism' (a term borrowed from painting), with the new American architecture.[20] 'Everything can be tolerated in the *fin-de-siècle* artist, except base imitation,' wrote Berlage in the year in which he designed the Muntplein building. Oddly enough, the article from which this is taken, the much quoted 'Architecture and impressionism', shows striking similarities with a German article describing the Berlin building. Berlage had replaced 'naturalism' with 'impressionism', but the meaning was the same: the modern building, he believed, should have an austere ornamentation and a simply constructed main form with a 'characteristic outline'. He used purely practical arguments to explain the necessity of working 'impressionistically': namely, that the lack of time and money in the building industry forced simplicity on the architect. Without putting forward any argument – only a passing reference to the beauty inherent in good construction – he made a virtue of necessity, stating that this lack of time and money in fact liberated the architect from his dependence on 'expensive' materials, forms and ornamentation. Beauty was independent of money, he claimed: 'this is definitely not a paradox, but a truth that should be loudly proclaimed, to which I should like to add: the less money available for luxury, the better the chance of achieving character'.[21]

In the late twentieth century art historians hailed this article as an important theoretical statement, even the first theory of modern Dutch architecture.[22] In the personality-centred account in which Berlage is seen as the key figure of the modern movement, this is both logical and understandable. In his personal development 'Architecture and impressionism' was indeed a milestone, a verbal farewell to his Renaissance past. However, in the broader context of the new movement it was, to use a twentieth-century analogy, the manoeuvre of the no longer young virtuoso who had changed lanes and been forced to overtake in order to do so. Kromhout considered the article interesting enough to the readers of *De Kunstwereld* to summarize it, though he warned that 'many of the ideas expressed have been ventilated on earlier occasions' – here he was probably thinking of his own publications.[23] At issue, after all, was not only the *Deutsche Bauzeitung* article's reference to 'naturalism', but also the entire composite of ideas and designs concerning both the fine and the applied arts, from England, the United States, Germany, Belgium and the Netherlands, and had for some years been incorporated into the new movement, in the Netherlands as elsewhere. It seems as if Berlage was trying to defend himself in advance against the allegation that he had been slow in seeing what was happening: 'It is truly not from a desire to imitate, or to parade the new movement, that I express my conviction that this is the path architecture should follow. Architecture should become impressionistic' because that was what the present era called for.[24]

In this way Berlage presented his 'discovery' as an original and objective diagnosis of the spirit of the times. He made no mention of any sources or examples, or of any names that had inspired his new ideas. 'Everything can be tolerated from the *fin-de-siècle* artist, except base imitation.'

'The style of upholsterers and furniture manufacturers': Art Nouveau

In the eyes of the many writers airing their dissatisfactions in *Architectura*, *De Opmerker* and *Bouwkundig Weekblad*, one of the expressions of 'unsightliness and falsehood' referred to on p. 182 was Art Nouveau. The resistance to Art Nouveau in the Netherlands was much fiercer than the resistance to building 'in style', and was much more widespread in the architectural community, crossing the borders of generations, of coteries and of movements. This is a curious phenomenon. The earliest examples of Art Nouveau architecture, the buildings in Brussels by Paul Hankar (1859–1901) and Victor Horta (1861–1947) referred to earlier in this chapter, showed an ahistorical simplicity which in 1895 was still inconceivable in the Netherlands. But why did this architecture, seemingly an answer to the problem of the century, stir up such a deep aversion? Undoubtedly lurking somewhere here was a feeling of national identity that for decades had been reinforced by the habit of scoffing at the 'coarseness' of Germany and the frivolity and fickleness of the French and the Belgians – in other words, what was at issue here was 'our serious national character'.

An opposition between superficiality and seriousness also existed, as we have noted, between the new movement and the upholders of traditional values. It was as if the tension was released in a shared burning indignation at an outsider, Art Nouveau. That the traditionalists were up in arms may hardly come as a surprise, but that the young with their subjective aesthetics were perhaps even more critical is remarkable. Were they shocked by what they saw in Art Nouveau? Was this how their urge for freedom had manifested itself, was this the reality of a subjective

Fig.103
Lambert van Meerten
House, Delft (1893),
designed by Adolf le
Comte and
J. L. Schouten. Le
Comte taught
ornament drawing at
the Polytechnic
School at Delft. This
experiment with the
new simplicity, in
collaboration with the
engineer Schouten,
preceded Berlage's De
Algemeene office
building, but was
taken seriously
neither by
Amsterdam's 'new
movement' nor, later,
by architectural
historians: it simply
did not fit into the
evolution theory of
modern Dutch
architecture.

aesthetic, of the architecture of feeling that delighted the eye – and did they now shrink from it? Kromhout, the champion of artistic freedom, wrote in 1900: 'Art Nouveau is the style of upholsterers and furniture manufacturers, the style of twists of seaweed, a farce, an aesthetic without a backbone, the product of a morbid fantasy, an imported article attracting everyone who wants to be at the forefront of modernism.'[25] Formulated in architectural terms, Kromhout argued, 'foolish acts' had been committed with the 'honourable' building materials bluestone, iron and wood, due to a lack of a 'serious principle' – here he can only have been referring to the principle of truth. In *De*

Kroniek the young H. W. Mol gave the Belgian painter and architect Henry van de Velde (1863–1957) something to think about when he characterized his work as 'conspicuous manifestations of the new … restricted to purely superficial matters'; the furniture of Van de Velde, he continued, demonstrated a 'voluptuousness' and a 'violation of wood so deeply insulting to pure feelings; in every respect one feels a morbid hunger for new forms at all costs'. *De Opmerker* in 1899 typified his work as 'lethal poison'; 'the Belgian style' had caused 'real havoc' inside and outside Belgium. Richard N. Roland Holst (1868–1938) and other members of the Dutch applied-arts movement fought against the Belgian 'style of twists and twirls', not least because it did not respect the 'laws of logic'.[26]

In 1898 a furniture business called Arts and Crafts opened in The Hague, offering furniture and decorative art made by Art Nouveau designers. Two years later, with a few others, Berlage established in Amsterdam the firm 't Binnenhuis (Domestic Interior). On offer were 'sound' products intended to counterbalance the 'dubious non-

Fig. 104
Karel P. C. de Bazel's design (1895) for a front and back cover of *De Architect*, the journal published by Architectura et Amicitia, issues 3–4, 1896. The gifted artist was experimenting – on paper – with the new ahistorical beauty developed by the Art Nouveau movement. He went no further with this when, a short time later, Berlage and his followers started a campaign against 'morbid' Art Nouveau.

Dutch movement'. For was not the 'so-called' Art Nouveau of Van de Velde the opposite of the 'sound principle', Berlage asked. 'Has this style not failed totally precisely because he applies this principle most inappropriately or not at all?' Jacob van den Bosch (1868–1948), Berlage's kindred spirit and manager of 't Binnenhuis, two years later wrote: 'Obvious as it may seem to say this about our own circle of designers, so far the best things have been made in Holland.'[27]

This barrage of invective against Art Nouveau demonstrates above all that it was regarded as an insult to truth. Only in The Hague did the Dutch flirt with this 'morbid art'; the end-of-the-century artistic climate of The Hague was not insensitive to 'decadence'. However, the new movement in Dutch architecture was mostly an Amsterdam affair, and, as we have seen, the Amsterdam cultural circles liked to see themselves as logical, serious and sound. But while Berlage was still struggling with his brick vaults, Horta designed and built his Maison du Peuple in Brussels (1895–9), in its space and in its construction, and with its glass and iron façade, a remarkable and very original building. To a highly idiosyncratic creative talent Horta and Hankar added a profound knowledge and control of their building materials, the result not only of their talent but also of the training they had received from the great masters of Flemish Renaissance, the Belgian architects Hendrik Beyaert and Jean Baes.[28] Van de Velde, trained as a painter but self-taught as a furniture designer and architect, acquired an international reputation with his innovative creations. But the talents of the Belgian architects were disparaged and ridiculed in Amsterdam, while suggestions were made that they were mere incompetents. Of Van de Velde Berlage sneered in 1898: 'No, truly, architecture is not an art that can be practised as a side-line.'[29]

The aversion to Art Nouveau intensified during 1898–9. Was it that it had become too successful? Perhaps there was a deeper cause. As we have seen, the tendency towards individual artistic subjectivity and freedom was followed by a reaction, led by Berlage, promoting the re-establishment of an objective universal aesthetic – but this time as an ideology, as the dogma inherent in that one sound principle: the simple, straightforward construction. It cannot but be that the mud-slinging aimed at Art Nouveau had been instrumental in this transformation, this maturing of spirits. Berlage and his followers, required a repellent image of 'morbidity' to lend weight to their 'sound' principles. Others, even Kromhout, may have wanted to demonstrate their belief that artistic freedom had its limits and that architecture could not exist without some kind of discipline.

OPPOSITE, BOTTOM
Fig.105
Carel Henny House, The Hague (1898), dining room and furniture, designed by H. P. Berlage. 'Sound principles' and the 'laws of logic' were intended to counterbalance the 'dubious non-Dutch movement of so-called Art Nouveau'.

Fig.106
Johan Mutters' Lensvelt Nicola Bakery and Tea Room, The Hague (1895): the first example of Art Nouveau architecture and interior design in The Hague, the only city in the Netherlands with a cultural climate in which Art Nouveau could thrive.

Now that everybody agreed, for whatever reasons, that an 'idiotic' style like Art Nouveau – the words of H. W. Mol – could not show the way forward, it was time to put into practice the long-held conviction that the Netherlands must pursue an architectural concept that suited its serious national character, headed by the architect who best exemplified it.

Fig.107
The showroom of Jan Willem Bosboom's, E. Beekman Iron Foundry, The Hague (1898). This shop in the centre of the city illustrates the radical breakthrough that took place in these years: here was an experimental 'immaterialization' of architecture demonstrated not only in the façade but also in the interior – its floors had undivided open spaces vertically connected in the middle of the building.

OPPOSITE
Fig.108
H. P. Berlage's Royal Lunch Room in his Stock Exchange. A few frequently repeated images of the Exchange (two façades and the produce exchange hall) reinforced Berlage's reputation as an innovator. But rarely published pictures of parts of the Exchange such as this one show him as a designer who, artistically speaking, still had a strong relation with the past.

Character and ornament

In the 8os, the debates on truth in architecture were in a way pseudo-debates. The real differences of opinion related to the character, the 'message' of architecture. In

the 90s, rampaging individualism and diminishing theoretical interest made the concept of character even more diffuse and subjective. Whereas according to the old tradition ornament had been seen as the perfect means of manifesting a building's character because of its 'adaptability', by the end of the 80s ornament was becoming very much its own thing, judged more on its own visual merits than as a means of expressing character. And the new art education, in which traditional ornamentation was replaced by floral motifs, was part of an international development. The new approach aimed to develop individual talents rather than collectivizing taste within the context of a 'style'. The much used work by Th. M. M. van Grieken, *The Plant as Ornament* (1888), articulated this new awareness.

We do not contend that students must copy ornaments in all their variation or be taught what the precise difference is between this style and that style. On the contrary, that would only lead to servile imitation, to resuscitating forms and methods of ornamentation inappropriate for this era, while the main objective of art education – learning to see forms and colours, sharpening creativity, learning to create new forms – would be ignored.[30]

This was in fact the formulation of a fundamental change. The point of copying and making minute distinctions between historical style details used to be to *understand* the ornament and the style. But Van Grieken had something totally different in mind. What he was concerned with was individual originality, new design and learning to *see*. His method illustrated the process that was already happening, irreversibly and all over: the change from a theoretically based, objectively reasoned concept of architecture to one in which architecture was conceived as a visual image to be experienced at a more subjective level – like a beautiful object that has no need of an all-embracing theory to explain it. The disappearance of the theoretical basis and the focus on a more personal, original ornamentation also implied that ornament was released from its causal relationship with the construction. How *could* the new floral motifs explain the 'idea' of a single architectural element, let alone the idea of a building as a whole? To go one step further – if an ornament was no longer the expression of an idea and became a beautiful yet 'empty' image, there was no longer any need for a relationship between architecture and ornament. And the paradox was that the emancipation of decorative art resulting from the new study of ornament implied a twentieth-century architecture *without* ornament.

When the old theory of ornament with its codified

meanings disappeared, the concept of character remained. Even the young generation, which had not taken the concept of truth very seriously, maintained the concept of character. When by the beginning of 1893 the conflict of the generations was in full swing, *De Opmerker* wrote that the design of a public building should speak an understandable language – 'only the decadent and their impressionist friends' would say otherwise.[31] The fact was that the new movement too wanted an understandable architecture – it was just that it was speaking a different language from the older generation – or, rather, different languages. It has to be said, though, that the disintegration of any consensus on character ended in unintelligibility. Depending on which critic happened to be speaking, Berlage's Stock Exchange had the character of a factory or of a North Italian palazzo, not by any estimation that of a modern financial centre or a contemporary Amsterdam building. For those trained according to convention, the designs entered for competitions by De Bazel, Walenkamp and Bauer were confusing because the function of the buildings could not be understood from the exterior. In 1898 De Bazel made it even clearer that he was not favourably disposed towards the traditional idea of character when he published a series of pictures of Cuypers' Central Station. Through these images, rather than with words, he expressed his great admiration for this work, and apparently had no objection whatsoever as regards the appropriateness, for the modern monarchy in the context of a station,[32] of a royal waiting room in the form of a medieval ciborium. As far as concerned competitions – and, for that matter, the designs for the Stock Exchange and the Central Station too – designers were allowed an exceptional artistic freedom. In everyday practice the client tended to be more demanding about the expression that his new building would assume, as a result of which character was treated more traditionally. Kromhout's American Hotel (1900–2) exemplifies this: rich ornaments and exuberant eclectic transformations of historical style elements form the generally understandable and therefore conventional vehicle through which the festive and luxurious character of the building is expressed.

A complicating factor for us is that the new movement rejected some of the conventions to do with character while retaining others. It dismissed, for example, the entire repertoire of the 'national' style but developed new normative metaphors. Most striking was the character of the 'profoundly flat'. Primitive simplicity, absence of ornament, became the character of contemporary architecture. The invention of the visual image of the modern was, as discussed before, part of a new

international visual culture. Notwithstanding the emphasis placed on 'honest construction', that the concept of character was better attuned to this than was the concept of truth is understandable. Since the eighteenth century, character had been a matter of *feeling*. Despite the lack of theoretical clarity, the importance of character was at least as great as it had been before, precisely because the visual culture had gained in importance over the verbal, theoretical culture. In the previous decades architects had applied the concept of truth to distinguish themselves from the 'unqualified'. In the visual culture of the 1890s something else was acquired to make this extra dimension

Fig.109
The American Hotel
with its Café-
restaurant Américain,
Amsterdam (1900–2),
by Willem Kromhout.
By 1900 Ed Cuypers'
American Hotel no
longer met modern
requirements, and it
was demolished
together with the
adjacent Police
Headquarters
(Fig.73). It was
replaced by this
building, the most
significant work of
the architect who,
with his 'Everything
into the sewer' (1891),
had marked the birth
of the 'new
movement' in Dutch
architecture.

to their work apparent: namely, architecture with a modern character, as an expression of modern times. It was not the first time that an old theory – the idea that character is closely related to style – proved topical. According to the definition given by Quatremère de Quincy around 1790, style was the representation of the character of a people, its morals and customs, and the geographical and climatological circumstances. In the 1880s this notion had yielded many of the features of a national architecture. After the early 90s' reaction against everything that could be called 'style', Berlage and his followers again saw to it that the situation was reversed and style was once more understood as an expression of the character of the people. This time, however, it centred not on a historical but on a not yet existing, future identity – that of modern society. This character, the *modern style*, became the new myth of architecture when the old metaphysics – the character of the past – was exhausted.

The 'modern style' and metaphysics
The word 'metaphysics' is not used haphazardly here.

Character *was* metaphysics. Lauweriks propagated the belief that architecture was in essence the representation of an 'ideal' – in his case, the idea of a transcendental mystical reality. He saw architecture, including the design and construction of a building, as the expression of a process in which matter expressed a spiritual truth and in which other ideas and higher thoughts manifested themselves in matter.[33] In 1898 De Bazel described the objective of architecture as 'the representation of the divine order, building a union of earth and heaven, of the material nature of man and his spiritual soul'; the architect was the intermediary making 'high order and sacred meaning' visible in matter. 'The building as a whole is then a symbol and the embodiment of perfect harmony,' De Bazel said, making a distinction between the construction ('the stone that builds') and the ornamentation. The essence of stone for building purposes was serenity and balance, with ornamentation serving as the 'language' of the work, to explain its 'idea or function'. It is not difficult to see that these views perfectly attuned with the traditional aesthetics as taught by Gugel and Vogel. Only this time, they were arrayed in theosophical garb: 'We may expect of a work of art that, just like man, it will act as a *link between heaven and earth*.'³⁴

In this conviction lay the principal difference between Lauweriks and De Bazel on the one hand, and Berlage on the other. In 1898 Lauweriks described an unnamed architect who, after applying ornamentation to his architecture for many years, suddenly 'starts building in a severe manner, excluding all ornament as if it were vermin'. Such a sudden change could only, according to Lauweriks, be interpreted as following a fashion, the 'fashion of austerity and wilful simplicity under a veneer of economic considerations'.³⁵ For Lauweriks simplicity was not a quality in itself but the result of an internal, spiritual process. Did he have Berlage in mind here? Lauweriks, too, remembered Berlage renovating the Arti Building in 1894 in the Renaissance style; and with his building on the Muntplein and his article 'Architecture and impressionism' arguing that the pursuit of simplicity was an economic necessity. Two years later Lauweriks openly criticized Berlage, as we saw earlier, for knowing 'nothing or next to nothing' of the 'inner soul' of the art of building.

Berlage and his friends had an answer to this. The way they dealt with Lauweriks' thinking corresponded with the way in which they dealt with neo-Renaissance architecture and Art Nouveau: by denigrating them in the media while adopting useful elements from them. The socialist poet Henriëtte Roland Holst considered the resorting to mysticism an expression of the crisis felt by a bourgeoisie witnessing the loss of its power; the workers, on the other hand, sought consolation not in transcendental matters, but 'in the world itself[;] our security is in our consciousness'. The critic Jan Veth warned against the 'present peddlers of symbols and neomysticism'; there were so many suspicious characters that one must beware of spiritless charlatans, including those who called themselves spiritualists.³⁶ Meanwhile Berlage made his public gesture towards the spiritual basis of architecture, whereby his idea of a collective art became the 'new world concept', the secularized heaven in which all people would unite. In 1907 Van der Pek would explain that beauty originated in the sensory observation of the universe – the feeling of being 'united with the universe in the same way as in religion'. 'Reflecting on the universe made one feel at one with it, just like those who really know, just like the wise.'³⁷ And so, in Berlage's circle too, architecture became an art with an inner soul, a link between heaven and earth, even if that heaven was an earth-based utopia. And thus to them as well the architect became a priest, an intermediary revealing to society a higher reality, far removed from materialism and spiritless poverty.

The new eclecticism: the 90s' breakthrough
The new movement acknowledged the primacy of 'feeling', resisted the authority of tradition and of the establishment, and considered individual artistic freedom as a given – characteristics, also, of the artists of the Romantic movement in the late eighteenth century. It was about 1830 that these same characteristics had been introduced into architecture by Labrouste and the other young architects who called themselves eclectics. On many occasions Kromhout, with great eloquence, expressed this renewed Romantic mood. The young architect-to-be, he wrote, in 1894, should not rush to associate himself with his prominent colleagues in the hope of soon becoming one of them; he must not hide behind the fashionable debates on style and -isms, but form his own opinion. He should be happy to go through his own *Sturm-und-Drang* phase, and dare to stray from the beaten track. 'It is often forgotten that mountains veiled in clouds are also architecture, that the sea, the coasts, the rocks, the endless moorlands and hills, the forests, are also all architecture – the architecture of the vast building that is the earth, awakening in the artist the hunger for creation.'³⁸

If there was a breakthrough at all in the 90s, it was that the end of building 'in style' signified the beginning of a new, strong eclecticism. The manifesto of the new movement, '*Tout à l'égout*' (1891), in many ways shows that the deconstruction of the concept of style and of related -isms was in fact a metaphor for eclecticism: 'we do not want to *create* a style'; 'style is nothing other than the harmonious way in which an individual expresses himself, so that what he creates, says and does is merely the reflection of his own self and the society in which he lives'.³⁹ A few years later Van der Pek and Berlage fulminated against building 'in style' in words that were quite similar not only to those of '*Tout à l'égout*', but also to statements that the eclectic Leliman had made twenty years earlier. In fact, during the brief moment when the widespread fascination with building 'in style' was disappearing eclecticism was the only artistic viewpoint. It was to remain so until, a few years later, the search for a 'style', for objective rules and universal principles, started all over again, and the witch-hunt against free, styleless architecture resumed.

Eclecticism, as we have noted, was primarily an attitude – as an artist, the architect was free to choose what he wanted; and secondly it was a design method – the architect concentrated first on the functional requirements of the commission. For the eclectic, the design of a façade was the last and possibly least urgent stage of the design process, whereas for the 'style' architect it was the priority, controlling all aspects from beginning to end. 'Style' architects always thought in terms of the form of façades, even when they were describing the works of eclectics. Witness Berlage dismissing in just a few words the works of Paul Sédille and Charles Garnier (1825–98): 'It is simply that the French feel most at home in the opulent, unserious, exuberant architecture of the *roi soleil*, and this hunger for lavishness still characterizes even their best works.'[40] Indeed, Berlage always remained a style architect through and through: his brief departure in 1894 from building 'in style' was a mainly verbal intermezzo. His old colleague Leliman, who had found Berlage's renovation of the Arti Building little better than an insult, was still in 1898 the free spirit that he had been back in 1850. Conceptually speaking, he was the type of artist that Kromhout and his following wished to be. Leliman was the man who in 1889, only a few years before the publication of '*Tout à l'egout*', said:

You must know, gentlemen, that I have great respect for architecture for the sole reason that it must be pure and simple in order to become, and remain, beautiful and effective. What is the most important thing in architecture, the most difficult? It is the floor plan, the interior layout, because it tells one about the structure *and* about the exterior appearance. If the floor plan is good, if it is efficient, if the functional parts have been excellently arranged, if attention has been paid to light, air, outline and decorative elements, the onlooker will be able to see from the outside the interior's various parts and functions. If the architect thinks through the structure, the function and the decoration of each part of the interior there will be no need for him to choose a *style* in advance, for he will see it come forth spontaneously![41]

This was precisely what eclecticism was about.

Eclecticism, and the problematic word 'realism'

In the conventional history of 90s architecture, the concept of rationalism occupies a major place, such that one suspects that historians unconsciously went along with Cuypers' and Berlage's propaganda. Propaganda aside, though, rationalism had no particular significance because, as Kromhout noted, it was part of the training of every architect. If only because of the words just quoted, one would expect Leliman to have a place in the conventional rationalist picture of history. But, being no friends of Berlage, Leliman and his kindred spirits are absent from the story of the origins of modern Dutch architecture. Eclecticism, which as an artistic attitude and as a design method was such a driving force in those years, thus ended up in the dark vaults of history.

One of the causes for this is the professional fascination of art historians with style, in particular with the 'quest' for

a style. In 1891 the eclectic Ed Cuypers received a commission for a large furniture shop on the Spui Square in Amsterdam. The building, completed in 1892, had two lifts; the actual shop interior was luxurious, and the layout of the office and service parts was sober and efficient. The composition of the exterior was relatively simple, as were the details, and there were no 'protrusions, extensions, turrets, or any of those other excesses that have become almost indispensible'. The two façades on the street had very large windows, 'demonstrating that the building has been laid out as a shop-warehouse from top to bottom'. The necessary modern supporting structure of iron beams was visible in the design of the exterior.[42] The building has never been given a place in the history of the period that preceded the twentieth century – although it possessed all the characteristics that historiography could require: functionality, comfort, simplicity of design, the aesthetic elements of modern building and installation techniques, air, light and space. Not without significance, perhaps, is the fact Ed Cuypers did not belong to the small coterie that presented itself powerfully via Architectura et Amicitia and the media, despite being one of the young 90s generation – when he built the furniture shop at the Spui he was slightly older than Kromhout and three years younger than Berlage.

In order to understand the architecture of Ed Cuypers, the full significance of Leliman's words and the meaning of the 90s for the period that was to follow, we need to draw on other concepts than rationalism – namely, *idealism* and *realism*. Although at the time these concepts were hardly used, they were part and parcel of the thinking, the writing and the discussions on architecture. These two fundamentally different views had each its own long history, and a future that would extend into the greater part of the twentieth century.

Leliman's words of 1889 represented a view that was very common in Paris, Vienna and Germany. It drew on texts by Semper; by Parisian eclectics, especially Paul Sédille; by Germany theorists such as Richard Streiter and K. E. O. Fritsch, the editor of the *Deutsche Bauzeitung*; and by the Viennese architect Otto Wagner. As noted earlier, Sédille had played a major part in bringing up to date the eclecticism of the 1850s, which from then on was referred to as *le réalisme*. For realism as for eclecticism, there was no such thing as a problem of a contemporary style. By analogy with realism in painting and belles-lettres, realism in architecture focused on 'ordinary' matters such as functionality, economics and modern building techniques. In Germany and Austria a synonym for *Realismus*, *Sachlichkeit*, would put its stamp on twentieth-century architecture, the Netherlands included; hence the Dutch

Fig.110
H. F. Jansen & Son, furniture shop, the Spui, Amsterdam (1891–2), designed by Ed Cuypers: an example of the 'realistic' aesthetics of the eclectics expressing architectural truth and character in a new way. Historical ornaments, still thought necessary, embellish an efficient glass and iron architecture, but do not conceal it.

zakelijkheid ('matter-of-factness', 'realism'). Realism, in architecture, was the most far-reaching way of respecting the actual issues that expressed the value of a building, Richard Streiter postulated in 1896; it was the optimal fulfilment of the requirements of functionality, comfort and health-promotion – in one word, it was *Sachlichkeit*.[43]

The situation in the Netherlands was slightly different in one, not unimportant respect. The extensive commercial building of the previous decades had led to the concept of eclecticism becoming in France and Germany – as in the Netherlands – a word of abuse. But in those other two countries the process of updating it, as well as providing it with a new name, had restored its vital position in architecture. In the Netherlands, however, all public debate on the issue had been avoided, although there can no doubt that the phenomenon had not gone unnoticed. In 1886 Gugel had defined 'realism' as the quest to provide a work of art with the pretence of reality, without the intervention of aesthetic considerations arising from a 'poetic view'; realism did not aim to express an 'idea', he said, it was not a creation of the mind, but the pure representation of the visible reality of a concrete event[44] – a definition that would appear to be consistent with the objectives of eclecticism.

The reason why eclecticism in the Netherlands was not given the new name 'realism' was probably that there remained a link in the Dutch perception between realism and its pejorative connotations; realism remained 'coarse', 'low', 'dirty'. In previous decades 'realistic' building had been practised in the Netherlands, as we have seen, but in large urban developments and commercial buildings in city centres, outside the circle of the 'real' architects. In keeping with the cultural climate, the first experiments in 'unsightly' beauty were now witnessed in architectural circles – one account told of the pine interior of a house, in complete contradiction to tradition, being left unpainted.

Allard Pierson, a professor of art history and aesthetics in Amsterdam, attempted to breach the cultural blockade against realism in 1891 by explaining that art and beauty were not necessarily synonyms.[45] There were more aestheticians trying to convince the Dutch cultural elite to accept realism as a positive element in contemporary art. The art historian Jan Six, professor at the National Academy of the Visual Arts, made such an attempt in a lecture of 1893, entitled 'The meaning of the unsightly in Greek art', by demonstrating that realism existed even in Greek antiquity. Why did the Netherlands have such difficulty integrating the unsightly and the ordinary into art? Was it because political and religious ideologies had so powerfully determined the art and culture of the 80s and given idealism such a prominent place? As noted in Chapter 9, the young architects of the new movement remained faithful, unlike the young painters and writers, to an idealistic aesthetic, thus closing their eyes to a rapidly changing world. In 1898 their periodical *Architectura* wrote condescendingly about the first Dutch skyscraper, the White House in Rotterdam (1897–8, by Willem Molenbroek), showing absolutely no interest in 'realistic' considerations such as land prices and profitability, factors that were to influence architecture more and more.[46]

The contrast between idealism and realism (from now on referred to according to the meaning it was given by Sédille) calls for a theoretical definition. Idealism was based on the notion that architecture expressed an 'idea'. Depending on the context, this idea was the good, the beautiful, the true, together constituting an expression of the Divine in the opinion of architects such as Cuypers and De Bazel. Usually, though, what was at issue was a purely architectural concept: the ideal, the essential construction, which was the crux of the studies by Bötticher, Semper and Viollet-le-Duc: the essence of construction could become a material reality only through design, and only art was able to make design so meaningful, so 'layered', that it made the essential nature of construction understandable.[47] Such idealism was undoubtedly the main reason why architects did not rate the works of engineers as belonging to the domain of art. For the structures made by engineers resulted from technical calculations, and did not benefit at all from the kind of artistic treatment that exposed the higher idea via intuition and culture. For this reason, however impressive the skills employed, the works of engineers ranked lower than the works of architects.

Ornament and decoration (including elegant constructions in wood, brickwork bonds and combinations of building materials) were the instruments with which the idea of construction was interpreted. Berlage was perpetuating this old tradition when he wrote in 'Architecture and impressionism', 'it is the very construction that already contains all elements of art, no matter how simple'. Each type of building material even had its own 'idea', requiring individual expression. For instance, because a tree grows straight upwards, it was deemed unnatural for strips of wood to be bent using modern steaming techniques in order to produce a piece of Art Nouveau furniture. Such a treatment did not express the idea of wood and was therefore 'utterly peculiar', childish, full of affectation, morbid or 'impossible'.

Realism, on the other hand, could be characterized as having no higher, transcendental 'idea'. Its aesthetic profited from what it had learned in visual art and belles-lettres – namely, that the rejection of an ideal aesthetic could generate a completely new one – the aesthetic of the unsightly. Anyone who considered meaningless the convention that a piece of wooden furniture must consist of straight parts, discovered an enormous creative space that immediately opened up a new way of thinking, feeling and seeing. But realism also respected a completely different, equally immanent, idea, one based on practical experience and that could be verified in a practical way: the idea of the functional and efficient construction. The 'morbid' wooden armchairs of Van de Velde showed an entirely new, delicate balance between maximum solidity, maximum comfort and a minimum of materials. The proposition, mentioned earlier, that according to the 'idea' of iron and stone a light iron construction above a shop window could not possibly bear a stone façade, was equally erroneous, seen in this

Fig.111
Willem Molenbroek's White House office building, Rotterdam (1897–8). While Bosboom in The Hague (Fig.107) with his use of iron, glass and space presented an 'immaterial' architecture, Molenbroek with this skyscraper (after an American model) was questioning the dimensions of conventional aesthetics in another way. *Architectura* wrote in 1898: 'We hope that our country will be spared American products like this.'

light; such a construction was functional and efficient, and therefore *rational*.

Realism, function and beauty

That the emphasis during this decade shifted from idealism to realism is illustrated by the remarkable frequency with which the word 'efficiency' was used. Strictly speaking, the notion was in no way startling: already around the beginning of the Christian era Vitruvius with his *utilitas* noted something everyone knew already — that a building must be efficient. All we can say, perhaps, is that occasionally this idea attracted more attention, in particular when the architecture of the time set too much store by visual beauty to the detriment of a building's functionality and durability. The decades from 1750 to 1800 constituted such a period of shift, when Laugier, Lodoli, Hirt and later Schinkel and Hübsch redefined architecture as a constructional rather than a decorative art. Semper and Viollet-le-Duc stressed the relationship between construction and function as if they were referring to a law of nature. Around 1850 Semper drew analogies with animal skeletons so as to illustrate his ideas on the relationship between form, function and construction, and shortly afterwards Viollet-le-Duc referred to the wings of a

bird as a 'perfect machine' accurately expressing its function – 'as artists' he added, 'we need to do no more than that'.[48] We must handle this remark with caution. It should not be seen as exemplifying the naked functionalism of the twentieth century, but, rather, as belonging within the aesthetic framework of the nineteenth: architecture without ornament, to Viollet-le-Duc, would have been a contradiction in terms.

Gugel was one of those who formulated the nineteenth-century relationship between aesthetics and functionality. 'There can never be beauty if too little attention has been paid to efficiency or to proper construction,' he stated, but the function of a project could never dominate to the extent that aesthetic intuition had to give ground. 'The architect must therefore give shape to the building materials, as a result of which first the laws of construction and the practical object of the work are complied with, but he must never lose sight of the conditions relating to our aesthetic development.'[49] Gugel illustrated this with the 'very striking' observation of Schinkel's that the useful and the necessary are experienced as unpleasant unless they are presented as graceful and dignified. Beauty, therefore, was essential, deserving even more attention than functionality. Such statements illustrate what in the entire nineteenth century went virtually undisputed – namely, that beauty required functionality, but that functionality was subordinate to beauty, since beauty was the highest, all-embracing category closest to the purely conceptual 'idea', a view opposed to what was to become the credo of the twentieth century – that functionality creates beauty and determines its extent, and that absence of functionality is unsightly.

That this conceptual mutation originated in the 1890s is beyond dispute, but for the time being we can only surmise what the causes were. Once again it must be emphasized that this change was not the result of one theory or another: it was the result and expression of a common practice, to do with the interaction of clients, architects and their public. The advent of realism was something in which the entire architectural community took part – although architectural history has laid too much emphasis on the activities of the younger generation in this respect. To observers of the 90s, this conceptual mutation was much less noticeable than the conspicuous behaviour of some coteries. It was a stealthy process, at first only recognizable when looking back at the changes that had occurred over the past few years. The shift from an idealistic to a realistic aesthetic, which in fact meant an upgrading of functionality, was observed by *De Opmerker* in 1898, only after it had already taken place. Ten years earlier problems concerning construction had coincided with the question of beauty, but, *De Opmerker* wrote, today those two issues bore hardly any relation to one another and the issue of functionality had gained momentum. 'A new element, functionality, has come to dominate our architecture,' the journal added in 1899. 'This element is truly modern and will manifest itself even more in the course of the twentieth century.'[50] Clearly, there was an awareness that the transition from idealism to realism was to be a permanent one.

Evidence of the increased importance of functionality (efficiency, utility) can be found in many publications of the time. Here, we pinpoint the writings of two prominent architects. The first publication, which appeared in 1898 and was written by Constantijn Muysken, was aimed at the educated general public, and the second, pre-eminently intended for insiders, was the inaugural address delivered by Jacob Klinkhamer on the occasion of his appointment as professor at Delft Polytechnic in 1899.

The requirement nowadays is that dwellings be not only aesthetic, but also hygienic [Muysken wrote]. The demands that a modern society makes on an architect are all-important. More than ever before he must bring his art into line with these demands, taking into account above all else the means available to him. It is his task to provide proper lighting, heating and

ventilation, as well as gas, water and electricity, and to take into account the requirements of hygiene, including proper drainage and sewerage.[51]

Muysken was referring to quite ordinary things here. But this, precisely, was the whole point – that a prominent architect considered it important to explain the need for architects to concern themselves with such ordinary things because they were essential aspects of their job. Klinkhamer's discourse, demonstrating the same emphasis, concluded that whereas the peak of architectural performance was expressed in earlier ages via cathedrals and palaces, in the nineteenth century it was commercial and industrial buildings that performed the role. Klinkhamer himself enjoyed a solid reputation as a designer of factories. For him it was neither the architectural form nor, even less, the visual image that was important, but the functional success of the building's design. 'A factory is an organism where work and production take place, providing hundreds of people with jobs; and for these hundreds of people, the factory is their world, their existence.'[52]

Efficiency: the new ideal
The increased awareness of functional requirements, like

Fig.113
The ground-floor entrance hall of the office building of the Werkspoor Machine Factory, Amsterdam (1897), designed by Adolf L. van Gendt & Sons. The new architectural aesthetic was intent not on further developing the conventional idea of beauty, but on propounding the view that it is functionality that creates beauty.

Fig.114
The Flour and Bread Factory 'Holland', Amsterdam (1895), by Jacob F. Klinkhamer. Whereas in the past, Klinkhamer believed, it was cathedrals and palaces that represented the peak of architectural achievement, it was modern commercial works that fulfilled the same role at the end of the nineteenth century.

the other changes taking place at this time, was part of an international shift that was reflected in many publications. In matters of efficiency, the Unites States set the pace. Each year the New World provided new and ever more impressive evidence of what a further focus on efficiency could achieve. Efficiency was the miracle of more for less – more output for less money, more achievement for less effort, everything that much better and achieved that much more quickly, larger buildings on less land. During the 80s, by means of the turret trend, Dutch architecture had stretched the possibilities of height; the 90s witnessed the first commercial buildings inspired by American models. The unbridled vitality of American culture made efficiency a quality in itself. Schinkel's view – that the useful and necessary are experienced as unpleasant unless they are presented as graceful and dignified – which Gugel in 1886 still considered 'very striking', struck no chord in the United States. There, the useful and the necessary did not have to be beautiful in order to find favour – they automatically *became* beautiful if they performed successfully. In 1897 *De Opmerker* observed: 'efficiency determines everything [in American architecture]. Curious

shapes are never intended; they are always the natural result of demands set by efficiency'.[53]

In this context, in which efficiency became an international buzz word, circumstances forced the Dutch architectural profession to adapt itself with ever more intensity to practical daily reality. It became painfully clear that if architects were to continue as before and on making efficiency subservient to beauty, they would make themselves redundant. The public would no longer settle for beautiful but impractical, expensive buildings. The architects were constantly bombarded with news on this subject from home and abroad. In France and England, according to a report of 1894, artistic architectural issues were dominated by the financial and practical aspects. Consequently, the report continued, a client preferred to approach a building contractor for a design rather than an architect – it was generally agreed that an architect did more harm than good.[54] We have already observed this tendency in the Netherlands during the 70s and 80s, when the 'unqualified' and the engineers with their striving for efficiency, functionality and commercial success, were so despised by the architects, who saw themselves primarily as

Fig.115
Jacob van Looy's New York Life Insurance Company office building, Amsterdam (1891). Architecturally, this branch of the American company expresses 'America'. The composition and detail are adopted from New York commercial Beaux-Arts architecture; the elements of height and mass, also American, were new in Amsterdam, as the contrast with the adjoining buildings demonstrates.

artists. Now architects seemed to be starting to realize that the contempt they were expressing was making them victims of their own attitude.

This growing realization will have been the result not of wisdom or moral principle, but of learning the hard way.

The situation in which the architects found themselves as a professional group had become critical. But the main problem had less to do with an increasingly complex society setting more and more technical and organizational demands – these could be met by rethinking and specializing

208

Fig. 116
The Eugène Goulmy
& Baar Cigar Factory,
Amsterdam (1895),
designed by Abraham
Salm. The building,
in the middle of the
city, promoted the
new 'skyward trend'
and demonstrated the
increasing scale of
commercial
architecture. Like the
New York Life
Insurance offices
(Fig. 115), this
building referred
explicitly to America
– in this case to
George B. Post's
Union Trust Building
in New York
(1889–90). To the left
of the factory can be
seen an example of
first-generation
Dutch eclecticism: the
Vosje Café, with living
quarters above
(architect,
J. H. Leliman, 1859).

– and more to do with art itself, the architects' own domain. The criteria of truth and character by which they had always distinguished themselves from the unqualified hardly worked any more. Even the most prestigious critics were guided by their feelings and personal taste, and it was often a question of who they knew. When the last vestiges of a collective desire to define the profession in terms of architectural theory petered out, the distinction between 'real' architect and 'unqualified' was lost also. And none of this was the fault of the critics, who had simply made clear that the old artistic conventions and the old self-image of the architect were ripe for revision.

The need to 'professionalize'
It can be no coincidence that once there were no longer any objective criteria to indicate who was a 'real' architect and who was not, there emerged a new, non-artistic, but nevertheless objective criterion: this was found in regulation – not in respect of the art, but in respect of the architectural profession itself. In the 80s discussions had begun on the question of remuneration, and the 90s now witnessed a steady flow of articles on the need to professionalize generally. Many points were raised. Was an architect an artist, or was he a worker like any other? Should there be a qualifying examination? Should an architectural design have copyright protection because of its commercial value? Should the existing architectural associations, or a new union of architects, draw up a professional code in order to improve the conditions of competition between architects and to strengthen their position towards the client and the contractor? But no concrete results materialized. Individualism made it impossible to present a common front.

The architects' tendency to emphasize the visual qualities of architecture, as well as their 'quest for originality', entailed serious risks to the durability and functionality of their work. 'The architectural profession is really losing out,' the Dutch architect Jonas Ingenohl wrote in 1892, 'There are confirmed cases of wealthy, art-loving clients wanting nothing more to do with architects because they feel deceived by one particular "artist-architect" … this deception does not even have to have been deliberate; it may well be the consequence of indifference towards a practical layout, proper construction, durable materials – none of them matters that interest many artists.' The public, according to Ingenohl, often preferred an 'architect-contractor', who would, 'of course', have no aesthetic sense whatsoever but would know how to serve the public by building with regard to practicalities and economics. He would stick to the agreed budget, whereas the artist often did not know what he wanted and was prone to change all

kinds of things during the building process, thus incurring substantial incidental expenditure for the client.[55]

This dangerous tendency was only rectified because the architect was willing to give up his idealistic aesthetics and adopt the designer-craftsman's 'realistic' attitude. And documentary evidence does indeed confirm this truly revolutionary shift, so vital to the survival of the architectural profession. One article of 1896, reported in a remarkably positive and 'realistic' way on the 'speculative building'. Such an entrepreneur must, according to the writer, have a good sense of what the market wanted. After all, one bought a house not because it had a beautiful façade, but because it was solid, practical and comfortable.

There is often much for architects to learn from speculative builders. We have seen many a speculative building that is the last word in comfort. In general it can be said that the public is indifferent to the ideals that are today upheld by architects in this country, because it feels that they have very little practical use in everyday life. Does a man really care whether his house has been built according to the theory of Viollet-le-Duc, if it is to him gloomy and uninviting?[56]

'Idealism', individualism, and designing 'by system'
While the architects adapted themselves to daily reality, not least the fact that they had businesses to run, a time-honoured idealism was being defended with more vehemence than ever. More than the idealism of Bötticher or Semper, for whom the 'idea' of architecture was a purely *architectural* matter – such a version of idealism would now have been of no account – the idealism now at issue, and so prominently, had a collective dimension. And for this reason the debate focused on objective, architectural principles – in a word, on *style*. As we have seen, it was Berlage who assumed the leadership of the pro-style faction. It must have been curious, to many of his contemporaries, to witness Berlage's about-face so soon after his condemnation of building 'in style' and to see him embracing the ideal of the old generation. His resistance to artistic freedom had been noticed by Kromhout in 1894 in Berlage's lecture 'Architecture and impressionism'. 'When Berlage held his lecture', Kromhout wrote, 'I thought, why another "-ism", why not discuss an individualist architecture?'[57]

The opposition to individualist architecture seemed to start off objectively, neutrally, with designing 'by system' – a proportional system of triangles (or squares and circles) for determining the dimensions of a building and its components. From 1896 this concept received a fair amount of attention in the works of De Bazel, Lauweriks, Berlage

Fig.117–18
Around 1890
entrepreneurs bought
the country estate of
Boschlust, including
its park, on the
outskirts of The
Hague, both house
and park designed by
Jan David Zocher
(Fig. 117, 1836–8).
Immediately
afterwards building
contractors and
speculators moved in,
and the grounds were
successfully
developed into
middle-class terraced
housing (Fig.118).
These suburban
developments were at
Bezuidenhoutseweg,
The Hague.

and J. H. de Groot. De Groot, architect by training and art teacher by profession, published in 1896 together with Jacoba M. de Groot *Triangles for Design Purposes; for Home Study and for Schools*, which described how to design architectural ornaments using a triangle template with angles measured in multiples of 15°. His system was the result of a quest of many years aiming to emancipate decorative art from the 'plagiarism of nature' that had become customary in schools, De Groot wrote. His system of proportional triangles upheld, he had discovered, a time-honoured tradition and thus possessed a validity that transcended all styles; such a system had at all times been a guarantee of monumentality, harmony, rhythm and style. 'What De Groot had to say was something old, ancient even,' one critic wrote, 'probably already known at the time the pyramids were built, and perhaps older still – namely, the simple truth that art has its own rules, just as nature has its own rules, and that we who belong to the fast-fading nineteenth century must again realize and acknowledge their existence.'[58]

After De Bazel and Lauweriks (who used the geometrical figures as symbols of a mystical reality), Berlage also started to design 'by system'. On presenting

his designs for the Stock Exchange in 1898 he indicated that for the façades he had made use of the studies on proportion by Viollet-le-Duc, De Bazel, Lauweriks and De Groot. The entire building had been designed on the basis of Viollet-le-Duc's 'Egyptian' triangle – 'the pyramids, among other things, display these proportions'.[59] He went on to describe these proportions in such detail that his audience probably entirely forgot about his *unmentioned* sources of inspiration – American, German, Dutch, Italian. In 1900 De Groot published a new system, *A Few Notes on Designing in Architecture*, convinced that this offered the definitive solution for modern art. Berlage praised designing 'by system' as the modern manifestation of style. Another De Groot supporter was Berlage's friend Van den Bosch, the director of the 'sound' furniture shop 't Binnenhuis. Van den Bosch had invented his own system of proportions, which, he later wrote, 'enabled one to work not only on the basis of one's artistic sense of proportion, but with absolute confidence'.[60]

By 1900 a reaction had set in against the individualism and subjectivism that had been such a force in the 90s, leading to a moral campaign that discredited the period as one of confusion and decadence. Van den Bosch, calling on

's-GRAVENHAGE
Bezuidenhout

Dr. Trenkler Co., Leipzig. 13875

architects 'seriously [to] go in search of a sound foundation', fulminated against artists without principles – his principles:

[artists] intent only on pleasing others, like a beautiful woman who adorns herself with ribbons and sashes, but whose head is so deplorably empty that one can only regret her being so attractive. For many so-called artists, too, remain in the end little more than fashion plates, living according to the whim of the moment. Such people are not artists; they treat art like a whore, raping her daily, until they tire of it and ultimately perish in disgust at their own emptiness.[61]

Berlage: idealist or opportunist?

Berlage and his circle initiated the debate on a new style at a time when the word 'style' no longer seemed to mean anything; it was applied in every conceivable context, whether relevant or not.[62] For him, style retained its old meaning of a universal concept of form that expressed the character of society, but he ignored the question of its right to exist at all that had been at issue for over half a century. Because of the important position that it managed to secure for itself in history, we must examine closely this idea of a modern style.

The first question to ask is whether in 1900 architects had the cultural authority to determine, on behalf of society, its architectural expression. Reports on the matter do not inspire confidence in this respect. In the 1870s and 80s the public was already indifferent to the ideals of architects, as we saw earlier, and in the 90s the situation had become even worse, the public preferring to put their trust in contractors and house agents rather than in architects. But in an article in *De Kroniek* early in 1895 Berlage gave a very different impression. People were finally starting to appreciate architecture, he wrote. 'It has became an art again – that is to say, it has become a public affair – and this renewed interest is promoting it to heights that it has not reached since before the seventeenth century. There can no longer be any doubt about it: the next century will have art again, art of and for the people, of and for the community.'[63] By contrast, *De Opmerker* noted that the public had once again shown no interest in architecture. But according to Berlage, 'the democratic principle, developing by leaps and bounds' necessitated the introduction of a simple, 'impressionistic' kind of architecture, because democracy 'very rightly regards luxury as wastefulness': the money must be used to build housing for the workers, and schools. *De Opmerker* responded that architecture was by nature aristocratic, not democratic; the will of the majority led to the lowest common denominator; the masses were interested in one thing only: utility.[64] Berlage then cited the Parthenon and the medieval cathedrals as examples of the democratic nature of architecture, produced as it was by a wide diversity of craftsmen: 'If such structures had not been undertaken with the greatest dedication of all concerned, if the people had not cared for such splendid, idealistic works, they would simply not have been built.' Nowaways such dedication was lacking because capitalism had turned into a matter of money – therefore the nineteenth century had been unable to produce an architecture of its own. However, he concluded, there were signs of improving social conditions, inspired by a communal ideal: love for the community itself. This would make possible the creation of a new style.[65]

It is a fact of historiography that the contemporary notion of the common people having no interest in art has been left unnoticed, whereas modern historians have no doubts that Berlage, at the age of almost forty, and finally embarking on a successful career, had suddenly become an idealist. Of course, it is not impossible that *De Opmerker*, which regarded him as an opportunist, and Lauweriks, who reproached him for not understanding architecture's inner essence, were mistaken. However, the questions remain.

When outlining the new architecture in 1895, Berlage seemed to be thinking primarily of his own work: the new movement would be in the nature of a medieval renaissance, he said, referring to the design of his Muntplein building. His later publications confirm that he was not capable of dissociating the problem of a modern architecture from his personal concept of it – this is not to imply that he was not an idealist, only that this idealism may have been rather limited. Certainly, his stance on the democratic nature of architecture and on the people's love of art hardly tallies with his highly pragmatic collaboration with the new governing elite, with whom he negotiated the commission for the Stock Exchange in total secrecy. The plutocrats imposed their community art undemocratically, wrote a critic in 1897 – anyway, the working classes simply did not have the time to concern themselves with idealistic matters such as art.[66]

Berlage's idealism may also be questioned because of the ease with which his own contribution to architecture and that of a few artist friends were turned into a matter of vital national cultural importance; it is clear from their written works that they did not wait for a public reaction to their suggestions for a 'community art', but busied themselves with cultivating a support network of politicians,

intellectuals and especially the press. Through the press they did their best to discredit the multiformity of the 1890s as reflecting a state of confusion, turmoil, anarchy, social division, extravagance and decadence. They also used the press to voice their alternative: an art incorporating harmony, a culture with eternal laws, supported by society, and an abundance of spiritual richness – in fact, 'unity in diversity'. Jan Veth commented in 1894, and again in 1904, that it had too often been accepted that art must reflect its own period. But art of that kind would be as ephemeral as life lived from one day to the next, he insisted. Great art, on the other hand, struggled to discover the absolute beyond mere appearance, and was rooted in the everlasting. At present society was structurally weak; the overconfident doctrine of rampant individualism had resulted in fragmentation, in a fruitless and impoverishing particularism. But 'we', concluded Veth, have thought better of it and are trying to revive community art, which almost bled to death because of this all-pervading individualism.[67]

In the years that followed it became increasingly clear that Berlage made the fight against multiformity and the idealization of communality his personal mission.[68] He became the leader, first of the younger architects, then of the entire Dutch architectural profession. But what has never become clear is who or what there was, in fact, to lead; outside of Berlage's small circle, architecture had become irrepressibly multiform.

As an architect, making one's professional opinions public has always had business implications, especially to do with risk. Like all the other architects, Berlage was involved in a competitive market, in which context a clear favourable media image could be very useful. As we have already observed, his fierce public criticism of Art Nouveau cannot be seen as genuine artistic indignation, given the evidence that at precisely this time he was incorporating certain Art Nouveau elements into his own work.[69] Art criticism served as a weapon against the competition and as publicity for one's own business, while Berlage's 'style' was very much bound up with a segment of the commercial market that had been developed by clients – such as the businessman Carel Henny and the chairman of the diamond-cutters' union Henri Polak[70] – who found Berlage 'useful'. Clients such as these would not have stood for the straightforward, pragmatic aesthetic propagated by 'Architecture and impressionism'. What they required was an ideological aesthetic underpinned with the alluring dialectic of their own version of twentieth-century Modernism – a dialectic motivated by a power-hungry opportunism, in which language assumed an arbitrary quality, robbing it of its meaning: thus 'idealism' was in fact 'realism', 'austerity' meant 'abundance', to simplify form was 'awfully difficult',[71] the administrative elite equalled the community; the new style was the fabrication of a coterie.

Architecture and the people

Berlage's observations of January 1895 on the democratic community art to come followed his reading of Jan Veth's translation (1894) of Walter Crane's *The Claims of Decorative Art*. After 1894 Crane's work, and especially that of William Morris and John Ruskin, had an immediate and profound influence on applied art in the Netherlands,[72] particularly in relation to the pursuit of a new, simple beauty. The social views of Morris and Ruskin were reflected in the new Dutch architectural ideal as defined by Berlage. Ruskin and Morris wrote with distaste about the modern industrial age with its commercialization of the arts, and about the deteriorating morals and large-scale social disintegration that it brought with it. Medieval art and society, when artists understood their craft and craftsmen worked with dedication and a natural sense of beauty, drew their admiration. In the Middle Ages, art and society were one. Then came the Renaissance, which placed the individual in the limelight; the arts became a matter for the upper classes, and were increasingly alienated from ordinary people. The division of labour and the fragmentation of the arts, which alienated the craftsman from the product, gained momentum with modern capitalism, which intensified and accelerated these processes to an extent that changed the very fabric of society.

Ruskin's writings, in particular, struck the right chord with Dutch architects. Gosschalk may have been exaggerating when in 1899 he noted that nothing was ever published on architecture nowadays that did not contain some quote or other by Ruskin, but the outpouring of admiration that his death in 1900 unleashed in the *Bouwkundig Weekblad*, *Architectura* and *De Opmerker* reflected the esteem in which he was held. Designers such as Weissman and Jacob van den Bosch, despite their widely differing opinions, were united in their respect for Ruskin.

Berlage's concept of style clearly profited from this Europe-wide interest in an ideal unity of art and society. But how, exactly, should that general interest be understood in the context of the 1890s? Did it indicate the existence of a collective ideal, something that people were prepared to work towards, or was it a Ruskin-inspired enthusiasm for a past world, a beautiful collective dream, a splendid cultural perspective that made one forget for a moment the harsh reality – the daily routine in which many architects were

happy to receive any unpretentious commission, adding the merest personal touch here and there? What was new in Ruskin's argument that gave it a European appeal?

For forty years Alberdingk Thijm had been arguing that the Renaissance had destroyed the ideal culture of the Middle Ages. For over thirty years, backed by well-heeled clients who had enabled him more or less to maintain the unity of the arts, P.J.H.Cuypers had been building according to traditional methods based on medieval models. Since the 1850s Leliman had dedicated himself to improving the craftsmanship skills and the social position of building workers, and he, Gosschalk and Rose had been the first prominent architects to recognize the importance of adequate housing for workers and to play a role in the forming of opinions on the social aspects of architecture. Carel Vosmaer observed as early as 1861: 'In our country, art and the people had a strange relationship with one another. Art is practised and enjoyed by a very limited number of intellectuals, while the masses are almost totally devoid of art.[73] For many years, in an effort to bridge the gap between art and 'the people', Vosmaer did his best, both as an art critic and as a publicist, to educate his readers in artistic matters. The 70s had witnessed, through architects such as De Kruyff, a transformation in the applied arts, which was motivated - as was Morris's Arts and Crafts Movement – by a disapproval of the industrial and commercial production practices and by the ideal of 'artistic applied art', using traditional methods and utensils.

In view of this background, it is hardly surprising that in the Netherlands Ruskin's and Morris's ideals fell on fertile ground. The only question is why this had to wait to happen until the 90s, and why it aroused so much enthusiasm. The most admired Ruskin texts were, after all, already quite old: *The Stones of Venice* dated from 1853, *The Seven Lamps of Architecture* from 1849. Morris's socialist ideals had proved unworkable in practice; his workshops, where love for the craft was paramount and mechanized labour outlawed, produced art that could be afforded only by the rich. What must have given Ruskin special credence in the 90s was his belief in the pointlessness of attempting to base a contemporary architecture on the rules of historic architecture. Every rule based on a procedure, he wrote, would become worthless the moment circumstances changed or a new building material appeared. The only laws that endured were those based on human nature.[74] The vehemence of Ruskin's attack on the 'pestilent' Renaissance must have appeared quite modern in tone and content. His image of the Middle Ages was topical because it was possible to project the social problems of the 90s on to that period, and because the solution that he offered was presented so compellingly. His incisive writing style, his fierceness of expression on moral and aesthetic matters, based not on extensive philosophical reasoning but on 'feeling', must have seemed highly appropriate at that moment.

Various articles in the architectural journals give the impression that the admiration for Ruskin was not solely artistic and literary; there were some who advocated, apparently, a more comprehensive revival of medieval values. The anarchist-socialist Willem C. Bauer, for instance, urging in 1892 that society was in need of social reforms, fervently argued for a return of the simplicity and the religions and social values of the Middle Ages; as late as 1897 he held up the high-minded intellectual life of the Middle Ages as a model for his own materialistic era. In 1894 Jan Ernst van der Pek had described the dedication and love with which the labourer worked 'in the heyday of Christianity', reflecting that it would perhaps be more accurate to call him an artist, and ascribed the dissolution of the guilds to the ending of this glorious era. In the same year H. W. Mol wrote of the sharp decline in architecture as the result of the disappearance of the spiritual ideal after the Middle Ages. In 1896 Lauweriks wistfully wrote that the Middle Ages, because of their community art, could be considered 'for us Christians' the purest culture period of all. Berlage too, who in 1895 predicted for modern times an art with all the characteristics of a medieval renaissance, and who had praised medieval architecture for its community art and rational approach, continued well after 1900 to extol the Middle Ages.[75] No wonder, in view of such widespread enthusiasm for the period, that P. J. H. Cuypers occupied the loftiest position on Mount Olympus.

Does not all this demonstrate without a doubt the powerful influence that Ruskin's ideas had on the new movement's views on architecture? Or, to put it another way, did he not express precisely the sentiments that were to be encountered in the Netherlands at that time? No brief or simple answer can be given to these questions. The impulse for change came from all sides. Take the Dutch term *gemeenschapskunst*, 'community art'. It is customary to examine English examples for its source. When it was first used in the Netherlands in 1894–9, its sister term *Gemeinschaft* also meaning 'community' had already been the subject of debate in Germany for about seven years. Its premise can be attributed in particular to the much talked about book *Gemeinschaft und Gesellschaft* (Community and Society, 1887) by the German sociologist Ferdinand Tönnies. Tönnies described *Gemeinschaft* as the communal, 'true' way of living together, the way in which a neighbourhood, a family or a people feel and behave as one.

This 'natural' *Gemeinschaft* is, however, increasingly threatened and sometimes even eradicated by *Gesellschaft*, a way of living that is defined by purely functional or geographical characteristics (the state with its laws and its civic rights and duties, the metropolis, the large industrial complexes). Much pressure is put on the values of *Gesellschaft*, such as love and respect for man and nature, by the everyday struggle for life, resulting in selfishness, exploitation and moral decline. Tönnies' analysis of the processes transforming society in the nineteenth-century industrial state is especially interesting here for his use of the term 'communal' and the ideas it evokes, suggesting as it does a social ideal for future society. It is important to understand that in the Netherlands, without a metropolis to compare with London, Paris or Berlin, the problem of the community did exist. The social and political content of the term 'national' had been unclear ever since the 70s, and the emergence of nationalism in the next decade proved to be only a temporary solution. With the institutions of the old class-based society now eroded, new kinds of social organization, new social interests, monopolized public attention. What happened in the architectural circles of the 90s – loss of traditional values and standards, individualism, fragmentation and loss of coherence – was taking place in society in general. Under these circumstances the desire for a real community was an understandable reaction, but it must also have been clear that creating such a community would require superhuman effort.

More than 150 years ago Dutch architects – small in number – had started a debate on the essentials of the fine art of building. In those days the demands that architecture and architects had to meet were not too different from what for a long time had been the usual thing to do. An occasional steam engine and two or three short railway lines made up the miracles of the modern era; sending a letter by home-pigeon was still the fastest way to communicate. By 1900 this world did not exist anymore. It had relatively dense and global railway and telegraph networks, transatlantic ocean-liners, electricity, a few motor-cars and experimental aircraft. At that time, how could the architects have admired the Middle Ages and the Renaissance as sincerely, and in such a dedicated way as their predecessors had done in 1850? In his preface to the second edition of *The Seven Lamps* (1880) Ruskin himself wondered why his work was so widely appreciated again – this book was the most useless one he had written: it had little to do with daily reality.

Still, the art of building, having no fixed rules now to guide itself or to specify its relationship with society, was

's · GRAVENHAGE
Grand Bazar
d. l. P.-Façade

's-Gravenhage
Grand Bazar de la Paix Intérieur

construction methods and certain types of ornament, which characterized their art, the cultural unity of contemporary artists is to be found in their common reverence for the idea that one must express one's personality in the purest way possible.'[76]

One must express one's personality – but, as an architect, always in the context of society. There was no need for a more precise definition, or for rules: it was a natural fact.

In 1906 in The Hague the Grand Bazar de la Paix, designed by J. C. van Dorssers opened its doors. With a floor area of eight thousand square metres, it was the first large department store in the Netherlands to have been built according to the spatial and constructional concept of the Parisian *grands magasins*. The construction time of six months had been astonishingly short.

The Grand Bazar did not need to be explained by an idealist 'community art' theory. The massive public turn-out at its opening was proof enough of architecture's irresistible power to create a community – in this case a transient twentieth-century community of individuals with transient common desires and demonstrating transient communal behaviour. But this building has not even achieved the status of a footnote in the history of Dutch architecture – even though, at one glance, it is clear that its architectural principles have a much stronger relationship with the icons of the Modern Movement, such as the Van Nelle factory in Rotterdam (Johannes A. Brinkman, Leendert C. van der Vlugt, 1926–30), than has the traditional, somewhat conservative architecture of Berlage, who has received all the accolades.

Here we are defining architecture in a way that is very

Fig. 119–20
J. C. van Dorssers'
Grand Bazar de la
Paix, The Hague
(1906): the first large
modern department
store in the
Netherlands, echoing
famous *grands
magasins* in Paris,
photographed on the
day of its opening.
Because this building
was not a part of the
idealist aesthetic of
historiographers, it
has remained
invisible, and has been
allotted no place in
the history of Dutch
architecture.

not to lose its position as an art, or its special status of being the most public art. Worrying about these two characteristics had been the driving force behind the architectural debates throughout the nineteenth century. In the 1890s it became clear that the problem was only apparent. What started in 1891 with Kromhout and his audience, burning with enthusiasm, united in their rejection of artistic authority, could be summarized by Ed Cuypers in 1904 as a fact of artistic life. As in the past, he wrote, there was one single ideological and cultural attitude that characterized the present era. It manifested itself in all areas, and it was called individualism. Paradoxically, he said, whereas in the past the predominant characteristic had been similarity, today it was diversity; and it used the present artistic diversity that constituted the contemporary style. 'Whereas in the past artists belonging to the same period were linked by a common preference for certain different from the art-historical convention that sees the main theme of a building in the 'style' of its façade. This is also very different from the nineteenth-century vision of the art of building as a refined and inspired construction. In the architecture of the Grand Bazar there was no pursuit of artistic beauty; its purpose was to facilitate mass distribution and mass consumption, for which a certain degree of beauty – or an absence of beauty – could be useful. The building demonstrated that aesthetics was no longer a fundamental law that must be obeyed, but rather an instrument to be used when appropriate, then discarded when not needed.

If this was where aesthetics now found itself, what remained of truth and character? The architecture of the twentieth century would provide an answer. Truth can be pursued as long as the architect is prepared to play the old game with a wink and a nod at the insiders, his fellow architects. Character is the narrative that client and architect wish to relay to the public: their cultural ideals, edified or vulgar; their commercial, functional or artistic messages; their hidden intellectual or emotional meanings, their cheap fantasies or glorious illusions. Twentieth-century architecture would find new fundamentals outside of itself; tools for its further development that were perhaps richer and more multiform than ever before. The expression of truth and character changed, but they remained an ineradicable, an essential part of architecture in a non-theoretical, de facto way: like the taste of a fruit, or the smell of a flower.

Notes

1. *De Opmerker* 31 (1896) no. 14, 107–9; see also *De Opmerker* 31 (1896) no. 45, 357–9, on the fashion of stuccoing façades so as to produce a flat surface. Marijke L. A. J. T. Brekelmans 1989, 35 cites E. Gugel, J. H. W. Leliman 1902 on the dissemination of the Belgian 'flat façades' concepts via *L'Émulation*, of which the Helios building, Amsterdam (1896, architect G. van Arkel), was an example.
2. W. Kromhout 1891, 379.
3. Kromhout: *De Opmerker* 27 (1892) no. 12, 95; the primitive: *De Opmerker* 31 (1896) no. 47, 377.
4. W.C.B. [W. C. Bauer] 1897a; J. L. M. Lauweriks 1898a.
5. Lieske Tibbe et al. 1987, 21–2; Lieske Tibbe 1994, 123–4.
6. Hermann Muthesius 1907, 6, 61.
7. Art institutions: Adi Martis 1990, 178ff.; applied arts: Lieske Tibbe 1985, M. Simon Thomas 1988 and M. Simon Thomas 1996 ch. 3. Micro-organisms: A. Hofmann 1894, 176 and in particular Ernst H. P. A. Haeckel 1899–1904.
8. 'Almost full-blown movement': B. 1897b, 69; London: *De Opmerker* 33 (1898) no. 16, 122.
9. E.g. *De Opmerker* 30 (1895) no. 4, 27–8 and no. 25, 196.
10. *Architectura* 3 (1895) no. 25, 103–4; no. 26, 105–7.
11. Sacré-Cœur: H. J. Jesse 1891, 83–4. Romanesque church building: the German architectural journals published several examples of this new trend in church building which were occasionally translated in the Dutch journals, for example: 'De St Anna-kerk te

Münchén' ('The Church of St Anna at Munich'), *De Opmerker* 30 (1895) no. 26, 204–5. Lauweriks: Frans van Burkom, Marty Bax 1989, 19.
12. Lectures: for example, J. C. D. di Gazar 1890; courses: for example, J. R. de Kruyff 1890. Lauweriks and De Groot: Manfred Bock 1975, 35.
13. E.g. 'Feestversieringen' ('Festive decorations'), *Bouwkundig Weekblad* 18 (1898) no. 38, 295–6; and reports on the restoration of the neoclassicist city gate Willemspoort (Amsterdam 1840): 'Berichten' (Reports), *Bouwkundig Weekblad* 19 (1899) no. 33, 266; 'De Willemspoort', *Bouwkundig Weekblad* 19 (1899) no. 45, 347–8.
14. H. P. Berlage 1895b, 70.
15. Berlage's imitation of Italian architecture from Romanesque and early Gothic models has been well documented and analysed by Pieter Singelenberg 1972 and by Manfred Bock 1983, p.286–93 and 364.
16. *Architectura* 6 (1898) no. 20, 82–4.
17. Berlage's imitation of American Romanesque architecture: A. W. Reinink 1970 and Manfred Bock 1983, 294–6.
18. P. [J. E. van der Pek] 1895.
19. Some examples: H. P. Berlage 1891a; H. P. Berlage 1895–6, 214–16; H. P. Berlage 1897a. Cautious praise: H. P. Berlage 1910b, 151, 155.
20. The relationship between Berlage's Muntplein building and the Künstlerhaus [Art Institute] zum St Lucas, Berlin (1889–90, architect B. Sehring) was discovered by Manfred Bock 1983, 26–5, and further developed by Iain Boyd Whyte 1993, 176–8 (also, the comparison with America, 177).
21. 'Except base imitation': H. P. Berlage 1894, 99; 'not a paradox': 109.
22. Manfred Bock 1983, *passim*.
23. W. K. Cz. [Kromhout] 1894 no. 13, 6. It was clear also from the unexciting summary of the speech in which he first presented his impressionism notion that Berlage was not offering his audience any new perspectives: *Architectura* 2 (1894) no. 13, 53.
24. H. P. Berlage 1894, 105.
25. W. Kromhout 1900.
26. H. W. Mol 1898; *De Opmerker* 34 (1899) no. 31, 244. Roland Holst: Lieske Tibbe 1994, 121–2.
27. H. P. Berlage 1905, 74; 56–7; Van den Bosch: Lieske Tibbe et al. 1985, 23.
28. Jos Vandenbreeden, Françoise Dierkens-Aubry 1994, 134–40.
29. B. [H. P. Berlage] 1898.
30. Th. M. M. van Grieken 1888, preface. An important moment in the Dutch reception of the Arts and Crafts Movement was Vosmaer's translation and adaptation of Lewis Foreman Day's popular book *Everyday Art. Short Essays on the Arts not Fine* (London 1882) (Carel Vosmaer 1884, 1st edn, 1886, 2nd edn). An overview of the applied arts in the crucial decades 1870–90, with special attention to the study of nature: M. Simon Thomas 1996, ch. 3.
31. *De Opmerker* 28 (1893) no. 1, 4.
32. For criticism of the character of the Stock Exchange: A. W. Reinink 1975, 92–3. Lack of clarity of De Bazel's and Bauer's drawings: *De Opmerker* 34 (1899) no. 3, 18–19. De Bazel and the Central Station: K. de B. [K. P. C. de Bazel] 1898.
33. See, for instance, J. L. M. Lauweriks 1897, 8: 'in the first place, our rationality and higher thoughts form the basis. Second is its material couterpart, which is a set of rules tested by experience. Finally then the building material, that has to be investigated in every single detail. Thus practice would come connected to theory, confirming the firmness of the one part in the enduring conclusiveness of the other.'
34. K. de B. [K. P. C. de Bazel [1898, in particular 32 (on the objective of architecture), 35 (on the character), 44 (on the function of ornament); J. L. M. Lauweriks 1896, 301.
35. J. L. M. Lauweriks 1898a, 86.
36. H. Roland Holst in 1897–9, cited by Lieske Tibbe 1994, 145; Jan

Veth 1904, 37.

37. H. P. Berlage 1905, 80–1; J. E. van der Pek 1907, 12–13.
38. W. K. Cz. [Kromhout] 1894 no. 27, 4.
39. W. Kromhout 1891, 389.
40. H. P. Berlage 1895–6, 425–6.
41. J. H. Leliman 1889, 170.
42. C. T. J. Louis Rieber 1829b, 296.
43. Richard Streiter, 'Aus München' ('From Munich'), *Pan* 1896 no. 3, 249, cited by Stanford Anderson in his introduction to Hermann Muthesius 1902 (1994), 40 note 38.
44. E. Gugel 1886, 2nd edn, 12.
45. Unpainted pinewood panelling: the architect E. F. Ehnle 1891, 275, 'very unsightly (…), as if it was only meant to be temporary'. Pierson: *De Portefeuille* 13 (1891) no. 12, 831–3.
46. *Architectura* 6 (1898) no. 27, 114.
47. The concept of dressings (*Bekleidung*) developed by Bötticher and Semper was also expressed a little later by Viollet-le-Duc in his *Dictionnaire* as part of the important headword 'style': 'l'architecture, c'est-à-dire (…) la structure revêtue d'une forme d'art'.
48. Eugène-Emmanuel Viollet-le-Duc 1854–68, headword 'style', on the bird: 'ses ailes sont une machine parfaite lui permettant de voler. La machine est l'expression exacte de la fonction qu'elle remplit; nous autres artistes, nous n'avons pas besoin d'aller plus loin.' On the organicist analogies and backgrounds of Semper and Viollet-le-Duc: Caroline van Eck 1994, 216–39.
49. E. Gugel 1869, 1st edn, 24, and 1886, 2nd edn, 24.
50. *De Opmerker* 33 (1898) no. 26, 202; *De Opmerker* 34 (1899) no. 1, 2.
51. C. Muysken 1898, 159.
52. J. F. Klinkhamer 1900, 6–7. For silos designed by Klinkhamer around 1899: Dirk Baalman 1989.
53. *De Opmerker* 32 (1897) no. 1, 2.
54. *Architectura* 2 (1894) no. 29, 127–8.
55. J. Ingenohl 1892, 172–3.
56. *De Opmerker* 31 (1896) no. 26, 204.
57. W. K. Cz. [W. Kromhout] 1894 no. 14, 6.
58. Luctor 1896.
59. Berlage's presentation: R. [C. T. J. Louis Rieber] 1898, 111 and *Architectura* 6 (1898) no. 17, 70. The triangle system in the Stock Exchange design: Pieter Singelenberg 1972, ch. 9 and Manfred Bock 1983, 60–70.
60. Van den Bosch's autobiography (1937), cited by Dirk Baalman 1982, contains an analysis of his 'sphere system'; also in C. Schoemaker 1987, 54–6.
61. Jacob van den Bosch 1900, 391–2.
62. A selection in *Architectura* 2 (1894) no. 46, 195; no. 47, 200; no. 48, 205, in which six prevailing definitions are discussed.
63. H. P. Berlage 1895c, 9.
64. H. P. Berlage 1894, 106. Contra: *De Opmerker* 29 (1894) no. 26, 201–2, also *De Opmerker* 30 (1895) no. 2, 10.
65. H. P. Berlage 1895d, 59.
66. 'Democratie and kunst' ('Democracy and art'), cited by A. W. Reinink 1975, 70–1.
67. Jan Veth in the preface to his translation of Walter Crane 1894, v.
68. See, for example, H. P. Berlage 1905, in particular 76–83.
69. Berlage's Art Nouveau designs: Annelies van der Stoel 1996.
70. On Henny and Berlage: Marjan Boot 1974.
71. H. P. Berlage 1895d. 59.
72. Lieske Tibbe 1985; Lieske Tibbe 1993; Lieske Tibbe 1994, 109ff.
73. Carel Vosmaer 1861, 7.
74. John Ruskin 1989, 3.
75. W. C. Bauer 1892; W. C. B. [W. C. Bauer] 1897a and 1897b; J. E. van der Pek 1894, 229; H. W. Mol 1894b, 197–8; L. [J. L. M. Lauweriks[

1896; H. P. Berlage 1895–6, 424; H. P. Berlage 1895d, 59; H. P. Berlage 1897b; H. P. Berlage 1905, 76ff; H. P. Berlage 1908, 132.
76. Ed Cuypers 1904, 132.

Bibliography

The following abbreviations have been used:

Arch	*Architectura*
BB	*Bouwkundige Bijdragen*
BT	*Bouwkundig Tijdschrift*
Bulletin KNOB	*Bulletin Koninklijke Nederlandse Oudheidkundige Bond*
BW	*Bouwkundig Weekblad*
DDW	*De Dietsche Warande*
DNS	*De Nederlandsche Spectator*
NK	*Nederlandsche Kunstbode*
NKJ	*Nederlands Kunsthistorisch Jaarboek*
Opm	*De Opmerker*
Porte	*De Portefeuille*

J. A. Alberdingk Thijm 1858a: 'Willen wij alleen de Gothiek?', *DDW* 4 (1858), 171–80.

—— 1858b: 'Nieuwe Bouwwerken, -voltooyingen en -herstellingen in Nederland IV. kerken (III). VI. St. Laurentius te Alkmaar I', *DDW* 4 (1858), 355–68.

—— 1858c: *De Heilige Linie. Proeve over de oostwaardsche richting van kerk en autaar, als hoofdbeginsel der kerkelijke bouwkunst*, Amsterdam 1858 (also published in *DDW* 3 [1857], 195–238, 331–73, 374–482).

—— 1864: 'De kerken van den architekt Petr. Jos. Hub. Cuypers', *DDW* 6 (1864), 104–15, 249–55, 560–3.

A. Th. [J. A. Alberdingk Thijm] 1876: 'Snuggere theoristen ("deskundigen")', *DDW* (new series) 1 (1876), 600–2.

[J. A. Alberdingk Thijm] 1883: 'Eeen heuglijk verschijnsel', *Opm* 18 (1883) no. 48, 443–4.

E. Allard 1883: 'De nationale tentoonstelling van bouwkunst te Brussel', *BW* 3 (1883) no. 40, 255–6, 258–9.

B. 1844: 'Iets over den stijl in de kunst', *Kunstkronyk* 4 (1844), 69–70.

—— 1893: 'Het Universiteitsgebouw te Utrecht', *Arch* 1 (1893) no. 36, 155–6.

—— 1897a: 'De bouwkunst der negentiende eeuw', *Opm* 32 (1897) no. 50, 397–8.

—— 1897b: 'Keuze tentoonstelling van Nederlandsche moderne kunsnijverheid in de Lakenhal te Leiden', *Arch* 5 (1897) no. 12, 69–70.

Dirk Baalman 1982: 'Het proportiesysteem van Jacques van den Bosch. Een herwaardering van de Quadratuur', *Kunstlicht* 3 (1982) no. 8, 7–12.

—— 1989: 'Bij de sloop van de graansilo Korthals Altes in Amsterdam', *Bulletin KNOB* 88 (1989) no. 2, 8–20.

—— 1991: 'Nederlands eerste hoogleraar bouwkunde: Eugen Gugel', *De Sluitsteen* 7 (1991) no. 2/3, 43–66.

J. Th. M. Bank 1990: *Het roemrijk vaderland. Cultureel nationalisme in Nederland in de negentiende eeuw*, The Hague 1990.

W. C. Bauer 1888: 'Bij de plaat. Pittoresk', *Opm* 23 (1888) no. 43, 343–4.

—— 1892: 'Kunst en hervorming', *Opm* 27 (1892) no. 9, 72–3; no. 10, 80–1; no. 13, 105–7; no. 14, 113–15; no. 15, 122–3; no. 16, 130–1.

—— 1893: 'De Nes', *Arch* 1 (1893) no. 10, 44.

W. C. B. [W. C. Bauer] 1897a: 'Eenvoud', *Arch* 5 (1897) no. 2, 10.

—— [W. C. Bauer] 1897b: 'Geloof', *Arch* 5 (1897) no. 3, 13–14.

B. [K. P. C. de Bazel] 1898: 'Geometrie in de bouwkunst', *Arch* 6 (1898) no. 32, 133.

K. de B. [K. P. C. de Bazel] 1898: 'Bouwkunst', *Bouw-en sierkunst* 1 (1898), 32–5, 42–4, with illustrations.

K. P. C. de Bazel et al. 1916: *Dr. H. P. Berlage en zijn werk*, Rotterdam 1916.

D. J. F. van Beeck Calkoen 1802: *Euryalus over het schoone*, Haarlem 1802.

Adolf Behne 1926 (1996): *Der moderne Zweckbau*, Munich 1926 (*The Modern Functional Building*, with introduction by Rosemarie Haag Bletter, Santa Monica, Calif. 1996).

H. L. Berckenhoff 1875: 'Iets over de kunst bij de Grieken', *NK* 2 (1875) no. 4, 29–30.

Hetty E. M. Berens 2001: *Willem Nicholaas Rose (1801–1877). Stedenbouw, civiele techniek en architectuur*, Rotterdam 2001.

H. P. Berlage 1883: 'Amsterdam en Venetië [Amsterdam and Venice]. Schets in verband met de tegenwoordige veranderingen van Amsterdam', *BW* 3 (1883) no. 34, 217–19; no. 36, 226–8; no. 37, 232–4.

—— 1884: 'Gottfried Semper. Vrij overgenomen, naar eene levensschets door Herman Hettner', *BW* 4 (1884) no. 21, 142–6.

—— 1886: 'Indruk van de jubileumtentoonstelling te Berlin', *BW* 6 (1886) no. 34, 203–7.

—— 1889: 'Blijde inkomsten en steden in feesttooi', *BT* 9 (1889) vol. 3, 23–35.

—— 1891a: 'Bouwkundige schetsen II', *Porte* 12 (1891) no. 46, 585–7.

—— 1891b: 'Bouwkundige schetsen VI', *Porte* 12 (1891) no. 12, 829–31.

—— 1892a: 'De kunst in stedenbouw', BW 12 (1892) no. 15, 87–91; no. 17, 101–2; no. 20, 121–4; no. 21, 126–7.

—— 1892b: 'Bouwkundige schetsen XII', Porte 14 (1892) no. 51, 1274.

—— 1894: 'Bouwkunst en impressionisme', 2 (1894) no. 22, 93–5; no. 23, 98–100; no. 24, 105–6; no. 25, 109–10 (American edition: 'Architecture and impressionism', in Hendrik Petrus Berlage 1996, 105–21).

B. [H. P. Berlage] 1895: 'Kritiek', De Kroniek 1 (1895), 250–1.

H. P. Berlage 1895a: 'IJzer en steen', De Kroniek 1 (1895), 362–3.

—— 1895b: 'Iets over gothiek', Arch 3 (1895) no. 17, 70–2; no. 18, 73–6; no. 21, 86–7; no. 23, 93–5; no. 24, 97–8.

—— 1895c: 'Over architectuur', De Kroniek 1 (1895), 9–10.

—— 1895d: 'Over Architectuur', De Kroniek 1 (1895), 58–9.

—— 1895–6: 'Over architectuur' ('On architecture'), Tweemaandelijksch Tijdschrift 1 (1895), 417–27; 2 (1896), 202–35.

—— 1896: 'De arbeiderswoningen aan de gedempte Lindengracht', De Kroniek 2 (1896), 360–1.

—— 1897a: 'Duitsche Architectuur', De Kroniek 3 (1897), 59–60.

—— 1897b: 'Dr. P. J. H. Cuypers', De Kroniek 3 (1897), 153.

B. [H. P. Berlage] 1898: 'Over architectuur', De Kroniek 4 (1898), 295.

H. P. Berlage n.d. [1904]: Over stijl in bouw- en meubelkunst (On Style in Architecture and Furniture), Amsterdam n.d. [1904] (Rotterdam 1908, 2nd edn, 1917, 3rd edn, 1921, 4th edn).

—— 1905: 'Beschouwingen over stijl' ('Thoughts on style'), De Beweging 1 (1905) vol. 1, 47–83 (German edition Gedanken über Stil in der Baukunst, Leipzig 1905; American edition 'Thoughts on style in architecture', in Hendrik Petrus Berlage 1996, 122–56).

—— 1908: 'Eenige beschouwingen over de Klassieke Bouwkunst', De Beweging 4 (1908) vol. 3, no. 8, 115–34 ('Some reflections on classical architecture', in Hendrik Petrus Berlage 1996, 259–76).

—— 1910a: Studies over bouwkunst, stijl en samenleving, Rotterdam 1910.

—— 1910b: 'Iets over de moderne Duitsche architectuur en de Brusselsche tentoonstelling', De Beweging 6 (1910) vol. 14, no. 11, 151–6.

—— 1925: De ontwikkeling der moderne bouwkunst in Holland, Amsterdam 1925.

Hendrik Petrus Berlage 1996: Thoughts on Style, 1886–1909 (ed. Harry F. Mallgrave), Santa Monica, Calif. 1996.

C. Bernheiden 1992: 'Gegen die "Stilmengerei": August Reichensperger und seine Stellung zur Architektur der Gorik und der Renaissance', in Petra Krutisch, Anke Hufschmidt (ed.) 1992, vol. 6, 224–34.

A. C. Bleys 1886a: 'De excursie', Opm 21 (1886) no. 36, 289.

—— 1886b: 'Ingezonden. Nog eens de excursie', Opm 21 (1886) no. 38, 305.

François Blondel 1675–83: Cours d'architecture enseigné dans l'Académie Royale d'Architecture, Paris 1675–83; facsimile of 2nd edn (1698) Hildesheim/New York 1982.

Jacques-François Blondel 1771–7: Cours d'architecture, ou traité de la décoration, distribution et construction des bâtimens, Paris 1771–7.

Manfred Bock 1975: Architectura. Nederlandse architectuur 1893–1918, Amsterdam 1975.

—— 1983: Anfänge einer neuen Architektur. Berlages Beitrag zur architektonische Kultur der Niederlande im ausgehenden 19. Jahrhundert, The Hague/Wiesbaden 1983.

Tiede J. Boersma 1989: 'Christiaan Kramm en zijn betekenis voor het bouwkunst-onderwijs en het "Gotische Architectuurteekenen" aan de Utrechtse Stadsscholen voor Teken en Bouwkunde, 1822–66', De Sluitsteen 5 (1989), 3, 83–113.

—— 1993: '"Het oefenperk der kunst": ontwerp en architectuurbeschouwing in de prijsvragen van de Maatschappij tot Bevordering der Bouwkunst (1842–1880)', De Sluitsteen 9 (1993) 3/4, 10–42.

—— Coert Peter Krabbe 1992: 'Geschiedbeeld en toekomstvisie. Daniël David Büchler (1787–1871), de eerste voorzitter van de Maatschappij tot Bevordering der Bouwkunst', Jaarboek Monumentenzorg 1992, Zwolle/Zeist 1992, 181–99.

Germain Boffrand 1745 (1969): Livre d'architecture contenant les principes généraux de cet art, Paris 1745 (facsimile edn 1969).

J. Boomgaard 1984: '"Hangt mij op een sterk licht". Rembrandts licht en de plaatsing van de Nachtwacht in het Rijksmuseum', NKJ 35 (1984), 327–49.

Marjan Boot 1974: 'Carel Henny en zijn huis; een demonstratie van "goed wonen" rond de eeuwwisseling', NKJ 25 (1974), 91–122.

Symen Bosboom 1821: Cort onderwijs van de vijf kolommen door Vincent Scamozzi geordineert en nu door Symon Bosboom, Stadts Steenhouwer tot Amsterdam in minuten gestelt, Amsterdam 1821.

—— 1854: Vijf colom orden, met der zelve deuren en poorten weleer door wylen Sijmon Bosboom uit den beroemden Venetiaanschen bouwmeester Vincent Scamozzi in minuten overgebracht en nu met verklaringen opgehelderd ... door Caspar Philips en Jacobus Houthuisen, Amsterdam 1854.

Jacob van den Bosch 1900: 'Versieringskunst', Arch 8 (1900) no. 46, 371–2; no. 47, 380–1; no. 48, 391–2.

Eveline Botman, Petra van den Heuvel 1989: Het tekeningenarchief A.N.Godefroy. Architectuurtekeningen 1841–1896, Rotterdam 1989.

Carl G. W. Böttcher 1844–52 (1874): Die Tektonik der Hellenen (Greek Architecture), Potsdam 1844–52, Berlin 1874, 2nd edn.

Friedrich Bouterwek 1830: Grondbeginselen der leer van het schoone (Principles of the Theory of Aesthetics), Leiden 1830.

W. C. Brade 1827–34, (1842–4): Theoretisch en practisch Bouwkundig (Theoretical and Practical Building) handboek ten dienste van ingenieurs, architecten, opzigters, timmerlieden, metselaars en verdere bouwkundigen, The Hague 1827–34 (4 vols); The Hague/Amsterdam 1842–4 2nd extended edn (5 vols).

Ernst Branding 1895: 'Overzicht', Arch 3 (1895) no. 9, 38–40.

Marijke L. A. J. T. Brekelmans 1989: 'Hollandse Renaissance als bron van de Nieuwe Kunst. Analyses van gebouwen van G. van

Arkel (1858–1918) en H. P. Berlage (1856–1934), architecten te Amsterdam', *Bulletin KNOB* 88 (1989) no. 2, 23–41.

Willem Bruls, Dorothée van Hooff 1991: *Grand Hotels van de Benelux*, Amsterdam 1991.

D. D. Büchler 1845: *Over de bouwkunst van ons vaderland* (On the Art of Dutch Building). *Beantwoording van den vraag: Waarin ligt de reden van de weinige vorderingen der bouwkunst in ons vaderland, in vergelijking van die bij andere volken, en welke zijn de middelen om haar bij ons hooger op te voeren?*, n.p. 1845.

Jacob Burckhardt 1855: *Der Cicerone. Eine Anleitung zum Genuss der Kunstwerke Italiens*, Basel 1855.

—— 1860: *Die Cultur der Renaissance in Italien. Ein Versuch*, Basel 1860.

—— 1867: *Baukunst der Renaissance in Italien* (vol. 4 by F. Kugler, *Geschichte der Baukunst*), Stuttgart 1867.

Edmund Burke 1757 (1990): *A Philosophical Enquiry into the Origin of our Ideas of the Sublime and the Beautiful*, London 1757 (ed. and introduced by Adam Phillips, Oxford/New York 1990).

Frans van Burkom, Marty Bax 1989: 'Lauweriks en Cuypers, een langdurig afscheid', *Jong Holland* 5 (1989) no. 4, 8–19.

Nicolas le Camus de Mézières 1780 (1992): *Le génie de l'architecture; ou, L'analogie de cet art avec nos sensations*, 1780 (trans. with introduction by D. Middleton, *The Genius of Architecture; or, The Analogy of that Art with our Sensations*, Santa Monica, Calif. 1992).

Richard Chafee 1977: 'The teaching of architecture at the École des Beaux-Arts', in Arthur Drexler (ed.) 1977, 63–109.

Bernard Colenbrander (ed.) 1993: *Stijl. Norm en handschrift in de Nederlandse architectuur van de negentiende en twintigste eeuw*, Rotterdam 1993.

Peter Collins 1971: *Changing Ideals in Modern Architecture, 1750–1950*, London 1971, 3rd edn (1965, 1st edn).

Walter Crane 1894: *Kunst en samenleving* (trans. and adaptation of *The Claims of Decorative Art* by Jan Veth), Amsterdam 1894.

H. W. A. Croiset van Uchelen 1887: 'Het moderne woonhuis', *Opm* 22 (1887) no. 51, 409–12; no. 52, 418–22.

Crook, J. Mordaunt 1987: *The Dilemma of Style. Architectural Ideas from the Picturesque to the Post-Modern*, London 1987, repr. 1989.

Kathleen Curran 1992: 'Gärtners Farb- und Ornamentauffassung und sein Einfluss auf England und Amerika', in Winfried Nerdinger (ed.) 1992, 185–217.

L. Custers 1995: *Dáár was de bron. De Beweging van Tachtig in de ogen van Albert Verwey*, Maarssen 1995.

Ed Cuypers 1904: 'Bestaat er een moderne stijl?', *Het Huis* 2 (1904) no. 11, 122–32.

J. Th. J. Cuypers 1888: 'De tentoonstelling van werken door den bouwkundige J. van Lokhorst, uitgevoerd onder het Departement van Binnenlandsche Zaken', *BW* 8 (1888) no. 49, 302–3; no. 50, 308–9.

P. J. H. Cuypers 1895: 'Antwoord van Dr. Cuypers', *Arch* 3 (1895) no. 22, 91.

D. J. 1884: 'Over verschillende methoden tot opleiding van

architecten in het buitenland', *Opm* 19 (1884) no. 26, 230–2.

Daniel (pseud.) 1898: 'Een praatje uit Amsterdam', *Opm* 33 (1898) no. 12, 93–4.

August van Delden 1881: 'Onderzoek naar de oorzaken van strijd op het gebied der bouwkunst in Nederland', ('An investigation into the causes of the struggle for Dutch architecture') *BT* 1 (1881), 4–12.

W. Denslagen et al. (ed.) 1993: *Bouwkunst. Studies in vriendschap voor Kees Peeters*, Amsterdam 1993.

Alphons Diepenbrock 1895: 'De wijze bouwmeester', *De Kroniek* 1 (1895) no. 22, 169–70.

A. Dietze 1993: 'Mislukt? Jan de Haan (1845–1920): steenhouwer, architect en uitgever tussen praktijk en theorie', *De Sluitsteen* 9 (1993) nos 1–2, 38–51.

Arthur Drexler (ed.), *The Architecture of the École des Beaux-Arts*, London 1977.

H. van Dulken et al. (ed.) 1986: *Kunst en beleid in Nederland*, Amsterdam 1986.

Thomas H. von der Dunk 1994a: 'Jhr Victor de Stuers en het Rijksmuseum. De controvese inzake de zege van Cuypers bij de prijsvraag van 1875 nader bezien', *Bulletin van het Rijksmuseum* 42 (1994) no. 1, 37–76.

—— 1994b: 'De St. Augustinus aan de Oudegracht. De bouwgeschiedenis van Utrechts enige neoclassicistische kerk', *Jaarboek Oud-Utrecht* 1994, 142–70.

Caroline van Eck 1994: *Organicism in Nineteenth-century Architecture. An Inquiry into Its Theoretical and Philosopical Background*, Amsterdam 1994.

—— 1995: 'Par le style on atteint au sublime: the meaning of the term "style" in French architectural theory of the late eighteenth century', in Caroline van Eck et al. (ed.), *The Question of Style in Philosophy and the Arts*, Cambridge 1995, 89–107.

E. F. Ehnle 1891: 'Tracht naar het goede en erken het goede in anderen', *BW* 11 (1891) no. 44, 266–9; no. 45, 273–5.

Titus Eliëns 1990: *Kunst, nijverheid, kunstnijverheid. De nationale nijverheidstentoonstellingen als spiegel van de Nederlandse kunstnijverheid in de negentiende eeuw*, Zutphen 1990.

G. E. Engberts 1977: *De Nederlandse en Amsterdamse bouwactiviteiten 1850–1914. Een poging tot raming van de omvang met behulp van technische en economische samenhangen*, Deventer 1977.

Enrichetta (pseud.) 1883: 'De grenzen van het realisme', *Porte* 4 (1883) no. 49, 429–31.

Marijke Estourgie-Beijer 1993: 'Schoonheid, waarheid en karakter: Lelimans denken over bouwkunst', *De Sluitsteen* 9 (1993) no. 3–4, 51–72.

Henri Evers 1886: 'Heinrich von Ferstel', *Opm* 21 (1886) no. 51, 409–12; no. 52, 419–21.

F. Ewerbeck 1883–8: *Die Renaissance in Belgian und Holland* (The Renaissance in Belgium and the Netherlands). *Sammlung von Gengenständen der Architektur und Kunstgewerbe in Originalaufnahmen* (also pub. in French, *La Renaissance en Belgique et Hollande*), Leipzig 1883–8.

Flâneur 1883: 'Zou dat de bedoeling wel zijn?', *Opm* 18 (1883) no. 13, 129.

Flanor [Carel Vosmaer] 1882: *see* Vosmaer.

Georg Galland 1882: *Die Renaissance in Holland in ihrer geschichtlichen Hauptentwicklung dargestellt* (The Renaissance in the Netherlands treated in its Historical Development), Berlin 1882.

—— 1890: *Geschichte der Holländschen Baukunst und Bildnerei im Zeitalter der Renaissance, der nationalen Blüte und des Klassicismus* (A History of Dutch Architecture and Visual Arts during the Renaissance, the National Golden Age and Classicism), Frankfurt am Main 1890.

J. C. D. di Gazar 1890: 'De Acropolis en hare bouwwerken', *Opm* 25 (1890) no. 22, 185–8.

Georg Germann 1972: *Gothic Revival in Europe and Britain: Sources, Influences and Ideas*, London 1972.

P. A. M. Geurts et al. (ed.) 1992: *J. A. Alberdingk Thijm 1820–1889. Erflater van de negentiende eeuw*, Baarn 1992.

Sigfried Giedion 1941: *Space, Time and Architecture*, Cambridge, Mass. 1941, 1st edn, with many reprints.

A. N. Godefroy 1860: 'Antwoord op de vraag "Wat behoort men te verstaan door nationale bouwkunst? Heeft zoodanig eene kunst in vroegere tijden bestaan, of bestaat zij nog, zoo ja, bij welke natiën? Welke kenmerken strekken daarvan ten bewijze, en bestaat er mogelijkheid dat zoodanige kunst zich in onzen tijd en meer bepaald bij one natie ontwikkele – welke zijn daartoe de voorwaarden?"', *BB* 11 (1860), 356–67.

—— 1867: introduction and trans. of 'Prospectus van César Daly, *Motifs historiques d'architecture et de sculpture, d'ornement pour la composition et la décoration extérieure des édifices publics et privés*', *BB* 15 (1867), 69–76.

—— 1893: 'Voordracht gehouden in vergadering van 1 Febr. 1893', *Arch* 1 (1893) no. 10, 41–4; no. 11, 46–8.

Pierre-Jacques Goetghebuer 1827: *Choix des monumens, edifices et maisons les plus remarquables du Royaume des Pays-Bas* (The Choice of Monuments), Ghent 1827.

Adolf Göller 1887: *Zur Aesthetik der Architektur* (Aesthetics of Architecture). *Vorträge und Studien*, Stuttgart 1887.

—— 1888: *Die Entstehung der architektonischen Stilformen. Eine Geschichte der Baukunst nach dem Werden und Wandern der Formgedanken* (The Shaping of Architectural Style: A History of the Art of Building, treated as the Origin and Development of the Idea of Architectural Form), Stuttgart 1888.

I. Gosschalk 1864: 'Museum Willem I', *DNS* 1864, 130–2, 148–50, 164–5.

—— 1867: 'Iets over bouwen met gebakken steen', *Volksalmanak Maatschappij tot Nut van 't Algemeen* 1867, 174–90.

—— 1868: 'Onze hedendaagsche wijze van bouwen, vergeleken met die van den tijd der renaissance', *Volksalmanak Maatschappij tot Nut van 't Algemeen* 1868, 182–91.

—— 1871: 'Wanneer is de bouwkunde bouwkunst?', *Volksalmanak Maatschappij tot Nut van 't Algemeen* 1871, 161–74.

—— 1876: 'In welken stijl moeten wij bouwen?', *Volksalmanak Maatschappij tot Nut van 't Algemeen* 1876, 137–49.

—— 1899: 'Bij de platen, betreffende het nieuwe station te Groningen', *BT* 17 (1899), 57–73.

Th. M. N. van Grieken 1888: *De Plant in hare Ornamentale Behandeling* (The Plant as Ornament) *met eene inleiding over de Zinnebeeldige Voorstelling*, Groningen 1888.

Frans Grijzenhout, Carel van Tuyll van Serooskerken (ed.) 1989: *Edele eenvoud. Neo-classicisme in Nederland 1765–1800*, Haarlem/The Hague/Zwolle 1989.

J. H. de Groot 1900: *Iets over ontwerpen in architectuur* (A Few Notes on Designing in Architecture), Maassluis 1900.

J. H. and Jacoba M. de Groot 1896: *Driehoeken bij het ontwerpen van ornament. Voor zelfstudie en voor scholen* (Triangles for Design Purposes; for Home Study and for Schools), Amsterdam 1896.

W. J. de Groot 1886: 'Boekbeoordeeling. De Bouwmeester', *BW* 6 (1886) no. 11, 66–7.

G. Ulrich Grossmann 1992: 'Die Renaissance der Renaissance-Baukunst. Eine Einführung mit Blick auf den Weserraum', in Petra Krutisch, Anke Hufschmidt (ed.) 1992, vol. 6, 201–23.

E. Gugel 1869 (1886), *Geschiedenis van de bouwstijlen in de hoofdtijdperken der architectuur* (A History of Styles in the Main Architectural Periods), Arnhem 1869, 1st edn (2nd, 'much extended' edn 1886; 2nd edn also pub. in instalments from 1884).

—— 1880–8: *Architectonische Vormleer* (Architectural Morphology), Amsterdam 1880 (Part I), The Hague 1887 (Parts II and III), The Hague 1888 (Part IV).

—— J. H. W. Leliman 1902: *Geschiedenis van de bouwstijlen in de hoofdtijdperken der architectuur*, Rotterdam 1902 (3rd extended edn by E.Gugel 1869).

Cornelius Gurlitt 1886–8, 1888: *Geschichte des Barockstiles, des Rococo und des Klassicismus in Belgien, Holland, Frankreich, England*, Stuttgart 1886–8 (in instalments), Stuttgart 1888 (pub. in 2 vols).

Jannes de Haan 1986: *Villaparken in Nederland. Een onderzoek aan de hand van het villapark Duin en Daal te Bloemendaal 1897–1940*, Haarlem 1986.

Ernst H. P. A Haeckel 1899–1904: *Kunstformen der Natur*, Leipzig/Vienna 1899–1904, 11 vols.

Louis Hautecœur 1955: *Histoire de l'architecture classique en France 6: La restauration et le Gouvernement de Juillet 1815–1848*, Paris 1955.

Henry Havard 1874–7: *La Hollande pittoresque* (The Picturesque Netherlands), vol. 1: *Voyage aux villes mortes due Zuiderzée* (Paris/The Hague 1874, 2nd edn 1875, 3rd edn 1880); vol. 2: *Les frontières menacées. Voyage dans les provinces de Frise, Groningue, Drenthe, Overyssel, Gueldre et Limbourg* (Paris 1876); vol. 3: *Le cœur du pays. Voyage dans la Hollande méridionale, le Zélande et le Brabant* (Paris/Amsterdam 1877, 2nd edn 1878).

—— n.d. [1875]: *Verleden en heden. Een togt langs de kusten van de Zuiderzee*, Haarlem n.d. [1875] (trans. of *Voyage aux villes mortes du Zuiderzée*).

—— 1876, 1877: *Amsterdam et Venise* (Amsterdam and Venice), Paris 1876, 1877, 2nd edn.

—— 1881: *La Hollande à vol d'oiseau* (The Netherlands as the Crow Flies), Paris 1881.

Wolfgang Herrmann 1984: *Gottfried Semper. In Search of Architecture*, Cambridge, Mass./London 1984.

Th. van Herstelle [J. A. Alberdingk Thijm] 1869: 'Over nieuwe Nederlandsche bouwwerken', *DDW* 8 (1869); 385–400.

Alois Hirt 1809: *Die Baukunst nach den Grundgesätzen der Alten*, Berlin 1809.

Henry-Russell Hitchcock 1929: *Modern Architecture, Romanticism and Reintegration*, New York 1929.

—— 1958: *Architecture, Nineteenth and Twentieth Centuries*, Harmondsworth 1958, 1st edn.

E. J. Hobsbawm, Terence Ranger (ed.) 1983: *The Invention of Tradition*, Cambridge 1983.

A. Hofmann 1887: 'De Fransche bouwkunst tijdens de Derde Republiek', *BW* 7 (1887) no. 34, 205–7; no. 35, 210–13; no. 36, 217–19; no. 39, 236–8; no. 43, 261–3 (trans. adapted from original text pub. in *Deutsche Bauzeitung*).

—— 1893: 'Punten van aanraking in het artistieke tusschen bouwkunst en ingenieurswetenschappen', *BW* 13 (1893) no. 27, 165–7; no. 28, 169–72; no. 29, 176–9; no. 30, 182–4.

Guido Hoogewoud 1974: 'De Amsterdamse Beursprijsvraag van 1884', *NKJ* 25 (1974), 277–359.

Pauline Houwink 1973: *Watertorens in Nederland (1856–1915)*, Nieukoop 1973.

Heinrich Hübsch 1828 (1992): *In welchem Style sollen wir bauen?*, Karlsruhe 1828 (Wolfgang Herrmann [ed.], *In What Style Should We Build? The German Debate on Architectural Style*, Santa Monica, Calif. 1992, 63–101).

—— 1847 (1992): 'Die verschiedenen Ansichten über Baustil gegenüber der heutigen Zeit' = *Die Architektur und ihr Verhältniß zur heutigen Malerei und Skulptur*, Chapter 14, Stuttgart/Tübingen 1847, English edition 'The Different Views of Architectural Style in Relation to the Present Time' in Wolfgang Herrmann (ed.) *In What Style Should We Build? The German Debate on Architectural Style*, Santa Monica, Calif. 1992, 169–77.

J. J. van IJsendijck 1880–1889, [1905–7]: *Documents classés de l'art dans les Pays-Bas du Xe au XVIIIe siècle*, Antwerp 1880–1889 (5 vols); by A. W. Weissman extended new edn entitled *Documents classés de l'art dans les Pays-Bas du Xme au XIXme siècle*, Utrecht [1905–7].

J. Ingenohl 1891: 'Esthetische beschouwingen over de hedendaagsche bouwkunst', *Opm* 26 (1891) no. 3, 18–20; no. 4, 26–9.

—— 1892: 'Kunst en publiek', *Opm* 27 (1892) no. 19, 154–7; no. 21, 172–3.

J. 1896: 'Critiek', *Arch* 4 (1896) no. 46, 185–6.

H. G. J. [H. G. Jansen] 1889: 'De bekroningen der Parijsche tentoonstelling', *Opm* 24 (1889) no. 40, 327–8.

Ida Jager 1992: *Willem Kromhout Czn. 1864–1940*, Rotterdam 1992.

J. B. Jager 1886: 'Hedendaagsche kunst', *Opm* 21 (1886) no. 5, 33–4.

H. J. Jesse 1891: 'Eene herinnering', *BW* 11 (1891) no. 13, 77–8; no. 14, 81–4.

André Jolles 1897: 'Het Cuypers-feest in het Rijks-Museum', *De Kroniek* 3 (1897), 162.

Erik de Jong 1989a: 'Eenvoudige grootheid. Architectuur in Nederland 1765–1800', in Frans Grijzenhout, Carel van Tuyll van Serooskerken (ed.) 1989, 44–71.

—— 1989b: 'Schoon en schilderachtig. De landschappelijke tuinstijl', in Frans Grijzenhout, Carel van Tuyll van Serooskerken (ed.) 1989, 72–87.

—— 1992: 'Architectuur en landschap. Jacob Otten Husly (1738–96) als theoreticus. Een verkenning', in H. Krop, P. Sonderen (ed.) 1992, 79–96.

J. A. de Jonge 1976: *De industrialisatie in Nederland tussen 1850 en 1914*, Nijmegen 1976, 2nd edn (1st edn 1968).

K. 1884: 'Bouwwerken en hun omgeving', *Opm* 19 (1884) no. 34, 297–8.

—— 1885: 'De Amsterdamsche Beursprijsvraag', *Opm* 20 (1885) no. 25, 217–18.

—— 1895: 'De invitatie-tentoonstelling van den Haagschen Kunstkring in het academiegebouw te 's Hage', *Arch* 3 (1895) no. 30, 124.

J. C. K. 1884: 'Een Amerikaansche curiositeit op bouwkundig gebied', *Opm* 19 (1884) no. 34, 298–9.

Peter Karstkarel 1988: 'Het treurig aanzien tot nieuwe luister. Het ideaalplan-Van Asch van Wijck 1827', in Ko Jacobs, L. Smit (ed.), *De ideale stad. Ideaalplannen voor de stad Utrecht 1664–1988*, Utrecht 1988, 27–52.

J. F. Klinkhamer 1881: 'De in aanbouw zijnde prachtbouwwerken te Weenen', *BW* 1 (1881) no. 28, 144–7; no. 29, 149–51.

—— 1900: 'Rede uitgesproken bij de aanvaarding van het Hoogleeraarsambt in de Bouwkunde aan de Polytechnische School te Delft, den 2den October 1899', *BT* 18 (1900) part 1, 1–7.

Paul Knolle 1989: 'Edele eenvoudigheid. De waardering voor klassieke kunst bij Nederlandse kunsttheoretici', in Frans Grijzenhout, Carel van Tuyll van Serooskerken (ed.) 1989, 33–44.

J. Kok 1884: 'Karakter en stijl der Amsterdamsche Beurs', *BW* 4 (1884) no. 51, 338–9.

—— 1894: 'Het nieuwe gebouw voor de "Algemeene" te Amsterdam', *BW* 14 (1894) no. 9, 59–60.

Coert P. Krabbe 1998: *Ambacht, kunst, wetenschap. Bevordering van de bouwkunst in Nederland (1775–1880)*, Zwolle/Zeist 1998.

W. Kromhout 1887: 'Bij de plaat', *BW* 7 (1887) no. 5, 26.

—— 1888a: 'De bouwkunst aan de Loire', *BW* 8 (1888) no. 3, 15–17; no. 4, 21–2; no. 5, 27–31; no. 6, 34–5.

—— 1888b: 'La Trinité', *BT* 8 (1888) no. 2, 8–9.

—— 1889: 'Bij de plaat', *Opm* 24 (1889) no. 2, 12.

—— 1891: 'Tout à l'égout' ('Everything into the sewer'), *Opm* 26 (1891) no. 46, 369–72; no. 47, 378–80; no. 48, 387–90; no. 49, 395–7.

—— 1893: 'Het rationalisme in Frankrijk', *Arch* 1 (1893) no. 1, 2–3; no. 2, 5–6; no. 3, 10–11; no. 5, 18–20; no. 6, 25–7.

W. K. Cz. [W. Kromhout] 1894: 'Architectuur', *De Kunstwereld* 1 (1894), weekly column.

W. Kromhout 1894a: 'De nieuwe Stadsschouwburg', *Arch* 2 (1894) no. 35, 149–50; no. 36, 153–4; also publ. in *De Kunstwereld* 1 (1894) no. 36, 5; no. 37, 3–4.

—— 1894b: 'Het Kasteel "de Haer" te Vleuten', *De Kunstwereld* 1 (1894) no. 29, 3; no. 30, 4; no. 31, 4; no. 32, 6; no. 33, 3–4.

—— 1894c: 'Eenige gebouwen en ontwerpen', *De Kunstwereld* 1 (1894) no. 16, 5–6; no. 18, 3–4.

—— 1895: 'Het nieuwe museum aan de Van Baerlestraat te Amsterdam', *Arch* 3 (1895) no. 38, 165–7.

—— 1900: 'Vijf verloren jaren?', *Arch* 8 (1900) no. 34, 265–6.

H. Krop, P. Sonderen (ed.) 1992: 'Esthetica tussen klassiek en romantiek', *Geschiedenis van de wijsbegeerte in Nederland. Documentatieblad werkgroep Sassen* 3 (1992) no. 3.

Kruft, Hanno-Walter 1994: *A History of Architectural Theory from Vitruvius to the Present*, trans. Ronald Taylor, Elsie Callander and Antony Wood, London 1994.

Petra Krutisch, Anke Hufschmidt (ed.) 1992: *Renaissance der Renaissance. Ein bürgerlicher Kunststil im 19. Jahrhundert* (Schriften des Weserrenaissance-Museums Schloss Brake, vols 5 and 6), Munich/Berlin 1992.

J. R. de Kruyff 1876: *De Nederlandsche kunst-nijverheid in verband met dan internationalen wedstrijd bij gelegenheid van de in 1877 te Amsterdam te houden tentoonstelling van kunst toegepast op nijverheid*, Amsterdam 1876.

—— 1881: 'Ons weekblad', *BW* 1 (1881) no. 1, n.p.; also published in *Opm* 16 no. 19 (7.5.1881), under the title 'Bouwkundig Weekblad'.

—— 1885: 'Hollandsche renaissance', *BW* 5 (1885) no. 10, 66–7; no. 12, 77–80; no. 15, 97–8; no. 16, 101–4.

—— 1888: 'Schoonheidsleer der bouwkunst. 1', *BW* 8 (1888) no. 8, 45–50.

—— 1890: 'Prae-adviezen', *BW* 10 (1890) no. 20, 124–5.

F. Kugler 1841–2: *Hanbuch der Kunstgeschichte* (History of Art Handbook), Stuttgart 1841–2 (publ. in instalments); 1848, 2nd edn; 1856–9, 3rd edn; 1861, 4th edn.

Jan Jaap Kuyt, Norbert Middelkoop, Auke van der Woud 1997: *Bouwmeesters van Amsterdam. G. B. Salm and A. Salm*, Amsterdam/Rotterdam 1997.

H. Laudel 1991: *Gottfried Semper. Architekur und Stil*, Dresden 1991.

Marc-Antoine Laugier 1753 (1977): *Essai sur l'architecture*, Paris 1753 (trans. and introduction by Wolfgang and Anni Herrmann, *An essay on Architecture*, Los Angeles 1977).

L. [J. L. M. Lauweriks] 1896: 'Tentoonstelling Dr. Cuypers in het kunstnijverheidsmuseum te Haarlem', *De Kroniek* 2 (1896), 263.

J. L. M. Lauweriks 1896: 'De laatste wandschildering van A. J. Derkinderen voor het Bossche raadhuis in verband met de kunst van bouwen', *Opm* 31 (1896) no. 38, 399–301.

—— 1897: 'Aan Dr. P. J. H. Cuypers op zijn zeventigsten geboortedag 17 Mei 1897', *Arch* 5 (1897) no. 20, 6–9.

—— 1898a: 'Aan de Nederlandsche architecten. Over eenvoud, soberheid en economie', *Arch* 6 (1898) no. 21, 85–7.

—— 1898b: 'Het nieuwe postkantoor', *De Kroniek* 4 (1898), 196–7; also publ. in *Arch* 6 (1898) no. 35, 144–5.

A. J. C. van Leeuwen 1995: *De maakbaarheid van het verleden. P. J. H. Cuypers als restauratiearchitect*, Zwolle/Zeist 1995.

W. R. F. van Leeuwen 1987: 'Rationeel en schilderachtig. Isaac Gosschalk en het begin van de neorenaissance in Nederland', *Archis* 1987 no. 2, 30–39.

—— 1993: 'Woning- en utiliteitsbouw', in Harry W. Lintsen et al. (ed.) 1993, vol. 3, 194–231.

J. H. Leliman 1860a: 'Welke regels moet men volgen bij het afkeuren van gebouwen?', *BB* 11 (1860), 1–12.

—— 1860b: 'Antwoord op de vraag: "Waaren is toe schrijven de weinige belangstelling van het nederlandsche volk in de schoone bouwkunst, en wat kan gedaan worden om die belangstelling te doen toenemen?"', *BB* 11 (1860), 116–21.

—— 1860c: 'Antwoord op de vraag: "Is het uitwendig pleisteren van nieuwe, in baksteen uitgevoerde openbare gebouwen, aan te prijzen, uit een technisch en aesthetisch oogpunt?"', *BB* 11 (1860), 137–41.

—— 1860d: 'Antwoord op de vraag: "In welke opzichten is de tegenwoordige tijd in vergelijking met den goeden ouden tijd, dien de meerbejaarden in het bouwvak roemen, daarboven al dan niet te verkiezen?"', *BB* 11 (1860), 368–83.

—— 1860e: 'Iets over den bouwstijl de Amsterdamsche woonhuizen van de zeventiende en achttiende eeuw, naar aanleiding van de slooping en den herbouw van het koffijhuis: "Het Vosje", op het Rokin te Amsterdam', *BB* 11 (1860), 421–58.

—— 1864: 'National gedenkteeken voor 1813', *DNS* 1864, 201–2.

—— 1865: 'National monument voor 1813', *BB* 14 (1865), 179–83.

—— 1867: 'De naamlooze vennootschap: Paleis voor Volksvlijt. Een oordeel over haar prospectus, hare prijsuitschrijving en haar gebouw', *Opm* 2 (1867) no. 2, 5–6; no. 3, 9–11; no. 4, 13–15; no. 5, 17–18.

—— 1869: 'Antwoord op de vraag: "In welke opzigten is de industrie aan de schoone bouwkunst al of niet bevorderlijk, vooral met het oog op de meer algemeene toepassing van ijzer?"', *BB* 16 (1869) appendix 1, 134–8.

—— 1870a: 'Antwoord op de vraag: "Heeft men in vroegere tijden de klassieke bouwstijlen goed gekend?"', *BB* 17 (1870), appendix to doc. 3, 68–74.

—— 1870b [on behalf of the board of the Society for the Advancement of the Art of Building]: 'De schoone kunsten en het onderwijs daarin, in verband tot de bouwkunst', *BB* 17 (1870), 89–100.

—— 1871: 'Antwoord op de vraag: "Op welken grond spreken sommigen over *onzen oud-Nederlandschen Bouwstijl*, en zijn de door hen bedoelde bouwvormen thans geschikt te achten voor publieke, monumentale en burgergebouwen?"', *BB* 18 (1871), appendix to doc. 1, 85–92; also publ. in *Opm* 5 no. 47 (19.11.1870).

—— 1884: 'Ons vak, ons loon en ons lot', *Opm* 19 (1884) no. 10, 85–8.

—— 1888: 'Avondkout over het schoone', *BW* 8 (1888) no. 27, 168–70; no. 29, 180–3.

—— 1889: 'Causerie, den 20 Maart 1889 in het Genootschap "Architectura et Amicitia" voorgedragen', *Opm* 24 (1889), 167–71.

J. H. W. L. [J. H. W. Leliman] 1898: 'Het kasteel Haarzuylen', *BW* 18 (1898) no. 16, 117–18.

Neil Levine 1977: 'The romantic idea of architectural legibility: Henri Labrouste and the néo-grec', in Arthur Drexler (ed.) 1977, 333–57.

—— 1982: 'The book and the building: Hugo's theory of architecture and Labrouste's Bibliothèque Ste-Geneviève', in Robin Middleton (ed.) 1984, 2nd edn, 138–73.

Michael J. Lewis 1993: *The Politics of the German Gothic Revival. August Reichensperger*, Cambridge, Mass./London 1993.

Hugo Licht 1884: 'De Berlijnsche architectuur', *BW* 4 (1884) no. 26, 173–5.

Harry W. Lintsen et al. (ed.) 1993: *Geschiedenis van de techniek in Nederland. De wording van een moderne sameleving 1800–1890*, Zutphen 1993 (6 vols).

Arjen J. Looijenga 1900: *Van Waterstaatskerk tot kathedraal. De St. Josephskerk te Haarlem en het werk van de Waterstaatsarchitect H. H. Dansdorp*, Haarlem 1990.

—— 1995: 'Kleur tot meerdere glorie Gods. Constructieve en geschilderde polychromie in negentiende-eeuwse Nederlandse kerken', *Jong Holland* 11 (1995) no. 2, 65–83.

Wilhelm Lübke 1872, 1882: *Geschichte der deuschen Renaissance* (The History of the German Renaissance) (vol. 5 by F. Kugler, *Geschichte der Baukunst*), Stuttgart 1872, 1st edn, 1882, 2nd edn.

Richard Lucae 1869: 'Über die Macht des Raumes in der Baukunst', *Zeitschrift für Bauwesen* 19 (1869).

Luctor 1896: 'De regels der kunst', *Opm* 31 (1896) no. 50, 397–9.

F. Luthmer 1885: *Malerische Innenräume moderner Wohnungen*, Frankfurt am Main 1885.

M. [J. A. Alberdingk Thijm] 1850: 'Protestantsche architectuur. De nieuwe Zuider-kerk te Rotterdam, door den Heer A.W. van Dam', *De Spektator* 9 (1850), 73–84.

De M. 1883: 'Oorspronkelijkheid of niet?', *Opm* 18 (1883), 117–18.

H. Mackowsky (ed.) 1922: *K. F. Schinkel, Briefe, Tagebücher, Gedanken*, Berlin 1922.

Jan De Mayer (ed.) 1988: *De Sint-Lucasscholen en de neogotiek 1862–1914*, Leuven 1988.

—— 1992: 'Katholiek reveil, kerk en kunst', in P. A. M. Geurts et al. (ed.) 1992, 81–102.

Harry F. Mallgrave 1993: 'From realism to *Sachlichkeit*: the polemics of architectural modernity in the 1890's, in Harry F. Mallgrave (ed.) 1993, 281–321.

—— 1996: *Gottfried Semper. Architect of the Nineteenth Century*, London 1996.

—— (ed.) 1993: *Otto Wagner. Reflections on the Raiment of Modernity*, Santa Monica, Calif. 1993.

——, Wolfgang Herrmann 1989: *G. Semper, The Four Elements of Architecture, and Other Writings* (introduction and trans.), Cambridge/New York/Melbourne 1989.

——, Eleftherios Ikonomou 1994: *Empathy, Form, and Space.*

Problems in German Aesthetics 1873–1895, Santa Monica, Calif. 1994.

J. de Man et al. (ed.) 1993: *Kunst op schrift. Een inventarisatie van Nederlandstalige publikaties op het gebied van kunsttheorie en esthetica 1670–1820*, Leiden 1993.

Adi Martis 1979: 'Het ontstaan van het kunstnijverheidsonderwijs in Nederland en de geschiedenis van de Quellinusschool te Amsterdam (1879–1924)', *NKJ* 30 (1979), 79–171.

—— 1990: *Voor de kunst en voor de nijverheid: het ontstaan van het kunstnijverheidsonderwijs in Nederland*, Amsterdam 1990.

J. M. Mauch 1832–9: *Vergleichende Darstellung griechischer Bauordnungen*, Potsdam 1832–9.

—— 1845: *Neue systematische Darstellung der architectonische Ordnungen der Griechen, Römer und neuen Baumeistern*, Potsdam 1845.

R. Meischke et al. 1993–6: *Huizen in Nederland. Architectuurhistorische verkenningen aan de hand van het bezit van de Vereniging Hendrick de Keyser*, Zwolle/Amsterdam 1993–6, 3 vols.

Robin Middleton et al. (ed.) 1984a: *The Beaux-Arts and Nineteenth-century French Architecture*, London 1984, 2nd edn (1982, 1st edn).

—— 1984b: 'Hittorff's polychrome campaign', in Robin Middleton 1984, 2nd edn, 174–95.

——, David Watkin 1980: *Neoclassical and Nineteenth-century Architecture*, New York 1980.

Constance D. H. Moes 1991: *Architectuur als sieraad van de natuur. De architectuurtekeningen uit het archief van J. D. Zocher jr. (1791–1870) en L. P. Zocher (1820–1915)*, Rotterdam 1991.

H. W. Mol 1894a: 'Architectuur philosophie', *Arch* 2 (1894) no. 40, 170–2, continuation of 'Ingezonden', no. 42, 179–80.

—— 1894b: 'Enkele opmerkingen over kunstleven en architectuur', *Arch* 2 (1894) no. 46, 197–8; no. 47, 200–1; no. 48, 205–6; no. 49, 210–11.

—— 1898: 'H. van de Velde', *De Kroniek* 4 (1898), 376–7.

H. W. M. [H. W. Mol] 1900: 'Iets over hedendaagsche architectuur', *Arch* 8 (1900) no. 44, 355–6.

L. M. Moolenaar 1885: 'Hedendaagsche bouwkunst', *Opm* 20 (1885) no. 52, 446–7.

—— 1888: 'Het vormen-vraagstuk en de hedendaagsche bouwkunst', *Opm* 23 (1888), 400–2, 416–18.

—— 1895: *Een theoretische grondslag voor de afmetingen, verhoudingen en karakteriseering van bouwkunstige vormen*, Amsterdam 1895.

Müller et al. 1878: 'Antwoord op de vraag: "Op welke wijze kan in ons land het verband, tusschen de bouwkunst en de andere beeldende kunsten, verbeterd worden?"', *BB* 24 (1878), appendix 2 to doc. 1, 139–40.

Hermann Muthesius 1994 (1902): *Style-Architecture and Building-Art: Transformations of Architecture in the Nineteenth Century and its Present Condition*, Santa Monica, Calif. 1994 (trans. of original text of 1902, with introduction by Stanford Anderson).

—— 1907 (1976): *Kunstgewerbe und Architektur*, Jena 1907 (facsimile, Nendeln 1976).

C. Muysken 1881: 'Het Kasteel "Oud Wassenaar" bij 's Gravenhage', *BT* 1 (1881) vol. 1, 1–2; vol. 2, 17–18; vol. 3, 33, with illustrations.

—— 1898: 'Bouw- en beeldhouwkunst', in P. H. Ritter (ed.), *Eene halve eeuw 1848–1898. Nederland onder de regeering van Koning Willem den Derde en het Regentschap van Koningin Emma door Nederlanders beschreven*, Amsterdam 1898, vol. 2, 139–62.

Winfried Nerdinger (ed.) 1992: *Friedrich von Gärtner. Ein Architektenleben 1791–1847*, Munich 1992.

—— et al. (ed.) 1900: *Revolutionsarchitektur. Ein Aspekt der europäischen Architektur um 1800*, Munich 1990.

Jean-François de Neufforge 1757–80: *Recueil élémentaire d'architecture, contenant des distributions de bâtimens bourgeois*, Paris 1757–80.

E. J. Niermans 1886: 'Parijsche toestanden', *BW* 6 (1886) no. 14, 80–3.

J. J. van Nieukerken 1885: 'Oude gebouwtjes', *BT* 5 (1885) no. 3, 37–42.

—— 1887: 'Ingezonden', *Opm* 22 (1887) no. 51, 442.

F. J. Nieuwenhuis 1888: 'Indrukken', *BW* 8 (1888) no. 51, 315–17.

—— 1883: 'Karakter, ook in de kunst. Eene studie', *Opm* 18 (1883), 441–2, 449–50, 465–6.

H. C. J. M. van Nispen tot Sevenaer 1894: 'Leizing voor het genootschap "Architectura et Amicitia", 29 November 1893', *Arch* 2 (1894) no. 1, 6–8; no. 2, 11–12; no. 3, 14–15; no. 4, 18–19.

L. Noiré 1874: *Die Entwicklung der Kunst in der Stufenfolge der einzelnen Künste*, Leipzig 1874.

M. Olin 1986: 'Self-representation: resemblance and convention in nineteenth-century theories of architecture and the decorative arts', *Zeitschrift für Kunstgeschichte* 49 (1986), 376–97.

J. Oosterhoff et al. 1988: *Bouwtechniek in Nederland 1, constructies in ijzer en beton. Gebouwen 1800–1940, overzicht en typologie*, Delft/Zeist 1988.

C. W. Opzoomer 1875: *Het wezen en de grenzen der kunst*, Leiden 1875.

A. Ortwein 1871–80: *Deutsche Renaissance. Eine Sammlung von Gegenständen der Architektur, Dekoration und Kunstgewerbe in Original-Aufnahmen*, Leipzig 1871–80.

Aart Oxenaar 1989: *Centraal Station Amsterdam. Het paleis voor de reiziger*, The Hague 1989.

—— 1993: 'Op zoek naar een schilderachtig straatbeeld: de stadswoonhuizen van P.J.H. Cuypers in de Vondelstraat (1867–71)', in *Amsterdam. Het beschouwen waard*, Amsterdam 1993, 75–87.

Corjan van der Peet, Guido Steenmeijer (ed.) 1995: *De rijksbouwmeesters. Twee eeuwen architectuur van de Rijksgebouwendienst en zijn voorlopers*, Rotterdam 1995.

J. E. van der Pek 1889: 'Bij de plaat', *Opm* 24 (1889) no. 45, 377–9, with illustrations.

—— 1894: 'Bouwen-in-stijl', in H. P. Berlage 1895–6, 223–33.

P. [J. E. van der Pek] 1895: 'Niet Amerikaansch', *De Kroniek* 1 (1895), 218–19.

J. E. van der Pek 1895: 'Het Gemeente-Museum te Amsterdam', *De Kroniek* 1 (1895), 322–4.

—— 1896: 'Een nieuw bouwwerk', *De Kroniek* 2 (1896), 223–4; 235.

—— 1907: *Over het begrip en het wezen der bouwkunst*, Amsterdam 1907.

J. J. Penn 1841: *Handboek der Schoone Bouwkunst* (Handbook of the Fine Art of Building), Breda 1841.

Claude Perrault 1683 (1993): *Ordonnance des cinq espèces de colonnes selon la méthode des anciens*, 1683 (*Regulation of the Five Kinds of Columns after the Method of the Ancients*, Santa Monica, Calif. 1993, with introduction by Alberto Perez-Gomez).

C. H. Peters 1894: 'Oud-Hollandsche baksteen-bouw', *Arch* 2 (1894) no. 12, 49–51; no. 13, 53–5; no. 14, 57–8; no. 15, 62–3; no. 16, 65–7.

Nicholaus Pevsner 1936: *Pioneers of the Modern Movement*, London 1936, 1st edn (1949, 2nd edn).

—— 1970: *Pioneers of Modern Design. From William Morris to Walter Gropius*, Harmondsworth 1970, 5th edn (1960, 1st edn) (adaptation of N. Pevsner 1936).

—— 1972: *Some Architectural Writers of the Nineteenth Century*, Oxford 1972.

Klaus Jan Philipp 1990: '"Von der Wirkung der Baukunst auf die Veredelung der Menschen". Anmerkungen zur deutschen Architekturtheorie um 1800', in Winfried Nerdinger et al. (ed.) 1990, 43–7.

Allard Pierson 1868: *Schoonheidszin en levenswijsheid* (Beauty and Wisdom). *Twee voorlezingen*, Arnhem 1868.

Sergio Polano et al. 1988: *Hendrik Petrus Berlage. Het complete werk*, Alphen aan den Rijn 1988 (*Hendrik Petrus Berlage Opera Completa*, Milano 1987).

M. H. Port 1995: *Imperial London. Civil Government Building in London 1850–1915*, New Haven/London 1995.

C. B. Posthumus Meyjes 1885: 'Het Paleis van Justitie te Brussel', *Opm* 20 (1885) no. 8, 70–1; no. 9, 77–80.

—— 1887: 'Onze villa', *Opm* 22 (1887) no. 10, 73–6.

O. Praamstra 1991: *Gezond verstand en goede smaak. De kritieken van Conrad Busken Huet*, Amstelveen 1991.

Niels L. Prak 1991: *Het Nederlandse woonhuis van 1800 tot 1940*, Delft 1991.

Lut Prims, Ronny de Meyer 1993: *Het Zuid (Antwerpen 1875–1890). Architectuur en maatschappij*, Antwerpen 1993.

Il Puttino 1883: 'Stijl, school en oorspronkelijkheid', *BW* 3 (1883) no. 12, 71–2.

Antoine-Chrysostome Quatremère de Quincy 1788–1825: *Encyclopédie Méthodique*, vol. 1, Paris 1788; vol. 2, Paris 1825.

R. 1886: 'Bouwmaatschappij tot verkrijging van eigen woningen', *Opm* 21 (1886) no. 19, 152.

—— 1887: 'Uit de Sleutelstad', *Opm* 22 (1887) no. 53, 428–9.

A. W. Reinink 1965 (1993): *K. P. C. de Bazel, Architect*, Leiden 1965 (Rotterdam 1993, 2nd edn, with afterword).

—— 1970: 'American influences on late nineteenth-century architecture in the Netherlands', *Journal of the Society of Architectural Historians* 29 (1970) no. 2, 163–74.

—— 1975: *Amsterdam en de Beurs van Berlage*, The Hague 1975.

A. Reyding 1885: 'Bouwkunst. *Het Rijksmuseum te Amsterdam* door A. W. Weissman', *Porte* 7 (1885) no. 24, 382.

—— 1886: 'Tentoonstelling van architectonische ontwerpen, enz. in het gebouw der Mij. tot Bevordering der Bouwkunst', *Porte* 10 (1886) no. 3, 45–6.

C. T. J. Louis Rieber 1884: 'De Beursplannen', *BW* 4 (1884) no. 49, 321–5.

—— 1885: '1884–1885', *BW* 5 (1885) no. 1, 3–5.

—— 1887: 'Een oordeel over Nederlandsche bouwkunst', *BW* 7 (1887) no. 14, 83–4.

—— 1892a: '"De Maatschappij tot Aanmoedigning der Bouwkunde" en de toestand der bouwkunst in den aanvang der 19e eeuw', *BT* 12 (1892), 1–35.

—— 1892b: 'Het nieuwe meubelmagazijn der heeren H. F. Jansen en Zonen te Amsterdam', *BW* 12 (1892) no. 49, 296–7.

—— 1897: 'Johan Frederik Metzelaar', *BW* 17 (1897) no. 5, 27–8.

R. [C. T. J. Louis Rieber] 1898: 'De nieuwe Beurs te Amsterdam', *BW* 18 (1898) no. 15, 109–12 (report of a lecture by H. P. Berlage).

E. Rittner Bos 1888: 'Stijl en karakter', *Porte* 10 (1888) no. 1, 2–3.

H. Romers 1981: *De spoorwegarchitectuur in Nederland 1841–1938*, Zutphen 1981.

S. E. W. Roorda van Eysinga 1869: 'Materialisme en gebrek aan een waardigen bouwstijl', *Opm* 4 no. 29 (17.7.1869).

R. v. E. [S. E. W. Roorda van Eysinga] 1884: 'De nauwkeurigheid in de kunst. Een studie uit de esthetische zielkunde', *Opm* 19 (1884) no. 15, 126–9.

W. N. Rose 1854: 'Over de algemeene voorwaarden, waaraan een voortbrengsel der schoone bouwkunst moet beantwoorden', *BB* 8 (1854), 351–72.

—— 1856–7: 'Over het mythische en conventionele in de schoone bouwkunst bij het verschil tusschen klassische en romantische stijlen' ('On the Mythical and the Conventional in Architecture in relation to the Difference between the Classical and Romantic Styles'), *Verhandelingen van het Koninklijk Instituut van Ingenieurs* 1856–7, 49–63.

—— 1858a: 'Antwoord op de vraag: "In hoever is de instandhouding der oude gebouwen en gedenkteekenen van vroegeren tijd wenschelijk en bevorderlijk aan den bloei der vaderlandsche bouwkunst?"', *BB* 10 (1858), 175–84.

—— 1858b: 'Antwoord op de vraag: "Waarin is de waarde van de geschiedenis der schoone bouwkunst gelegen, en hoe moet die geschiedenis worden voorgedragen?"', *BB* 10 (1858), 264–70.

—— 1860a: 'Antwoord op de vraag: "Waaraan is toe te schrijven de weinige belangstelling van het nederlandsche volk in de schoone bouwkunst, en wat kan gedaan worden om die belangstelling te doen toenemen?"', *BB* 11 (1860), 101–11.

—— 1860b: 'Antwoord op de vraag "Wat behoort men te verstaan door nationale bouwkunst? Heeft zoodanig eene kunst in vroegere tijden bestaan, of bestaat zij nog, zoo ja, bij welke natiën? Welke kenmerken strekken daarven ten bewijze, en bestaat er mogelijkheid dat zoodanige kunst zich in onzen tijd en meer bepaald bij onze natie ontwikkele – welke zijn daartoe de voorwaarden?"', *BB* 11 (1860), 349–55.

—— 1863a: 'Antwoord op de vraag "Welke vorderingen zijn in de bouwkunst op te merken, sedert den tijd dat de gothische bouwstijl minder algemeen is toegepast geworden?"', *BB* 13 (1863), appendix to doc. 5, 29–41.

—— 1863b: *De leer van het ornament* (The Theory of Ornament). *Met teekeningen toegelicht*, Delft 1863.

—— 1865: 'Over de vermeerdering der hulpmiddelen in de schoone bouwkunst', *BB* 14 (1865), 1–26.

—— 1869a: 'Is de smaak, zoo als die in het dagelijksch leven wordt begrepen, geschikt om over de waarde van de schoone kunsten te oordeelen?', *BB* 16 (1869), 289–300.

—— 1869b: 'Maakt de kunstgeest, dien beeldhouwers en schilders moeten hebben, hen ongeschikt om over de bouwkunst te oordeelen?', *BB* 16 (1869), 185–94.

—— 1871a: 'Antwoord op de vraag: "Welke beteekenis moet men geven aan het woord *karakter* in de bouwkunst, en naar welke regelen moet dat kunstkarakter aanschouwelijk worden gemaakt, opdat het voor beoefenaar en leek rijke vruchten drage?', *BB* 18 (1871), appendix to doc. 1, 75–84.

—— 1871b: 'Antwoord op de vraag: "Tot welke voor- en nadeelen kan een idealistische rigting in de bouwkunst en hare praktijk leiden?"', *BB* 18 (1871), appendix 2, 64–72.

—— 1871c: 'Antwoord op de vraag: "Wat beteekent *aesthetika* in de kunst? Hoedanig behoort het onderwijs daarin te zijn, bijzonder wat de bouwkunst betreft? Welke schrijvers kan men raadplegen en wie hebben voor ons land het meeste gezag?"', *BB* 18 (1871), appendix 2, 73–8.

Paul T. E. E. Rosenberg 1995a: 'Van Lokhorst, bloemetje van den kouden grond', in Corjan van der Peet, Guido Steenmeijer (ed.) 1995, 235–66.

—— 1995b: 'De Metzelaars, een halve eeuw justitiegebouwen', in Corjan van der Peet, Guido Steenmeijer (ed.) 1995, 301–28.

—— 1872: 'Verhandelingen over de aesthetica der beeldende kunsten en in het bijzonder die der schoone bouwkunst' (On the aesthetics of the visual arts with particular reference to the fine art of building), in *BB* 19 (1872), 89–184, 225–80.

—— Guido H. P. Steenmeijer 1995: 'Warnsinck en Pierson, rijksbouwkundigen avant la lettre', in Corjan van der Peet, Guido Steenmeijer (ed.) 1995, 149–64.

E. Rouyer 1882: *La Renaissance de François 1er à Louis XIII. Décorations intérieures, lambris, panneaux*, Paris 1882.

John Ruskin 1849 (1989): *The Seven Lamps of Architecture*, 1849 (1880, 2nd edn, 1898, 6th edn, new edn of 1880: New York 1989).

—— 1985 (1853): *The Stones of Venice*, New York 1985 (J. G. Links ed., with original 1853 text).

S. 1889: 'Der Städte-bau nach seinen künstlerischen Grundsätzen vom Architekt Camillo Sitte', *BW* 9 (1889) no. 31, 182–4; no. 40, 236–7.

M. Saboya 1991: *Presse et architecture au XIXe siècle. César Daly et la Revue Générale de l'Architecture et des Travaux Publics*, Paris 1991.

J. W. Schaap 1877: 'Antwoord op de vraag: "Ontegenzeggelijk is het gebruik van de bekende ordeboeken van Bosboom en Vignola op den achtergrond of bijna geheel in onbruik geraakt. Mag dit als een gunstig verschijnsel op het gebied der bouwkunst bij ons te lande aangemerkt worden, en is de beoefening der zoogenaamde bouwworden in de genoemde boeken vervat, voor den leerling in de bouwkunst alsnog al dan niet aan te bevelen?"', *BB* 23 (1877), appendix, 87–92.

Carol Schade 1981: *Woningbouw voor arbeiders in het 19de-eeuwse Amsterdam*, Amsterdam 1981.

—— 1993: 'Architect Van der Pek en beeldhouwer Zijl', *Jong Holland* 9 (1993) no. 4, 50–3.

P. H. Scheltema 1887: 'Het bouwkundig onderwijs', *BW* 7 (1887) no. 13, 77–81.

Jeroen Schilt, Jouke van der Werf 1992: *Genootschap Architectura et Amicitia 1855–1990*, Rotterdam 1992.

Lidwien Schiphorst 1992: '"Een samengevat korps van knappen kunstenaars." De beginjaren van Cuypers' werkplaatsen', *De Sluitsteen* 8 (1992) no. 3, 79–96.

Freek H. Schmidt 1999: *Pieter de Swart. Architect van de Achttiende Eeuw*, Zwolle/Zeist 1999.

C. Schoemaker 1987: 'Meubels en interieurontwerpen', in Lieske Tibbe et al. 1987, 44–85.

A. Schoy 1878: *L'Architecture néerlandaise au XVIIme siècle*, Brussels 1898.

—— 1879: *Histoire de l'influence Italienne sur l'architecture dans les Pays-Bas*, Brussels 1879.

U. Schütte 1981: '"Als wenn eine ganze Ordnung da stünde…" Anmerkungen zum System der Säulenordnungen und seiner Auflösung im späten 18. Jahrhundert', *Zeitschrift für Kunstgeschichte* 44 (1981), 15–37.

Mitchell Schwarzer 1995: *German Architectural Theory and the Search for Modern Identity*, Cambridge 1995.

Helen Searing (ed.) 1982: *In Search of a Modern Architecture. A tribute to Henry-Russell Hitchcock*, Cambridge, Mass/London 1982.

Paul Sédille 1885: 'De tegenwoordige bouwkunst en de daarmede in verband staande kunstnijverheid', *BW* 5 (1885) no. 33, 206–7; no. 34, 209–11; no. 36, 223–4; no. 37, 229–31.

Gottfried Semper (1852) 1966: *Wissenschaft, Industrie und Kunst, und andere Schriften über Architektur, Kunsthandwerk und Kunstunterricht* (Science, Industry and Art: Proposals for the Development of a National Taste in Art at the Closing of the London Industrial Exhibition), Mainz 1966 (new edn, ed. Hans M. Wingler, of original edn 1852. English trans. in Gottfried Semper 1989, 130–67).

—— 1860–3: *Der Stil in den technischen und tektonischen Künsten, oder praktische Aesthetik. Ein Handbuch für Techniker, Künstler*

und *Kunstfreunde* (Style in the Technical and Structural Arts, or Practical Aesthetics. A Handbook for Engineers, Artists and Art Lovers), Frankfurt 1860 (I), Munich 1863 (II).

—— 1878–9: *Der Stil in den technischen und tektonischen Künsten, oder praktische Aesthetik. Ein Handbuch für Techniker, Künstler und Kunstfreunde*, Munich 1878–9, 2 vols (2nd rev. edn by Semper 1860–3).

—— 1989: *The Four Elements of Architecture, and Other Writings* (introduction and trans. by Harry F. Mallgrave, Wolfgang Herrmann), Cambridge/New York/Melbourne 1989.

M. Simon Thomas 1988: 'Het ornament, het verleden en de natuur – drie hoofdthema's in het denken over vormgeving in Nederland 1870–90', *NKJ* 39 (1988), 27–60.

—— 1996: *De leer van het ornament. Versieren volgens voorschrift, 1850–1930*, Amsterdam 1996.

Pieter Singelenberg 1972: *H.P. Berlage, Idea and Style. The Quest for Modern Architecture*, Utrecht 1972.

—— 1976: 'Sempers Einfluss auf Berlage', in E. Börsch-Supan et al., *Gottfried Semper um die Mitte des 19. Jahrhunderts*, Basel 1976, 303–14.

Camillo Sitte 1889 (1991): *Der Städtebau nach seinen künstlerischen Grundsätzen* (Town Planning according to Artistic Principles), Vienna 1889 (Dutch trans. with afterword: *De Stedebouw volgens zijn artistieke grondbeginselen*, by Auke van der Woud, Rotterdam 1991).

J. Six 1893: *De beteekenis van het leelijke in de Grieksche kunst* (The Meaning of the Unsightly in Greek Art), Amsterdam 1893.

J. P. Smits 1995: *Economische groei en structuurveranderingen in de Nederlandse dienstensector, 1850–1913. De bijdrage van handel en transport aan het proces van 'moderne economische groei'*, Amsterdam 1995.

Spectator 1884: 'Stijl', *Opm* 19 (1884) no. 38, 329–30.

Ronald Stenvert 1995: 'Die Wiederentdeckung der Renaissance in der niederländischen Architektur', in Petra Krutisch, Anke Hufschmidt (ed.) 1992, vol. 8, 113–32.

A. B. J. Sterck 1889: *Eerlijkheid in de kunst. Gothiek of Renaissance?*, Amsterdam 1889.

Annelies van der Stoel 1996: 'Berlage als ontwerper van straatmeubilair omstreeks de eeuwwisseling', *Jong Holland* 12 (1996) no. 4, 38–49.

C. M. Storm van 's Gravesande 1843, 1850, 1863: *Bouwkundige leercursus ten gebruike der Koninklijke Academie. Handleiding tot de kennis der Burgerlijke en Militaire bouwkunst voor de Kadetten der genie* (Royal Academy Architectural Course on the Civil and Military Art of Building for Cadets in Military Engineering), [Breda] 1843, 1st edn, 1850, 2nd edn, 1863, 3rd edn.

Johannes van Straaten 1825. *De Vignola der ambachtslieden, of gemakkelijke wijze om vijf bouwworden te teekenen* (The Vignola of Craftsmen, or a Simple Way to Draw the Five Orders), Amsterdam 1825.

—— 1828–32: *Afbeeldingen van antieke en moderne bouwkundige voorwerpen, ontleend aan Grieksche, Romeinsche en Oostersche tempels, paleizen, schouwburgen, badstoven en andere nog voorhanden gebouwen of der zelver gedeelten en ruinen*

(Illustrations of Ancient and Modern Structures, Borrowed from Greek, Roman and Eastern Temples, Palaces, Theatres, Baths and Other Extant Buildings or Parts Thereof, including Ruins), Amsterdam 1828–32.

Toos Streng 1988: 'Drieërlei opvatting over kunst en kritiek in Nederland tussen 1835 en 1839', *De Negentiende Eeuw. Documentatieblad werkgroep 19e eeuw* 12 (1988), 98–111.

—— 1992: 'Het dualisme van geest en stof. Esthetica in Nederland in het tweede kwart van de negentiende eeuw', in H. Krop, P. Sonderen (ed.) 1992, 121–40.

—— 1995: *Realisme in de kunst- en literatuurbeschouwing in Nederland tot 1875*, Amsterdam 1995.

Hein Strijder 1877: 'Ingezonden. Aan de lezers van De Opmerker en de Dietsche Warande', *Opm* 12 no. 51 (23.12.1877).

A. A. Stuart 1843: *De bevordering der bouwkunst in verband met de zedelijke beschaving der bouwlieden*, Amsterdam 1843.

Victor de Stuers 1873 (1975): 'Holland op zijn smalst' ('Holland at its Most Narrow-minded'), *De Gids* 37 (1873) part 3, 320–403 [facsimile edition, Marijke Beek et al., introduction, *Victor de Stuers. Holland op zijn smalst*, Bussum 1975].

—— 1874: 'Interetur decoctum', *De Gids* 38 (1874) part 4, 314–52.

—— 1875: *Da Capo. Een woord over regeering, kunst en oude monumenten* (Da Capo. Another Word on Government, Art and Historic Monuments), The Hague 1875.

—— 1877: 'Een bouwkunstig spook' ('An architectural ghost'), *De Gids* 41 (1877) vol. 3, 521–49.

—— 1897: *Dr P. J. H. Cuypers*, Haarlem 1897.

C. A. van Swigchem 1965: *Abraham van der Hart 1747–1820, architect, stadsbouwmeester van Amsterdam*, Amsterdam 1965.

W. Szambien 1987: *Symétrie, goût, caractère. Théorie et terminologie de l'architecture à l'age classique, 1550–1800*, Paris 1987.

J. L. Terwen 1858: *Kingdom of the Netherlands, represented in a Series of Picturesque Drawings from Nature*, Gouda, 1858.

M. Thijssen 1986: 'De Maatschappij Arti et Amicitiae 1839–70. Over het ontstaan en de betekenis van een kunstenaarsvereniging in de negentiende eeuw', in H. van Dulken et al. (ed.) 1986, 9–83.

L. Tibbe 1985: 'Theorie versus praktijk. De invloed van Engelse socialistische idealen op de Nederlandse kunstnijverheid sbeweging', in *Industrie en vormgeving in Nederland 1850/1950*, Amsterdam (Stedelijk Museum) 1985, 31–43.

—— 1993: 'Bron van troost of coffee-table book. De receptie van Walter Crane in Nederland', in W. Denslagen et al. (ed.) 1993, 528–39.

—— 1994: *R. N. Roland Holst 1868–1938. Arbeid en schoonheid vereend. Opvattingen over gemeenschapskunst*, Amsterdam 1994.

—— et al. 1985: *Jacob van den Bosch 1868–1948*, Assen/Eindhoven 1985.

J. Tideman 1894: 'Een drietal studiën op het gebied van de geschiedenis der bouwkunst in Nederland', *Opm* 29 (1894) no. 1, 2–5; no. 2, 9–12; no. 3, 17–20.

A. J. Ubels 1966: 'Een koninklijk architect', *Jaarboek Die Haghe* 1966, 42–60.

G. G. Ungewitter 1849: *Vorlegblätter für Ziegel- und Steinarbeit* (Patterns of Brick and Stonework), Leipzig 1849.

Untersuchungen 1788 (1986): *Untersuchungen über den Character der Gebäude; über die Verbindung der Baukunst mit den schönen Künsten und über die Wirkungen, welche durch dieselben hervorgebracht werde sollen*, Leipzig 1788 (facsimile edn, with introduction by Hanno-Walter Kruft, Nördlingen 1986).

V. 1884: 'Haagsche bouwkunst en nog wat', *Opm* 19 (1884), 79–80.

Jos Vandenbreeden, Françoise Dierkens-Aubry 1994: *De 19de eeuw in België. Architectuur en interieur*, Tielt 1994.

Karin M. Veenland-Heineman 1985: 'Lucas Hermanus Eberson (1822–89), een "volkomen onbeduidende architect"?', in *Bouwen in Nederland. Vijfentwintig opstellen over Nederlandse architectuur opgedragen aan prof ir J. J. Terwen*, Delft 1985, 467–93.

Veritas 1884: 'Het auteursrecht van dan architect in de pers', *Opm* 19 (1884) no. 27, 241.

Jan Veth 1894: *In het Rijksmuseum. Met twee brieven van Jozef Israëls*, Amsterdam 1894.

V. [Jan Veth] 1895: 'Gulden woorden', *De Kroniek* 1 (1895) no. 21, 163.

J. V. [Jan Veth] 1898: 'De Beurs van Amsterdam', *De Kroniek* 4 (1898), 85.

Jan Veth 1904: *Kunstbeschouwingen. Algemeene onderwerpen, reisbrieven, monumenten, oude Nederlandsche kunst*, Amsterdam 1904.

Eugène-Emmanuel Viollet-le-Duc 1854–68: *Dictionnaire raisonné de l'architecture française du XIe au XVIe siècle*, Paris 1854–68, 10 vols.

—— 1863: 'Over den stijl in de bouwkunst', *BB* 13 (1863), 197–214.

—— 1863–72 (1977): *Entretiens sur l'architecture* (Discourses on Architecture), Paris 1863–72 [facsimile edn Liège/Brussels 1977].

—— 1865: 'Over den smaak in de bouwkunst', *BB* 14 (1865), 27–44.

—— 1870a: 'Smaak (translated from the *Dictionnaire raisonné de l'architecture française du XIe au XVIe siècle*)', *BB* 17 (1870), 65–82.

—— 1870b: 'Beschouwingen over de bouwkunst', *BB* 17 (1870), 165–71.

J. van Vloten 1865: *Aesthetica of schoonheidskunde, in losse hoofdtrekken* (Aesthetics, or the Theory of Beauty). *Naar uit- en inheemsche bronnen, voor Nederlanders geschetst*, Deventer 1865.

—— 1871: *Aesthetika, of leer van den kunstsmaak, naar uit- en inheemsche bronnen, voor Nederlanders bewerkt*, Deventer 1871, 2nd edn (2nd, extended edn by J. van Vloten 1865).

H. P. Vogel n.d. [1863, 1888]: *Handleiding tot beoefening van den Griekschen bouwstijl* (Guide to the Practice of Greek Architecture), Den Haag n.d. [1863, 1st edn, 1888, 2nd edn], with illustrations.

—— 1872, n.d. [1888]: *Grondbeginselen der schoone bouwkunst. Een handboek voor den bouwkunstenaar en een leiddraad bij het onderwijs op de teekenschollen* (Fundamental Principles of the Art of Building: A Handbook for the Architect and a Guide to Teaching for Art Schools), Amsterdam 1872, 1st edn, Rotterdam n.d. [1888, 2nd edn].

—— 1885: 'Critische beschouwing', *Opm* 20 (1885) no. 40, 343–6.

Carel Vosmaer 1856: *Eene studie over het schoone en de kunst* (A Study on Beauty and Art), Amsterdam 1856.

—— 1861a: 'Het huis', *Volksalmanak Maatschappij tot Nut van 't Algemeen* 1861, 161–73.

—— 1861b: 'Volk en kunst', *Kunstkronyk* 2 (1861), 7–8.

—— 1864: 'Eenige geschriften over het nationaal gedenkteeken', *DNS* (1864), 281–4; 289–93.

—— 1879: *De Kunst voor ieder. Atlas der kunstgeschiedenis ten gebruike bij het onderwijs en eigen oefening, in school en huis, tot kennis der kunst, der geschiedenis, der zeden, zoowel als ter opheldering van het gelezene. Van de oudste tijden tot het einde der 18de eeuw. Part 1: Bouw- en beeldhouwkunst der Grieken en Romeinen [etc.]; Part 2: Beeldhouwkunst der Renaissance (slot)* (trans. from German), Leiden 1879.

Flanor [Carel Vosmaer] 1882: 'Vlugmaren', *DNS* 1882, 185–7.

Carel Vosmaer 1884, 1886: *De kunst in het daaglijksch leven (vrij naar het Engelsch van Lewis Foreman Day)*, The Hague 1884, 1st edn, 2nd, extended edn The Hague 1886.

—— 1885: 'Het nieuwe museum te Amsterdam', *DNS* 1885, 263–5; 269–72; 277–9.

Vox 1881a: 'Kunst een modezaak', *NK* 3 (1881) no. 16, 122–3.

Bert Vreeken, Ester Wouthuysen 1987: *De Grand Hotels van Amsterdam. Opkomst en bloei sinds 1860*, The Hague 1987.

A. de Vries 1984: 'De Amsterdamse Beurs 1825–40; prijsvraag en polemiek', *Jaarboek Amstelodamum* 76 (1984), 140–59.

D. de Vries 1881: 'Antwoord op de vraag "Ware het niet wenschelijk, op het voetspoor der groote Italiaansche meesters, de samenwerking der drie zusterkunsten: Bouwkunst, Schilderkunst en Beeldhouwkunst, te bevorderen?", *Opm* 16 no. 39 (24.9.1881).

W. 1884: 'Oud-Amsterdam', *Opm* 19 (1884) no. 29, 257–9.

R. Wagner-Rieger (ed.) 1969–81: *Die Wiener Ringstrasse: Bild einer Epoche. Die Erweiterung der inneren Stadt Wien unter Kaiser Franz Joseph*, Wiesbaden/Vienna 1969–81, 11 vols.

I. Warnsinck 1840: *Bouwkundige aanmerkingen op het onlangs tentoongestelde model van eene koopmansbeurs voor de stad Amsterdam*, Amsterdam 1840.

—— 1849: 'Wenk omtrent de bewaring van vaderlandsche kunstvoorbrengselen van vroegeren tijd', *BB* 5 (1849), 113–16.

A. W. Weissman 1881: 'Iets over bouwkunst', *NK* 3 (1881) no. 47, 369–72.

—— 1882: 'Schoonheidsleer (meer speciaal het inwendige onzer woonhuizen)', *Opm* 17 no. 22 (3.6.1882).

—— 1883: 'Schetsen naar de natuur', *Opm* 18 (1883) no. 22, 214–15.

—— 1885: 'Hedendaagsche kunst', *Opm* 20 (1885) no. 47, 401–3; no. 48, 409–11.

T. van Westrheene 1869: 'Feestrede, uitgesproken bij gelegenheid der viering van het vijf-en-twintigjarig bestaan van de Maatschappij tot Bevordering der Bouwkunst op Woensdag 7 Augustus 1867', *BB* 16 (1869), 1–20.

Iain Boyd Whyte 1993: 'Modernist dioscuri? Otto Wagner and Hendrik Petrus Berlage', in Harry F. Mallgrave (ed.) 1993, 157–93.

Johann Joachim Winckelmann 1764 (1993): *Geschichte der Kunst des Altertums* (History of the Art of Antiquity), Dresden 1764 (facsimile edn Darmstadt 1993).

Auke van der Woud 1998: *De Bataafse hut. Denken over het oudste Nederland (1750–1850)*, Amsterdam 1998, 2nd edn.

X. 1861: 'De jongste werken van den rijksbouwmeester', *DNS* 1861, 318–22.

—— 1884a: 'Restaureeren', *Opm* 19 (1884), 39–9.

—— 1884b: 'En dan nog zeggen: er zijn te veel architecten in Amsterdam', *Opm* 19 (1884), 306.

—— 1886: 'Critiek', *Opm* 21 (1886) no. 47, 377–8.

—— 1890: 'Ter overweging', *Opm* 25 (1890) no. 23, 193–4.

X.X. 1876: 'Plans voor een Rijksmuseum te Amsterdam', *Opm* 11 no. 47 (19.11.1876).

—— 1887: 'Aan wien de schuld?', *BW* 7 (1887) no. 33, 197–8.

Y. 1881: 'Darwinisme en schoonheidsleer', *Opm* 16 no. 17 (23.4.1881).

David Van Zanten 1977: 'Architectural composition at the École des Beaux-Arts from Charles Percier to Charles Garnier', in Arthur Drexler (ed.) 1977, 111–324.

—— 1982: 'The beginnings of French Romantic architecture and Félix Duban's Temple Protestant', in Helen Searing (ed.) 1982, 64–84.

—— 1984: 'Architectural polychromy: life in architecture', in Robin Middleton et al. (ed.) 1984a, 196–215.

—— 1987: *Designing Paris. The Architecture of Duban, Labrouste, Duc, and Vaudoyer*, Cambridge, Mass./London 1987.

—— 1994: *Building Paris. Architectural Institutions and the Transformation of the French Capital, 1830–1870*, Cambridge, Mass. 1994.

Cornelis Zemel 1847: 'Naar welken stijl zal ik mij bij het bouwen regelen?', *BB* 4 (1847), 307–18.

Figure Acknowledgements

The author and publishers would like to thank the following institutions for permission to publish photographs of items in their collections (references are to figure numbers):

Municipal Archives Amsterdam: jacket, frontispiece, 2, 4, 11, 25, 29, 36, 38, 39, 43, 46, 47, 55, 56, 64, 65, 68, 69, 70, 72, 73, 80, 81, 83, 84, 85, 88, 93, 99, 108, 109, 110, 115.
Municipal Archives, Arnhem: 63.
Municipal Archives, Dordrecht: 8.
Municipal Archives, The Hague: 28, 41, 42, 44, 48, 57, 58, 60, 117, 118, 119, 120.
Municipal Archives, Rotterdam: 14, 17, 45, 71, 100, 111.
Municipal Museum, Breda: 75, 76.
Nederlands Architectuurinstituut (Institute of Dutch Architecture), Rotterdam: 1, 10, 15, 18, 19, 21, 27, 31, 33, 40, 50, 51, 52, 54, 61, 62, 67, 77, 79, 82, 86, 87, 90, 91, 92, 94, 95, 96, 97, 98, 101, 102, 103, 104, 105, 106, 107, 113, 114, 116.
Rijksdienst voor de Monumentenzorg (National Heritage Department), Zeist: 3, 7, 9, 12, 13, 20, 24, 26, 32, 37, 53, 74.
Rijksgebouwendienst (State Building Department), The Hague: 78.
Royal Archives, The Hague: 34, 112.
Royal Library, The Hague: 5, 6, 16, 22, 23, 30, 35, 66, 89.
Technical University of Delft Library: 59.
University of Groningen Library: 49.

Index

References in italics are to pages on which black and white illustrations appear